The Scarce State

States are often minimally present in the rural periphery. Yet a limited presence does not mean a limited impact. Isolated state actions in regions where the state is otherwise scarce can have outsize, long-lasting effects on society. *The Scarce State* reframes our understanding of the political economy of hinterlands through a multi-method study of Northern Ghana alongside shadow cases from other world regions. Drawing on a historical natural experiment, the book shows how the contemporary economic and political elite emerged in Ghana's hinterland, linking interventions by an ostensibly weak state to new socio-economic inequality and grassroots efforts to reimagine traditional institutions. The book demonstrates how these state-generated societal changes reshaped access to political power, producing dynastic politics, clientelism, and violence. *The Scarce State* challenges common claims about state-building and state weakness, provides new evidence on the historical origins of inequality, and reconsiders the mechanisms linking historical institutions to contemporary politics.

Noah L. Nathan is an Associate Professor of Political Science at the Massachusetts Institute of Technology. He is the author of *Electoral Politics and Africa's Urban Transition: Class and Ethnicity in Ghana* (2019).

Cambridge Studies in Comparative Politics

General Editor

Kathleen Thelen *Massachusetts Institute of Technology*

Associate Editors

Catherine Boone *London School of Economics*
Thad Dunning *University of California, Berkeley*
Anna Grzymala-Busse *Stanford University*
Torben Iversen *Harvard University*
Stathis Kalyvas *University of Oxford*
Melanie Manion *Duke University*
Susan Stokes *University of Chicago*
Tariq Thachil *University of Pennsylvania*
Erik Wibbels *University of Pennsylvania*

Series Founder

Peter Lange *Duke University*

Other Books in the Series

Christopher Adolph, *Bankers, Bureaucrats, and Central Bank Politics: The Myth of Neutrality*
Michael Albertus, *Autocracy and Redistribution: The Politics of Land Reform*
Michael Albertus, *Property without Rights: Origins and Consequences of the Property Rights Gap*
Santiago Anria, *When Movements Become Parties: The Bolivian MAS in Comparative Perspective*
Ben W. Ansell, *From the Ballot to the Blackboard: The Redistributive Political Economy of Education*
Ben W. Ansell and Johannes Lindvall, *Inward Conquest: The Political Origins of Modern Public Services*
Ben W. Ansell and David J. Samuels, *Inequality and Democratization: An Elite-Competition Approach*
Ana Arjona, *Rebelocracy: Social Order in the Colombian Civil War*
Leonardo R. Arriola, *Multi-Ethnic Coalitions in Africa: Business Financing of Opposition Election Campaigns*

Continued after the index

The Scarce State
Inequality and Political Power in the Hinterland

NOAH L. NATHAN
Massachusetts Institute of Technology

CAMBRIDGE
UNIVERSITY PRESS

CAMBRIDGE
UNIVERSITY PRESS

Shaftesbury Road, Cambridge CB2 8EA, United Kingdom

One Liberty Plaza, 20th Floor, New York, NY 10006, USA

477 Williamstown Road, Port Melbourne, VIC 3207, Australia

314–321, 3rd Floor, Plot 3, Splendor Forum, Jasola District Centre, New Delhi – 110025, India

103 Penang Road, #05–06/07, Visioncrest Commercial, Singapore 238467

Cambridge University Press is part of Cambridge University Press & Assessment, a department of the University of Cambridge.

We share the University's mission to contribute to society through the pursuit of education, learning and research at the highest international levels of excellence.

www.cambridge.org
Information on this title: www.cambridge.org/9781009261104

DOI: 10.1017/9781009261111

First published 2023

A catalogue record for this publication is available from the British Library.

ISBN 978-1-009-26110-4 Hardback
ISBN 978-1-009-26112-8 Paperback

Contents

Figures

Maps

Tables

Acknowledgments

As it goes to press, I have been working on this book, or at least thinking about it, for fourteen years. In some sense, it is still my first academic project.

I first traveled to Northern Ghana in 2008 to interview members of the Konkomba community for an undergraduate thesis about the violence that gripped the region in 1994 and 1995. My coursework had taught me to expect that the formal state would be "weak" and incapable in remote towns like Saboba, unable to project much authority. And it became clear quickly that the state's presence there was limited. I still have a vivid memory of spending the dark pre-dawn hours of a July morning waiting at the Saboba bus station – with only one outbound bus a day, you really didn't want to miss it – sitting with one of the lone employees of the district post office. Originally from Accra, far to the south, he complained about his misfortune of having been assigned to such a distant place. He confided that he spent as little time at his job as he possibly could – just enough to not get fired – and otherwise was back in the city with his family. That's what he was waiting for the bus to go do. It would be easy to conclude from our conversation that the state couldn't possibly be very powerful in a place where its (already few) employees shirked their duties to try to stay away.

But this view of the state clashed significantly with what my interview respondents in Saboba had kept trying to tell me during the preceding days. In their accounts, the state was *absolutely central* to what had happened during the 1994–1995 conflict: the state created the underlying grievances that generated conflict, its actions helped directly spark the violence, and it was the state whose recognition and attention the competing parties were fighting over. Everything I heard kept boiling back down to the state and all the ways it had influenced and reshaped local communities. How could it be that the central state was both so limited in what it could do, and yet, in residents' eyes, still the core causal force behind some of their most important political experiences?

Since 2008, two things have remained stuck in my mind: on one hand, how to explain the paradox that is at the heart of the book – how a state could both be "weak" in all traditional senses of the term and yet so clearly powerful in its ability to influence society; on the other hand, a desire to try to retell the story of the Konkomba and their neighboring communities more properly once I had the tools and skills to do better than a novice college student.

After I finished my first book, I pivoted back to this project to try give both my best shot. While the book's scope has broadened, ideas dating to 2008 are still at its heart. I've now spent the last two years writing it in the midst of a pandemic, witnessing what the literature tells us is instead a "strong" state – my own, held up so often as the reference against which African states get lazily compared – fail repeatedly at basic tasks of state capacity. This has only deepened my conviction that something is off with how we political scientists think about state power and weakness, a theme I return to in the following pages.

I am indebted to many people who helped make this book possible. I thank all the Ghanaians who spoke with me in interviews over many years. I hope I have done their experiences some justice, though I'm sure I've also failed to understand things along the way.

I also thank Robert Bates, Emmanuel Akyeampong, and especially Nahomi Ichino for introducing me to Ghana and encouraging me to undertake the initial research that became this book. Bob and Nahomi both subsequently became valued mentors to whom I remain very grateful. Marek Kowalik, James Suran-Era, Edward Salifu Mahama, and Ubindam Jacob were incredible hosts in 2008, helping a clueless outsider find his way. I also thank Jon Kirby, Deborah Pellow, and Carola Lentz. Although they each probably don't remember meeting me this many years later, I appreciate their help back then in first guiding me into the literature on the North.

The more recent phases of the project depended on a large number of dedicated research assistants. I thank Alhassan Ibn Abdallah, Paul Atwell, Anthony Bilandam, Frimpong Bilandam, Salahudeen Abubakari Dumah, Moustafa El-Kashlan, Eve Hillman, Solomon Nagob, Megan

Ryan, Josephine Samani, and Erik Williams. Paul Atwell's work was especially helpful for digitizing the census data. For help navigating the field and accessing data, I'm also indebted to Didacus Afegra, Yaw Haratu Amadu, Dominic Ayine, and Charles Nyojah; Philomena Nyarko, Rosalind Quartey, and the Ghana Statistical Service; Alexander Essien, Christopher Koki, and the National House of Chiefs; the staff of the Northern Regional Archives, Tamale, and Martha Wilfahrt for prodding me to go check them out; and Franklin Oduro, Paul Osei-Kuffour, and the wonderful team at the Ghana Center for Democratic Development (CDD-Ghana). Also special thanks to Gidi and Gladys Lustig for providing such a home away from home.

This book was written between the University of Michigan and a sabbatical at the Center for Advanced Study in the Behavioral Sciences (CASBS). At Michigan, I am grateful to Allen Hicken for his mentorship and friendship, as well as to Nancy Burns, Justine Davis, Mark Dincecco, Chris Fariss, Edgar Franco-Vivanco, Nahomi Ichino, Brian Min, Anne Pitcher, and Dan Slater for their advice and support. At CASBS, early versions of the manuscript benefitted from the comments of Mike Albertus, Michael Brownstein, David Ciepley, Guy Grossman, Michael Hiscox, Margaret Levi, Jennifer Pan, and the other fellows.

Special thanks go to the anonymous reviewers for their helpful feedback, as well as to Dan Slater and the Weiser Center for Emerging Democracies for hosting my book workshop and to Dan, Leo Arriola, Justine Davis, Mark Dincecco, Allen Hicken, Eric Kramon, Janet Lewis, Lauren Maclean, Jan Pierskalla, and Martha Wilfahrt for their incredible suggestions. At other points, individual elements of the manuscript benefitted from the feedback and suggestions of Catherine Boone, Sarah Brierley, Kim Yi Dionne, Sima Ghaddar, Adam Harris, Kimuli Kasara, David Laitin, Evan Lieberman, Avital Livny, Sara Lowes, Eddy Malesky, Daniela Osorio Michel, George Ofosu, Tom O'Mealia, Dan Posner, Zara Riaz, Joan Ricart-Huguet, Amanda Robinson, Benjamin Schneer, Robert Schub, Ariel White, and audiences at Berkeley, Columbia, Duke, MIT, Nuffield College, Stanford, UCLA, Vanderbilt, and several American Political Science Association, Midwest Political Science Association, and Working Group in African Political Economy conferences. I also thank Rachel Blaifeder and the great team at Cambridge University Press, Kathy Thelen and the editors of the Comparative Politics series, Dennis Akuoku-Frimpong, Nii Obodai Provencal, and Vivian Unger.

Finally, my most important thanks go to Solomon and Mai. Solomon's arrival coincided with writing this book, offering the most joyous excuse that I can possibly think of to set the manuscript aside and focus my attention on more important things. Mai has unflinchingly provided support, encouragement, and her love throughout the research process, offering more feedback and insight into the ideas here than everyone else combined. Every time I got stuck in a rut of self-doubt, she was there to lead me out. I am so grateful to have her as a partner. I dedicate this book to them.

PART I

INTRODUCTION

I

The Politics of State Scarcity

In 2020, Anthony Karbo was the Member of Parliament (MP) for Lawra, a town in Ghana's far northwestern periphery. Beyond his role as MP, he doubled as the country's Deputy Minister of Roads and Highways, with influence over a vital resource for his hinterland region. He is not the first member of his family to become a powerful elite. His father, Edward Puowele Karbo, is Lawra's paramount chief, the area's most senior traditional leader. His father's uncle, Abeyifaa Karbo, was the previous chief, serving for almost three decades. Before that, Abeyifaa had been Lawra's most influential politician, elected as the area's first ever MP in 1954 while Ghana was still under colonial rule. Abeyifaa's own father, Jorbie Akodam (J. A.) Karbo, was chief from 1935 to 1967. Before him, J. A.'s brother Binni was chief as well.[1]

To many scholars, a central governance challenge in developing countries is the existence of what the Latin Americanist Guillermo O'Donnell (1993) famously termed "brown areas" on the map: subnational regions in which societal elites capture entrenched power in place of an absent state, leveraging their wealth or status to engage in clientelist politics that distort accountability, or even undermining state sovereignty through the private provision of violence.[2] In the words of Migdal (1988), poor governance outcomes in these regions arise from the ability of "strong societies" – and the elites like the Karbos who lead them – to dominate "weak states."

---

[1] Lentz (2006, 61, 324), Awedoba et al. (2009, 52–53), Brankopowers (2017).
[2] Bardhan and Mookherjee (2006), Acemoglu and Robinson (2008), Acemoglu et al. (2014).

Lawra lies within a region of persistent state weakness that has long been an afterthought to state leaders. Across the colonial period and successive post-independence regimes, they kept the state's footprint light in Northern Ghana, the hinterland to the north of the country's more prosperous forest belt and coast. Fearing little political threat from the population, and with little wealth to extract, the state made consistently limited investments. The communities surrounding Lawra exemplify this experience at the state's margins. Remote and seemingly cut off from the rest of the country for most of the twentieth century by a low quality road network, residents used to refer to the area as "overseas" and joke that they were "going to Ghana" when traveling south to the country's cities.[3] Into the 1980s, residents described the region as experiencing near "total neglect" from the state.[4]

State weakness in Northern Ghana parallels other hinterlands in the developing world, both within and beyond Africa.[5] Weakness is most immediately visible in hinterlands through the state's limited presence: the formal trappings common to any state – its administrative offices and physical infrastructure – are often simply not there, with basic public services distant and hard to reach.[6] This limited "territorial reach" often goes hand-in-hand with incapacity – the state's inability to act on its leaders' dictates.[7] Building from Hersbt (2000), it is often assumed that regions of limited state presence are where the state is least impactful – least able to change society or displace pre-existing realities of governance.

This long-standing assumption that weak states in the rural periphery are subordinate to society continues to inform major research agendas on African politics, with parallels in related literatures on other developing regions.[8] Those seeking to explain local public goods provision in rural areas like Lawra now often probe the role of nonstate societal elites like the Karbos,[9] or instead study the norms and identities

---

[3] Bob-Milliar (2011, 466).

[4] Bob-Milliar (2011, 459).

[5] O'Donnell (1993), Herbst (2000), Scott (2009).

[6] Brinkerhoff, Wetterberg, and Wibbels (2018).

[7] Mann (1988), Soifer (2008).

[8] Such claims are common throughout the literature on African states (Ekeh 1975, Bayart 1993, Chabal and Daloz 1999, Englebert 2000).

[9] Baldassarri and Grossman (2011), Acemoglu et al. (2014), Grossman (2014), Baldwin (2015, 2019a, 2019b), Baldwin and Mvukiyehe (2015), Gottlieb (2017).

that inform self-provision and collective action,[10] rather than explore the direct actions of the state itself. Scholars of political violence explain conflict in hinterlands as a function of the state's absence and inability to police grievances in society.[11] Others are increasingly focused on the present-day effects of precolonial societal institutions that pre-date the modern state altogether.[12] The assumption underlying much of this latter research is that pre-existing societal institutions persist and explain modern outcomes because the weak state has been incapable of displacing them.[13] Overall, each set of scholarship reasons that if the state is so weak in peripheral rural areas, we must look elsewhere to understand key features of politics.

This book pushes back against this reasoning. I propose a new approach to the rural periphery in Africa and beyond, departing from existing research in two key ways. First, I challenge the common assumption that a state's limited physical presence indicates an inability to have large effects on society and politics. In many peripheral regions, states are not merely absent, they are *scarce*. The economic language of scarcity – rather than more common terms like "limited state presence," "limited territorial reach," or the vague "state weakness" – provides a more appropriate metaphor for understanding the impacts of these states. Their actions and the resources they control are in short supply relative to demand for them in rural society. Much as the scarcity of a good in a marketplace increases its price, the scarcity of the state increases the relative economic weight that its isolated actions can have. The result is that even very absent and seemingly incapable states with limited "infrastructural power"[14] and limited autonomy from societal elites – the most common definitions of state weakness – can still be incredibly impactful states. Because a scarce state's actions have outsize effects in places that otherwise have limited contact with the state, relatively absent states may be

---

[10] Miguel and Gugerty (2005), Habyarimana et al. (2007, 2009), Cammett and Maclean (2014), Larson and Lewis (2017), Wilfahrt (2018). Paller (2019) extends a similar research agenda to urban areas.

[11] Fearon and Laitin (2003), Buhaug and Rod (2006), Elfversson (2015), Rudolfsen (2017), Lewis (2020), Muller-Crepon et al. (2020).

[12] Englebert (2000), Gennaioli and Rainer (2007), Nunn (2008), Nunn and Wantchekon (2011), Michalopoulos and Papaioannou (2013), Wilfahrt (2018), Kramon (2019), Paine (2019), Michalopoulos and Papaioannou (2020).

[13] Gennaioli and Rainer (2007, 185–186).

[14] Mann (1988).

potentially even more impactful at re-shaping society than in subnational regions where the state is less scarce and more capable. Simply counting a state's physical footprint – its offices, infrastructure, and bureaucrats – does not provide a strong measure of its potential impact.[15]

Second, I argue that a state that appears weak relative to a "strong society" can still have had such a large impact that it can be, paradoxically, the actor who forcefully made that society what it is, creating the very societal elites and institutions who now dominate it. Even in so-called brown areas – where the state appears weakest subnationally – society is not a pristine entity free of the state's effects; these areas cannot be studied independently from the history of the state's actions, however isolated and limited in scope those actions might appear. Taking these two claims together, the book implies that rather than zones of near statelessness, as Herbst's (2000) framework suggests viewing rural regions with limited states, these areas are instead where the footprints of the state's actions may be most visible in society and politics.

At the heart of this theory is the observation that the state's scarcity – the fact that the state has so few points of contact with society and makes so few attempts at governing – is itself what allows the isolated actions that the state does take to have outsize effects. In regions with limited economic development, even very absent states still regularly control the allocation of resources far more valuable than those otherwise available in society. When such a state acts, it typically distributes some resources to society. But because the state is limited and incapable, these resources are often targeted narrowly – to small sets of beneficiaries – rather than reaching society at large. These beneficiaries receive economic windfalls that elevate them in socioeconomic status relative to everyone else.

Crucially, if the state remains scarce and takes few new actions that benefit new beneficiaries, the advantages created by earlier state actions compound over time. Seemingly minor and isolated state actions can then have large long-term effects on socioeconomic inequality, creating new elites and sparking substantial changes to societal institutions. In turn, state-generated inequality affects how societal actors contest with each other for political power. By contrast, and counterintuitively, in

---

[15] This echoes a broader observation from literature on the African state outside political science that the state's substantive effects can diverge from the state's concrete "materiality," or the simple sum of its physical parts, including because of the endogenous ways that societies respond to state absence (Hagmann and Peclard 2010, Nugent 2010*b*). Also see Mitchell (1999).

subnational regions where the state is more active, less resource advantaged relative to a more developed private sector, or both, the same specific state actions will be less impactful on society and politics. In line with the metaphor above, reductions in state scarcity give the state's actions less substantive weight, or value.

The book explores this argument through a multi-method study of Northern Ghana, an archetypical hinterland in Africa, and also extends the theory to cases from other developing world regions, including Peru and the Philippines. Drawing in part on a natural experiment, the main analyses process trace the causal pathways through which Northern Ghana's contemporary societal and political elite emerged, linking actions of the scarce modern state to new forms of economic and social stratification and then demonstrating how these socioeconomic changes determined access to political power, the nature of clientelist politics, and patterns of contemporary political violence.

I show that elite families like the Karbos of Lawra are very much creations of the modern state, not pre-existing societal actors who maintain power in spite of it. In an early attempt to keep the state's footprint small, state leaders delegated grassroots authority, arbitrarily selecting families like the Karbos to serve as new "traditional" intermediaries in communities like Lawra. Simply gaining privileged contact with the scarce state set up this narrow group of families to benefit from future distributions of state resources, especially with the introduction of the public education system decades later. In turn, economic advantages from early access to state resources allowed these families to sustain political dynasties and consolidate power. This all occurred in a context in which the state was persistently weak in most ways the concept is defined, and despite the few actions it took not being implemented successfully by an incapable bureaucracy. Yet by delivering windfalls of resources more valuable than those in society, the state's few actions had large, at times unintended, effects, helping to create the "strong societies" that later seemed to overpower the weak state.

This is a book about the politics of state scarcity. Rather than stopping at the observation that the state has a limited presence, immediately assuming it has had a limited impact, and looking elsewhere to explain rural society and politics, I take the state's scarcity as my starting point and explore that scarcity's consequences. I push back against common assumptions about the nature of state weakness in the developing world and question how scholars typically conceptualize the politics of the rural periphery. I also suggest new approaches for understanding the origins of economic and political inequality and studying the historical legacies of colonial and precolonial institutions.

I focus on state–society relations in the *hinterland*. Hinterlands lie at the state's periphery. While this is often the geographic periphery – distant from the capital and major cities – the periphery is better defined through a region's political and economic relationship to the central state. I view hinterlands as economically marginal rural areas where the state makes limited attempts to project authority.[16] Hinterlands are where the politics of state scarcity come into sharpest relief. Going out to the limit, to the weakest parts of a weak state, and still uncovering evidence of the state's ability to transform society and politics can help illustrate the flaws in existing approaches to studying state-building.

I define the state as the set of bureaucratic organizations that acts out the orders of state leaders as they attempt to govern. Although standard in political science,[17] this organizational conceptualization of the state is narrower than in more anthropological literature that focuses on the state as a social imaginary and process of political contestation, including by examining the roles that societal actors political scientists would typically label as "nonstate" can play in also performing state-like functions.[18] This latter work is useful in suggesting ways that the state's effects can extend beyond the physical contours of the state's bureaucratic presence, but I maintain the simpler and standard definition here for conceptual clarity. And while a large literature focuses on the private incentives and principal–agent relationships that determine interactions among actors within the state – such as between local bureaucrats and national state leaders[19] – these distinctions are outside the scope of my argument. I instead simplify and collapse to viewing the state as a unitary organ that follows its leaders' directives. I focus on national state

---

[16] In many cases, geographic, political, and economic peripheries overlap. But there are exceptions – geographically distant regions that are "core" to a state's political attention and economic interests – such that geography alone cannot define the hinterland. Pierskalla et al. (2019) show that distance from the capital does not always account for where African states historically projected the most authority subnationally.

[17] Skocpol (1985).

[18] Mitchell (1999), Lund (2006), Blundo and Le Meur (2009), Hagmann and Peclard (2010), Bierschenk and Olivier de Sardan (2014). On nonstate provision in political science, see Cammett and Maclean (2014).

[19] Berwick and Christia (2018), Hassan (2020).

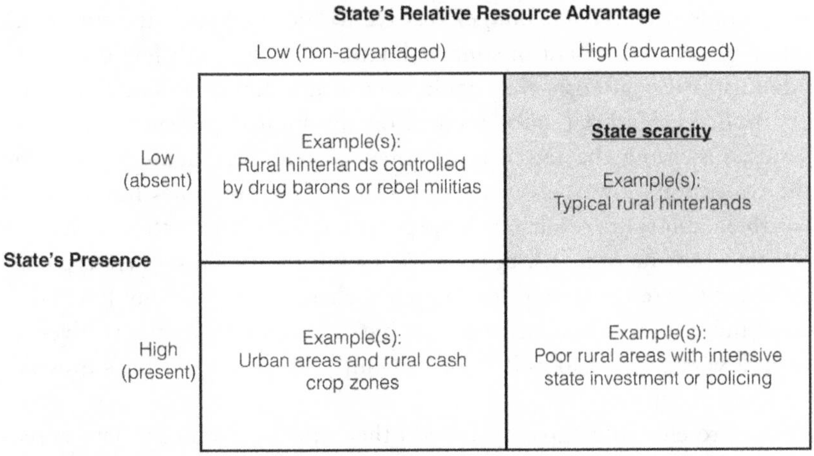

State's Relative Resource Advantage

	Low (non-advantaged)	High (advantaged)
Low (absent)	Example(s): Rural hinterlands controlled by drug barons or rebel militias	**State scarcity** Example(s): Typical rural hinterlands
High (present)	Example(s): Urban areas and rural cash crop zones	Example(s): Poor rural areas with intensive state investment or policing

State's Presence (row label on left)

FIGURE 1.1 Subnational regions defined by state presence and resource advantages. The state's presence and relative resource advantages define four categories of subnational region. The book primarily focuses on the condition of state scarcity in the top-right cell.

leaders – whether autocrats or elected politicians – as the decision-makers guiding the state's behavior.

In this definition, state and society are separate but in constant interaction, with each attempting to control and alter the other.[20] State–society boundaries can be blurry in practice.[21] In many African contexts, for example, traditional societal elites, such as chiefs, exercise forms of public authority separately from formal state institutions.[22] But it is still analytically useful to focus on a more parsimonious division between formal state leaders and bureaucrats, on one side, and actors within society who may at times assist or complement the state's activities, on the other.[23] This is in part because the interview subjects featured in the remainder of this book themselves make this distinction, referring to societal elites like traditional chiefs as part of a shared "us" – members of their own communities – while labeling state leaders and bureaucrats as a distinct and distant "them" from which their communities demand resources.

Figure 1.1 situates hinterlands relative to other subnational regions using two core variables: the state's *presence* and the extent to which the

[20] Mann (1988), Migdal (1988), Hassan, Mattingly, and Nugent (2022).
[21] Mitchell (1999).
[22] Lund (2006).
[23] Similarly, see Nugent (2010b).

state holds *resource advantages* relative to society. States are only minimally physically present in some subnational areas, with few officers or administrative outposts that could even begin implementing state leaders' policies. Herbst (2000) focuses on the limited presence of African states, observing the few officials they post to peripheral regions and the constraints low road density and difficult geographies have created for their ability to reach far-flung populations.[24] The state's capacity – whether bureaucratic, fiscal, coercive, or informational[25] – will typically be lower where the state is less present: where there are many fewer officials, the state will generally be less able to execute leaders' directives. In turn, low capacity makes it more difficult to expand the state's presence into new territories.

But presence and capacity are still theoretically distinct.[26] The stereotypical bloated urban bureaucracy controlled by a machine party represents an incapable, but very present state – with (too) many offices and employees, even if ineffective at implementing policies amidst corruption and clientelism. More importantly, the state's relative absence in a given territory is often a strategic choice, not simply an outcome of limited capacity. Herbst (2000) suggests that limited state presence primarily results from the cost of projecting power across distance – that it is too hard for weak states to extend across difficult terrain. But Boone (2003) demonstrates that postcolonial African leaders often kept the state much more absent than they were capable of in some regions as a form of bargaining with local elites.[27] States remain especially absent in some hinterlands because state leaders see little political or economic benefit from making the state more present, not because it is too far.[28] In the absence of natural resources or cash crops, there may be too few economic rents to extract from the local economy to justify new state investment. Alternatively, the lack of a serious political challenge may render a region not worth actively coopting or coercing.

---

[24] For other examples, see O'Donnell (1993), Acemoglu et al. (2015), Soifer (2015), Muller-Crepon et al. (2020), and the many studies of African politics using distance from the capital as a proxy for state strength.

[25] Evans et al. (1985), Levi (1988), Weber (1946 [1919]), and Scott (1998), respectively.

[26] Capacity and territorial reach form separate dimensions within Mann's (1988) "state infrastructural power" (Soifer 2008).

[27] Other scholars similarly document African leaders' strategic manipulation of their states' presence across territory by choosing where to draw administrative boundaries and site offices. For example, Grossman and Lewis (2014), Hassan (2016), and Hassan and Sheely (2017).

[28] Outside the African context, see Slater and Kim (2015).

The second dimension in Figure 1.1 is the state's *resource advantage* relative to society. States in the developing world are often what Chandra (2016, 33) labels "dominant states," with control over economic resources that significantly exceed those in the private market.[29] By resources, I mean that states retain discretionary control over a wide range of economically valuable private and local public goods. States have the ability to decide which areas receive infrastructure investments and access to basic services like health and electricity, as well as to allocate private goods to individuals such as employment, land rights, and opportunities to develop human capital through public education. What is crucial to Figure 1.1 is not that the state has control over a large *absolute* amount of resources, but that it is *relatively* advantaged versus its society – *that the ratio between the economic value of what contact with the state can provide to what is otherwise available in the private market is high.*

Even as many states in the developing world appear poor from a cross-national perspective, they still regularly control resources far greater than in their local economies. A central feature of political competition in many developing countries, especially in Africa, has long been that the state serves as an incredibly valuable prize to compete to control because that control provides access to economic returns not available elsewhere.[30] In the postcolonial world, the infrastructure of the modern state mostly emerged exogenously to society, endowed from the start with significant external resource advantages. In Africa, postcolonial states inherited many of the colonial state's advantages and then were able to sustain them despite limited fiscal capacity through access to natural resource rents, relatively easy to enforce taxes on exports, and external development assistance.[31] In addition, the sources of the state's resources can be highly concentrated in space: extraction is often focused subnationally on more prosperous regions, while remaining relatively minimal elsewhere. The result is that in less developed subnational regions, such as many hinterlands, the state can have far more resources to spend than are present in society.

That many developing states' relative resource advantages have emerged exogenously to local societies is important for understanding the

[29] Alternatively, in the words of Bates (1983), these states disproportionately control the scarce benefits of "modernity."
[30] Bates (1983, 2008).
[31] Bates (1981), van de Walle (2001).

effects these states can have. Traditional conceptualizations focus on the state's role as an extractor – even a predator or bandit – that has resources only insomuch as it takes them.[32] But where the state's resource advantages are accumulated externally to a local society, it is more likely to become a *net provider*, giving out more than it takes back. In hinterlands where there is relatively little wealth worth attempting to extract, the short-run risk of increased taxation from contact with the state can be quite minimal; effects of the state are most likely from the resources it gives, not via society's attempts to avoid its extraction.[33]

Viewed in combination, these two variables define four broad categories of subnational regions represented by the cells of Figure 1.1. These cells can be labeled by their combination of the two dimensions: {presence, resource advantages}. Most hinterland regions in the developing world, including the example of Lawra in Northern Ghana described above, fall within the top-right of Figure 1.1, in the {low, high}, or {absent, advantaged}, cell. These regions are zones of *state scarcity*: they correspond to underdeveloped rural areas in which the state has a limited formal presence, yet also has control over the distribution of resources that dwarf those otherwise available in the local economy.[34] Demand for the state's resources in society significantly outpaces supply, creating scarcity. Subnational hinterlands with scarce states are the primary focus of the book.

By contrast, diagonally across from these hinterlands in the bottom-left of Figure 1.1 are subnational regions in the {high, low}, or {present, non-advantaged}, cell. These are areas where the state is instead much more active and in which the private economy is more developed, reducing the gap in value between any resources potentially provided by the state and those that can be secured independently in society. This cell represents political and economic core regions of developing countries. The difference between the {absent, advantaged} and {present, non-advantaged} cells is not purely rural versus urban. Examples of the {present, non-advantaged} cell include both urban areas and rural areas

---

[32] Or at least convinces society to give them to it. Levi (1988), Tilly (1990), Olson (1993), Scott (1998, 2009).

[33] This contrasts notably with the approach in Scott (1998, 2009).

[34] Limited economic development is endogenous to state scarcity. The economy is typically least developed where the state is least capable of providing economic infrastructure and enforcement (Besley and Persson 2009, Dincecco 2018). Meanwhile, state leaders often invest the least in expanding the state's presence in the first place in resource-poor regions with little economic potential (Boone 2003).

that are cash crop zones or other sites of high value economic activities (e.g., mining), where the state has incentives to invest in building up a presence to extract.

The two other off-diagonal cells in Figure 1.1 are relatively less common but still exist in subnational pockets in some developing countries, providing an opportunity to consider broader implications and scope conditions of my theory. The {low, low}, or {absent, non-advantaged}, cell represents a second, more extreme, type of hinterland in which private societal actors have come to control resources that rival those of the state itself. Contemporary examples include areas dominated by drug cartels, rebel militias, or mafias, such as the sections of rural Colombia controlled by paramilitaries or the broad swaths of rural Mali and Somalia controlled by militants. Similar to the state's resource advantages in {absent, advantaged} hinterlands, the private resources of these societal actors often also emerge exogenously to the economies of local communities, drawn from illicit international markets or military arms and financing provided by external powers.[35] While hinterlands in the {absent, non-advantaged} cell may be particularly salient in the popular imagination, they are more exceptions than the rule. In Africa, for example, the vast majority of rural areas, even if not entirely peaceful, do not have powerful rebels or militias who rival the state. This is true even within conflict-prone countries.[36] My primary focus is on more typical hinterlands that better fit in the {absent, advantaged} cell.

The final set of subnational regions characterized by Figure 1.1 are areas in the {high, high}, or {present, advantaged}, cell. These are regions where the state retains its resource advantage over society – for example, because they are not zones of major economic activity – and yet in which the state has nonetheless decided to invest in a relatively substantial presence. This may be because the region is strategically vital for a potential inter-state conflict, such as some border regions. Alternatively, it may be because state leaders face an especially pressing political threat, despite the area's underdevelopment, and reduce the state's scarcity to ensure

---

[35] For example, Lee (2020). Alternatively, as discussed in more detail in Chapters 2 and 9, the advantages of private actors in this cell of Figure 1.1 may emerge from past actions of the state itself.

[36] In conflict event data from the Armed Conflict Location and Event Data (ACLED) project (2016), no rebel activity between 2015 and 2020 was reported in 55 percent (25 of 46) of countries in sub-Saharan Africa. In those that had rebels, the median case had rebel activity in just 17 percent of its second-tier administrative units, leaving large swaths of the rural periphery unaffected.

compliance.[37] I consider examples of these off-diagonal cells – {absent, non-advantaged} and {present, advantaged} – in Chapters 2 and 9.

1.2 THEORY: THE LARGE EFFECTS OF SCARCE STATES

The theory explores how the relative resource advantages of scarce states allow them to transform society and politics, having large effects even where existing accounts assume the state should be inconsequential. The central focus is thus on the effects of state action *within* regions in the {absent, advantaged} cell. More broadly, however, I also suggest that the effects of most individual state actions may in fact be largest in these regions compared to the other cells of Figure 1.1. In the aggregate, across multiple state actions, this implies that it is not necessarily true that the state will have had its smallest effects on society where it is persistently absent and has the lowest capacity.

By state effects on society, I mean the causal effect of the state: a state with large effects changes pre-existing societal institutions and hierarchies in major ways through its actions. This concept is related to existing notions of state power. Building from Dahl (1957), Lindvall and Teorell (2016) argue that a state is only "powerful" insomuch as it can make societal actors do things that they would not otherwise do. A state with large effects on its society is certainly a state that makes society do things it would not otherwise do. But many conceptualizations of power, including Mann's (1988), also incorporate intent: can the state make society do what the state wants it to do?[38] My focus is instead broader, on a more latent or implicit type of power: I recognize that the state's most meaningful impacts on society in hinterland regions may at times come through unintended consequences of policies adopted for other reasons, or that were not executed as planned. In this view, the state can have large effects on society – with the state's actions fundamental to understanding why society has come to be the way that it is – even where the state is quintessentially weak and does not have significant power in any traditional sense.

I consider state effects in two stages. First, I focus on effects on society, both direct and indirect. I then focus on downstream effects of the societal changes induced by the state on competition for political power. I summarize each set of claims here and develop them further in Chapter 2.

---

[37] Boone (2003).
[38] For a broader discussion of state power, see Kashwan et al. (2019).

1.2.1 Direct and Indirect Effects on Society

When states with resource advantages act, they step into society with a huge weight behind their footsteps. Their actions can leave large imprints – with cascading distortionary effects over time – even if their policies are not executed as intended, and especially if they are scarce and only attempt a few policies overall. Indeed, that scarce states only attempt few interventions into society is itself what helps make those actions so impactful. State effects can be both direct – with state resources reordering social hierarchies and institutions – and indirect – with the possibility of accessing state resources incentivizing society into endogenous, bottom-up responses.

The most direct manifestation of scarce states' impact on hinterland regions may be their ability to create new forms of socioeconomic inequality, both within and between rural communities. When the state intervenes in these regions, it typically confers some of its resources on the population, giving out more than it takes back. This creates winners and losers: benefits accrue to some people or places, but not others. Building a local public good like a clinic or road benefits the communities in its catchment area, but not elsewhere. Hiring local agents to provide services or delegating tasks to local intermediaries delivers a private benefit to those selected to perform the work that does not similarly extend to those not selected. Moreover, by virtue of the incapacity caused by the state's limited presence, any benefits are unlikely to be evenly or widely distributed. Instead, the more absent the state is, the more likely the winners of its actions are to be narrowly concentrated.

Because the state's resources dwarf those in society, beneficiaries of state actions gain a new advantage. Privileged contact with the state becomes an economic *windfall* potentially far more valuable than what could otherwise be accumulated. This is true regardless of whether the state confers a private benefit to individuals or a local public good to specific communities.

Economic windfalls from the state create new socioeconomic inequality on two time scales. In the short run, inequality emerges because winners of state action gain resources relative to losers. Longer term, this new inequality sticks and becomes entrenched *if* the state remains scarce and takes few subsequent actions that allocate further windfalls to new recipients. Continued state scarcity magnifies the state's earlier actions, giving them long afterlives; inequality compounds over time when early access to state resources provides an economic head start that sets early winners of state action off on a better trajectory. There are often few nonstate paths to wealth accumulation in the {absent, advantaged} cell of Figure 1.1, leaving early losers little outside opportunity to catch up.[39] Breaking out of this path-dependent divergence between the initial winners and losers of state action requires either substantial changes to the local economy that create new private sector paths to wealth accessible to those initially left behind or instead a dramatic subsequent increase in the state's presence, and resulting distribution of new state resources to new recipients.

When a scarce state acts is thus important for understanding the effects it has. Early interventions into a resource-poor society with limited baseline economic stratification can have long-lasting effects even if the interventions are quite small. New actions that occur later must be comparatively larger to have similarly sized effects; the baseline level of stratification and wealth in society will have risen as a result of earlier state action. To close socioeconomic gaps that its earlier actions have opened, the value of any new resources delivered by a state later on must be greater than the initial windfalls; simply providing the same benefit later will not necessarily undermine the compounded inequality that has emerged. The result is that as long as the state remains relatively scarce, its very first steps into hinterland regions are likely to have had the comparatively most important implications for the subsequent trajectory of society.

The scarce state's actions can also have significant indirect effects on society. In regions of persistent state scarcity, the losers who do not benefit from initial windfalls – and end up on the bottom of emerging socioeconomic hierarchies – must consider several possible responses. They may simply cope with the state's neglect, self-providing resources in its absence.[40] They may violently resist the state, pushing back against the new inequality it has brought.[41] But where the state's relative resource advantages are high, neglected communities may instead face the strongest incentives to respond by proactively seeking the state out, taking steps to attract it to their communities in the hopes greater contact will bring windfalls to themselves. New societal elites and institutions that best facilitate improved access to the state can emerge endogenously, as communities shift their behavior on their own. The state's mere presence

---

[39] Alesina et al. (2019) find persistently worse intergenerational economic mobility in subnational regions in Africa in which state investment has been most limited over time.

[40] Cammett and Maclean (2014).

[41] Scott (1998, 2009).

as a reserve of resources more valuable than what is available in society can be powerful enough to incentivize bottom-up social changes that alter the basic structure of society, even without the state's intent.

An additional implication of this argument is that the societal effects of the same specific state actions may, counterintuitively, be smaller in other subnational regions. Where the state is less resource advantaged relative to society, any individual action it takes is less likely to have the ability to reorder existing distributions of wealth and political power in the short run. In turn, where the state is more present, the long-run effects of any individual action will be smaller because the state is more likely to soon take additional actions that distribute new windfalls to additional recipients, offsetting earlier actions. In the {present, non-advantaged} ({high, low}) cell of Figure 1.1, representing a country's core regions, both dynamics are at play. In the aggregate, even if the state takes many more actions overall in regions where it is less scarce, it is not necessarily the case that the state's overall impact on society will be greater compared to where the state nominally appears weaker.

1.2.2 Political Consequences: Capture, Clientelism, and Violence

In turn, the societal changes brought about by the state's scarcity reshape the politics of hinterlands. The distribution of economic resources affects how contests for power unfold, defining the tools available to societal actors as they seek political authority. While political effects can appear across multiple domains, I focus on three salient examples for many developing countries: elite capture, clientelism, and political violence.

First, isolated state actions in hinterlands create conditions for elite capture. The new elites who emerge from early state windfalls gain economic advantages that allow them to dominate politics, with economic inequality manifesting as political inequality. During autocratic periods, state-created elites can use their new local advantages to muscle aside rivals and attract further rents from state leaders. In electoral periods, these same elites can use their advantages to buy voters' support. Elite capture rooted in state-generated inequality may take the form of *dynastic politics*, in which politicians from the same small sets of families wield quasi-oligarchical power across generations.[42]

---

[42] Dal Bo et al. (2009), Chandra (2016), Jensenius (2016), Querubin (2016), Smith (2018).

Second, state-generated economic inequality sustains clientelism. In addition to candidates and officeholders, elites placed at the top of new socioeconomic hierarchies by the state's actions can become clientelist brokers, coordinating and delivering local votes in return for further state resources.[43] If the elites acting as brokers have influence over community members' political behavior, but are not accountable to those community members to hold onto their own positions of power, they may exploit their role as intermediaries for private gain, trading away community members' votes while capturing many of the benefits. This becomes more likely where these elites were elevated artificially by state actions, lacking organic, deeply-rooted social accountability to community members.[44] In this way, clientelism that emerges from state-created inequality may also help further undermine democratic accountability in hinterlands.

Third, the societal changes caused by scarce states can also produce political violence. Contrary to common claims, this violence is not an outcome of the state's incapacity, but emerges because the state's actions fuel new grievances. Where many residents view the state as a net provider, this violence will often not explicitly target the state, as in a civil war, but instead take the form of nonstate communal conflicts in which actors within society compete for the state's attention. Violence becomes a tool to improve one's relative position in the hope of increasing the odds of securing valuable state resources for yourself. Violence emerges between separate communities or ethnic groups, with those that see themselves as the losers of isolated state actions rising up against the new dominance of neighboring winners. Alternatively, intra-communal violence erupts as residents contest the new intra-ethnic hierarchies emerging from the state's isolated distribution of resources.

1.3 CONTEXT: NORTHERN GHANA AND THE MODERN AFRICAN STATE

I examine this argument in the context of the modern African state. I follow Young (1994) in defining the modern state as beginning at the onset of colonial rule, in contrast to the premodern, precolonial states that preceded it. Postcolonial state institutions in many African countries evolved directly from their colonial analogs. Young (1994) observes that "the colonial state lives, absorbed into the structures of the independent

---

43 Baldwin (2015), Holland and Palmer-Rubin (2015), Koter (2016), Mares and Young (2016), Gottlieb (2017).
44 Acemoglu et al. (2014), Gottlieb (2017).

polity"; it is "deeply embedded within its postcolonial successor."[45] My focus on continuities across the colonial and postcolonial periods also echoes Herbst (2000) in recognizing that although the identity (and normative legitimacy) of state leaders changed, their state-building task remained similar. Whether state leaders are European or African does not change the ability of isolated state actions to reshape hinterland regions.[46]

Existing characterizations of the modern African state present an enigma. The same states are portrayed as disastrously weak, unable to govern or deliver services, and yet also capable of having major impacts. The modern African state is a "mirage" and "facade," "vacuous" and "institutionally feeble," and cannot control or act separately from its society.[47] It is persistently unable to project power across its territory, with "limited ambitions" for rule, administering society "on the cheap" in a way that has failed to displace precolonial realities of governance.[48] It is barely even "empirically" a state,[49] minimally touching the lives of citizens in the rural periphery.[50] And yet, it is also a "crusher of rocks";[51] the origin of new social identities and modes of social control;[52] a "vampire" sucking its society's blood,[53] whose policy choices and institutional structures profoundly affect citizens' behavior.[54] At times, the state appears to straddle both worlds within the same study. Although Migdal (1988) principally describes the Sierra Leonian state as captured by society, his historical account also implicitly suggests it was also more than powerful enough to have radically remade key elements of that society. My argument helps resolve these competing characterizations of the modern

---

[45] Young (1994, 2, 10). More recently, Young (2004) suggests that the period from the 1990s onward may represent an end of the "postcolonial" state, given changes to state authority wrought by democratization and structural adjustment. While important, this distinction is not directly relevant to the argument here; my main analyses all focus on state actions prior to the 1990s. Moreover, to whatever extent structural adjustment weakened the state's ability to intervene further in society, it only magnifies the importance of understanding the long-term effects of earlier state actions.

[46] Moreover, this focus on historical continuity addresses a key shortcoming Hagmann and Peclard (2010) identify in some other political science work on the African state – that state "weakness" is viewed from too ahistorical a lens.

[47] Chabal and Daloz (1999, 8, 16, 1, and 2, respectively). Migdal (1988) makes a related set of claims.

[48] Herbst (2000, 73 and 75, respectively).

[49] Jackson and Rosberg (1982).

[50] Zolberg (1966), Hyden (1980).

[51] Young (1994).

[52] Vail (1989), Mamdani (1996).

[53] Frimpong-Ansah (1991).

[54] Bates (1981, 1983, 1989, 2008), Maclean (2010).

African state by suggesting that the state's very weakness – as evinced through its scarcity – may often be what helps magnify the impacts of its actions.

I demonstrate this by focusing empirically on a modern African state with a large hinterland in which that state was persistently scarce. Formerly the British Gold Coast, Ghana is a nation of over 30 million people with an economy historically dominated by cash crops (primarily cocoa) and gold mining. Southern Ghana spans the country's coastal regions, including the economically booming national capital Accra and the cash crop zones in the central forest belt surrounding Kumasi, capital of the precolonial Ashanti Empire. Northern Ghana – the shaded region in Map 1.1 – instead comprises the less populated and poorer areas north and east of the Black Volta River.[55] This region has 17 percent of Ghana's present-day population – now approximately 5 million of 30 million. Unlike the more densely populated, forested, and fertile South, the country's North is mostly flat, low-density savannah extending to the lower fringes of the Sahel. The Northern hinterland is highly diverse, with over thirty indigenous ethnic groups. In the precolonial period, it was a mix of *acephalous* societies – without political centralization – and small kingdoms that were peripheral vassal states of Ashanti.

The North's marginalization has continued under both British and independent rule, with the state maintaining a persistently limited presence. In the colonial period, it was governed separately from – and far more minimally than – the rest of the country, set aside as the separate Northern Territories of the larger Gold Coast colony. The British made "only the feeblest of efforts" at institution-building and economic development in the North;[56] with no cash crops or natural resources, the region was not a priority for the colonial regime, colonized more to prevent other European powers from colonizing it than for its economic value to the Empire. By the 1920s and 1930s, this territory roughly the size of Virginia was overseen by a skeleton staff of as few as thirty British officers, of all types, thinly spread across fewer than a dozen towns.[57] Until World War II, there were as few as 100 European residents at any

---

[55] This is the Northern, North East, Savannah, Upper East, and Upper West Regions. From 1983 to 2018, these were the Northern, Upper East, and Upper West Regions.

[56] Ladouceur (1979, 44).

[57] In the 1921 census, two decades into colonial rule, there were twenty-seven British officers resident in the Northern Territories and just thirty-six non-African residents *total*.

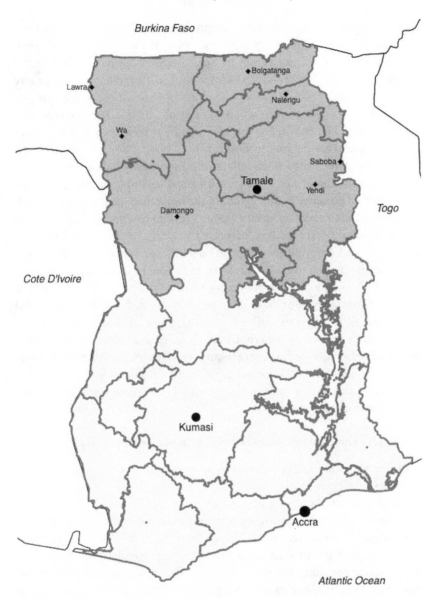

MAP 1.1 Map of Ghana. Northern Ghana is the shaded region. The western, southern, and eastern borders of this region are framed by the Black Volta River, Lake Volta, and the Oti River, respectively.

time.[58] Missionary activity was sharply limited to a few outposts until the 1950s. Data on the geographic footprint of the colonial state introduced in Chapter 3 suggests that by 1945, residents of over 87 percent of Northern Ghana's towns and villages would still have had to walk more than 10 km (6.2 miles) to reach *any* formal state office, police post, or other administrative station where they could have direct contact with state officials. The British left this hinterland, in their own words, "more than half a century behind the South."[59]

The North remained politically and economically subordinate to the South after independence in 1957, with state leaders continuing to maintain a limited presence in the region. In the immediate postcolonial period, Northern Ghana serves as one of Boone's (2003) examples of a peripheral region in which state leaders intentionally kept the state away, delegating power to existing local elites rather then deconcentrating the state's bureaucratic presence in a serious attempt to govern more directly. Decentralization reforms first adopted in 1988 and gradually accelerated after democratization in 1992 have only recently created a more meaningful grassroots state apparatus. The combined result of nearly a century of state scarcity is that Northern Ghana has received dramatically lower investment in basic infrastructure and services than Southern Ghana. Even as Ghana has experienced rapid economic development over the last several decades, a substantial overall North–South gap in poverty and infrastructure remains.[60]

1.3.1 Three Interventions: Chiefs, Schools, and Property Rights

Despite its minimal overall footprint, however, the modern state did make three interventions in Northern Ghana over the course of the twentieth century that are the core empirical focus of the book. I highlight these three actions because they are each, by far, the most significant efforts that the state undertook to conduct three of the most central governance activities attempted by all states: administering the population, distributing services, and providing the rule of law. The first action involved delegating authority to administer society cheaply. The second was the provision of public education. The third was a belated decision about whose property rights over land to legally recognize.

---

[58] For example, the 1931 census records 107 total non-African residents, many of whom were Lebanese and Indian traders, not British officials.

[59] Quoted in Bening (1990, 255).

[60] Abdulai and Hickey (2016).

In line with the claim above that state scarcity often emerges through an intentional choice of state leaders, rather than as a simple outcome of limited capacity,[61] each of these actions was undertaken with the explicit intention of facilitating state absence: delegating authority allowed the state to keep its formal staff small; education was initially provided only insomuch as it made delegating authority more effective; and the state reallocated property rights to reduce its need to provide its own oversight. Moreover, on their own, each intervention initially struggled to achieve its intended objectives, indicative of the scarce state's consistently limited capacity. Yet they all eventually combined to have large, mutually reinforcing effects on society and politics. I outline each in turn here.

First, operating with such a minimal staff, the British quickly turned to administering society through local intermediaries instead. Delegating authority to local elites, including traditional chiefs, would soon become a common strategy across British colonies in Africa.[62] It represents a widely applied approach adopted by many state-builders in peripheral regions around the world, even far beyond the examples of African colonialism or the policies formally labeled "indirect rule."[63]

The British faced a challenge, however: not all communities had existing leaders to whom they could delegate authority. The region's precolonial kingdoms had well-established chiefs; among these already-centralized ethnic groups, such as the Dagomba, Gonja, and Mamprusi, the British co-opted and reinforced pre-existing leadership structures. But these kingdoms account for only approximately one third of the region's population. The remaining population was instead acephalous, without an existing authority structure that reached beyond individual extended families. From as early as 1902, just a year after formal colonial rule began, British officials instead set about inventing new chieftaincy institutions from scratch in many acephalous communities.[64]

---

[61] Boone (2003).

[62] Young (1994).

[63] Gerring et al. (2011), Slater and Kim (2015). Matsuzaki (2019) details that the delegation of authority to local intermediaries has also been a common feature of state-building in Southeast Asia (and twenty-first-century Iraq and Afghanistan). Mamdani (1996) and Boone (2003) argue that commonly discussed differences between British "indirect" and French "direct" rule in Africa are overblown – in practice, the French also relied on various similar local intermediaries in many subnational regions of their African colonies.

[64] I use the word "invention" to refer to the creation of new forms of traditional chieftaincy in a non-normative sense in line with the substantial historical literature on the topic that uses this term. See Ranger (1983), as well as Spear (2003) (for a critical reappraisal).

Intervening in societies about which they know very little, British deci-sions about who to appoint as chiefs were often deeply ad hoc, arbitrarily installing families into offices that could potentially become hereditary across subsequent generations. The imposition of these new political insti-tutions was not immediately successful – many new chiefs only very gradually amassed social authority and legitimacy in their communities over the coming decades.[65] But over the colonial period, as the scope of their authority gradually increased, opportunities eventually emerged for chiefs and their families to receive windfalls from their privileged link to the scarce state.

Crucially for my analysis, the British only imposed chieftaincy insti-tutions among a subset of acephalous ethnic groups. Others were left without their own state-recognized local leaders, placed instead under the nominal control of neighboring ethnic groups while defaulting in practice to pre-existing clan and family leadership. The difference between these two sets of ethnic groups – those with invented chiefs and those without them – was largely due to an arbitrary colonial border briefly in effect at the outset of the colonial period (see below and Chapter 4).

Overall, this initial variation in the delegation of authority to chiefs represents a *critical juncture* that set ethnic groups in Northern Ghana on three distinct, path-dependent trajectories of state–society relations over the next century: there are societies in Northern Ghana that *always* had chiefs, dating to the precolonial period; societies with colonially *invented* chiefs, with new elites imposed in the early twentieth century; and those that were *never recognized* as independent ethnic groups by the state and left largely without independent chiefs into the postcolonial period. Con-sistent with the argument above about path dependence and historical sequencing, this first state intervention became the most significant overall of the three, and correspondingly receives the most focus in the subse-quent chapters, because it came first and changed baseline conditions in society in ways that the state's subsequent actions would then have to grapple with.

The second major intervention was the halting creation of a public edu-cation system, the main public service that the state extended to the North throughout the twentieth century. Between 1945 and 1960, the education

---

In some ways, this was more an "imposition" than an invention, though there was also considerable African participation and agency over time in the design of these new institutions (Spear 2003).

[65] Lentz (2006), Grischow (2006).

system in Northern Ghana expanded from just 17 primary schools and 0 secondary schools to 216 primary schools and 2 secondary schools. Although this meant that fewer than 6 percent of Northern communities had schools and enrollments remained very low, schools became the most present state institution in the North by a wide margin.

For the small first generation of students able to attend school, education served as a windfall from the state. School "pioneers" received a head start in human capital accumulation relative to the rest of the population.[66] These benefits nested on top of the state's first major intervention – the imposition of chieftaincy – because of chiefs' role as the main point out of contact between their communities and the state. Chiefs were central in lobbying for and building schools, such that more schools were built in communities with chiefs than those left without these leaders. In turn, chiefs were given significant input into early enrollment decisions, allowing their own children to attend before children from other families. This allowed colonially imposed chiefs to use advantages originating from the state's first major action to disproportionately capture the benefits of its second.

The third major state intervention occurred deeper in the postcolonial period. It again nested on top of the first by increasing the advantages of the earliest winners of state action – chiefs. Under British rule, the state claimed ownership of all land in Northern Ghana, but did little with it. Colonial-era land policies continued after independence. In the majority of Northern ethnic groups, especially those that had been precolonially acephalous, land remained *de facto* controlled at the community level by an earth priest – known as a "tendana" – not a chief.[67] But in the late 1970s, state leaders formally devolved land ownership to chiefs in an attempt to buy their political support.[68]

As with the first two interventions, the state initially lacked the presence and capacity on the ground to fully enforce or implement this new policy. But land reform opened up new opportunities for local actors to leverage their contact with the state to extract economic windfalls. The new policy increased the economic value of chieftaincy positions and *de jure* dispossessed ethnic groups who lacked their own hierarchies of state-recognized chiefs – the *never recognized* groups described above – from the land they had farmed for generations.

---

[66] Wantchekon et al. (2015), Ricart-Huguet (2021a).

[67] Rattray (1932), Tait (1961), Ladouceur (1979), Lund (2008).

[68] Baldwin (2014) shows that this was a common tactic by state leaders in post-independence Africa to shore up support in rural areas.

1.3.2 Observing the State's Impact

The subsequent chapters trace out how these three state actions had mutually reinforcing effects on society and politics. These actions changed society both directly, by producing new socioeconomic hierarchies and inequality, and indirectly, by incentivizing communities to change their own internal social institutions to seek out more contact with the state.

Directly, the state's invention of chieftaincy and introduction of education combined to create persistent intra-ethnic, intra-village economic inequality across rural Northern Ghana. In particular, I show in Chapter 4 that the *invented chiefs* ethnic groups – acephalous communities that experienced the colonial imposition of chieftaincy in the early twentieth century – have substantially more internal economic inequality today than the *never recognized* communities. The central mechanism underlying this effect is the educational opportunities that became differentially available to chiefs' children as the education system expanded in the mid-twentieth century.

More indirectly, the state's interventions unintentionally pushed *never recognized* communities to begin creating chiefs of their own in the late twentieth and early twenty-first centuries. Chapter 5 details the origins and mixed success of this bottom-up grassroots effort to attract more resources from the state. Recognizing that they had become the losers left behind by earlier state actions, and could now securely own land only if they also had traditional chiefs, these communities have begun doing to themselves what the colonial state did decades earlier elsewhere in Northern Ghana: inventing "traditional" institutions from scratch, in a major attempt to reorganize internal social structures.

In turn, these changes to society have combined to have each of the political effects described above. Chapter 6 documents how the specific families elevated by the invention of chieftaincy in the early twentieth century have remained the region's political elite over time, dominating access to elected office from Ghana's first elections in 1951 through to the present day. I show how these high levels of elite capture and dynastic politics have their origins in the windfalls bestowed on chiefs' families through their privileged access to human capital in the mid-twentieth century.

Chapter 7 then details how the invention of chieftaincy created conditions in which clientelism could thrive. Chiefs have used their privileged connections to the state to become clientelist intermediaries – community-level brokers who coordinate community votes on behalf of allied politicians and political parties. Chiefs whose authority stems from artificial state-imposed institutions are less accountable to community members today than those whose positions are rooted in institutions that evolved more organically within communities. As a result, more deleterious forms of brokered clientelism are common among the *invented chiefs* ethnic groups – where chieftaincy was imposed exogenously by the state – than in the *always chiefs* or *never recognized* communities.

Finally, Chapter 8 explores effects on political violence. I detail how endemic conflicts in the hinterland were caused directly by the scarce state's actions, which generated new grievances in society, rather than simply emerging as a side effect of the weak state's absence and inability to police its frontier. The imposition of chieftaincy institutions combined with the growing economic rents and political power available to chiefs to cause a series of intra-communal, even intra-family, violence over appointments and succession. At a larger scale, emerging inter-ethnic inequality, reinforced by the 1979 land reform, led to major inter-ethnic conflict between *never recognized* and *always chiefs* communities in the 1980s and 1990s. The violence was sparked by communities who were the losers of earlier state actions seeking to take matters into their own hands to acquire scarce state resources for themselves.

1.4 DATA AND METHOD

I demonstrate these effects by drawing on a range of micro-level data, a multi-method design, and extended field research dating to 2008.[69] The quantitative data includes a series of new datasets on chieftaincy institutions and appointments, historical school enrollments and locations, and other types of early state activity coded from archival sources. I also use highly localized community- and individual-level census data from three national censuses – 2010, 2000, and 1960. The 2010 data includes individual-level returns located to each individual community, creating a dataset of up to 2.5 million observations.[70] The 1960 data has been digitized and geo-coded for the first time.

The qualitative data includes archival materials and over 110 in-depth interviews.[71] Elite interviews were conducted with politicians, including

---

[69] The main data collection occurred in 2018 and 2019.

[70] This is a 10 percent representative, random sample of individual records within every tract, or Enumeration Area.

[71] More details on these interviews, including sampling and questionnaires, are in the Appendix.

a random sample of 20 current MPs, as well as other government and
political party officials and civil society leaders. In addition, I draw heavily throughout the book on oral history interviews conducted with chiefs,
tendanas (earth priests), and other community elders in twelve rural communities spanning the three main categories of ethnic groups introduced
above. A relatively uncommon source in the literature on state-building,
the oral histories allow me to anchor my analysis in community members' own narratives and collective memories, as well as to include their
voices throughout the following pages. Central elements of my theory
arise directly from participants' own explanations of how the state has
impacted their communities.

The research design primarily relies on process tracing of the over-
time effects of state actions within a single hinterland region, focusing
on the {absent, advantaged} cell of Figure 1.1. I devote careful attention
to concerns over both internal and external validity. Regarding internal validity, many of the central analyses are "large-N" subnationally.
At the heart of the research design is a natural experiment. For a brief
15-year period at the outset of colonial rule, roughly one quarter of
Northern Ghana was part of a neighboring German colony – Togoland.
It was then absorbed into the British Gold Coast during World War I.
The initial Anglo-German border split the region's population in a highly
arbitrary manner – indeed, British officials themselves referred to this border as an "arbitrary boundary."[72] It serves as the critical juncture that
assigned communities originally placed on each side to different subsequent trajectories of state–society relations. Most importantly, almost all
precolonially acephalous communities initially under British rule experienced the imposition of chieftaincy – becoming the *invented chiefs* groups
described above – while otherwise similar communities under initial German rule did not – becoming the *never recognized* groups. Because the
next two major state actions – education and land reform – nested on top
of this initial assignment of communities to chiefs, the 1899–1914 Anglo-
German border provides a plausibly exogenous source of leverage with
which to estimate the effects of state actions across time.

I detail the external validity and scope conditions of the main argument
by drawing on shadow cases. The most direct comparison is to the parallel experiences of Southern Ghana, where the state was both much more
active and less resource advantaged versus society than in the North. The
South's urban areas and rural cash crop zones serve as the most natural

[72] *Northern Territories Annual Report for 1917* (1918, 11).

comparison to Northern Ghana in the {present, non-advantaged} cell of Figure 1.1, allowing me to vary the two main dimensions in the argument above while holding state leaders and institutions fixed. In addition, in Chapters 2 and 9, I include additional shadow cases that capture the two less common, off-diagonal cells of Figure 1.1, exploring state-building in the rural hinterlands of Peru and the Philippines. These additional cases demonstrate that the two variables highlighted above – the state's presence and resource advantages – serve as the principal scope conditions for my theory.

1.5 CONTRIBUTIONS

This book challenges common claims about the state. I show that scholars need to rethink the concept of state weakness to better explain the politics of developing countries, especially in their rural hinterlands. The book also provides new evidence about the origins of economic and political inequality in the postcolonial world, reconsiders the mechanisms linking historical institutions to contemporary politics, and refines existing theories about traditional leaders' role in modern African politics.

1.5.1 The State and the Rural Periphery

Even amidst substantial urbanization,[73] rural hinterlands remain critical to understanding the politics of the developing world. Many of the most pressing political and economic challenges in developing countries – poverty, elite capture, clientelism, violence, and limits to service delivery and the rule of law – are often most extreme in the hinterland. Accurately diagnosing why these challenges persist requires closely examining the politics of peripheral regions.

Scholars who do so often start from the premise that the most central characteristic of hinterlands is the state's relative absence – that hinterlands are where the state matters least. At the extreme, to Scott (2009), hinterlands are "ungoverned" spaces beyond the state's reach. They are O'Donnell's (1993) "brown areas" on the map that the state cannot penetrate. In the study of African politics, exemplified by Herbst (2000), hinterlands are often seen as spaces where modern states have consistently projected the least power from the outset of the colonial period to the present day. These types of claims underlie a significant body of research

---

[73] Nathan (2019).

on both rural Africa and other rural regions of the developing world, encouraging scholars to look beyond the state to explain contemporary rural politics.

I suggest that this is the wrong analytic framework for these regions. Even as they are the zones where the state's formal footprint is small, hinterlands may in fact be among the *easiest* areas for the state's actions to transform because this is where the state's relative resource advantages over society are often most extreme. I show that in Ghana's northern hinterland, understanding the large impacts of the state's historical steps into society is necessary to explain essentially all major facets of contemporary politics – in spite of that state's sustained absence and incapacity.

Most broadly, this demonstrates an important theoretical imprecision in widespread characterizations of developing states as "weak." As commonly used in the literature, "state weakness" confuses cause and effect, collapsing underlying features of states with outcomes of state leaders' contingent choices.[74] I show that knowing that a state is scarce, has limited infrastructural or coercive power, or is bureaucratically incapable does not imply weakness in all other dimensions, especially an inability to fundamentally transform society. In fact, I show that the state's ability to reorder society may be what helps first create the very phenomena that often then get cited as evidence of state weakness: elite capture, clientelism and its associated limits to service delivery, and political violence. These are better viewed as *outcomes* of a scarce state's strong effects on society. As a result, when scholars such as Migdal (1988) or Chabal and Daloz (1999) categorize the African state as a "mirage" or "facade" by pointing to elite capture and the state's lack of autonomy from society, they risk underplaying the degree to which the state itself is a powerful cause of what they observe.

The book also suggests an alternative understanding of the legacies of colonial and postcolonial state-building. Existing research on colonial rule, especially recent quantitative scholarship, overwhelmingly focuses on how colonial regimes and their affiliated actors affected long-run political and economic outcomes in the subnational regions in which they were *most active*: the effects of colonial rule are typically studied by observing impacts on the main places where the plantations, railroads, missionaries, and other institutions of occupation and extraction *were* – not where they were not.[75] By contrast, I show long-run effects of early state actions

---

[74] Lindvall and Teorell (2016).

[75] Nunn (2010), Cagé and Rueda (2016), Jedwab and Moradi (2016), Lowes and Montero (2018), Roessler et al. (2020), Ricart-Huguet (2021*b*).

even in a subnational region where colonial rule was at its *most absent* – finding large impacts within an area typically only studied as the control condition against which most analyses evaluate more intensive state interventions elsewhere.[76] Contrary to Herbst (2000), this demonstrates that the African colonial state could still very much be Young's (1994) "crusher of rocks" even in subnational regions in which its power to change precolonial realities of governance has been most dismissed.

Similarly, through my examination of public education and land reform, I show how the actions of the postcolonial state also continued to significantly reshape society even where post-independence leaders otherwise strategically chose to project the *least* state authority. In particular, even in the depths of Africa's late-twentieth-century economic crisis – at a point when the postcolonial state had essentially bottomed out in its formal capacity[77] – the 1979 land reform in Northern Ghana helps demonstrate how *de jure* state policies could still have powerful effects despite poor implementation. Rather than viewing independence as a hard break that radically changed trajectories of state-building, my findings reemphasize Young's (1994) call to study the postcolonial African state as a continuation of its colonial predecessor, able to reshape society for similar reasons and in similar ways.

1.5.2 The Origins of Political and Economic Inequality

In addition, the book provides new evidence on the origins of economic and political inequality, and the close relationships between them. A key focus is to explain who – down to the level of specific families like the Karbos in the opening example – becomes a socioeconomic and political elite, and why. While the qualitative historical literature provides rich examples of the connections between colonial policy and elite formation in Africa,[78] existing literature has rarely explored elite origins so systematically as an outcome variable.

Many scholars instead take the existence of societal and political elites as a given and build theories out from there.[79] But this presents an inferential problem if these elites emerged through the same political and economic processes being explained. At the extreme, some explicitly view

---

[76] For example, Roessler et al. (2020).
[77] Chazan (1982), van de Walle (2001).
[78] For example, Schatzberg (1980) on the paths to elite status in colonial Lisala, Congo, or Tignor (1976) on elite formation in colonial Kenya.
[79] For example, see Slater (2010) and Riedl (2014).

economic stratification as exogenous and antecedent to state-building:
Boix (2015) assumes that economic stratification develops separate from
the state and that initial state institutions then emerge as responses to the
crises of social order produced by that inequality; Olson (1993) similarly
puts the causal arrow from economic conditions to demand for the state.
I show instead that for the postcolonial world, bottom-up demands for
the state in society are often a second-order outcome of the inequality
and distributional conflicts that the state's own earlier actions have generated. Studies that primarily focus on societal responses to state-building
through the lens of grassroots resistance, such as Scott (1998, 2009), may
significantly understate the degree to which residents of regions of state
scarcity have incentives instead to actively seek the state out and make
themselves more legible to it so they can also benefit from its resources
and rise in the new social order it is creating.

Moreover, empirical literature on the origins of economic inequality
in Africa overwhelmingly explores the impacts of colonial rule on
overall inter-regional or inter-ethnic inequalities, such as between entire
subnational jurisdictions subjected to different government policies.[80] We
have a large body of evidence, for example, for why Northern Nigeria is
poorer than Southern Nigeria and other similar regional disparities. Little
scholarship has instead established the degree to which colonialism and
later post-independence state actions created micro-level, intra-ethnic
stratification between and within individual rural communities,[81] empirically documenting, as I do, why some villages became more egalitarian
than others, why some families became wealthier, or how either effect
persists.[82]

This focus on the long-run legacies of state action also helps understand the origins of micro-level political inequality, especially elite capture
in the form of dynastic politics. Recent scholarship on dynasties focuses
overwhelmingly on how the legislative incumbency advantage sustains
families in power in modern democracies.[83] But I show that much
deeper sources of advantage – long pre-dating democratization – may
also explain which families dominate modern elections, especially where
economic mobility is otherwise limited.[84]

---

[80] Huillery (2009), van de Walle (2009), Archibong (2018), Roessler et al. (2020), Ricart-
Huguet (2021*b*).

[81] Nugent (2010*b*, 37), in particular, has directly called for more research on this topic.

[82] Wantchekon et al. (2015) and Meier zu Selhausen et al. (2018) are partial exceptions
discussed in Chapter 2.

[83] Dal Bo et al. (2009), Chandra (2016), Querubin (2016), Smith (2018).

[84] Jensenius (2016).

1.5.3 The Persistent Effects of Past Institutions

The book also contributes to our understanding of the legacies of historical institutions. Drawing on Murdock's (1967) atlas of ethnic groups, there is now widespread evidence of correlations between societies' precolonial characteristics and modern outcomes.[85] Much of this work focuses on long-run effects of precolonial political centralization.[86] A key open question in this research agenda is to better identify the mechanisms linking precolonial centralization to contemporary conditions. Many scholars argue that these relationships are due to the direct effects of institutions that persist in some form today. The assumption is that institutions dating to the precolonial period still have active, contemporary effects.[87] But most studies cannot directly unpack the channels of transmission from past to present because the available cross-national data does not allow them to systematically observe how ethnic institutions have evolved over time. In Austin's (2008) phrase, they are left to "compress history," viewing before and after, but not what has occurred in-between.[88] The actions of the postcolonial state, in particular, often simply drop out of the analysis.

By diving deeply into a single case, where "decompressing" history becomes more possible, the book calls into question whether these correlations truly represent the *effects of persistent institutions* or instead the *persistent effects of past institutions*. These are very different mechanisms.[89] In the latter, precolonial institutions may have changed long ago, but still predict contemporary outcomes indirectly through their downstream effects on other variables, especially how societies with initial institutional differences were then treated by the modern state.[90]

---

[85] Englebert (2000), Wig (2016), Kramon (2019), Paine (2019), Michalopoulos and Papaioannou (2020).

[86] Osafo-Kwaako and Robinson (2013).

[87] Gennaioli and Rainer (2007), Michalopoulos and Papaioannou (2013), Wig (2016), Kramon (2019), and Houle et al. (2019) all claim that the main mechanism underlying their findings arises from a direct effect of institutions that still exist.

[88] Wilfahrt (2021) offers a related critique.

[89] Wilfahrt (2018, 2021) makes a similar distinction for Senegal: precolonial institutions do not correlate with contemporary outcomes because they still exist, but because they led to the formation of strong social identities that persist even without the institutions that first birthed them.

[90] Beyond Africa, Dell (2010) provides a vivid example of this latter category of mechanisms: forced labor in colonial Peru ceased centuries ago, but still predicts contemporary development indirectly through its prior effects on migration and economic investment.

I show that ethnic groups' internal institutions changed *massively* through contact with the modern state. The common claim that precolonial institutions persist does not withstand close scrutiny in this region. Many of Northern Ghana's precolonially acephalous groups are not acephalous at all today, but have state-created chieftaincy institutions that can be just as (or more) powerful as those in precolonially centralized groups. Moreover, groups that still remain officially acephalous now have their own nascent chieftaincy institutions, emerging only in the last few decades. Even chieftaincy within Northern Ghana's precolonially centralized kingdoms does not reflect an unbroken legacy of precolonial politics.[91]

Correlations between precolonial institutions and present-day outcomes may not reflect anything specific about those institutions themselves, but more that groups with different initial institutions were set out on different long-run trajectories of state–society relations when they first came into contact with the modern state. This has exposed them to different bundles of state policies over time that have cumulatively created their modern conditions.[92] To understand why ethnic groups in Africa with different precolonial institutions experience different governance today, we must avoid the trap Austin (2008) warns of and closely examine what the state has done in-between, not write off the state's power, bracket decades of colonial and postcolonial state-building, and assume that precolonial institutions themselves still affect modern politics.

1.5.4 Traditional Governance

Finally, the book speaks to several debates about the role of traditional leaders in modern Africa. First, in contrast with Baldwin's (2015) argument that most traditional chiefs have consistent incentives to act as "development brokers," representing community interests in their pursuit of resources from politicians, I suggest that whether chiefs' role as electoral intermediaries is beneficial for their communities is highly contingent on the institutions of social accountability that connect chiefs to

---

[91] Chapters 7 and 8 describe how, in efforts to resolve succession disputes and exert political control, both the colonial and post-independence states have altered key features of these institutions.
[92] Archibong (2019).

their subjects. Internal accountability can vary greatly across groups,[93] depending on how state actions reshaped societal institutions.[94]

Second, Mamdani (1996) famously describes the deleterious consequences of the new forms of traditional authority – or "decentralized despotism" – imposed by colonial rule. Yet other scholars have suggested that the impact of the colonial imposition of chieftaincy is overstated,[95] including by arguing that many artificially imposed chiefs lost their political influence after independence and have not become deeply embedded in society.[96] In one sense, the evidence in the subsequent chapters provides strong support for Mamdani's (1996) view, detailing how these new institutions have had persistent political effects over time. I demonstrate a key mechanism – preferential access to early schooling for chiefs' descendants – by which these effects could persist in society irrespective of the present-day political influence of chiefs themselves.

But in line with Spear (2003), the book also suggests that there was much more variation and African agency in the imposition of chieftaincy institutions than Mamdani's (1996) account of a monolithic colonial state allows. The extent to which chiefs fit within Mamdani's categorization of "despots" varied – and continues to vary – greatly at the local level. The extent to which these institutions were pure impositions, rather than shared creations of local communities, also varies; many local populations came to embrace artificial chieftaincy institutions, even where the state lacked the ability to install them by force. Moreover, the invention of chieftaincy is not purely a colonial story, but remains active to the present. In response to the incentives created by the state's scarcity, some communities are still hard at work inventing new "traditional" institutions of their own design.

1.6 ROADMAP FOR THE BOOK

In the remainder of Part I, Chapter 2 develops the book's core argument about the potential for scarce, resource-advantaged states to have large effects. Chapter 3 introduces the Northern Ghanaian case. The chapter focuses on the three main state interventions into society described above.

---

[93] Baldwin and Holzinger (2019) richly document such variation across sub-Saharan Africa.

[94] Acemoglu et al. (2014) similarly tie the behavior of contemporary chiefs in Sierra Leone to early colonial intervention in institutions governing the selection of chiefs.

[95] Spear (2003).

[96] Tignor (1976), Koter (2016).

The empirical analysis begins in Part II, exploring the societal effects of state action. Chapter 4 examines the direct effects of the scarce state on inter- and intra-ethnic economic inequality, focusing on how the invention of chieftaincy combined with the introduction of formal education to produce persistent micro-level socioeconomic stratification. Chapter 5 explores the indirect effects of state scarcity, documenting a bottom-up, very modern movement among communities from the Konkomba ethnic group – the largest *never recognized* group – to impose chiefs on themselves.

Part III then examines the downstream political effects of these societal changes. Chapter 6 focuses on elite capture and the emergence of dynastic politics, showing how the families of early colonial chiefs continue to dominate access to elected office. Chapter 7 explores modern-day clientelism, often facilitated by traditional chiefs, and connects historically rooted modes of social accountability that have emerged between chiefs and their community members to the distributive impacts of contemporary electoral competition. Chapter 8 links the history of intra- and inter-ethnic political violence to the state's three interventions into society.

Part IV considers the broader implications of the book's theory and findings. Chapter 9 switches focus to shadow cases – Southern Ghana, Peru, and the Philippines – that exemplify the other cells of Figure 1.1 in order to demonstrate the external validity and scope conditions of the argument. Chapter 10 concludes by presenting a paradox suggested by the book's findings: that many features of developing states often viewed as evidence of their inherent limits may instead be endogenous outcomes of the state's significant ability to have transformed society, potentially making the state the forceful creator of its own weakness.

2

The Large Effects of Scarce States

Many scholars observe that the state's presence is limited in peripheral regions. They see that there are few officials posted into an area, that service provision is minimal, or that the road network is underdeveloped, leaving most communities hard for the central state to reach. Based on this, they label the state "weak," implying that the state is not as important or impactful for shaping local political dynamics as compared to where it is more present, and thus, stronger.

This common chain of reasoning is a fallacy. The first observation – that the state is relatively absent – does not imply the second – that the state is less influential or impactful than where it is more present. Instead, the fact that the state is not very present in a peripheral region means that the few actions it does take can have substantially larger effects than those same actions would have had elsewhere. What might seem like comparatively insignificant interventions by the state in hinterlands can still profoundly reshape local society and politics.

This chapter demonstrates this fallacy by explaining the three core steps in the book's argument, which is meant to apply widely across the developing world. First, I begin by considering the potential for *direct* state effects on society through the distribution of state resources. What is most important for understanding how states remake social institutions and reallocate societal power is less the total number of actions that the state takes or the aggregate amount of resources it distributes than the degree to which the state's actions change inequality, or the *relative distribution* of resource access within society. The latter depends on how concentrated the benefits of the state's actions are, how big they are relative to pre-existing inequality in society, and when historically they happen.

The effect on society of a given state action is likely to vary with two factors: (i) the state's *presence* and (ii) the state's *resource advantages* versus society. The state's presence is typically limited in poor hinterland regions, while its relative resource advantages are typically highest, rendering the state *scarce*. In these regions, the impacts on society of isolated state actions that distribute state resources to local actors can be very high, with the ability to create new forms of inequality and social hierarchy. By contrast, effects of the exact same actions are lower in regions with other combinations of these two variables. In the aggregate, the cumulative impact of the state's interventions into society is not necessarily smaller in poor hinterland regions compared to where the state is more active.

Second, I suggest that isolated state actions can have effects through a more *indirect* channel as well. Where the state's resource advantages are high, but the state's presence is limited, leaving it relatively incapable of extracting from society, citizens face strong incentives to change their behavior and societal institutions to better seek out the state and its resources on their own. Unlike classic studies that principally focus on rural responses to state-building as a process of grassroots resistance,[1] this implies instead that residents of hinterland regions with scarce states often respond to the state's absence by mobilizing around demands for its increased presence. The result is that the scarce state's actions can also have large unintended effects in hinterlands, transforming society even if the state's formal capacity to implement its policies and wield coercive power remains quite low.

Third, the societal changes produced – directly or indirectly – by isolated state actions have downstream consequences for who wields political authority and how local actors contest for political power. State-generated inequality and social hierarchy create the conditions for elite capture in hinterland regions. The emergence of inequality also encourages clientelism – with actors with privileged access to the state and its resources leveraging their positions for political influence – as well as political violence – with contestation between the societal winners and losers of state action.

---

[1] Scott (1998), Scott (2009).

2.1 DIRECT EFFECTS OF STATE ACTION

Imagine a state was intervening in a local region to do something routine that nearly all states do, such as build a primary school.[2] Any new school confers some positive economic benefit to the area that receives it, particularly to the subset of families whose children get to enroll. But where will this individual school have the biggest impact on society? The answer is simple: in an area that does not already have a school, especially if the state has few plans to build additional schools in the near future. The effect of the same school will be lower in an area that already has (or will soon have) other public schools, or that already has good private alternatives. This is the straightforward intuition for why individual state actions are likely to be much more impactful in hinterland regions than in regions with more robust private economies or greater state presence and activity.

To develop this logic further, I first explicate four central assumptions implicit in this anecdote and then show the implications of the argument across the different subnational regions formed by the combination of the the state's presence and relative resource advantages.

2.1.1 Four Starting Assumptions

Four assumptions underlie my claims about the direct effects of state action. These assumptions are purposefully general and meant to apply widely both to the distribution of private goods to individual recipients or local public goods (club goods) to small sets of recipients, such as individual rural communities. They are also meant to apply to any state, including regardless of whether it is a colonial, postcolonial, or contemporary state.[3]

First, the effects of state interventions in society are best conceptualized as *relative effects* rather than defined by their absolute size or scope. The key dependent variable is the distribution of *relative* advantage within society, either among individuals or across local communities. Understanding how societal institutions work and how political power is distributed typically means understanding how society is ranked: how

---

[2] Paglayan (2020).
[3] Young (2004).

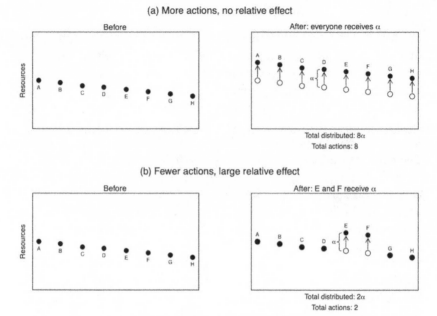

FIGURE 2.1 Relative effects vs. total actions. The left column is the distribution of resources in society at baseline. In panel (a), all eight members are given α – eight actions, with aggregate value 8α. There is no change in inequality. In panel (b), just two members are given α – just two actions of aggregate value 2α. Inequality increases, with a larger effect on society despite fewer, less valuable actions.

much individual-level or inter-communal inequality is there in access to wealth and other resources? State actions that induce larger changes in relative hierarchy – increasing or reducing inequality and reshuffling the relative distribution of resources – will have more meaningful effects on how local society and politics actually operate. By contrast, even large absolute influxes (or extractions) of resources that do not change inequality and hierarchy may have comparatively insignificant impacts on societal institutions and behavior.

Figure 2.1 provides a stylized example of this distinction.[4] The left column shows the baseline distribution of resources in a hypothetical eight-member society (alternatively, this could be considered an eight community society if viewing inequality at the community level). The

---

[4] Figures 2.1, 2.2, and 2.3 each show state action as a positive shock of resources, but the logic would be the same if α were instead visualized as a negative shock (taxation or extraction).

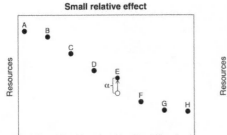 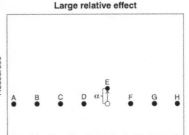

FIGURE 2.2 Relative effects by baseline inequality. The same action – a benefit of fixed size α to person E – has different relative effects on inequality depending on the baseline distribution of resources. In the left panel, the rank order of society is unchanged. In the right panel, E is now the new elite, with a significant increase in inequality.

right column of panel (a) shows society after the state takes eight total actions, passing out a benefit of size α to each person (community). Panel (b) instead shows the distribution of resources after the state makes a more limited set of interventions: just two actions, passing out private benefit α to just two members of society. Although the number of actions and total amount distributed are higher in panel (a), there is no effect on relative status: inequality remains completely unchanged. By contrast, in panel (b), the state's interventions have significantly re-ranked the society. A more concentrated allocation can have a larger relative effect even if smaller in absolute amount.

Second, how big a relative effect a given state action has depends on the existing level of inequality. This is visualized in Figure 2.2. Even a seemingly small distribution of resources can have large effects on relative status within previously flat societies with little inequality (right panel). By contrast, where there is already substantial stratification – such as might have emerged through a robust private sector economy – distributing the exact same amount of resources may have a comparatively tiny effect on inequality (left panel). The more wealth and economic stratification that have already emerged, the less likely any new disbursement of resources is to upset the stats quo.

The third assumption is that initial resource advantages often compound over time, as represented by Figure 2.3. Imagine two individuals (or communities) with similar wealth and identical economic opportunities to grow that wealth (i.e., who have similar rates of return). The state now provides one with a windfall of arbitrary size (α). As long as we assume that this lucky beneficiary's future rate of return remains at

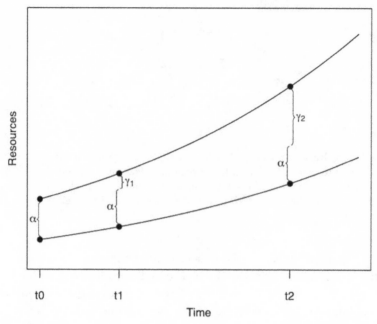

FIGURE 2.3 Early advantages compound. In the first time period ($t0$), one individual gains an advantage of α resources over the other. Over time, even if both individuals' resources compound at the same rate, the relative advantage of the first increases. The same initial benefit (α) is no longer enough to close the gap; catching up later ($t2$) requires a bigger added payoff ($\gamma_2 > \gamma 1$) than earlier ($t1$).

least as high as the non-beneficiary's, the windfall provides an economic head start.[5] Over time, simply providing the same initial benefit (α) to the other person (or community) will no longer be enough for them to catch up; the more time passes, catching up requires an increasingly large additional benefit (γ) above the value of the initial windfall. This could be significant new wealth that becomes available through changes to the private sector economy or a substantial increase in the size of the new windfalls that state provides to other members of society instead.

Fourth, I assume that the private value of many state resources to their recipients is declining in how many others already have the resource. This is summarized in Figure 2.4. Imagine a rural town that gets electrified by the state utility at a time when no other towns in the surrounding region have electricity. Not only do the town's residents gain personal

[5] In practice, greater initial wealth can open up even higher rates of return, speeding up the dynamic shown in Figure 2.3.

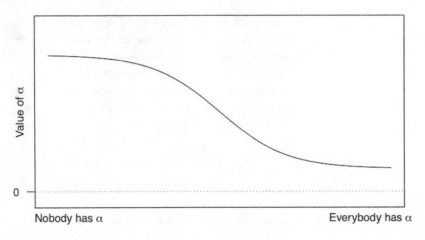

FIGURE 2.4 Diminishing marginal value. The private benefit to the recipient (individual or community) from receiving a good of fixed size (α) is often declining in the number of others who already have access to that same good.

boosts to productivity and well-being, but the town is likely to attract new investment that fuels growth as business activities in the surrounding region relocate to the electrified area. By contrast, if another town is the 157th in its region to get electrified, the overall benefit is likely still positive, but smaller: residents may get similar direct boosts to well-being, but little growth-producing investment is likely to pour in because electricity is no longer scarce in the surrounding economy. An identical dynamic can play out for many private goods that states target to individuals. In the following text and in the later chapters, I focus on the effect of being among the first in a region to get formal education. All else equal, the private labor market returns to education should be higher when education is scarce than if a recent graduate enters a labor market flush with many others with similar qualifications.[6]

These last two assumptions are closely related, suggesting that the timing of when and how often state resources are distributed matters for their effects. Earlier interventions by the state can be much more impactful than

---

[6] I do not suggest that this dynamic is universal. Some goods may also have positive externalities and economies of scale, with private benefits that are (at least initially) growing in the number of others who also have the good. For example, if only you had a phone when nobody else did, the initial benefits would be muted: who could you call? My assumption is only that the logic in Figure 2.4 applies to a broad subset of goods that developing states distribute.

later ones of the same size because the fourth assumption magnifies the importance of the third assumption: if the value of the initial resource (α) that created a gap between the two individuals in Figure 2.3 is itself declining over time as additional other people also receive it, the extra payoff (γ) needed to subsequently close the gap between the two individuals will be even larger.[7] This implies both: (a) that there should be a premium to receiving windfalls of resources early, before everyone else; and (b) that this premium will be largest in settings in which future distributions to new recipients are less frequent and happen later, allowing initial advantages more time to compound.

2.1.2 Direct Effects across Subnational Regions

Figure 2.5 applies the underlying logic of these four assumptions to consider where subnationally the same exact state action – *holding fixed that action's size and scope* – would have the largest effects on society based on variation in two characteristics of the state: how present the state is in an area and how resource-advantaged it is relative to the population.

Where the state's presence is limited, it takes fewer actions over time and has less capacity to deliver benefits to a wider cross section of the population. Where the state is resource-advantaged relative to its population it may not be wealthy, or have a large absolute number of resources at its disposal, but the ratio of what the state is able to distribute compared to what society already has available is high. I work through predictions for the expected relative effects of the same action in each cell in Figure 2.5, labeled by {presence, resource advantages}. In the short run, we can view the placement of subnational regions in different cells of Figure 2.5 as fixed. But in what follows, I also consider how subnational regions can move across these cells over time, shifting types as state leaders choose to significantly increase or reduce their state's presence, or as shocks to the local economy change the balance of resources between state and society.

Taken together, the predictions in Figure 2.5 do not imply that, in the aggregate, the total effect of all state actions together is greater in one cell of Figure 2.5 than another. But building from the assumptions above,

---

[7] For example, if in an initial period one community is electrified and another is not, simply giving the second community electricity years later will not close the economic gap between them, both because the first community's initial advantages have since compounded (Figure 2.3) *and* because the marginal value of electrification has itself declined in the meantime, as many other communities are also now electrified (Figure 2.4).

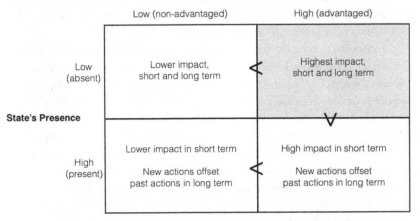

FIGURE 2.5 Impact of an isolated state action. Holding the size and scale of the action fixed.

the differences in Figure 2.5 are still crucial because they imply both that: (a) we cannot assume that any specific state action or policy has smaller effects where the state is least active; and (b) we cannot assume *ex ante* that the cumulative impact of the state on society will be lowest in regions with the most limited state presence. Instead, if the state's resource advantages are sufficiently large, the increased relative effect of its actions may plausibly be high enough that the state is at least as impactful overall in areas of limited presence as where it is more active. Ultimately, because of its scarcity, the state can still be *the* central force shaping hinterland society and politics even as it appears incredibly weak.

The {Absent, Advantaged} Cell

The {absent, advantaged} cell ({low, high}) of Figure 2.5 characterizes most rural hinterlands, especially those that are not cash crop or mining regions. These are peripheral zones where the state often either struggles to project a large presence due to difficult distance and geography or chooses not to try to project a large presence because there are few economic or political incentives to do so. These subnational regions are also typically poorer and less developed than core regions, with less wealth available through the private sector that could generate high baseline rates of inequality.[8] The state's relative resource advantages are often very high

---

[8] Underdevelopment in the hinterland is both a cause and consequence of state absence: states are less likely to expand their presence in regions of limited economic potential,

and access to the state's resources can be incredibly valuable. For example, in much of the African periphery, state employment is one of, if not the, only avenues into the formal economy.[9]

Moments of contact between the state and society in these regions benefit at least some local residents with access to state resources. This includes whenever the state attempts to fund local public goods, provide services, or hire residents into the bureaucracy. Benefits even flow to the population when the state takes actions explicitly meant to limit its presence. Something almost all states do in peripheral regions is attempt to delegate authority to local intermediaries who can govern in the absence of distant central state officials.[10] This confers economic benefits on those who are selected as intermediaries, including any rents they can extract from their positions.

State actions that distribute what are in essence large windfalls of benefits relative to what is available in the local economy have the potential to generate new forms of inequality – at two time scales. First, in the short run, because the state's absence limits its capacity, its actions rarely distribute benefits evenly within the local population. Instead, most benefits are narrowly concentrated, or particularistic. Some villages receive roads and schools, but budget constraints mean that many others do not. Within communities, some students get to enroll in school, but there is not enough space for many others. A few local actors are tapped as state intermediaries, receiving the benefits that come with these positions; other eligible candidates are passed over. The resulting infusion of resources to narrow recipients immediately reorders the relative distribution of socioeconomic status, as displayed in Figure 2.1; this is even more so because, due to their overall underdevelopment, most areas in the {absent, advantaged} cell have limited inequality to begin with, as in Figure 2.2.

Second, over the long run, new inequality becomes entrenched if the state remains absent and takes few new actions that confer new windfalls on different recipients, which otherwise might have offset the compounding advantages of the initial winners (Figure 2.3). Persistent state-generated inequality is especially likely in the absence of a robust

---

and economic potential remains more limited where a less present state provides fewer investments and is less able to support markets.

[9] The only other alternative is to exit – migrating to urban areas or to mining or cash crop regions.

[10] Gerring et al. (2011), Slater and Kim (2015), Matsuzaki (2019).

private sector that provides the losers of initial state allocations an outside means to catch up. Even if the state belatedly starts providing the same initial resource to a wider set of recipients, it may no longer be enough to close the gap, especially if the resource's marginal value has declined over time, as explained by Figure 2.4. Moreover, in the meantime, the initial winners of state action may be able to use their early advantages to position themselves and their families to benefit most from any new windfalls of state resources that do eventually come along, only further reinforcing state-generated inequality over time.

Wantchekon et al. (2015) vividly illustrate an example of this logic in Benin, where just four schools were built in the hinterland in the first two and a half decades of colonial rule. These schools bestowed windfalls on the small number of boys who were able to attend, providing economic advantages that persist over a century later among their extended descendants. These benefits were so large and sustained *because* the colonial education system remained so scarce: no one else had access to similar human capital until much later. Similarly, in a more qualitative analysis of class formation in a small hinterland community in Congo, Schatzberg (1980) meticulously documents how early contact with the colonial state – especially through the first opportunities to attend school – explain the intergenerational concentration of wealth and social status in particular local families decades into the postcolonial period.

Crucial to these types of path-dependent dynamics is that the state stays relatively scarce over time, remaining within this same cell of Figure 2.5. If either dimension – the state's relative absence or resource advantages – were to have subsequently changed in a substantial way, new elites could have emerged and offset the effects of the state's earlier actions. The logic for why follows from the predictions for the remaining cells of Figure 2.5.

The {Present, Advantaged} Cell

Moving from the top-right to bottom-right of Figure 2.5, the {present, advantaged} cell ({high, high}) instead represents regions where the state is both relatively active in society and has significant resource advantages. The greater local presence of the state reduces the ability of a given action to reshape society, in two ways. First, with more state officials and higher local capacity, there is a greater chance that some state resources are distributed in a less concentrated fashion, even holding fixed the amount distributed. If the benefits of state actions are delivered more evenly, there is less chance that state windfalls generate new inequality, even in the short run (Figure 2.1).

Second, and more importantly, even if the benefits of a given action remain narrowly concentrated, a more present state will take more actions beyond the first that distribute additional sets of resources. This comparatively reduces the ability of any individual action to have long-run effects if new allocations of new windfalls to new recipients close the gaps created by earlier actions. This may happen either because new distributions of state resources occur in the near future, before advantages created by initial actions have time to compound, or instead because subsequent access to state resources for others in society is so large that future state actions offset initial advantages (Figure 2.3).[11]

Returning to the stylized example of building a school, a {present, advantaged} area would be one where there are no private schools available. The first public school built by the state could have a big initial impact on inequality, benefitting the students who get to enroll over those who do not. But unlike in Wantchekon et al. (2015), any lasting effect of that one school will likely soon be washed out by the construction of additional schools in the near future by a more active state.

Chandra (2016) demonstrates a related dynamic in her analysis of the formation of the Indian political elite. She describes the Indian state as having significant resource advantages over its society, such that contact with and positions in the state provide central avenues for extracting the resources needed to become an elite. But these benefits have not accrued to the same set of actors over time. In many parts of India, earlier elite families that emerged from privileged contact with the state in the colonial period have been replaced by new elites elevated through much more recent opportunities to benefit from an increasingly active and well-resourced state. Today, most elite political families only have been elites for a few decades, with more recent access to benefits that has fully offset other elites' earlier advantages. But, importantly, Jensenius (2016) shows that the families of colonial-era elites still disproportionately dominate local politics in the poorest, most rural regions of India – the {absent, advantaged} areas where the state has remained comparatively scarcest over time and there have been the fewest opportunities to access new windfalls that would allow new families to catch up.

---

[11] Unless there is complete capture of *all* future benefits by the same first set of winners, each new state action provides some chance for new recipients to gain access to resources.

The history of major state interventions into rural Latin America – explored in more detail for the example of Peru in Chapter 9 – provides another example of how an increase in the local presence of the state can offset the long-run effects of earlier actions. Consistent with the predictions for the {absent, advantaged} cell, the Spanish colonial state created new forms of inequality in many hinterlands of Latin America by providing land grants and labor concessions to small sets of families who then dominated for generations as a state-generated rural planter elite.[12] But Albertus (2015) shows that these elites do not still dominate today in many countries because states subsequently became much less scarce. Redistributive land reform greatly expanded the scope of the state's intervention in the rural periphery, and shifted these regions into the {present, advantaged} cell. By expropriating and reallocating elites' property, land reform was a sufficiently large subsequent state intervention that it offset and wiped out compounded advantages of the earlier winners (Figure 2.3).

This latter example helps demonstrate what can happen when subnational regions shift cells of Figure 2.5 over time. If the state toggles on and off its presence – punctuating long periods of absence with moments of intense occupation and extraction – a region can shift back and forth between the {absent, advantaged} and {present, advantaged} cells. As it does so, the state's actions may create multiple separate waves of elites, rather than entrenching a single set of elites through an early and isolated state action. Chapter 9 shows that this is exactly what has happened at multiple points in rural Peruvian history: state actions provided targeted windfalls that elevated new elites in rural society, those elites then stuck through prolonged periods of state scarcity, only to be wiped out, with their wealth expropriated and reallocated when the state's presence subsequently increased.

The {Present, Non-advantaged} Cell

Moving to the bottom-left of Figure 2.5 is the {present, non-advantaged} cell ({high, low}), where the state is neither absent nor resource advantaged. These are politically and economically core regions where the state is more active and in which a more robust private sector both creates more baseline inequality and provides nonstate paths to acquiring similar resources to what the state can provide.

---

[12] Gilbert (1977).

In the stylized example of building a school, these would be areas
both where there are already private schools and in which the state will
soon construct more public schools. Building any one school has a lower
individual impact on society in the short term: pre-existing private schools
mean that human capital is already available and inequality in education access has likely already emerged, with a single new allocation of
resources of a given size comparatively less able to re-rank society (Figure
2.2). Moreover, in the long term, additional new public schools will likely
soon come on line before initial advantages provided by a single school
have sufficient time to compound (Figure 2.3).

Within Africa, the {present, non-advantaged} cell represents major cash
crop regions and urban areas.[13] In these areas there are often more robust
private paths to wealth and economic stratification. This even includes
for African populations during the colonial period, when new economic
elites at times emerged separately from the state through the agricultural and export economies.[14] Moreover, in many core regions of Africa,
especially in British colonies, missionaries – including indigenous missionaries operating beyond the direct supervision of Europeans – played a
large role in the non-state provision of education, making human capital
available to a much wider cross section of society than in Wantchekon
et al.'s (2015) example of hinterland Benin.[15] For example, Meier zu Selhausen et al. (2018) demonstrate how access to missionary education
among previously non-elite families combined with a robust private sector
labor market in urban Uganda to create a relatively fluid class structure,
in which new elites emerged in each generation, rather than the earliest
winners in access to education becoming entrenched over time.

Consistent with these predictions for the {present, non-advantaged}
cell, Alesina et al. (2019) show that across most of Africa, there is greater
intergenerational economic mobility in urban areas, regions with longer
histories of state infrastructure investment dating to the colonial period
(e.g., cash crop zones), and regions with greater contact with nonstate

---

[13] At the most extreme, another interpretation of the {high, low} cell would be advanced
industrial democracies. While there is intergenerational persistence in wealth in the US,
for example, it is notable that at the very top of the income bracket there is significant
turnover, with new entrants from the private economy, not intergenerational capture by
those with privileged ties to the state. Nearly three quarters of the current wealthiest
people in the US (on the Forbes billionaires list) are "self-made," not inheritors of family
fortunes (Scheuer and Slemrod 2019, 3).

[14] Hill (1963), Akyeampong (2014), Roessler et al. (2020).

[15] Frankema (2012).

education through missionaries. In these regions, advantages created by individual state actions are less likely to stick over time compared to zones of state scarcity.

The {Absent, Non-advantaged} Cell

Lastly, to the top-left of Figure 2.5 is the {absent, non-advantaged} cell ({low, low}). In the hypothetical example of building a school, these would be areas where there is already private education despite the absence of public schools. As in Figure 2.2, constructing a single public school is less likely to upset existing hierarchy in society compared to regions where there is no existing inequality because there is no private school either (the {absent, advantaged} cell). In turn, with less ability for an isolated state action to generate new inequality in the short run, there is also less potential for that action to cause long-term changes either.

Examples of the {absent, non-advantaged} cell include areas that are not just rural hinterlands, but have limited state sovereignty, with the state overshadowed by militias, rebel groups, or criminal cartels that have amassed private resources that equal or exceed those controlled by the state. The state's power to reshape society through isolated actions will be quite limited, with the state finding it especially difficult to displace entrenched elites.

But, crucially, not only are these situations in hinterland regions relatively rare compared to the {absent, advantaged} cell, as explained in Chapter 1, but they also often emerge endogenously from the dynamics described for the {absent, advantaged} cell, providing another example of how regions can shift across the cells of Figure 2.5 over time. Windfalls provided by early state actions can allow the initial winners to subsequently extract enough rents and amass enough local influence to eventually close the resource gap between state and society, foreclosing on the state's continued ability to significantly reshape society. This is especially likely when an exogenous shock to local economic conditions – a change in the global markets or an international conflict – subsequently opens access to new resources from which elites put in place by earlier state actions are suddenly in an advantaged position to disproportionately benefit. In this way, the state's limited influence in {absent, non-advantaged} areas may often simply be a downstream, longer-run outcome of the state's significant power to reshape society in {absent, advantaged} areas.

For example, in the Philippines, also described in more detail in Chapter 9, rural oligarchs with private militias challenged basic state sovereignty in some areas in the early postcolonial period.[16] These oligarchs' advantages did not pre-date the modern state, however. They were created through the actions of the Spanish and American colonial states, which provided valuable windfalls of resources to narrow sets of new elites in the form of land rights, arms, and control over new local government positions as they delegated authority to local intermediaries in the rural periphery.[17] Amidst a significant opening to the global economy in the 19th century, and then especially amid a flow of external arms to local forces resisting the Japanese occupation during World War II, these new rural elites initially elevated by prior actions of the state were able to transform into powerful oligarchs controlling private armies too powerful for the state to confront directly.[18]

Similarly, the militias and drug cartels that have dominated the state in some rural hinterlands of Central and South America often initially emerged as a direct consequence of previous state actions that powerfully reshaped local politics and society. In some rural frontier regions of Colombia, both the leftist FARC (*Fuerzas Armadas Revolucionarias de Colombia*) rebels and the right-wing paramilitaries who emerged to oppose the FARC initially benefitted from access to the state and its resources. In each case, actions by the Colombian state helped these non-state actors first amass wealth and consolidate control, as described for the {absent, advantaged} cell.[19] Subsequently, shifts in the global drug economy offered new opportunities for some of these armed groups to begin amassing new economic resources and become independent of the state that first created them. Many of Mexico's cartels were similarly initially nurtured by corrupt state officials under the long-running PRI (*Partido Revolucionario Institucional*) regime, first gaining power by leveraging connections to resources from the local state apparatus before attracting enough independent external resources through the drug trade to gain a resource advantage over the local state that had birthed them.[20]

---

[16] McCoy (1993), Slater (2008, 2010).
[17] Anderson (1988), Hutchcroft (2000), Matsuzaki (2019).
[18] Larkin (1982), Anderson (1988), McCoy (1993).
[19] Ballve (2020). The FARC initially benefitted from government decentralization initiatives (Ballve 2020, 39–45). Right-wing paramilitaries received important direct support from the Colombian military (Ballve 2020, 53).
[20] Medel and Thoumi (2014), Trejo and Ley (2018).

2.2 INDIRECT STATE EFFECTS IN THE HINTERLAND

The remaining steps in the argument focus on the downstream implications of state actions within hinterlands with scarce states in the {absent, advantaged} cell of Figure 2.5. When scarce states act – such as by delegating authority to local actors or investing in local public goods – their actions can directly reshape society and generate new socioeconomic hierarchies by providing economic windfalls to the winners of state action. But these same actions can also change society *indirectly*, incentivizing endogenous responses from the losers – those who did not benefit from the state's resources.

Existing literature on state-society relations in the rural periphery places a dominant focus on grassroots resistance to the state. The influential work of Scott (1998, 2009) describes how societies have sought to undermine, pervert, and violently avoid attempts by central states to exert greater control in hinterlands.[21] Scott (2009) characterizes the hinterlands of Southeast Asia as being fundamentally defined by attempts to flee from the state's grip – with societies evolving new economic behaviors and forms of social organization to keep repressive states away.

Others instead describe strategies of societal accommodation to the state's absence. Maclean (2010) details how the persistent scarcity of the formal state in rural Ghana could produce compensatory changes in informal village institutions, with some communities organically developing new forms of internal social insurance provision and risk sharing that did not emerge in otherwise similar regions of Cote d'Ivoire where the state was comparatively more active at the local level. More broadly, scholars have long documented the many forms of nonstate public goods provision that can emerge in regions where state provision is most limited.[22]

But resistance and accommodation are not the only possible responses to endemic state scarcity. The increased presence of the central state raises the specter of repression and social control. Yet it also offers opportunities to access desired economic benefits. These possibilities are in tension, but the latter may often swamp fears of the former. Rather than resist, many local populations in hinterland areas face powerful incentives to seek out the state. Similarly, while some communities may be able to make do without the state in some domains, accommodating themselves as best they can to its absence, the prospect of greater contact with the

---

[21] Also see Hyden (1980), Koren and Sarbahi (2017), and Ying (2020).
[22] Cammett and Maclean (2014), Baldwin (2015).

state – and with it, the ability to forego the costly self-provision of resources – is an enticing proposition.

The response of many communities to state scarcity may instead be to act on their own to try to draw the state closer and reduce its scarcity by changing societal practices in ways that make society more legible – easier for the state "to see," per Scott (1998). Where the state is resource advantaged, the state's resources represent a highly valued bundle of goods. Meanwhile, the state's absence itself limits the state's capacity to extract back from the population. Hinterland populations in the developing world often confront extremely limited direct tax burdens.[23] And indeed, as noted above, the state's limited fiscal capacity in the hinterland is endogenous: the state never invests in building up fiscal capacity in these regions because there is little worth attempting to extract. Along these lines, Slater and Kim (2015) contest Scott's (1998) assumption that all states even *want* to make every subnational region legible in a way that would allow for improved extraction.

In such a context, the immediate threat of state contact highlighted by Scott (1998, 2009) may be significantly overstated. To whatever limited extent the state acts, it often becomes a *net provider* of resources, not a net extractor. State absence may then not be a condition that rural societies work to achieve through resistance, or a situation to which they simply accept and adapt, but a problem they proactively seek to resolve. While similarly critiquing Scott (1998), Walker (2015) argues that some rural populations may instead have a demand for "eligibility," not a fear of "legibility:" where the state is a net provider, rural citizens actively want to be "seen by the state" so that they become eligible for state resources they have previously been denied, not attempt to avoid the state to protect themselves.

Incentives for proactive, bottom-up actions that increase contact with the state are especially strong among the losers of the state's earlier actions: they observe others benefitting from state windfalls and change their own behavior to access new windfalls for themselves. This can lead to changes in the basic ways societies organize and identify politically. For example, drawing on a rich anthropological literature, Bates (1983) describes how the basic structure of ethnic identities in independence-era

---

[23] Bates (1981) famously details how regimes often focus instead on easier to collect revenues from natural resource rents, import–export tariffs, or indirect price controls through monopsony buying schemes.

African societies was at times explicitly refashioned by newly emerging societal elites seeking to better access state resources. Whereas the amalgamation and homogenization of ethnic identities in rural areas has long been a central state-building effort of more active states seeking to make their populations legible,[24] these rural African societies engaged in similar efforts to forge new, large-scale ethnic identities largely on their own, from below.[25]

Grassroots efforts to improve state legibility may also lead to reforms to local institutions that re-rank society and produce new hierarchies. Entrepreneurial leaders may emerge endogenously based on their perceived ability to link their communities to the state resources, upsetting pre-existing institutions. At the extreme, and even more fundamentally, the losers of earlier state action in the hinterland may also just proactively get up and move, migrating in search of state presence and better state services. A particularly common response of hinterland populations across the developing world is exit. But in contrast to Herbst's (2000) and Scott's (2009) focus on migration as a means to evade the state, most out-migration from hinterlands is to urban areas, where the state is most present. This is the opposite of what one would do if seeking to resist and flee.

This last example – rural out-migration – was at times what state leaders had hoped to induce through the state's neglect of the hinterland. In some African colonies, including Ghana (see Chapter 3), converting hinterland regions into a migrant "labor reserve" was a justification colonial leaders used to avoid more sustained state investment that might produce local economic growth.[26] But the other changes outlined here, such as the emergence of new rural elites who can best link communities to the state, will occur regardless of whether state leaders intend them to happen. Simply by providing scarce resources to some parts of society but not others, the state's actions can create changes to society by unintentionally inducing other actors in the {absent, advantaged} cell of Figure 2.5 to alter their own behavior in response.

---

[24] See Weber (1976), for example, on the French state's forced homogenization of the countryside.
[25] For a further summary, and critique, of these arguments about ethnicity, see Vail (1989).
[26] Grischow (2006).

2.3 IMPLICATIONS FOR POLITICAL POWER AND CONTESTATION

Finally, and in turn, the changes to hinterland societies produced by state action – whether directly or indirectly – affect who wields political power and how local actors contest for it. I explore how state actions re-rank societies above because how society is ranked affects how politics unfolds. I focus on three downstream political effects of state action in the hinterland.

First, the distribution of socioeconomic status defines who most easily becomes a political elite. In democracies, wealthier politicians are better able to buy their way to electoral victories. In autocracies, wealthier politicians can use their resource advantages to buy loyalty and build grassroots followings that get them a seat at the bargaining table with regime elites. Focused more on political threats in cities and cash crop regions, authoritarian governments in postcolonial Africa often found it easier to ensure the acquiescence of rural hinterlands by paying off and working through existing socioeconomic elites rather than attempting more costly efforts to mobilize mass support among rural populations.[27] Such efforts from central governments simply deepen the socioeconomic advantages of elites in hinterland regions that were first elevated by earlier state actions. As socioeconomic inequality becomes entrenched over time, political inequality is likely to become entrenched as well, resulting in elite capture.

State-induced changes to inequality also affect how societal actors contest for political power. The second example of a political outcome affected by state action in the hinterland is clientelism, a form of political competition often directly rooted in economic inequality. Clientelism is often explicitly hierarchical, feeding on voters vulnerability, with elites leveraging their wealth or access to the state into political influence over the poor.[28] Central to many clientelist exchanges are brokers – intermediaries or middlemen who link politicians (patrons) with voters (clients).[29] In regions of state scarcity, isolated state actions that delegate grassroots wealth and authority to narrow sets of local actors will often elevate new sets of community-level brokers. These local deputies of a distant state are then in an advantageous position to wield their privileged access to that state – and the highly valued resources it controls – to reshape

---

[27] Zolberg (1966), Bates (1981), Boone (2003), Riedl (2014).
[28] Hicken (2011), Nichter (2018).
[29] Stokes et al. (2013), Mares and Young (2016).

local political behavior. If they do so to their own private benefit, rather than in the best interest of the communities they represent, these new brokers can undermine democratic accountability and reduce the quality of governance.

Third, the use of violence as a form of political contestation is also likely to be changed by state-generated inequality in hinterlands. Hinterlands are often assumed to be particularly violent subnationally because they are areas where it can be easiest to organize beyond the watchful eye of state officials.[30] But violence in the hinterland may be as much a direct outcome of the changes to society created by the state's actions as it is something produced by the state's inability to police.

Existing research on violence in the hinterland focuses predominately on anti-state violence, such as civil war.[31] This fits with the broader focus in the literature on hinterlands on grassroots resistance to the state, described above. But if the combination of the state's absence and relative resource advantages instead creates powerful incentives to seek out the state, rather than resist it, a principal effect of state actions in the hinterland may instead be on nonstate violence – targeted internally within society, not at state leaders. Societal actors will fight with each over the terms of their access to the state's scarce resources, rather than simply resist its incursions into society outright.

As the state's isolated actions create new winners and losers by providing windfalls of valuable resources in otherwise poor regions, its actions generate new grievances both within and between ethnic groups. The losers of state action resort to violence to capture windfalls for themselves, with violence becoming one tool to pursue the forms of indirect, endogenous societal change described above. Internal conflict becomes part of the process of changing pre-existing societal institutions to better access the state. In addition, the new winners of state action may turn to violence to cement their gains, reinforce state-generated elite capture, and maintain their new privileged political and economic positions. Across these channels, endemic political violence in the hinterland becomes an explicit outcome of the scarce state's substantial ability to reorder local societal hierarchies, not simply evidence of the state's incapacity to prevent conflict.

---

[30] Fearon and Laitin (2003), Lewis (2020), Muller-Crepon et al. (2020).
[31] Fearon and Laitin (2003), Buhaug and Rod (2006), Tollefsen and Buhaug (2015), Ying (2020).

2.4 CONCLUSION

This chapter has introduced the three main steps in the book's argument. State scarcity in the hinterland allows the few actions the state does take to have especially large effects on society – to the point that we cannot assume the state has smaller impacts in areas where it is least present and least active. The state generates new forms of inequality and social hierarchy by providing valuable windfalls of resources to the narrow beneficiaries of its isolated actions, as well as by indirectly encouraging societal actors to change their own institutions and behavior to seek out state windfalls for themselves. In turn, these societal changes affect who holds political power in the hinterland and how they contest for it.

Moving forward, Part II focuses on the direct (Chapter 4) and indirect (Chapter 5) societal effects of the state's isolated actions, zooming in on the theory's predictions for hinterland regions in the {absent, advantaged} cell of Figure 2.5. Part III then turns to the downstream effects of these societal changes on the three political outcomes described in this chapter: elite capture (Chapter 6), clientelism (Chapter 7), and intra-communal violence (Chapter 8). Part IV (Chapter 9) explores the implications of the argument across the other cells of Figure 2.5.

3

Northern Ghana's Scarce State

That was the time when the white man was going back. [Q: You mean around independence?] No. Not in the independence time. But when he wasn't coming here ... Later he decided to come back again.
    – Traditional chief, north of Bolgatanga, May 2019

While interviewing a chief north of Bolgatanga, I was struck by a particular turn of phrase used to retell the oral history passed down about his community. At least in his telling, during the early decades of the colonial period the experience of British rule in this community – located off the main road, just before the Burkina Faso border – was not one of a sustained, intensive occupation, but instead a series of very specific, isolated moments of contact still salient in the community's collective memory a century later. He recalled discussion of individual times "the white man came" – such as to appoint the community's first chief – and then described other periods as "when the white man was going back." I was confused, and asked if he meant the period after Ghana's independence in 1957. He clarified that no, he was referring to decade-long stretches in the early twentieth century between British officials' visits when he believed his community had little, if any, direct interaction with the colonial regime.[1] From the community's perspective, these were periods when the British might as well have gone back to where they came from.

[1] Interview with chief and elders, community #2, Bolgatanga District, 21 May 2019. The oral history interviews are introduced in Chapter 4 and more details are provided in the Appendix.

The footprint of colonial states was not uniform. In urban areas or rural zones of major economic extraction, the colonial state could be highly visible and active. Elsewhere, especially in hinterland areas like Ghana's northern frontier, the state often remained very absent. This does not mean that colonial rule was somehow benign. But populations in peripheral areas could go long periods without contact from distant state officials. Moreover, to the extent these areas offered few economic opportunities and posed little political threat to post-independence regimes, state absence often persisted long after colonial rule ended.

This chapter traces the history of the modern state in Northern Ghana. Similar to Herbst's (2000) account, there is a great deal of continuity in the minimal projection of state authority in this region spanning from the precolonial period, before the modern state emerged, through to post-independence politics. I document that state scarcity and explain why it occurred and, only recently, has begun to recede. I then detail the three major actions the modern state still took in the periphery across the colonial and postcolonial periods. These actions did not occur in spite of the state's absence, but as exigencies of it. At the outset of colonial period, the British quickly began substituting for the minimal direct presence of colonial officials by delegating some administrative authority to local traditional chiefs, even where this meant imposing new forms of chieftaincy that never previously existed. Later, seeking more effective administrators who could continue to govern in their place, the British slowly began building out a basic education infrastructure. In turn, post-independence leaders, seeking a politically expedient alliance with the region's colonially empowered chiefs, delegated further powers to chiefs through changes to land tenure laws that made the state even more absent.

I introduce and explain each of these three actions in the following sections, drawing on historical literature as well as administrative data, oral histories, and primary archival sources. The chapter concludes by putting Northern Ghana in comparative perspective, showing how the region's experience of state scarcity is representative of many hinterlands.

3.1 THE SCARCE STATE

The defining feature of the state in Northern Ghana, even before colonial rule, has been its scarcity. In this section, I present quantitative evidence documenting the state's absence in the North and then qualitatively detail the origins and nature of state scarcity across the precolonial, colonial, and postcolonial periods.

3.1.1 State Presence across Time and Space

When taking a bird's eye view, the state's prolonged absence in Northern Ghana jumps off the page. I show the state's persistently limited footprint by drawing on a representative sample of over 2.5 million individual-level returns from Ghana's 2010 census.

Lee and Zhang (2017) demonstrate that heaping in ages reported by census respondents indicates a state's territorial reach and capacity. As an illustrative example, the left panel of Figure 3.1 plots the distribution of the ages self-reported by adults (ages twenty through ninety-nine). Rather than a smooth distribution, as would reflect the true distribution of ages, the data is instead disproportionately "heaped" into ages ending in zero or five. This a common pattern across the developing world: where citizens have limited interaction and contact with the formal state – and a resulting lack of public school enrollment or access to government documents, such as birth certificates or identification cards – many do not have any means to recall their precise ages to census enumerators, instead rounding off to the nearest zero or five. The comparative degree of age heaping in a population is best measured using the Myers Score, an index of clustering in ending digits ranging from 0 (no age heaping)

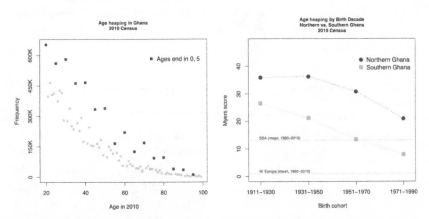

FIGURE 3.1 Age heaping in Ghana. The left panel demonstrates the presence of age heaping, an indicator of low state presence, among a random sample of 2.5 million respondents in Ghana's 2010 census; the right panel measures differences in age heaping by birth cohort between Northern and Southern Ghana using the Myers Score, as in Lee and Zhang (2017). For comparison, the horizontal lines indicate the mean overall age heaping values reported in Lee and Zhang (2017) for western European and sub-Saharan African censuses conducted between 1960 and 2010.

to 90 (all ages heaped on a single ending digit).[2] The mean Myers Score for censuses in western European countries between 1960 and 2010 was 0.98, indicating very little heaping. In the 2010 census, Ghana instead had a Myers Score of 13.8 among native-born adults (ages twenty through ninety-nine). This is typical for sub-Saharan Africa, close to the regional mean of 13.1.[3]

But age heaping in Northern Ghana has been dramatically greater than this. The right panel of Figure 3.1 shows a significant North–South divide in age heaping in Ghana, suggestive of differences in historical state presence between core and hinterland regions. The plot breaks out the data by region and birth cohort. Age heaping has gradually declined in both North and South among younger cohorts. But across generations, age heaping remains strikingly higher in Northern than Southern Ghana. For citizens born between 1931 and 1970, straddling the late-colonial and early postcolonial periods, the North-South gap in age heaping within Ghana is *larger* than the gap between highly developed states in western Europe and the average state in sub-Saharan Africa (over 13 points).

Map 3.1 instead visualizes this North–South gap in state presence geographically, calculating Myers Scores for each of Ghana's 275 parliamentary constituencies as of the 2016 election. Although there are some pockets with notable age heaping in the rural South, and a few isolated areas with less heaping in the North, age heaping in Ghana is *overwhelmingly* concentrated in the North, indicative of the state's persistent absence in this hinterland.[4]

3.1.2 The "Shatter Zone": Limited Precolonial Statehood

The stark pattern in Map 3.1 has deep roots. Northern Ghana has always been a hinterland. Borrowing Scott's (2009, 7–8) phrase, precolonial Northern Ghana could be described as a "shatter zone" – a region whose great ethnolinguistic diversity was produced by its location at the margins of other states. In medieval times, the region lay at the southeastern edge of the Sahelian empires, Mali and Songhai. In the fifteenth and sixteenth centuries, warriors splintering off from the empires pushed south. They created a series of small kingdoms that became integrated

---

[2] Lee and Zhang (2017) validate this measure. Also see Myers (1940).

[3] Lee and Zhang (2017, 126).

[4] Interestingly, the place in the North with the lowest age heaping (far upper-left) is around Nandom and Jirapa, where missionaries were initially most active in the 1920s and 1930s.

**Myers score by constituency
ages twenty to ninety–nine (c. 2010)**

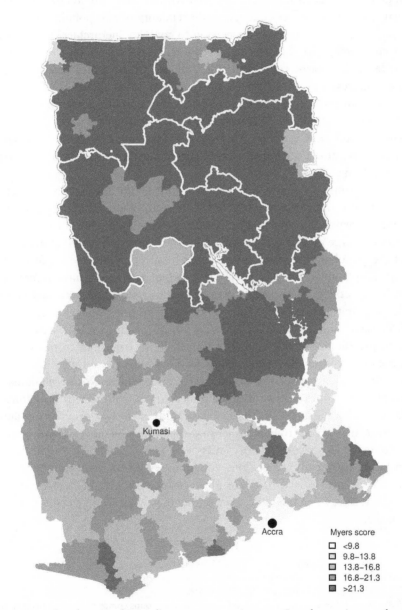

Myers score
☐ <9.8
☐ 9.8–13.8
▨ 13.8–16.8
▨ 16.8–21.3
▨ >21.3

MAP 3.1 Age heaping by parliamentary constituency. Local constituency-level estimates of age heaping (for ages twenty to ninety-nine) from the 2010 census. Darker shaded areas have more age heaping. The white polygons demarcate the five administrative regions (provinces) of Northern Ghana.

into trans-Sahelian trading networks.[5] These kingdoms, most prominently Dagbon, but also Gonja, Mamprugu, Wa, and Nanum, developed
systems of class stratification between royals – descendants of the original invaders – and commoners – descendants of the populations they
conquered – that governed succession to complex hierarchical structures
of chieftaincy (see Chapter 7). By the end of the seventeenth century,
however, European trade with the Atlantic Coast undercut the Sahelian empires, leading to the rise of a new dominant state to the south –
Ashanti, in present-day Southern Ghana. By the mid-eighteenth century,
the small kingdoms of Northern Ghana had become vassals of Ashanti.
The tributes they paid to Ashanti, a major exporter in the Transatlantic slave trade, included slaves captured from raids of surrounding
populations.[6]

Importantly, the kingdoms that emerged from the Sahelian invasions in
the fifteenth and sixteenth centuries never consolidated political authority
over the region,[7] controlling at most only roughly one third of the population.[8] Large swaths of Northern Ghana, comprising the large majority
of the population, remained populated by a highly diverse set of stateless, acephalous ethnic groups. These populations may have remained
so highly ethnically and linguistically fractionalized, and been unable to
develop state institutions, because of the constant pressure they faced
from slave raiding.[9] Much as Scott (2009) documents for Southeast Asia,
their precolonial institutions were shaped by strategic exit from the violence of surrounding states. Even up to the last decades of the nineteenth
century, well after the Transatlantic slave trade ended, Northern Ghana's
acephalous communities remained under attack from nearby kingdoms.
In particular, the late-19th-century slave raids of the warlords Samori and
Babatu still have a strong presence in the historical memory of many communities.[10] In my oral history interviews (see Chapter 4), respondents
in most historically acephalous communities dated their communities'
founding back only to the late nineteenth century, right before British
colonial rule, when their ancestors settled in new locations to better avoid
attacks.

---

[5] Staniland (1975), Wilks et al. (1986), Wilks (1989), Awedoba (2006).
[6] Grischow (2006), Lentz (2006).
[7] Grischow (2006), Lentz (2006), Talton (2010).
[8] By 2010, for example, these "always chiefs" ethnic groups comprised just 36 percent of
the North's population.
[9] Nunn (2008).
[10] Awedoba (2006), Grischow (2006), Lentz (2006).

Many of these acephalous groups shared key institutional similarities. Political authority was vested in family heads – the leaders of individual clans and lineage groups – not in any hierarchy of political institutions.[11] Land was managed by *tendanas,* or "earth priests," religious figures who controlled earth shrines and allocated plots among community members. The position of *tendana* typically fell (and still falls today) to a male elder of the original lineage group settled in each community, and had became a central institution in virtually every acephalous group in Northern Ghana prior to colonial rule.[12]

Studying Dagaba areas of the present-day Upper West Region, Lentz (2006, 2009) emphasizes that acephalous communities were not entirely without socioeconomic stratification in the precolonial period. By the late nineteenth century, individuals in some communities had begun to amass relative resource advantages over other community members through farming and trading, as well as through their efforts fighting off outside slave raiders. But overall, these communities lacked any clear hierarchical class structure or state-like political leadership, as had already developed in Dagbon, Gonja, Mamprugu, and the other kingdoms that emerged centuries earlier.

3.1.3 The Colonial State

Ghana's modern state began with the formation of the Gold Coast colony along the Atlantic Coast in the mid-nineteenth century. British rule only reached the North at the outset of the twentieth century, however, with present-day Northern Ghana incorporated into the colony as a separately governed satellite – the Northern Territories – from 1901. Until the 1890s, this northern frontier had remained untouched by colonial powers. Ghana's northern borders were initially drawn in the mid-1880s, prior to any European state establishing authority, or even having significantly explored or mapped the region. Lacking the capacity to project military force into the hinterland, the British struck a deal in 1889 with the Germans in Togoland to designate much of present-day Northern Ghana as a "neutral zone" until a real border could be demarcated.[13] In 1899, a

---

[11] Tait (1961), Lentz (2009).
[12] Rattray (1932), Lund (2008), Lentz (2006), Lentz (2009).
[13] For the decade this non-aggression pact was in effect, Britain and Germany both sent expeditions North – the British signed treaties with several precolonial kingdoms, while German forces reached Yendi. See Arhin (1974).

revised border divided the British Gold Coast from German Togoland.
By 1901, the British began governing their portion as the Northern Territories of the Gold Coast. After World War I, the Northern Territories
expanded to include territory originally under German control, which
Britain seized during the war (see Chapter 4).

The British immediately recognized that this hinterland offered few
opportunities for profit. Writing in 1912, an official observed:

> Many years will elapse, and many changes will have to be wrought ... before
> agricultural enterprises on at all a considerable scale can be undertaken with any
> prospect of financial success ... [M]oreover, there are no grounds for believing that
> the Northern Territories stand possessed of any natural [resource] advantages.[14]

Facilitating labor migration from the North to the South represented the
colonial regime's only economic interest. In effect, "non-development of
the north" became official policy.[15] Without major cash crops for export,
the region's agricultural economy remained centered on subsistence farming and food production and cattle-rearing for the domestic market.[16]
With such a limited private economy, the colonial state arrived in the
region with huge resource advantages over the population.

But with the region a low priority, the British dispatched incredibly
few officers, keeping the state's presence limited and governing indirectly
through local intermediaries – traditional chiefs. Until World War II, there
were typically less than one hundred Europeans resident in the region at
any time. For example, in 1921, two decades into formal colonial rule,
the colonial census reported that were less than thirty British officials
total in the Northern Territories, a region roughly the size of Virginia.
The all-African constabulary force of around 400 soldiers was overseen
by just 4 British officers by 1924.[17] At times, as few as eight District Commissioners managed the entire territory.[18] By comparison, the European
population in Southern Ghana – the focus of much more intensive British
rule – had reached 2,939 by 1921, including 768 British officers.[19]

From archival sources, especially colonial annual reports, it is possible to reconstruct the full record of construction of colonial government

---

[14] *Northern Territories of the Gold Coast: Report for 1912* (1913, 4).
[15] Grischow (2006, 55).
[16] The major crops were (and remain) yams, cassava, sorghum, millet, maize, and (in a few
  sufficiently irrigated areas) rice.
[17] *Northern Territories Annual Report for 1923–1924* (1924, 14).
[18] Bening (2010, 104).
[19] *Gold Coast: Report for 1921* (1923, 33).

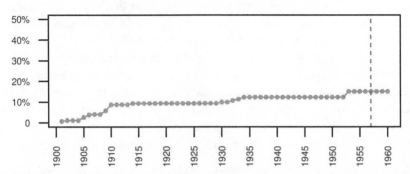

Communities within ten kilometers of state institutions (excluding schools)

FIGURE 3.2 Communities near state facilities (1901–1960). Communities in Northern Ghana within walking distance of any government facility (District Commissioner's office, police station, dispensary, etc.), measured using localities in the 2010 census. The year of Ghana's independence is marked by the vertical line.

facilities – such as administrative offices, police stations, hospitals, and agricultural research stations – in the Northern Territories from 1901 onward. Setting aside schools, examined in more detail below, Figure 3.2 plots growth in the other formal outposts of the colonial state over time. By 1931, three decades into British rule, just 10 percent of communities in the Northern Territories were with a ten kilometer radius of any British facility. By 1951, this had risen to only 12 percent of communities. The formal trappings of the state remained highly concentrated in just a dozen towns that served as district capitals.

In addition, the British limited the ability of missionaries – a major force in colonialism elsewhere – to operate. Catholic missionaries crossing over from French territory established a mission at Navrongo in 1906. As of 1921, there were still a grand total of three individual missionaries – all in Navrongo – in the entire Northern Territories.[20] These priests eventually won approval in the late 1920s and early 1930s to expand into several Dagaba communities, such as Nandom and Jirapa. But widespread missionary activity beyond a few enclaves did not pick up until the independence era.

One direct result of the state's formal absence was limited fiscal and bureaucratic capacity. Little revenue was collected, especially before

---

[20] *Gold Coast: Report for 1921* (1923, 33).

chiefs were deputized as tax collectors in 1936. Despite the low costs associated with deploying such a small staff, the Northern Territories operated at a major loss. In 1926, revenue extracted from the North represented just 9 percent of the (itself small) amount spent administering it, and less than 0.5 percent of revenues extracted in the rest of the Gold Coast.[21] To the extent that colonial officials eventually attempted to implement development initiatives, they struggled mightly to execute them.[22] As the Gold Coast transitioned to African internal rule in 1951, the overall picture created by state efforts in the Northern Territories was one of extreme neglect. Mumuni Bawumia, a major independence-era political figure,[23] reflects on the conditions left behind by the scarce state at independence:

Road infrastructure in the Northern Territories was poor; telephone and postal services were virtually non-existent. Apart from the poorly constructed and ill-equipped Tamale Hospital there were only a few dispensaries ... Treated pipe water supply was limited only to Tamale. The only gold mine ... closed down during the world war. The people of the North were left to undertake and to continue with the traditional subsistence farming. No cash exportable crops were introduced by the Colonial administration ... Northerners were not available [as civil servants] in the entire administrative system in the country.[24]

3.1.4 The State after Independence

Independence did not reduce the state's scarcity. The transition to independence began in 1951, with internal elections for an all-African colonial legislature. Kwame Nkrumah was elected as leader of government business, akin to Prime Minister. Upon formal independence in 1957, Ghana was briefly a democracy before Nkrumah and his Convention People's Party (CPP) consolidated authoritarian control in a one-party state.

Nkrumah aggressively attempted to supplant the authority of traditional chiefs in Southern Ghana, including by ratcheting up the state's administrative power at the local level.[25] The landed southern elite, led by Akan chiefs, represented the central political threat to his regime.

---

[21] *Northern Territories Annual Report for 1925–1926* (1926, 5). The 1926 budget shows revenues of £9,201 versus administrative expenditures of £100,792. By comparison, the revenues extracted in Southern Ghana were well over £3 million annually throughout the 1920s (e.g., *Gold Coast: Report for 1921*, 7).

[22] Gandah (2009, 93), Grischow (2006, 137, 183).

[23] Foreshadowing Chapter 6, Bawumia is the father of Ghana's current vice president, Mahamadu Bawumia.

[24] Bawumia (2004, 45).

[25] Rathbone (2000), Boone (2003).

But Nkrumah took a different approach in the North, leaving chiefs' powers largely unchallenged while courting them as potential allies.[26]

From the late 1960s, in the period after Nkrumah was deposed in a coup, Ghana's economy went into a tailspin, with negative growth between 1969 and 1979. During the economic crisis, the capacity of the post-independence state effectively bottomed out.[27] Weighed down by budget and staff shortages, the formal state became, if anything, even more absent across the North than in the late colonial period. Central state leaders responded to the economic crisis by intentionally limiting their ambitions to govern the periphery; government leaders decided that "central authorities are in a better position to ... minimize in their policies towards the relatively disadvantaged ... subregions" in order to focus on "development aims" in more economically vital areas.[28] The result was deterioration in the quality of what little state-provided infrastructure the North had, which only served to "exacerbate the remoteness of the north" from the state.[29]

On paper, the North was still governed from the same district capitals as in the colonial period during the authoritarian regimes that followed Nkrumah.[30] Yet Ayee (1993, 117-118) observes that "the achievements of most of the local councils [district governments] were limited to little more than paying staff emoluments. Most councils were unable to raise adequate revenue to support any meaningful development programmes at the district level." Even the staff who were paid were often absent; bureaucrats posted to the North were frequent no-shows in this period, preferring to remain in cities where they had other economic opportunities.[31] This left the formal state with incredibly limited capacity. In his memoirs, Bawumia (2004, 30), quoted above, argues that the state's neglect of the North continued unabated throughout the 1960s and 1970s: "no additional substantial development projects were visible in ... the Frafra, Kusasi, or South Mamprusi Districts," for example.

---

[26] Ladouceur (1979).

[27] Chazan (1982), Frimpong-Ansah (1991).

[28] Chazan (1982, 3).

[29] Drucker-Brown (1989, 102). Drucker-Brown (1989) documents significant reductions in the quality of (already meager) road, telephone, and post office infrastructure between the early 1960s and mid-1980s.

[30] Bening (2010). Other than two brief interludes with electoral politics in 1969–1972 and 1979–1981, Ghana was led by a series of dictatorships until 1992.

[31] Chazan (1982), Bob-Milliar (2011). Civil service absenteeism has remained a challenge in Northern Ghana into the twenty-first century, as recounted in the anecdote in the Acknowledgments.

After several more years of negative economic growth to begin the 1980s, economic reforms under Jerry Rawlings and his Provisional National Defense Council (PNDC) regime, in power from 1982, ended the crisis and set the country up for dramatic economic development in the subsequent decades.[32] But for most of the 1980s, the PNDC continued to rely on traditional chiefs as their main interlocutors with Northern communities rather than attempt to invest in building up a stronger local bureaucracy.[33]

It was only with decentralization reforms beginning from 1988 as an early step in Ghana's 1992 transition to democracy that the state's local presence began to slowly change across the North. The initial reforms expanded the number of local administrative districts from sixty-five to 110 nationwide – including up to twenty-four in the North – increasing the number of local bureaucrats and devolving more authority and funding to them.[34] Later governments engaged in several additional waves of administrative unit creation (studied in Chapter 7) – in 2004, 2007, 2012, and 2018 – creating an increasingly large bureaucracy in the North. The region is now split into fifty-three administrative districts, over four times as many as in the 1970s. Although the state still has serious limits to its capacity, it is now more present than ever before. But this is a recent change, still too nascent to have offset the accumulated effects of the century of extreme state scarcity preceding it.

3.2 THREE STATE ACTIONS

Despite its persistent scarcity, Northern Ghana's modern state still made three major interventions into society over the twentieth century. These actions are each among the most basic and minimal attempts a state could make at governance: decisions about how to delegate grassroots authority, how to provide elementary public goods, and how to allocate property rights. Perhaps counterintuitively, each action was only implemented with an eye by state leaders towards *keeping the state absent*; state leaders only approved these interventions insomuch as they would help avoid more costly and extensive interventions later on. And consistent with the state's

---

[32] Herbst (1993), Aryeetey (1996).

[33] Drucker-Brown (1989), Riedl (2014). For example, the Interim Management Committees initially created as the main local government bodies by the Provisional National Defense Council (PNDC) regime named chiefs to between one third to two thirds of all positions in the North (Ayee 1993).

[34] Ayee (1993, 120–124).

incapacity, all three actions faced major problems in implementation. Yet all three went on to have large effects on society and politics.

3.2.1 Inventing and Imposing Chiefs

The state's earliest institution-building came via the delegation of administrative duties to chiefs. British officers began deputizing chiefs as state agents in 1902.[35] The British turned to chiefs precisely because they wanted to keep the state's presence limited. The commissioner of the Northern Territories explained:

The policy of supporting and emphasizing the position of the ... native chief ... appears to me to be the only practicable system of administering this country, which has an area of 24,000 square miles ... and an available staff of some 18 British officers who are called upon to perform both civil and military duties.[36]

In the new administrative order that emerged, the British created parallel channels of state and traditional authority. The region was divided into districts, each led by an appointed British official, the District Commissioner, who then interacted with the population through chiefs. While indirect rule began informally right from 1902, the system was only formalized in the mid-1930s with the division of the region into Native Authorities specific to each ethnic group.[37] Before the mid-1930s, chiefs served as communities' only point of contact with British officials and were empowered as local judicial authorities. They also served as "labour contractors" – coordinating forced labor when requested by British officials and helping direct migrant workers South.[38] After the establishment of Native Authorities in the 1930s, chiefs also became responsible for small-scale tax collection as well as building and maintaining basic local public goods, such as markets and primary schools.

Native Authorities were territorial divisions led by an appointed council of chiefs from the respective ethnic group dominant in that area, and were headed by that group's paramount chief.[39] Modeled on pre-existing

---

[35] This was implemented via the Native Administrative Ordinance of 1902.

[36] *Northern Territories of the Gold Coast: Report for 1905* (1906, 3).

[37] Some groups were notably excluded from the Native Authority system, however, as explained below.

[38] Grischow (2006, 49).

[39] While most ethnic groups in Northern Ghana had a single paramount and Native Authority, a few, especially the Dagaba, had multiple co-equal paramounts leading separate Native Authorities.

kingdoms in the region, this system was pyramidal. At the top, the paramount chief, equivalent to a king, was responsible for appointing divisional chiefs, an intermediate tier of chiefs sited in the largest towns within the Native Authority. In turn, the divisional chiefs would appoint individual village chiefs for each rural community in the vicinity of their respective town.

As they began to work through chiefs, the British were forced to adapt to the varied pre-existing political institutions in the region. This has produced the three separate sets of ethnic groups outlined in Table 3.1. Among the pre-existing kingdoms described above, the British worked with pre-existing chiefs. The first column of Table 3.1 lists the present-day populations of ethnic groups that have *always* had chiefs since the pre-colonial period. Map 3.2 maps the present-day jurisdictions of chiefs from these groups. While the British made some changes to chieftaincy within these kingdoms (see Chapters 7 and 8), they kept the broad outlines of pre-existing institutions intact.

But much of the population did not have pre-existing chiefs who could be co-opted. In many precolonially acephalous ethnic groups, listed in the middle column of Table 3.1, the British instead resorted to *inventing* new chiefs from scratch.[40] This began immediately in the first decade of the twentieth century, with British forces moving systematically community by community, recognizing new leaders as they pacified acephalous areas.[41] In doing so, they "creat[ed] chieftaincy institutions among people for whom this institution was either unknown or at best peripheral."[42]

British officers did so from a position of near-complete ignorance about these societies. Initially, they believed that imposing chiefs was a means of re-establishing a "natural order" that had only recently been disrupted by slave raids. Writing of his early efforts to recognize chiefs, a colonial official described in 1907: "Much trouble has been made to divide these people up into their original divisions, and to come under the ... chiefs who they were in the habit of obeying before Samory and Barbatu overran the country."[43] But over time, the British realized that they were creating

---

[40] The Mo, a tiny group with less than 1 percent of Northern Ghana's population, do not neatly fit the coding scheme in Table 3.1. There were Mo chiefs in Southern Ghana during the colonial period (and perhaps earlier), but Mo chiefs only were state recognized in the North after independence. All analyses are robust to excluding Mo communities.

[41] Grischow (2006, 38–42).

[42] Awedoba et al. (2009, 3).

[43] *Northern Territories of the Gold Coast: Report for 1907* (1908, 8).

TABLE 3.1 *Ethnic groups and chieftaincy history in Northern Ghana*

Precolonial, colonial, and contemporary chiefs		Invented chiefs		Chiefs never independently recognized	
Group	Population Share	Group	Population Share	Group	Population Share
Dagomba	20.0%	Dagaba (Dagarte; incl. Lobi)	11.4%	Konkomba	12.7%
Mamprusi	5.6%	Frafra (incl. Nankansi, Talensi, Gurense)	8.4%	Bimoba	2.9%
Gonja	4.5%	Kusasi	5.7%	Hausa	2.0%
Kasena (Paga)	2.2%	Sisala	2.9%	Other Grusi (Templensi, Birifor, etc.)	2.0%
Nanumba	1.9%	Builsa (Kangyaga)	2.6%	Busanga	1.6%
Wala	1.6%	Namnam (Nabdom)	<1%	Chokosi (Anufor)	1.2%
		Mo (c. 1992)	<1%	Mosi	<1%
				Basare (Chamba)	<1%
				Wangara (Bambara)	<1%
				Nawuri	<1%
				Vagala	<1%
				Kotokoli (Tem)	<1%
				Salfalba (Sabulaba)	<1%
				Fulani	<1%
				Pilapila	<1%
				Zabrama	<1%
				Other Gurma	<1%
Total (2010): 1.5 million (36%)		Total (2010): 1.3 million (32%)		Total (2010): 1.1 million (25%)	

Group names and share of the Northern population from the 2010 census. The remaining 7% is southern or non-Ghanaian.

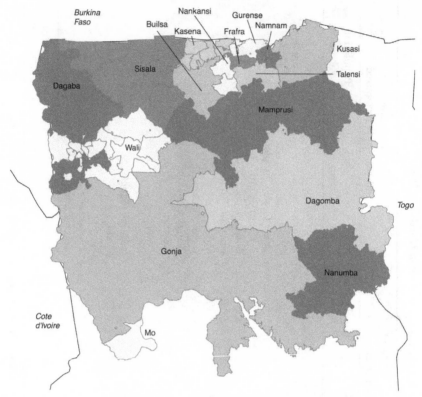

MAP 3.2 Traditional Councils in Northern Ghana. Modern-day jurisdictions of chiefs from "invented chiefs" and "always chiefs" ethnic groups, as listed in Table 3.1.

something entirely new. In a 1911 report, the Commissioner of the Northern Territories recognized that his officers were appointing chiefs in areas "where none previously existed."[44] The full novelty of the British imposition became apparent when colonial anthropologists began systematically attempting to understand the precolonial institutions of these groups in the 1930s, three decades after the British had already changed them.[45]

---

[44] *Northern Territories of the Gold Coast: Report for 1911* (1912, 20).

[45] The archives contain a notable 1936 exchange between a District Commissioner and the famous anthropologist Meyers Fortes, in which the colonial official asks basic questions about the Frafra society he governs – still unknown to the colonial state over thirty-five years into their control of the area. In response, Fortes observed that the new chiefly political order the British had already imposed was only very "distantly related" to what had come before. Northern Regional Archives, Tamale, Folio NRG 3 / 2 / 11.

In this low information environment, British decisions about who to elevate as a chief often appeared arbitrary, at odds with pre-existing social institutions. Lentz (2006, 2009) argues that at least in some Dagaba communities, the British tapped existing local "strongmen" as the chiefs – villagers who had already become relatively wealthier than the rest of the community. Writing in 1907, a British official observed that some communities were strategically offering forward men as chiefs who "have plenty of cattle, as on him falls the privilege of paying any fines that the Commissioner might impose on the town."[46]

But many narratives of the initial British selection of invented chiefs suggest that these appointments were typically far more *ad hoc*, unrelated to pre-existing distributions of wealth. Sometimes the tendana, a religious figure who lacked political authority, was simply given an additional role. Elsewhere within the same ethnic groups, selection could be more random. Lentz (2006, 44–45) describes cases in which the British summoned the tendana to a meeting, but the priest, suspicious of their intentions, sent a young man in his place, only to have the British turn around and empower that emissary – essentially their first interlocutor – as chief. Grischow (2006, 76) similarly recounts that "[w]hen the British toured the north to appoint chiefs, the land priests thrust forward commoners because they were suspicious of outsiders after the slave raids of the nineteenth century."[47] Simply being welcoming could be sufficient grounds to be elevated as a chief. Gandah (2009, 19) recounts that the first chief in his village was selected "because his family gave hospitality to the first white man who visited."[48] Grischow (2006, 39) summarizes that for acephalous groups in the present-day Upper East Region, the initial chiefs "were a diverse lot. Some of them had simply agreed to collaborate and were made chiefs, some were elders or former slaves or outcasts, and some had been minor [tendanas]. For the most part, they had little indigenous authority before becoming chiefs."

Oral history interviews in three randomly selected Dagaba communities and three randomly-selected Frafra communities suggest that communities' own narratives of how their chiefs were first chosen align with evidence that the British deviated from the pre-existing social

---

[46] *Northern Territories of the Gold Coast: Report for 1907* (1908, 8).

[47] Rattray (1932) and Lund (2008, 38) also report similar anecdotes.

[48] Relatedly, Lentz (2006, 50) writes of her interviews in Dagaba areas, "I frequently encountered the speculation that one's own village might have become the center of the new [Native Authority], or even the district headquarters, if only one's forefathers had not chased away the British or had not fled from them."

structure. In a Dagaba community near Nadowli, the regent (acting chief) narrated that his community's first chief – his own direct ancestor – was chosen simply because he was too old to flee when British forces first arrived, making him the first household head they met:

> During those times, there used to be war here and there ... So anytime people were coming, people were frightened. They would have to flee the area. But when the whites were coming, they saw them and they were all running from them. But [the first chief] being an old man ... he couldn't run very far. They chased after him and they caught up to him. They were explaining to him that they were not going to kill him. They brought him back and said 'ok he should take care of the community' ... He was basically just the first person they contacted.[49]

Respondents in a nearby community offered conflicting narratives of how their first chief was chosen; regardless of which is more accurate, both suggest the chief was not selected based on his pre-existing authority or wealth. A first respondent narrated that the first chief was selected after the British set up a contest in which the man who could run fastest would be made leader.[50] Directly matching Lentz (2006) and Grischow's (2006) anecdotes, another instead claimed that the British approached the tendana for a meeting, but he sent a young nephew (the same man described by the first respondent) to meet with them and that nephew was then chosen as the chief.[51]

Respondents in other communities emphasized that the British chose early chiefs with an eye towards administrative convenience. The tendana in a Frafra community near Zuarungu narrated that a recently settled outsider to their community was selected as the first chief because he happened to own a horse, which made it easier for him to oversee the communal labor team the British pressed into service to build the nearby road.[52] A particularly striking example came from another Frafra community. The current chief narrated that after first selecting a respected elder as chief through an election organized among community members, the British replaced him upon his death with his slave because the slave had developed a good working relationship with the District Commissioner from being sent on errands to and from his office miles away.[53]

---

[49] Interview with regent (acting chief), community #2, Nadowli District, 27 May 2019.

[50] Interview with chief's caretaker, community #1, Nadowli District, 27 May 2019.

[51] Interview with tendana, community #1, Nadowli District, 27 May 2019.

[52] Interview with tendana, community #1, Bolgatanga East District, 20 May 2019.

[53] Interview with chief and elders, community #2, Bolgatanga District, 21 May 2019. Of the initial selection, the chief explained: "What happened is that the whites, they were at Gambaga. So they came ... and if you want him to be the chief, the people will pick

This elevated the slave's descendants from the bottom rung of the community into a permanent "royal" family. Indeed, the arbitrary nature of these decisions is so important, in part, because many chieftaincy positions in the "invented chiefs" groups then became hereditary over time (see Chapter 7).[54]

Understandably, leaders imposed this arbitrarily were not immediately accepted by their communities. In the early decades, newly invented chiefs were often resisted, or simply ignored; the minimal British presence left most chiefs little power with which to enforce their dictates. Lentz (2006, 60) describes that, at first, "few [invented chiefs] managed to discipline their subjects with any kind of lasting effect," leading to "numerous complaints" among British officials that chiefs were failing to establish real authority.[55] One colonial official griped that "the majority of the natives in the Zouaragu [Zuarungu] District have been passive resisters, as far as obeying the chiefs was concerned" and described the need for more progress in "getting the people to realize that their chiefs are no longer to be considered figureheads."[56] Other officials complained of "intolerant and reactionary" household heads – the existing authority figures most directly challenged by chieftaincy – who "do everything in their power to counteract the growing authority of the Chiefs, for whom they retain a fanatical hatred."[57]

It would take three decades – into the 1930s – for many chiefs to gradually amass meaningful respect and influence.[58] Describing the period in the mid-1930s after Native Authorities were created and chiefs gained additional powers over tax collection and local administration, a colonial official observed, "[chiefs] have awakened to a sense of their responsibilities and are not afraid to use the powers conferred on them. At the beginning it was not an uncommon thing to find a chief who was too afraid or too apathetic to use the jurisdiction conferred on him. This has changed now."[59]

---

stones and heap them. This [man] will have plenty [of] stones, meaning you have so many people following you. That is why they picked ... We could call it an election in a way."

54 Awedoba et al. (2009).
55 Also see Grischow (2006, 73).
56 *Northern Territories of the Gold Coast: Report for 1911* (1912, 20).
57 *Northern Territories Annual Report for 1918* (1919, 18).
58 Lentz (2006, 34).
59 *Report on the Northern Territories 1933–1934* (1934, 5).

During the first decades after chiefs were imposed, the British attempted to prop up their authority in several ways, all constrained by the formal state's absence and incapacity. Armed force, via the colonial constabulary, helped enforce the authority of chiefs whose communities were close to existing state outposts.[60] But this was less viable for the many communities located much further away (see Figure 3.2). For example, the District Commissioner in Zuarungu pleaded with his superiors to increase the staffing of colonial officers to allow him to better help enforce chiefs' authority: "It seems ... unfair [to the chiefs] that a chief should be given an order ... to turn out his people for road work, and then, when some of the people refuse to turn out, and the chief appeals to the Commissioner to punish them for refusing to obey Government's order, nothing can be done."[61]

In lieu of the ability back up all chiefs' authority through force, the British cycled through chiefs in quick succession in some towns – hiring and firing in search of those best able to compel a community's respect on their own accord.[62] British officials also attempted to cultivate more organic support for chiefs by holding inter-community competitions, in which chiefs were awarded medallions for mobilizing community members, and by creating formal banners for chieftaincy positions – just as one might associate with a noble family in medieval Europe – in an attempt to generate pride in the institution.[63] Figure 3.3 shows a mockup for one such banner, created for the invented chief of Kaleo. These activities represented an attempt to draw on socially valued symbolism to draw people closer to these new authorities than the state could do through literal force.[64]

Many communities also gradually began to accommodate and work with these new leaders on their own, despite the state's lack of enforcement capacity. Chieftaincy provided new benefits. For example, chiefs' courts attracted participation because they provided more effective

---

[60] Lentz (2006, 55–57).

[61] Northern Regional Archives, Tamale, Folio NRG 3 / 2 / 11.

[62] Lentz (2006, 60); Gandah (2009, 29). That the selection of early chiefs was purposeful in at least some respects – such as screening for talent at leadership – is not a threat to the identification strategy in the subsequent chapters. The research design does not rely on any claim that the appointment of chiefs at an individual level was fully random (see Chapter 4).

[63] Gandah (2009, 29); Lentz (2006, 34, 68).

[64] Lund (2006) and Hagmann and Peclard (2010) theorize how state authority can be forged and legitimated through appeals to "symbolic repertoires" separate from the state's material resources.

FIGURE 3.3 Banner developed for the Kaleo-Na, Upper West Region. Northern Regional Archives, Tamale, Folio NRG 9 / 2 / 24.

avenues for centralized dispute resolution than what was previously available in acephalous societies.[65] Chiefs also offered community members their only means to access the colonial state – and the resources it could provide. Moreover, consistent with the potential symbolic and non-material value of the "state-ness" chiefs could confer,[66] Lentz (2006, 34) emphasizes that chieftaincy brought new social legitimacy and status to acephalous societies long dominated in the precolonial period by nearby kingdoms that already had chiefs: "[T]he adoption of chieftaincy allowed some groups ... to achieve a certain degree of 'progress'"; these communities "had been stigmatised as uncivilised ... regarded merely as booty for slave-raiders ... [T]he new political structures were attractive not only to chiefs, but also to ... [those] who sought the same status and respect as ... pre-colonial kingdoms."

However, a third category of groups – those in the final column of Table 3.1 – did not experience any similar efforts to invent and impose new chiefs from within local communities. Map 3.3 shows that in many Northern communities, the majority of the population is from an ethnic group *never recognized* by the colonial state. Most of these communities were also acephalous in the precolonial period, just like those that experienced the colonial invention of chieftaincy. The key distinction between them – detailed in Chapter 4 – is that most of the "never recognized" communities were originally in German Togoland and only incorporated into the Northern Territories after World War I.[67] The original Anglo-German border, in effect 1899–1914, is in Map 3.3.

Instead of being given their own chiefs, these communities were placed under the nominal oversight of neighboring "always chiefs" groups. Chiefs from these precolonial kingdoms made dubious historical claims to British officials of having had authority over neighboring acephalous peoples earlier in the nineteenth century (see Chapter 5). Regardless of their veracity, these claims provided over-stretched British officials a shortcut for governing this newly acquired German territory – which offered little

[65] Lentz (2006, 34).

[66] Lund (2006), Lund (2008).

[67] The only exceptions were incredibly small acephalous groups in the original Northern Territories, such as the Vagala and Birifo in the present-day Sawla-Tuna-Kalba and Wa West Districts, which each comprise less than 1 percent of Northern Ghana's population. These groups appear to have been too small to attract British attention and were also left without chiefs. They account for the smattering of "never recognized" communities to the far west of Map 3.3.

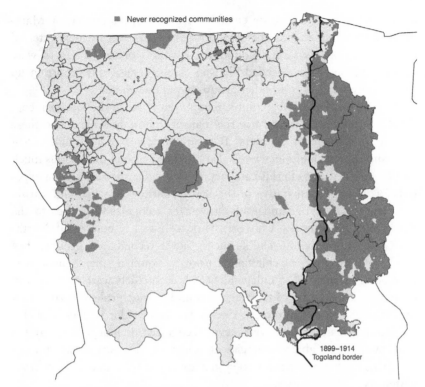

■ Never recognized communities

1899–1914
Togoland border

MAP 3.3 Communities with majority "never recognized" populations. Communities in the darkest color are from ethnic groups that have not had independent
hierarchies of state-recognized chiefs since the onset of colonial rule (see Table
3.1). The polygons indicate the official Traditional Council jurisdictions of groups
with state-recognized chiefs, as in Map 3.2.

new economic value – without having to invest more costly effort in trying
to prop up yet more newly invented chiefs.

This is exemplified by the Konkomba, a precolonially acephalous society, and by far the largest "never recognized" group (see Table 3.1). Most
Konkomba communities were left without their own state-backed leaders under British rule, defaulting to pre-existing clan governance while
being formally overseen by Dagomba, Nanumba, and Mamprusi chiefs.[68]
Chiefs from these other groups either officially ruled Konkomba communities from a distance, with little substantive authority on the ground,

[68] Tait (1961), Talton (2010).

or instead posted "surrogate chiefs" – Dagomba, Nanumba, or Mamprusi chiefs – into Konkomba communities to rule over them as external occupiers. In a few larger Konkomba towns, Konkomba elders were instead appointed as so-called "liaison chiefs," emissaries reporting up to supervising chiefs from other groups based elsewhere.[69]

Because the Konkomba comprise more than half of the "never recognized" population, they receive the majority of attention given to these groups in subsequent chapters. But similar forms of external, surrogate, and liaison chieftaincy were also practiced among the various much smaller ethnic groups in this category. In particular, the Konkomba experience is quite representative of the Basare, Birifor, Nawuri, and Vagala experience. The least similar of the "never recognized" groups to the Konkmoba is likely the Chokosi, who are just 1.2 percent of Northern Ghana's population. Unlike most "never recognized" groups, they did have some form of chieftaincy prior to colonial rule.[70] But rather than being recognized as independent, Chokosi chiefs were converted to dependent subsidiaries of the Dagomba under British rule, placed within the Dagomba Native Authority. Unifying this entire third category of ethnic groups was that they were never recognized as independent by the state, with chiefs able to exercise authority on their own, and did not experience colonial attempts to systematically elevate new leaders from within their communities.

Importantly, these colonial-era decisions about how to create (or not create) new chieftaincy institutions persist because key elements of the administrative system introduced under colonial rule were then kept intact long after independence. Ghana's post-independence authoritarian regimes initially maintained a facsimile of the colonial administrative system in the North. Districts were still headed by centrally appointed state officials similar to colonial District Commissioners. The Native Authorities persisted, with the same hierarchies of paramount, divisional, and village chiefs, but were relabelled Traditional Councils. Though chiefs relinquished their responsibilities for tax collection and goods provision, they still received state stipends and appointments to unelected assemblies that advised district leaders. As such, Northern chiefs operated in

---

[69] Dawson (2000).

[70] The historical record here is thin. However, pre-existing Chokosi chieftaincy is noted briefly in both Tait (1961, 8) and Arhin (1974, 97–102), for example. The quantitative analyses in subsequent chapters are robust to dropping the small set of Chokosi communities.

the initial postcolonial period in a fuzzy in-between space – as both quasi-state agents and nonstate societal elites who represented their communities' interests to state leaders.[71]

Decentralization reforms in 1988 introduced some democracy at the local level. The District Chief Executive (DCE), or mayor, the colonial District Commissioner's modern analogue, is still a central state appointee. But there is now also an elected District Assembly, akin to a city council. Chiefs no longer have guaranteed spots in this assembly or other roles in district administration, disconnecting them from any continuing claim to a formal state position.[72] However, the modern analogues of the Native Authorities, the territorially defined Traditional Councils for each state-recognized ethnic group still exist (Map 3.2), with authority over chieftaincy appointments, and, most importantly, since 1979, formal ownership of all land in their jurisdictions (described below).

3.2.2 Belatedly Building an Education System

The state's next major intervention came via the education system. This began under colonial rule and then continued as the most notable investment by the post-independence state in the region throughout the 1960s and 1970s. Overall, access to education was significantly lower compared to the rest of the Gold Coast by the end of the colonial period. In 1954, the Northern Territories had only 3 percent of the colony's schools (144 of 4,239), including just two of fifty secondary schools, despite having 20 percent of the population.[73] Missionary schools were also limited. While missionaries and churches were affiliated with 82% of schools in the South by 1954 (see Chapter 9), church schools accounted for only 10% in the North.[74]

Delayed education access was a symptom of the broader colonial goal to keep the hinterland underdeveloped and state absent. Colonial officials worried that schools would create a new educated class – "westernised elites and morally degenerate wage labourers" – who could challenge

---

[71] For more on the blurriness of the state-society boundary in African states, see Lund (2006), Blundo and Le Meur (2009), Hagmann and Peclard (2010), and Bierschenk and Olivier de Sardan (2014).

[72] Chieftaincy remains regulated by a non-partisan state body, the National House of Chiefs, but chiefs are no longer state agents or employees in any formal sense.

[73] *Education Statistics 1954* (1955, 1).

[74] *Education Statistics 1954* (1955, 6).

British authority, as they were increasingly doing in the South.[75] One
official put this bluntly in 1924, writing, "to give these ... children a more
advanced education ... might make them discontented with their lot."[76]

The British did allow for the construction of a small initial set of
schools, however. The first opened at Tamale in 1907, followed by Gambaga (1911), Wa (1917), Lawra (1919), and Yendi (1921).[77] The Catholic
missionaries at Navrongo opened a school in 1908, but it was only
intermittently active until the 1920s. Enrollments at these schools were
restricted to a few dozen children each. Many were boarders, recruited
by colonial officials from throughout the region. For higher education,
a small handful of graduates were sent South or to a middle school
eventually opened in Tamale.[78] The goal was to "educate a few selected
intelligent men of each tribe" who could become more effective administrators and interpreters for the colonial government.[79] As in other
British colonies, these early enrollments were aimed at "educating chiefs,
their sons and heirs as a means of enhancing their positions to facilitate
administration."[80] But enrolling the children of chiefs also emerged as a
practical necessity given the state's otherwise limited capacity. Suspicious
of what would happen to their children, many families initially refused
to allow them to enroll. Chiefs, especially those still struggling to develop
authority, were often unable to compel them to do so. But British officials had enough leverage over chiefs themselves to force them to send
their own children to meet the quota (see Chapter 4).[81] Ultimately, early
investments in education were an extension of the first major state action
above, serving as a component of indirect rule. And they only occurred
to the extent they helped British officials make indirect rule work better,
forestalling the need for a more direct state presence.

It was not until the late 1930s that the British allowed a series of community "day schools" – non-selective, non-boarding – to begin opening.
The transition to formal indirect rule in the mid-1930s included a switch
to direct taxation for the first time. This provided the Native Authorities,

---

[75] Grischow (2006, 69).

[76] Bening (1990, 49).

[77] The Lawra school soon closed due to low enrollment and only re-opened in 1935
(Gandah 2004, 36).

[78] Now Tamale Secondary School (TAMASCO), it was converted to a secondary school in
1951.

[79] Bening (1990, 3).

[80] Bening (1990, 62).

[81] Bening (1990, 7–8).

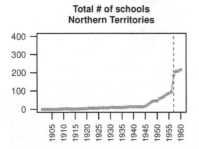
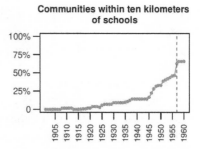

FIGURE 3.4 School access in Northern Ghana (1901–1960). Total number of schools constructed during the colonial period (left); percentage of communities (census Enumeration Areas) within a 10km radius of a school by year (right). Figures calculated from archival records, combining Annual Reports of the Northern Territories with school rosters from the Northern Regional Archives, Tamale.

the new district councils led by chiefs, with a pool of resources to finance local public goods. Using these funds, Native Authority day schools opened in a half dozen towns by 1945.[82] The state's biggest push for school construction only started from 1951, after the Gold Coast transitioned to internal African rule under Nkrumah. The principal policy demand of the newly elected Northern legislators was for funding to close the massive North–South education gap.[83] For the first time, state leaders (now Africans) supported the goal of mass education in the North, and the state financed the construction of hundreds of new primary schools.

Figure 3.4 plots the construction of schools in Northern Ghana over time. The number of communities with schools initially rose very slowly from two in 1915, to ten in 1930, to just seventeen by 1945. But by 1960, after a decade of internal rule, 216 Northern communities now had schools, mostly non-selective primary schools drawing from the surrounding area. There were also two secondary schools, with a third set to be opened that year. Using ten kilometers as the approximate maximum distance a non-boarding student could plausibly commute on foot, nearly two thirds of Northern communities (65 percent) were now within the catchment area of a primary school, up from less than 20 percent in 1945. By comparison, Figure 3.2 above shows that only 15 percent of communities were within 10km of any other state institution by 1960, indicative of the fact that primary schools had become the most present arm of the state by far.

[82] Grischow (2006, 98–102); Bening (1990, 88).
[83] Bening (1990, 198–199).

Nkrumah continued state investments in school construction into the 1960s. Most prominently, in 1961, he announced that primary education in the North would be free and compulsory for all children. But given the state's continued absence and bureaucratic incapacity, this was more a goal than anything remotely approaching reality. Universal attendance remained a mirage in the North for decades to come. Instead, newly opened primary schools in the 1950s and 1960s faced stark funding shortages, limiting enrollment, and still leaving many communities without easy access to primary education into the 1990s or even later. As a result, many of the initial wave of students attending school during the first major uptick in school construction in the 1940s and 1950s received a head start in education access of a generation or more compared to the broad majority of the population.

3.2.3 Delegating Land Rights

The state's third major intervention came in the late 1970s, with a change to the ownership of land. Separate land regimes developed between North and South during the colonial period. In the South, chiefs maintained control over land from the colonial period to present. In the North, the state instead formally granted ownership to itself. In practice, however, state control was very limited. Without cash crop agriculture, Northern land was of no particular value to the British. Little was ever expropriated, except for the construction of the small set of government facilities described above.[84] Precolonial land management practices continued undisturbed under the surface. While codifying and institutionalizing "neo-customary" land tenure institutions in rural areas was a principle aim of most colonial regimes in Africa,[85] the rulers of the Northern Territories devoted little attention to land at all, indicative of the state's broader absence in the hinterland.

In the "always chiefs" groups, this meant that chiefs continued to play a significant role allocating plots among community members. When these kingdoms emerged in the precolonial period, chiefs displaced and took on the powers of many of the pre-existing tendanas (earth priests).[86] But in the majority of Northern communities – populated by either the

---

[84] Lund (2008, 37) documents that between 1927 and 1951, the colonial state seized just eighty-two plots of land total in the Northern Territories.

[85] Boone (2014).

[86] Lund (2008, 44).

"invented chiefs" or "never recognized" ethnic groups – tendanas and individual family heads retained primary control over land.

Chiefs invented by the colonial state were largely not powerful enough to take on meaningful land authority and disturb pre-existing tenure regimes. Lund (2008, 19–37, 48) details how the British were so uninformed of local customary practices in the first decades of colonial rule that they initially did not even realize that the tendanas were still controlling most land; "[t]he majority of [land] transactions merely remained out of the legal and administrative horizon of government and the state" (37). Writing in 1948, the colonial Lands Commissioner observed, "These priests [tendanas] are in absolute control of the land under their jurisdiction both as regards tenure and the practical rules of agriculture, and can eject an occupier who is unsuitable ... They appear to keep in the background but have a strong influence."[87] Colonial-era land practices continued after independence. The state remained the formal trustee of all land but did little to exercise its authority.

This changed in the late 1970s. The initiative for land reform in the North did not come from major shifts to the underlying economy of the region, such as an increase in the economic value of land – a key reason that land tenure regimes have been renegotiated in the modern period elsewhere in Africa.[88] Instead, an exogenous political crisis emerging from Southern Ghana that threatened the military dictatorship of Ignatius Acheampong, in power since 1972, created an unusual opening in which Northern chiefs found themselves for the first time with sufficient leverage to extract a policy concession that they had already been demanding since before independence: the equalization of their legal powers with their Southern counterparts'.

Overseeing a collapsing economy, Acheampong faced mass protests from students and professionals in urban areas in 1976 and 1977, culminating in a general strike by labor unions demanding civilian rule. The regime agreed to a transition, but on its own terms, holding a referendum in 1978 on a proposal to establish a civilian one-party state, with the military retaining significant influence. In the lead-up to the vote, opposition against the referendum emerged throughout Southern Ghana, especially in urban areas. In response, the regime attempted to run up their margins in the rural North, including by wooing traditional leaders to deliver

---

[87] Quoted in Lund (2008, 40–41).
[88] Firmin-Sellers (2000), Boone (2014).

Northern votes.[89] To demonstrate his commitment to these chiefs and cement the bargain, Acheampong established a state inquiry, the Alhassan Commission, "to investigate the possibilities of divesting [Northern] land and turning control over it to ... traditional landowners."[90] The Alhassan Commission proposed returning all land in Northern Ghana from the state back to its "rightful owners," the chiefs. In effect, this recommendation was an attempt to make the formal state even more absent in Northern Ghana, by taking away one of its core duties and giving it back to society.

The 1978 referendum narrowly passed amidst low turnout and allegations of fraud, carried by overwhelming support from the North.[91] Two further coups – in 1978 and 1979 – meant Acheampong was out of office (and executed by firing squad) by the time the Alhassan Commission officially completed its work. But a version of the proposed changes were incorporated into the new 1979 Constitution, when Ghana briefly transitioned back to democratic rule, and then maintained by the new PNDC regime of Jerry Rawlings in the early 1980s, which also sought to co-opt Northern chiefs chiefs as valuable allies.[92] The new provisions declared that all land in the North "shall [now] vest in any such person who was the owner of any such land" – that is *before* the British colonial state had (officially) seized it.[93] Versions of these clauses continued in Ghana's (current) 1992 Constitution, clarifying that these owners are "the appropriate skin" – the local chief.[94]

Coming at a time when Ghana's state capacity was at its absolute nadir, these new provisions were not immediately implemented. The provisions were also legally vague. Who was the owner of each parcel before the state took control? The Alhassan Commission, whose members were drawn primarily from the "always chiefs" groups in which chiefs had been owners prior to British rule, meant for this to indicate chiefs. In 1982, after the PNDC took power in a further coup, some Lands Commission offices – the state agency with the legal ability to resolve this question – were shuttered for several years in the North,

---

[89] Chazan and LeVine (1979).

[90] Lund (2008, 53). Also see Jonsson (2009).

[91] Chazan and LeVine (1979).

[92] Riedl (2014).

[93] Talton (2010, 147–149).

[94] *Constitution of Ghana* (1992), Chapter 21, Article 257, Clauses 3 and 4. Chiefs sit on "skins" in Northern Ghana.

creating a vacuum into which local actors began interpreting the new legal provisions as they wished.[95]

Even without state capacity for full implementation, the new provisions nonetheless changed the status quo in three key ways. First, and most importantly, chiefs from the "always chiefs" groups now claimed to be the legal owners of all land occupied by the "never recognized" ethnic groups living within the formal jurisdictions of their chieftaincies. As explained above, the "never recognized" did not have independent state-recognized chiefs of their own, and as a result could not now legally own land – even plots their families had farmed for generations.

Second, in the "invented chiefs" groups, chiefs began issuing their own land permits and selling plots, putting them in direct conflict with the tendanas (earth priests). Sustained legal disputes developed in the courts about who exactly the "traditional" landowners in the North really were. Some tendanas began asserting in court that they also counted as "rightful owners," not only chiefs, as a means to continue their prior authority.[96] While chiefs still have no real land authority in some communities,[97] in others an uneasy dual system has emerged in which both the chief and tendana separately sign off on land transactions and can each extract their own rents. Third, and closely related, to the extent that chiefs did begin successfully intervening in the land market where they had not previously, the private economic value of holding chieftaincy positions increased substantially.

3.3 NORTHERN GHANA IN COMPARATIVE PERSPECTIVE

The dynamics outlined in this chapter are not unique, allowing the Northern Ghanaian case to speak to the broader study of state power in the rural periphery. The nature of the modern state in Northern Ghana notably differs from some subnational regions in sub-Saharan Africa subject to more intensive and extractive forms of colonial and postcolonial rule, such as cash crop regions and more urban and coastal areas (see Chapter 9).[98] But Northern Ghana is typical of many other peripheral rural areas in the developing world, especially in Africa.

---

[95] Lund (2008, 56).
[96] Lund (2008, 55–56).
[97] Yaro (2010).
[98] Ricart-Huguet (2021b) documents the subnational correlates of more intensive forms of colonial state-building.

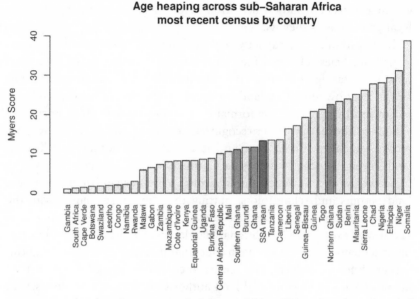

FIGURE 3.5 Age heaping across sub-Saharan Africa. Using data from Lee and Zhang (2017), the figure compares the degree of age heaping (Myers Score) among adult respondents in the most recent census available for each country or region. Ghana data is from the 2010 census, calculated by the author.

Similarly persistent state scarcity is a defining feature of rural hinterlands around the world.[99] In Africa, the British colonial state was similarly sparse across most rural areas – Herbst (2000, 78) notes that the British governed 43 million people in their African colonies with as few as 2,200 officials, most of whom were stationed in urban areas. In the contemporary period, Brinkerhoff et al. (2018) document a "negative spatial gradient" of service provision across rural Africa, with access to state services and facilities typically lowest in the most geographically remote regions. Returning to the age heaping measure introduced above, Figure 3.5 places Northern Ghana in comparison to the most recent census data available from other African countries. Ghana is a very typical case on the continent – its nationwide Myers Score for 2010 is virtually identical to the sub-Saharan African mean. Age heaping in Northern Ghana is also not unusual, but representative of many of the region's more incapable states, such as Togo, Sudan, and Sierra Leone.

[99] O'Donnell (1993), Herbst (2000), Scott (2009), Acemoglu et al. (2015).

Moreover, each of the three isolated state actions in Northern Ghana detailed above represent common interventions made by states in hinterland regions in Africa and elsewhere. First, the colonial imposition of novel traditional chieftaincy institutions occurred in many African colonies in a similar manner to Northern Ghana, for similar reasons.[100] There were also numerous other cases in which indirect rule varied subnationally, with pre-existing political institutions co-opted among some ethnic groups even as new institutions were invented for previously acephalous or non-centralized societies. Illustrative examples include Nigeria – where pre-existing institutions were co-opted in the North, but new institutions imposed in the Southeast[101] – and Zambia – where the colonial state co-opted Lozi chiefs in the West,[102] but imposed new leadership among the Tonga in the South.[103] The imposition of chieftaincy was also not isolated to British colonies. Boone (2003) documents related practices by the French among non-centralized societies in the Casamanche region of Senegal.[104] Even beyond the context of chieftaincy, the elevation of new local elites to facilitate indirect forms of governance in the face of state scarcity has been a common strategy of state-builders in the rural periphery around the world and is by no means a unique aspect of African colonialism.[105] Chapter 9 provides examples from Peru and the Philippines.

Second, the independence-era state's particular focus on education provision as its main activity in Northern Ghana is also representative of other postcolonial states. Schooling stands out as *the* principal local public good that many developing states still seek to provide even in subnational regions in which they otherwise underinvest in service provision. For example, by a wide margin, schools are the single most common local public good provided by the state to rural communities in Africa. I demonstrate this using data recorded in all 1,631 rural enumeration areas across the thirty-four African countries in the Round 7 Afrobarometer survey. In these recent surveys, eighty-one (81 percent) of

[100] Tignor (1971), Ranger (1983), Mamdani (1996), Spear (2003).
[101] Afigbo (1972) details the imposition of "warrant chiefs" in Igbo communities of Southeastern Nigeria and contrasts this with indirect rule in Northern Nigeria.
[102] Caplan (1970).
[103] O'Brien (1983).
[104] Boone (2014) further demonstrates that the delegation of authority, especially over land, to local traditional leaders was common across many subnational regions in other French colonies.
[105] Gerring et al. (2011), Slater and Kim (2015), Matsuzaki (2019).

rural Afrobarometer sampling locations had schools, compared to only 46 percent with a health clinic, 46 percent with electricity, 33 percent with piped water, 19 percent with police, and 10 percent with sewers.[106] Importantly, Brinkherhoff et al. (2018) find that education is the only public good for which there is not a negative spatial gradient across sub-Saharan Africa: unlike virtually all other services, they find that more remote, rural areas are not less likely to have schools compared to less peripheral regions. Education stands out as an especially important tool for state building,[107] and has been the central service provision focus in rural areas of many democratically elected African governments.[108]

Finally, the haphazard land reform effort the state adopted in Northern Ghana in 1979 echoes a similar phenomenon across Africa. Baldwin (2014) lists the Northern Ghanaian land reform examined here as one example among many of African governments strategically devolving land authority to traditional leaders in the postcolonial period in order to secure these leaders' political support. She documents related legal changes in postcolonial Burkina Faso, Cote d'Ivoire, Mozambique, Niger, South Africa, Zambia, and Zimbabwe, among other cases. More broadly, land reform efforts in the rural periphery were a common state initiative in many developing countries in the same time period; Albertus (2015) finds that one third of developing countries have engaged in efforts seeking to reallocate rights over rural land. Moreover, much like in Northern Ghana, these initiatives are often only incompletely implemented by these states, generating new conflicts over who truly has secure access to land.[109]

3.4 CONCLUSION

This chapter introduced the history of state-building in Northern Ghana. It documents the formal state's persistent scarcity in this rural hinterland across the precolonial, colonial, and postcolonial periods. It then outlines the three major interventions the modern state nonetheless still took in the region throughout the 20th century. The subsequent chapters

---

[106] Round 7 Merged Data, Afrobarometer Survey, subset to rural Enumeration Areas. Schools were the most common rural public good observed by enumerators in twenty-seven of the thirty-four countries surveyed. The exceptions are Cape Verde, eSwatini, Gambia, Morocco, Sao Tome and Principe, South Africa, and Tunisia.

[107] Weber (1976), Soifer (2015), Paglayan (2020).

[108] Stasavage (2005).

[109] Hassan and Klaus (2020), Albertus (2021).

consider the combined social and political effects of the invention of chief-taincy, the early expansion of the education system, and the formal devolution of land rights to traditional authorities. Each of these actions provided valuable windfalls to narrow subsets of the Northern population, creating new socioeconomic hierarchies and sparking new forms of political mobilization and activism by those cut off from these new benefits.

PART II

SOCIETAL EFFECTS

4

The Origins of Inequality

[He] was the first educated in this community ... He himself was the son of the first chief ... Now all of his children and grandchildren, they have been to school ... [But] the others didn't attend ... [They had] nobody to look up to who had been to school.

– Tendana and community elder, Nadowli District, May 2019

Almost all of the homes in a remote Frafra (Gurense) community included in my oral history interviews still have mud walls. Small structures are linked together to form shared courtyards for the extended families within, where meals are prepared outside over an open fire. The roofs are mostly thatch, though a few compounds have upgraded to thin metal sheets. Community members share a public toilet. Some have electricity. None have running water. Yet right in the middle of this village sits a large concrete house, freshly painted bright green. Its roof is modern corrugated metal, with a satellite TV dish on top. Its yard is enclosed by a painted fence. Running water flows into its kitchen and bathrooms, powered by an electric pump. Whose house is this? It was built by a long-time civil servant who has become a senior leader in Ghana's trade union movement. He lives in Accra, but grew up in the community. He stays in the house when visiting, and may soon retire back to it. In the meantime, his house is occupied by family members.[1]

Plainly visible inequality like this is a common sight in rural Northern Ghana: small sets of well-maintained "modern" houses – usually second homes of elites who work in the city – surrounded by residences of those

---

[1] Interview with chief and elders, Community #2, Bolgatanga District, 21 May 2019.

still near the very bottom of the national income ladder. But it is not ubiquitous: there are no concrete houses at all in one of the Konkomba communities also included in the oral histories. All homes are still mud. Even as this second village is less remote than the first, no elites hail from the community. In fact, the village only had its first ever secondary school graduate in 2011. He is now back home farming, unable to find work in the formal sector in part because he has no relatives already in elite professions who could advocate for him.[2]

This chapter shows how the modern state's first two major interventions into society explain the differences in inequality between these two communities. The invention of chieftaincy and the introduction of education worked in tandem to provide valuable economic windfalls to small sets of beneficiaries, giving them and their descendants a substantial economic head start. Creating new forms of intra-ethnic, intra-village economic inequality is one of the clearest *direct effects* that the state's isolated actions have had in this hinterland.

I show how the specific families elevated by the state as chiefs were put in a position to then benefit most from initial access to schooling. Importantly, these families did not benefit because chiefs had substantial power to extract rents from their positions. Instead, simply by virtue of gaining privileged contact with an otherwise scarce state, chiefs' families had unique opportunities to enroll their children in school. These school "pioneers," as they are known locally, were the first from their communities to enter the formal economy at a time when educated Northerners were incredibly rare. In turn, because the school pioneers often used their new income and positions of influence to support relatives back in the village, the advantages of early enrollment became concentrated within families, producing a new Northern elite and generating intra-communal inequality that persists through the inter-generational transmission of wealth.

But this process was much less likely to play out in the "never recognized" communities exemplified by the Konkomba village described above. Lacking chiefs to interface with the state, schools were typically only built much later on, when human capital was less scarce across the North and the marginal economic return to education had declined. And even in the subset of "never recognized" communities that did gain early access, the lack of chiefs meant enrollment was far less concentrated in specific families. The result was that new elite families were not similarly

---

[2] Interview with elders, Community #1, Saboba District, 17 May 2019.

elevated by the state in the late colonial and early postcolonial period, resulting in less intra-ethnic inequality today.

In their own words, residents explained today's local socio-economic hierarchy in precisely these terms. In the chapter's opening quote, a tendana (earth priest) in a Dagaba community near Nadowli narrated how the son of the community's state-invented chief was the first to graduate. He then returned in the 1950s to open the community's first school as its first teacher. Over his long career as an educator and civil servant, he ensured that his children and grandchildren attended as well, including by paying their school fees. His family now includes prominent lawyers and doctors living in Ghana's major cities, who financially support their relatives back home. But the tendana recounted that other local families, including his own, only began routinely enrolling their children much later and now count many fewer elites among their ranks.[3] As a member of a Sisala ("invented chiefs") royal family similarly explains, the state's early "education policy was skewed to favor children of chiefs," becoming "a huge resource to their advantage up to today."[4]

I demonstrate these effects of state action more systematically and quantitatively using the plausibly exogenous assignment of Northern ethnic groups to the invention of chieftaincy. While some precolonially acephalous ethnic groups, like the Frafra and Dagaba in the examples above, had chiefs imposed upon them in the early twentieth century, precolonially similar groups, such as the Konkomba, did not (see Chapter 3). The key difference between these communities was their location relative to the original, pre-1914 Anglo-German colonial border. Leveraging the treatment produced by this border – the colonial invention of chieftaincy – I find that there is significantly more intra-communal, intra-ethnic economic inequality today in communities from the "invented chiefs" groups than the "never recognized" groups. I then show that the primary mechanism is privileged access to schooling for chiefs' families in the mid-twentieth century.

The chapter begins by explaining the research design, detailing how the pre-1914 colonial border creates an opportunity to estimate long-run effects of the colonial state's imposition of new intra-ethnic elites. I then introduce the data and explain how inequality is measured. The analysis first establishes a strong correlation between the invention of chieftaincy and inequality today, comparing the "invented chiefs" and

[3] Interview with tendana, Community #1, Nadowli District, 27 May 2019.
[4] Interview with Sisala royal and academic, Tamale, 27 June 2018.

"never recognized" communities. I then explain how the state's selective provision of education accounts for this relationship. The final section rules out a series of alternative explanations and mechanisms. In Chapter 9, I return to the study of education using the shadow case of Southern Ghana to show how early access to human capital had different effects on socioeconomic inequality in a subnational region in which the state was instead less scarce.

4.1 EXOGENOUS COLONIAL INVENTION?

The chapter focuses on a comparison of the "invented chiefs" and "never recognized" communities to examine the effect of the imposition of a new intra-ethnic social hierarchy by the early colonial state through its invention of chieftaincy. Because the British did not create new chiefs within the "never recognized" communities, and most "never recognized" and "invented chiefs" communities were similarly acephalous prior to colonial rule (see Chapter 3), the "never recognized" groups can serve as a control group against which to compare otherwise similar "invented chiefs" communities.

By contrast, chieftaincy and intra-ethnic socioeconomic hierarchy had already endogenously developed among the "always chiefs" groups prior to colonial rule. This makes it difficult to disentangle whether contemporary inequality among this third set of ethnic groups is due to the actions of the state, or is instead simply a legacy of pre-existing stratification from the precolonial period. I present descriptive evidence on inequality within the "always chiefs" groups, but they are dropped in the main analyses to focus the comparison on groups that started at a similar place at the outset of colonial rule.

Restricting to the "invented chiefs" and "never recognized" groups, the British colonial state's decision to invent chiefs is plausibly exogenous to the pre-existing characteristics of communities. The vast majority of "never recognized" communities were initially in German Togoland (see Figure 3.6), divided by what British officials themselves referred to as an "arbitrary boundary."[5] Not drawn to include any particular ethnic group in either territory, the border split precolonial kingdoms, including

---

[5] Discussing the death of a Dagomba chief, a British official narrates that the chief was "given the Karaga Stool [chieftaincy] by the King of Yendi before the arbitrary boundary fixed between Togoland and the Northern Territories of the Gold Coast placed Yendi ... under German Control." *Northern Territories Annual Report for 1917* (1918, 11).

Dagbon, Gonja, and Mamprugu.[6] This occurred because the border was decided with limited knowledge of local populations, prior to formal colonial rule on either side.

Britain and Germany only began encroaching into the northern hinterlands of their respective colonies in the 1890s.[7] In 1889, they had agreed to set aside most of present-day Northern Ghana as a large "neutral zone" – defined purely by latitude and longitude – because "German and British forces were at that time ill-equipped for a race against each other" given their very limited ability to project military power into the remote interior.[8] They agreed to avoid expanding into the area until a proper border could be demarcated. This happened in 1899, with the Germans agreeing to give Britain much of the zone (among other concessions) in return for islands in the Pacific, especially Samoa.[9]

The final border primarily followed the Daka River, a minor tributary of the Volta. Historical accounts provide no evidence the Daka was chosen because it represented any meaningful geographic, economic, or political break between territories. Instead, it appears to have simply been the most readily available geographic feature along which a border could be drawn. The only contention in Anglo-German negotiations was a single town – Salaga – a trading hub at the southern edge of the neutral zone that was a starting point for caravan routes into and out of Ashanti.[10] Using the Daka allowed the Germans to give Salaga to Britain (in exchange for Pacific concessions), even as it meant splitting precolonial kingdoms.

This border arbitrarily assigned communities on each side to different experiences of the state's imposition of chieftaincy. As detailed in Chapter 3, the British started inventing chieftaincy among virtually all acephalous ethnic groups on their side starting from the first decade of the twentieth century. The Germans did not similarly create new chiefs during their brief rule. Although they began implementing indirect rule through traditional chiefs in southern Togoland, and made preparations to do the

---

[6] The division of Dagbon into separate colonies quickly became an administrative headache because the Ya Na, the Dagmoba king at Yendi, was put in German territory, even as most of the Dagomba population was in British territory (Staniland 1975). If the border had been purposefully drawn with detailed knowledge of local political dynamics, this mistake presumably would not have been made.

[7] Arhin (1974).

[8] Stoecker (1986, 90).

[9] Kennedy (1974), Knoll (1978).

[10] Knoll (1978, 35–36).

same in the North starting from 1913, this was immediately interrupted by World War I. Mostly, the Germans made little effort to interfere in pre-existing community leadership institutions in the North because "they lacked the financial and military means to enforce their decisions" and "feared that they might provoke [an uprising] against the government."[11] Indeed, into the 1910s, a single officer was nominally responsible for the entire area that would ultimately join Northern Ghana.[12]

After capturing part of Togoland in 1914, the British faced uncertainty over both the legal status of the territory and where the new border with French-occupied Togoland (now Togo) would be drawn.[13] The new German territory was formally designated as a League of Nations trust, but was placed under the supervision of British officials in the Northern Territories of the Gold Coast, effectively annexed into the existing colony. Seeking a short-term means to extend their limited footprint into a new territory of minimal economic value, the British decided that an easier interim means of administering it was to simply extend the jurisdictions of chiefs already in the Gold Coast into Togoland, rather than engaging in the difficult work of recognizing new chiefs from scratch among new ethnic groups.[14] This decision was never revisited. As a result, assignment to British vs. German rule between 1899 and 1914 explains almost all variation in where chiefs were invented.

Moreover, the "invented chiefs" and "never recognized" groups did not otherwise differ substantially in cultural characteristics: these were similarly poor, flat societies without substantial pre-existing wealth stratification (see Chapter 3); almost all had similar clan-based social organizations and non-matrilineal inheritance; and they widely shared land-owning and religious practices, with land controlled by the tendana via worship of an earth shrine.[15] The colonial anthropologist R.S. Rattray observed that precolonial institutions were highly similar across most acephalous groups in the region: "Over the whole area ... we had, it

---

[11] Knoll (1978, 48–49).

[12] Knoll (1978, 43–45).

[13] Bening (1983). Anglo-French negotiations over the new international Gold Coast-Togo border continued throughout the 1920s.

[14] The British did recognize Nanumba chiefs, an "always chiefs" group closely related to the Dagomba that had signed a treaty with British emissaries in the mid-1880s (Ladouceur 1979).

[15] Lund (2008, 38), Tait (1961), Ladouceur (1979). Moreover, both the "invented chiefs" and "never recognized" groups are now majority Christian, unlike the overwhelmingly Muslim "always chiefs" groups. The widespread presence of missionaries occurred long after the invention of chieftaincy (see Chapter 3).

was found, a people who possessed a practically uniform religion ... The outstanding feature ... was the *Tendana*."[16]

Many other colonial borders in Africa have been used to motivate natural experiments, with similar claims that they exogenously split pre-existing populations.[17] McCauley and Posner (2015) identify several shortcomings common to many such appeals to exogeneity. Fortunately, the 1899–1914 Anglo-German border avoids these main pitfalls. First, because it was only so briefly in effect, the border does not represent a bundled treatment of everything that ever happened on the respective sides. There was otherwise extremely limited governance of *either* Northern territory before the border went out of effect, such that other differences in British vs. German rule could not be considered alternate treatments. Beyond propping up new chiefs, the British made "only the feeblest of efforts" in other institution-building in the first decade-and-a-half of colonial rule in the North[18] – a period in which Chapter 3 documents that the British footprint was miniscule. By 1914, the Germans had still had "little interaction" with major ethnic groups, such as the Konkomba, in Northern Togoland.[19] "[L]arge areas remained unconquered and colonial [rule] did not develop much."[20] Missionaries and European firms were strictly forbidden from entering the German territory.[21] After World War I, the annexed portions of Togoland then experienced all of the same British and Ghanaian policy environment as the original Northern Territories of the Gold Coast. Importantly, any subsequent differences in how the state treated groups with and without invented chiefs are *post-treatment* to the initial invention of chieftaincy and causally downstream from it; they become part of the mechanism for the effects below, not an alternate treatment.

Second, the border does not correspond to meaningful discontinuities in environmental characteristics that would suggest British and German negotiators purposefully split their territories based on geographic differences that might separately affect contemporary economic outcomes. Northern Ghana is largely flat savannah, with similar terrain on each side of the Daka River. I validate this using rainfall, soil suitability, and slope

---

[16] Quoted in Lund (2008, 38).
[17] For example, Posner (2004) and Michalopoulos and Papaioannou (2013).
[18] Ladouceur (1979, 44)
[19] Talton (2010, 38).
[20] Stoecker (1986, 174).
[21] Stoecker (1986, 93). Both were instead very active in Southern Togoland.

(ruggedness) measurements from FAO (2012).[22] T-tests for the difference in means in each geographic characteristic between communities (census Enumeration Areas) lying just east and just west of the border reveal no substantive differences.[23] Nonetheless, all analyses below control for all three environmental characteristics.

Third, there is no historical evidence of large-scale sorting around the border during the brief period it was in effect. With such minimal colonial governance on each side, local populations had little reason to move across it. There was some migration across the border after Togoland was annexed into the Northern Territories, especially among the Konkomba ethnic group, the largest "never recognized" group. But this later migration is post-treatment to the state's intervention into Northern society, a downstream consequence of the absence of state-recognized Konkomba chiefs. I also show below that it does not provide an alternative mechanism for the results in this chapter.

4.2 DATA SOURCES

I rely on a series of data sources. I use highly localized census data from 2010. The 2010 data is a 10% sample of individual-level returns, geo-located by Enumeration Area (EA), or tract.[24] EAs are small, with less than 1,000 people on average, and mostly correspond to individual rural communities (villages). I subset to the 385,989 adults from Northern groups. Of these, 198,563 live in rural Northern Ghana, across 3,875 EAs.[25] I also use localized data from the 1960 census – Ghana's first modern census, which I have digitized for the first time. Data for 2,384 localities was linked to the 2010 census EAs through a combination of matching place names and manually geo-referencing a hand-drawn map of 1960 boundaries.[26]

---

[22] These data come in rasters of 9.2 km × 9.2 km grid cells, which I link to Enumeration Areas (EAs) of the 2010 census.

[23] There is no difference across the border in soil suitability. And while there are statistically significant differences in rainfall and slope, they are substantively trivial. FAO (2012) estimates a 3.59 millimeters (0.14 inch) discontinuity in average annual rainfall; this represents only a 0.035 standard deviation difference relative to the full variation across Northern Ghana. The difference on the slope index – with the east side of the border slightly flatter than the west – also represents only a 0.15 standard deviation shift compared to the variation across the full region.

[24] This is a representative, random sample of each EA.

[25] The remainder either live in northern cities (Tamale, Wa, Bolgatanga) or Southern Ghana.

[26] The 1960 data contains a much more limited set of variables than 2010, and is not at the individual level.

These sources are supplemented by the qualitative fieldwork. I draw again on the colonial annual reports and government correspondence housed at the Northern Regional Archives in Tamale, also examined in Chapter 3. I also employ oral history interviews. Oral histories were conducted in twelve rural communities – six from "invented chiefs" groups and six from "never recognized" groups. Three ethnic groups – Dagaba ("invented chiefs"), Frafra ("invented chiefs"), and Konkomba ("never recognized") – were purposefully selected to focus on the largest in each category (Table 3.1). Homogeneous rural communities from each group were then randomly selected after stratifying by the inequality outcome variable introduced below.[27]

While the oral histories do not include a representative sample of communities, they present an opportunity to hear community members explain the origins of inequality from their own perspective. In each community, separate interviews were conducted with the chief or senior-most elder or his representative (if the chief had traveled), the tendana, clan elders of the largest resident clans, the District Assemblymember (elected local government councilor), and a teacher in the local primary school (if available). This allows me to compare responses to the same questions across multiple actors within each community. Disagreements among respondents were common for questions about contested historical facts, especially the exact sequence of chieftaincy appointments in the community's early history, which inform the degree to which different families can make contemporary claims to eligibility for these positions.[28] But responses within the same community were largely very similar for the questions about education and inequality highlighted in this chapter. More details on the oral histories are in the Appendix.

4.3 MEASURING INEQUALITY

I measure contemporary economic inequality from factor analyses of the 2010 census, the only year for which individual-level returns are available to measure micro-level inequality within communities. Using outcome data from a century after the initial treatment has risks. One is that any major event in the intervening period that differentially affected

---

[27] The final sample included three Dagaba communities in the Nadowli District of Upper West Region, three Frafra (Gurense) communities split across the Bolgatanga (two) and Bolgatanga East (one) districts of Upper East Region, and six Konkomba communities split across the Mion (one), Saboba (two), and Nanumba North (three) districts of Northern Region.

[28] For more on chieftaincy disputes and their implications, see Chapters 7 and 8.

"invented chiefs" versus "never recognized" communities becomes a possible additional mechanism for an observed effect. I consider and rule out the most plausible alternatives in the final section below. Others are that 2010 data can mostly only show effects on subsequent generations, rather than on the initial beneficiaries of state windfalls, and net of out-migration, including the differential exit of better-educated residents to urban areas or abroad. But because my goal is to show how isolated state actions can have long-run effects that become entrenched, these latter two risks are better viewed as benefits. If anything, out-migration and generational turnover should bias against finding long-run effects of early state actions; still finding effects among subsequent generations in the rural North demonstrates the staying power of initial advantages created by the state. In line with Chapter 2, this makes clear how important it can be in hinterlands to receive state resources early in a context in which others faced barriers to catching up.

From the individual-level responses, I first create latent indices of wealth and human capital,[29] calculated from the first two dimensions of a factor analysis of assets, education, and employment variables listed in Figure 4.1. The indices are calculated over all adult Northerners throughout the country ($n = 385,989$), scaled with mean 0. Figure 4.1 displays correlations between each of the factors and the component variables. Each factor clearly maps to a distinct latent characteristic. The first – the "wealth index" – is highly correlated with not being a farmer and having a series of assets: a gas or electric stove, formal walls, access to a toilet, and a mobile phone. The second – the "human capital index" – is instead most highly correlated with human capital: having attended any school, being literate, and having attended secondary school.

To examine intra-community inequality, I focus on the wealth index, which varies widely at an individual level within the rural North, as indicated in the first two panels of Figure 4.2. I aggregate the individual-level wealth index from the factor analysis into a community-level inequality score. Following McKenzie (2005), I define inequality (I) as $I_c = \frac{\sigma_c}{\sqrt{\lambda}}$, where σ_c is the sample standard deviation of the wealth index among adults within each rural community (EA) in Northern Ghana, c, and λ is the variance of the wealth index across all rural northern adults.[30] Where I is greater than 1, there is more dispersion in wealth across individuals

---

[29] Filmer and Pritchett (2001), Filmer and Scott (2012). Income or wealth is not captured on the census.

[30] It is not possible to calculate a community-level Gini index; the Gini equation divides by mean wealth and cannot take negative values. Both are violated when using a factor analysis to measure wealth.

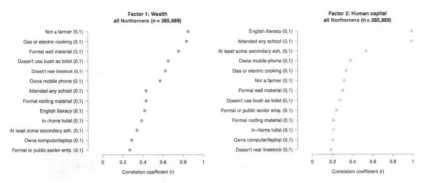

FIGURE 4.1 Correlations between factors and components. Factor 1 (wealth) and factor 2 (human capital), calculated for all adults from Northern ethnic groups nationwide.

within a community than among all Northerners, suggesting a very high rate of inequality. As I becomes lower than 1, there is increasingly less intra-community inequality. There is substantial variation in I across rural Northern Ghana (third panel, Figure 4.2).[31]

Moreover, because the large majority of rural communities are very ethnically homogeneous – 77 percent have 80 percent or more of their population from a single ethnic group – this also implies the presence of significant intra-ethnic inequality in wealth. I also recalculate I after restricting to residents from the largest ethnic group in each community. The two versions of I – for intra-community inequality alone, and the more restricted measure of intra-ethnic, intra-community inequality – are highly correlated ($r = 0.92$).

4.4 INTRA-VILLAGE, INTRA-ETHNIC INEQUALITY

4.4.1 Main Comparisons

I find that the invention of chieftaincy has had lasting effects on inequality within rural communities. Community-level inequality (I) is the outcome

---

[31] This index has several limitations. First, higher sampling error in the 10% census sample will produce more measurement error in I. For this reason, I drop the 112 smallest outlier EAs (bottom 3rd percentile) from all analyses, defined as those with fewer than 200 residents. The main specifications also control for population size, as measurement error should be mechanically related to the within-community sample size over which I is calculated. Third, substantive interpretation of I is complicated in administrative centers by the presence of civil servants with (relatively) high wealth who are not native to the town. The main specifications below drop the region's thirty-nine district capitals as of the 2010 census.

Societal Effects

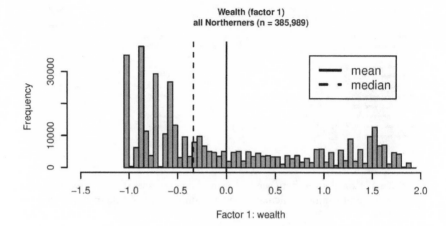

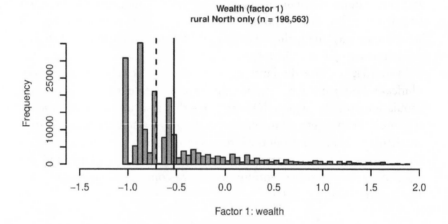

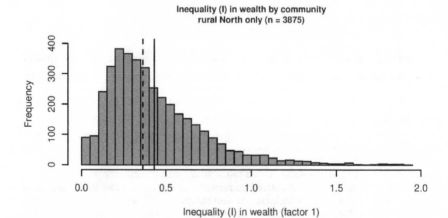

FIGURE 4.2 Distributions of the wealth and inequality indices

in Table 4.1, which presents several different approaches for estimating the effect of the state's imposition of chieftaincy. Panel (a) reports estimates for intra-community inequality (I) among all residents of each community; panel (b) reports the same models for intra-ethnic, intra-community inequality, with I restricted to the largest group within each community.

Column 1 begins with a descriptive comparison, regressing I on each community's population proportion from "invented chiefs" groups – which proxies for the presence of an invented chief.[32] Column 1 and the other models in Table 4.1 drop majority "always chiefs" communities, to isolate the comparison of "invented chiefs" vs. "never recognized" communities. I control for the median value of the wealth index in each community, to separate the analysis of inequality (dispersion) from overall differences in the wealth of the typical resident (levels). I also control for community size, ethnic diversity, and three pretreatment environmental characteristics from FAO (2012): agricultural soil suitability, average annual rainfall, and slope (ruggedness). Standard errors are clustered by the plurality ethnic group in each community.[33]

Columns 2–3 instead leverage the potentially exogenous assignment of communities to the invention of chieftaincy produced by the pre-1914 border. The simplest means to do so is via reduced form (intent-to-treat) models that compare previously acephalous communities assigned by the initial border to the invention of chieftaincy to those assigned to remain without chiefs. In column 2, the explanatory variable is a binary indicator for whether a community was already in the Gold Coast prior to 1914, and thus far more likely to have been subject to the colonial invention of chieftaincy. In column 3, to account for the possibility of post-1914 migration across the border, the explanatory variable is instead each community's population proportion from ethnic groups that were precolonially acephalous and had lived entirely on the British side prior to World War I.[34]

---

32 I cannot verify the presence of an invented chief in every single community in the census. But because the invention of chieftaincy was assigned at the group level, the vast majority of communities are homogeneous, and virtually all "invented chiefs" communities have chiefs, communities with larger "invented chiefs" populations are systematically more likely to have chiefs.

33 Because I is right-skewed (Figure 4.2), I can rule out the influence of outliers by dropping the top 5th percentile of communities. I find substantively identical results.

34 An alternative approach that I purposefully do not employ is a Regression Discontinuity Design (RDD) that examines variation in narrow bands right at the pre-1914 border.

TABLE 4.1 *Intra-village inequality: rural "invented chiefs" vs. "never recognized" communities*

	Panel (a): Intra-community inequality, all residents							
Outcome: Inequality (I) in wealth index (by EA, 2010, all residents)	1 OLS	2 OLS	3 OLS	4 2SLS	5 2SLS	6 OLS	7 2SLS	8 2SLS
"Invented chiefs" % in community	0.062** (0.022)			0.078* (0.035)	0.149 (0.093)	0.078** (0.027)	0.125*** (0.016)	0.133*** (0.039)
Gold Coast pre-1914 (0,1)		0.037** (0.014)						
Pop. % from acephalous groups in Gold Coast pre-1914			0.065** (0.018)					
Instrumental variable				GC	Pop %		GC	Pop %
Community-level controls	Y	Y	Y	Y	Y	N	N	N
N	2768	2768	2768	2768	2768	2769	2769	2769
adj. R^2	0.248	0.245	0.251	0.247	0.239	0.017	0.010	0.008
Standard errors	By group	By group	By group	By group	By group	By group	By group	By group

Panel (b): Intra-community inequality, plurality ethnicity only

Outcome: Inequality (I) in wealth index (by EA, 2010, largest group only)	1 OLS	2 OLS	3 OLS	4 2SLS	5 2SLS	6 OLS	7 2SLS	8 2SLS
"Invented chiefs" % in community	0.071*** (0.021)			0.077* (0.031)	0.140† (0.073)	0.083*** (0.023)	0.112*** (0.018)	0.134*** (0.039)
Gold Coast pre-1914 (0,1)		0.036** (0.014)						
Pop. % from acephalous groups in Gold Coast pre-1914			0.061*** (0.016)					
Instrumental variable				GC	Pop %		GC	Pop %
Community-level controls	Y	Y	Y	Y	Y	N	N	N
N	2765	2765	2765	2765	2765	2766	2766	2766
adj. R^2	0.243	0.239	0.244	0.243	0.237	0.021	0.018	0.013
Standard errors	By group	By group	By group	By group	By group	By group	By group	By group

† significant at $p < 0.10$; * $p < 0.05$; ** $p < 0.01$; *** $p < 0.001$. Communities with majority populations from the "always chiefs" groups are dropped. The instrument in columns 4 and 7 is an indicator for whether a community was already in the British Gold Coast prior to World War I. The instrument in columns 5 and 8 is the population proportion from precolonially acephalous ethnic groups that lived entirely on the pre–World War I British side of the border. Columns 6–8 exclude all controls.

As described above, the border cannot explain *all* variations in the presence of invented chiefs, however: some ethnic groups span the border, and others – especially the Konkomba – have gradually migrated across it after it went out of effect. To account for the resulting small variations in compliance with the border treatment, columns 4–5 report two-stage least squares (2SLS) regressions that instrument for the presence of an invented chiefs ethnic group in each community using the explanatory variables in columns 2 and 3, respectively, as instruments.[35] The final columns of Table 4.1 (6–8) repeat columns 1, 4, and 5 after dropping the controls to address concerns that some controls (e.g., median wealth) introduce post-treatment bias.

Overall, across approaches, Table 4.1 consistently shows that the invention of chieftaincy is directly related to greater present-day intra-communal, intra-ethnic inequality in wealth – even a full century after chiefs were invented. Fifteen of the sixteen coefficients of interest are statistically significant at conventional levels; the exception is the instrumented effect in Panel (a), column 5, which has $p = 0.1$. While the effect sizes vary across specifications, the estimated differences in inequality between "invented chiefs" and "never recognized" groups are substantively large, with "invented chiefs" communities scoring as much as half a standard deviation higher on the inequality index compared to "never recognized" communities.

The key identification assumption in columns 2–3 is that no pre-existing differences between previously acephalous groups on each side of the 1899–1914 border explain contemporary inequality. A similar assumption is required for the exclusion restriction to hold in the 2SLS models in columns 4–5. This is unlikely to be violated by environmental conditions, which are already controlled for in Table 4.1. Additional analyses in this chapter (Table 4.7) also use the latitude and longitude of each community to rule out the effect of other possible unobserved differences in economic geography, such as crops grown or exposure to different trade routes. Importantly, any differences in inequality between these sets of communities are also unlikely to be due to

There is not enough variation in ethnic groups living immediately at the border, especially between the "invented chiefs" and "never recognized" groups, to have a sufficient sample to estimate an RDD. Instead, my reduced form and 2SLS estimates make comparisons across the full region. This raises the limitation that other geographic differences than those I control for here (rainfall, slope, soil quality) could confound the results. I directly address this concern and find little support for it in the section on alternative mechanisms.

[35] The first stage for each 2SLS model easily passes an F-test to test for weak instruments.

other institution-building or government actions before the border went out of effect (in 1914), as governance by either Britain or Germany was otherwise extremely limited before the war (described above).

4.4.2 Additional comparisons

Additional tests highlight the substantive importance of the result in Table 4.1. First, these effects reflect the intergenerational transmission of advantage, rather than being concentrated among a specific age cohort. I recalculate I separately for three age cohorts in each community: residents fifty-five and older, born under colonial rule; residents twenty-five to fifty-four, raised in the initial post-independence period; and residents twenty-four and below, who have come of age since Ghana's democratization. Repeating column 1 of Table 4.1, the coefficient on the population from "invented chiefs" groups remains positive and statistically significant to at least the $p < 0.1$ level across each age cohort.[36]

Second, in a model similar to column 1 of Table 4.1, a homogeneous community from an "invented chiefs" ethnic group is signed as scoring higher on the inequality index than an otherwise similar community from an "always chiefs" ethnic group ($p = 0.12$). Overall, the mean value of I in majority "invented chiefs" communities is 0.46 compared to 0.44 in majority "always chiefs" communities. This is striking because the "always chiefs" communities have had some forms of class stratification since the deep precolonial period (Chapter 3), while similar distinctions only emerged in the "invented chiefs" communities when the colonial state began creating chiefs. These similar levels of inequality today suggest that the state's early actions were sufficiently powerful that the "invented chiefs" communities have now caught all the way up to (or even surpassed) inequality in the "always chiefs" communities. And because chiefs and their families in the "always chiefs" communities also received very similar advantages (described below) as in the "invented chiefs" communities, it also implies that the modern state's actions likely explain a greater share of the present-day inequality in the "always chiefs" groups than any longer-run effects of pre-existing stratification.[37]

---

[36] These new models drop communities in which there are so few people from a given age cohort that I cannot be credibly estimated (fewer than ten census records). It is not possible to examine even narrower age cohorts because there will not be sufficient sample sizes within communities.

[37] This is suggested by reasoning through the comparison with the "invented chiefs" communities. The "invented chiefs" communities had little pre-existing economic

Third, while Table 4.1 focuses on wealth, there are also notable differences in inequality in human capital. Similar analyses to Table 4.1 for the human capital index reveal no statistically significant differences. But such tests are misleading because most high human capital individuals from the communities in Table 4.1 no longer live there, as described in the opening examples in this chapter and in further detail in the remainder of this chapter. As is very common across Africa, most Northerners with high human capital migrate to large towns and cities, where formal employment opportunities are overwhelmingly concentrated, and then remit income back to family in rural home communities – helping to produce wealth inequality in the countryside.[38] Expanding scope to all ethnically Northern census respondents living nationwide (including in cities), Table 4.2 shows that the educated elite from "invented chiefs" groups is now substantially larger than from "never recognized" groups, both in raw numbers and percentage terms. This includes the proportion scoring at very high percentiles of the human capital index and in the proportions with tertiary education, formal or public sector employment, or who meet the definition of middle class status in Nathan (2019). Interestingly, the last two rows of Table 4.2 also indicate that the educated elite is largest among the "invented chiefs" ethnic groups even as these groups are the *poorest overall*, with the lowest mean and median scores on the wealth index nationwide among Northerners. This is consistent with the presence of significantly higher human capital inequality as well.[39]

4.5 THE MECHANISM: EDUCATION AS A MAJOR WINDFALL

Why did the invention of chieftaincy produce lasting inequality within rural communities? As described in Chapter 3, the power of invented chiefs to extract valuable rents was often quite limited in the colonial period. Instead, chiefs and their descendants benefitted most from their privileged contact with the scarce state. The central mechanism for Table 4.1 is that invented chiefs' families received preferential access

---

stratification and then received state-generated windfalls to chiefs (described below); the "always chiefs" communities had pre-existing stratification and then also received the same state-generated windfalls to chiefs. That both have roughly equal economic stratification today suggests that the state's windfalls are likely the more powerful causal force in explaining contemporary inequality.

[38] Ackah and Medvedev (2010), Young (2013).

[39] The elite capture facilitated by the invention of chieftaincy – examined closely in Chapters 6 and 7 – likely has led to worse overall economic outcomes for ordinary group members, even as a select few from the "invented chiefs" groups do very well.

TABLE 4.2 *Size of the elite by type of ethnic group*

	"Invented chiefs" ethnic groups	"Never recognized" ethnic groups	"Always chiefs" ethnic groups
Top 5th on "human capital" index (0,1)	5.7% (89,250)	4.2% (49,180)	6.3% (70,390)
Top 5th on both indices (0,1)	2.9% (45,070)	2.3% (27,030)	3.1% (34,540)
Middle or upper class (0,1)	4.0% (61,310)	2.4% (27,880)	4.2% (46,370)
Tertiary education (0,1)	3.5% (54,420)	2.2% (26,400)	4.3% (47,570)
Formal sector employment (0,1)	6.8% (106,650)	4.9% (57,690)	6.9% (77,070)
Public sector employment (0,1)	4.0% (62,870)	2.3% (26,640)	4.1% (46,120)
Median "wealth index"	−0.50	−0.32	−0.11
Mean "wealth index"	−0.12	0.04	0.12
Nationwide adult population (2010)	1,565,200	1,178,990	1,115,700

Figures for all adults (18 and above) nationwide on the 2010 census.

to human capital in the mid-twentieth century, amidst the state's initial expansion of school access. The state's provision of schooling generated intra-community, intra-ethnic inequality for two reasons. First, substantially more schools were initially built in "invented chiefs" than "never recognized" communities because chiefs played a key role in the early expansion of the education system. Second, early school enrollments were much more narrowly concentrated within specific families (chiefs' families) in communities that had chiefs. I show each dynamic in turn before demonstrating their combined effects on contemporary economic inequality.

4.5.1 Differential School Construction by Ethnicity

After World War II, the state finally began building primary schools at a large scale in Northern Ghana (Chapter 3; Figure 3.7). But this did not occur uniformly. Communities with chiefs were more likely to receive the first generation of Northern schools than those that lacked chiefs because chiefs played a direct role in creating the initial education system. Most schools built after 1932 were established by the Native Authorities, local administrative bodies headed by chiefs. This gave chiefs the authority to decide which communities would receive schools, and which would not. Gandah (2009) narrates that as far as the colonial state was concerned, "the consensus of the chiefs was considered to be the consensus of the people" (64) when it came to decisions about where to build schools.

Deference to chiefs' preferences continued throughout the 1950s into the post-independence period.[40] Although many Northern communities initially were suspicious of sending children to schools as the education system first emerged in the 1920s and 1930s (detailed below), over time, with the economic benefits of education gradually becoming clearer, many chiefs began actively lobbying state officials for schools for their communities, especially during the 1950s and 1960s. The archives from this period are filled with personal appeals from chiefs to both colonial and early postcolonial officials requesting school construction, with enclosed lists of prospective students they had already lined up to attend. Figure 4.3 shows an illustrative example of such a request. In turn, state officials made chiefs personally responsible for the upkeep of school facilities in their communities.[41]

Without their own chiefs to lobby for schools, "never recognized" communities were disadvantaged relative to "invented chiefs" communities. Because they lacked state-recognized leaders who could be deputized by education officials to supervise school construction, respondents in the Konkomba communities in the oral history interviews consistently narrated that often the only way to get a school in their communities was to eventually break down, pool their resources, and build their own, with volunteer teachers. The first school in five of these six communities was what is known colloquially as a "wing school" – gathering students under a shed or tree for basic primary lessons. In one Konkomba community, the wing school began in 1984 and was only replaced with a formal government school in 2006.[42] Another relied on its wing school from 1982 to 2003.[43] An MP from another "never recognized" ethnic group explained that because chiefs were responsible for coordinating school construction, the first primary school in his own home area (in

---

[40] For example, Bawumia (2004, 30–31).

[41] For example, see the school inspection reports in folio NRG 3 / 17 / 16, Northern Regional Archives, Tamale.

[42] Interview with clan elder, Community #3, Nanumba North district, July 5, 2019.

[43] Interview with clan elder, Community #1, Nanumba North district, July 4, 2019.

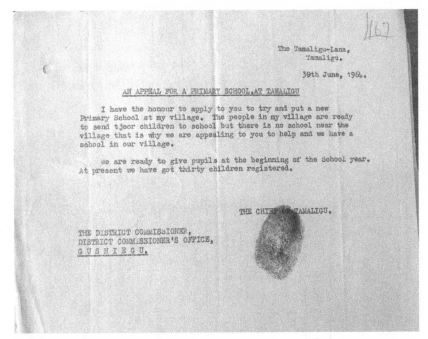

FIGURE 4.3 Example of chief's appeal for a primary school, with thumbprint signature. Northern Regional Archives, folio NRG 1/8/27, document 167.

the 1960s) went to a nearby village populated by a different ethnic group because this is where the chief lived: "When the teachers came to start the school, our village didn't have any accommodation for them and facilities. So they went to the next village – where the chief was" and could draw on local government resources to build a teachers' quarters. His own community eventually resorted to a wing school. "We had to put up sheds, makeshift sheds ... That's how the school started."[44]

Panel (a) of Table 4.3 draws on the same archival data as Figure 3.7 to track the proportion of communities from each major ethnic category falling within the approximate catchment area of a school (ten kilometer radius).[45] By 1945, a large gap in access had already opened: nearly 30 percent of "invented chiefs" communities were within walking distance of a school, compared to only 5 percent of "never recognized" communities.

---

[44] Interview with Birifor MP from Upper West Region, Accra, July 22, 2019.
[45] Ten kilometers is a 90-minute to 2-hour walk, an estimation of the maximum distance a student could plausibly commute each way per day on foot.

TABLE 4.3 *Ethnic disparities in early schooling in Northern Ghana*

Panel (a): Proximity to Schools

Year:	1915	1930	1945	1960
Communities w/in 10 km of school (n = 3923)	9 (0.2%)	360 (9.2%)	645 (16.4%)	2579 (65.7%)
"Always chiefs" communities w/in 10 km of school (n = 972)	6 (0.6%)	58 (6%)	91 (9.4%)	556 (57.2%)
"Invented chiefs" communities w/in 10 km of school (n = 1606)	1 (0.1%)	264 (16.4%)	473 (29.5%)	1418 (88.3%)
"Never recognized" communities w/in 10 km of school (n = 1144)	0 (0%)	28 (2.4%)	58 (5.1%)	497 (43.4%)

Panel (b): School Attendance (Boys) – 1960

	All Communities	"Always Chiefs" Communities	"Invented Chiefs" Communities	"Never Recognized" Communities
Mean % enrolled by community in primary or above (n = 3923)	9.9%	7.1%	14.0%	6.0%

Figures for panel (a) from archival records, combining Annual Reports of the Northern Territories with school rosters from the Northern Regional Archives, Tamale. Figures for panel (b) from the digitized, geo-coded 1960 census data.

By 1960, 88 percent of "invented chiefs" communities were near a school, compared to just 43 percent of "never recognized" communities.[46]

The disparity was also reflected in enrollments, which remained limited even where schools were built because of minimal state funding. Panel (b) uses the 1960 census data to show that even where schools existed, enrollments were low, with only 10 percent of eligible boys (approximately seven per community) enrolled on average.[47] Enrollments were highest in the "invented chiefs" communities (14% of eligible boys attending) and lowest in the "never recognized" communities (6 percent). Given how few schools were operating prior to the 1950s, students enrolled in 1960 were still among the very first to ever attend from their communities.

Table 4.4 confirms these patterns more systematically. In column 1 of Table 4.4, I use the community-level enrollment data from 1960 to show that by the early independence period, "invented chiefs" communities had significantly higher enrollment than otherwise similar "never recognized" communities. This is an identical OLS regression to column 1 of Table 4.1, but with 1960 enrollment as the outcome variable instead of 2010 inequality.[48] In columns 2 and 3 of Table 4.4, I repeat the 2SLS models from Table 4.1 with school enrollment now as the outcome and find that the invention of chieftaincy is likely causally related to 1960 enrollment.

Differences between "invented chiefs" and "never recognized" communities in primary school enrollment carried over to higher education as well, with direct implications for who could join the North's emerging economic elite. Many in the first generation of students in the North eventually dropped out. But for those who did complete primary education, two main forms of higher education prepared graduates for formal sector careers that provided paths into the emerging middle and upper classes. Most graduates were channeled into teacher training colleges to meet demand for qualified Northern teachers who could staff primary

---

[46] The "always chiefs" communities fell in the middle, with 57% within 10 km of a school by 1960. The difference between the increasingly Christian "invented chiefs" communities and largely Muslim "always chiefs" communities is most likely a function of religion. The British intentionally slow-rolled the state expansion of Western education in Muslim areas. This does not affect the chapter's core comparison of "invented chiefs" and "never recognized" communities, however, as both sets of groups are overwhelmingly non-Muslim.

[47] I restrict to male enrollment because it more consistently measures school access itself, rather than cultural attitudes about female education. Given restrictive gender norms, female enrollment was even lower – less than 1 percent of eligible girls on average.

[48] I also now control for Muslim population share; the British expanded education more slowly in Muslim areas.

TABLE 4.4 *Early access to education: rural "invented chiefs" vs. "never recognized" communities*

Outcome:	1 % boys enrolled in school in 1960	2 % boys enrolled in school in 1960	3 % boys enrolled in school in 1960
	OLS	2SLS	2SLS
"Invented chiefs" (%) in community	0.079*** (0.024)	0.163*** (0.049)	0.158* (0.078)
Community-level controls	Y	Y	Y
Instrumental variable		GC	Pop %
N	2766	2766	2766
adj. R^2	0.125	0.083	0.088

† significant at $p < 0.10$; *$p < 0.05$; **$p < 0.01$; ***$p < 0.001$. OLS (column 1) and 2SLS (columns 2–3) regressions, with standard errors clustered by plurality ethnic group. All models include the same restricted set of communities as in Table 4.1. The IV in column 2 is the indicator for being on the Gold Coast side pre-1914 border. The IV in column 3 is the population % from precolonially acephalous groups on the Gold Coast side pre-1914.

schools. Teaching was, by far, the principal form of formal sector employment available in the North in the post-independence period. A smaller set proceeded to secondary schools, qualifying them for other jobs in the civil service and opening the door to the professional class. In the oral history interviews, five of the six Frafra and Dagaba communities ("invented chiefs") had already had at least one secondary school graduate by the late 1960s. But the first secondary school graduates in five of the six Konkomba communities only came in the 1990s and 2000s, with the latest in 2011.

Table 4.5 displays data from archival registries of Northern students enrolled in both forms of higher education in the independence period. The first column is based on registries of the students enrolling in the three main teacher training colleges in the North – at Tamale, Navrongo, and Pusiga – between 1957 and 1960. The ethnicity of each enrolled student is coded based on their name, using an ethnic name dictionary.[49] While enrollee lists were not available for each year for each school, this provides a rough estimate of which types of students were entering

[49] The name dictionary was prepared with Sarah Brierley and George Ofosu. More details are available on request.

TABLE 4.5 *Admissions to higher education, by ethnic category*

	Teacher training college (1957–1960)	Secondary school in South (1956)	Population (%)
Invented chiefs groups	48.6% (126)	41.8% (36)	32
Never recognized groups	8.9% (23)	3.4% (3)	25
Always chiefs groups	24.7% (64)	43.0% (37)	36
Ethnicity unknown	17.8% (46)	11.7% (10)	–
	100% (259)	100% (86)	–

Column 1: Northern students admitted to the Tamale (1957–1960), Navrongo (1958), and Pusiga (1958) Teacher Training Colleges, coded by ethnic category. Students from Southern Ghana are dropped. Admissions records from Northern Regional Archives, Tamale, NRG 3/17/16, NRG 7/12/4, NRG 8/9/17; column 2: Northern students admitted to attend Secondary Schools in Southern Ghana in 1956, coded by ethnic category. Northern Regional Archives, Tamale, 7/12/2. Overall population proportions (2010) for comparison (see Chapter 3).

training college. Overall, starkly more students from the "invented chiefs" groups (48.6 percent of enrollees) reached training college than from the "never recognized" groups (8.9 percent of enrollees). The second column of Table 4.5 similarly codes the ethnicity of all 86 Northern students admitted to secondary schools in Southern Ghana in 1956. At this point, there was only one government secondary school in the North, at Tamale, which admitted roughly ninety students total per entering class (Form 1).[50] The students sent to Southern schools thus represent roughly half of all Northern secondary school students at the time. Again, there is a clear ethnic disparity in access to higher education: 41.8 percent of these early secondary school students came from the "invented chiefs" groups compared to just 3 percent from the "never recognized" groups.

Both columns of Table 4.5 show even greater disparities in access to higher education than Table 4.3 shows for access to primary school. The two disparities are related: even when students from "never recognized" ethnic groups were able to enroll in primary school by the independence era, a severe shortage of trained teachers from their groups meant that they often had to attend primary school in languages they did not speak, depressing their performance and causing more early dropouts. For example, a colonial official describing conditions at the new Native Authority primary school in Kpandai in 1948 noted that some students

[50] Estimated from the 1960 entering class, via folio NRG 8 / 9 / 34, Northern Regional Archives, Tamale.

were Nawuris and Basaris – two "never recognized" groups – but the teacher was educating students in Gonja, the language of the area's official chiefs: "The teacher, who can speak neither of these languages, is having a difficult time with [the Nawuri and Basari students] and has frequently to use interpreters from Class II to make himself understood. This language difficulty inevitably complicates the first year of school life and restricts progress considerably."[51] A senior education official described facing similar challenges starting up early schools in Konkomba communities.[52]

4.5.2 Differential Enrollment within Communities

Where primary schools existed, there were also disparities in who enrolled within communities. As already suggested by Table 4.3, Northern primary schools could initially only accommodate small classes sizes – with as few as twenty to forty students total per school. The first small set of schools built in the North – before the mid-1930s – were managed directly by state officials. Enrollments were highly selective and concentrated explicitly on chiefs' children. As of 1927, for example, 50 percent of students enrolled in Northern schools were the sons of chiefs.[53] In his memoir, Gandah (2004, 36), a Dagaba ("invented chiefs"), narrates how government teachers would go community by community demanding that each chief provide students from his household.[54] The goal was to use education selectively to train a new generation of chiefs who could be more effective agents of the colonial state.[55]

Yet enrollments remained *de facto* biased in favor of chiefs' children even after the state no longer purposefully sought to prioritize chiefs' families. This occurred after oversight over schooling shifted from British officials to the local Native Authorities in the mid-1930s. During the school construction boom of the 1940s–1960s (Figure 3.7), chiefs, deputized by the state to help build the schools, were still directly tasked with rounding up the first sets of students. Each of the oral histories

[51] Folio NRG 4/15/3, Northern Regional Archives, Tamale.
[52] Interview with retired senior education official, Saboba, June 23, 2018.
[53] *Annual Report of the Northern Territories for 1927* (1928, 8).
[54] The memoir of Ghana's recent president – John Dramani Mahama, a Gonja ("always chiefs") from Savannah Region – opens with a similar account of how is father, the son of a chief, was forced to become the first to attend school from his community (Mahama 2012).
[55] Bening (1990), Grischow (2006), Meier zu Selhausen et al. (2018).

in the "invented chiefs" (Frafra and Dagaba) communities consistently recounted that because chiefs were mandated with selecting students, children from their own households were *overwhelmingly* the first to enroll.

By contrast, to the extent schools existed, access was far less concentrated in particular families in many "never recognized" communities in the absence of village-wide leaders directly tasked with coordinating enrollment. Oral histories in the Konkomba communities offered much more varied explanations of who became the "pioneers" at school. Respondents in a town in Saboba District narrated that when colonial officials came in the early 1950s to demand students be sent to the new school nearby, the community's orphans were sent first because no family was willing to part with its children and there was no centralized leader to coordinate the selection of students.[56] The Konkomba respondents in a village in Nanumba North district similarly recounted that early attendance at school was spread widely across families, rather than concentrated in the family of the chief or other local elite.[57]

4.5.3 Implications for Inequality

Disparities across groups in where schools were built combined with these disparities within groups in enrollments to produce the higher levels of inequality in the "invented chiefs" communities. The relatively small set of students educated by the early postcolonial period benefitted from a major windfall from the modern state: highly valuable opportunities for human capital accumulation. The first school graduates in Northern Ghana – representing a very small share of the population even within communities that now had schools (Table 4.3) – entered the labor market at a time when educated Northerners were otherwise very rare. For example, in 1960, there were only roughly 800 total Northern students enrolled in either teacher training college or secondary school (at any level, Form 1 through Form 6).[58] Graduating into such a thin labor market provided privileged access to the first formal employment opportunities, often as the very first Northern civil servants. In a region with

---

[56] Interview with clan elder in community #3, Saboba District, 17 May 2019. As explained below, this does not reflect an initial difference in demand for school across ethnic groups, however. Most families across all ethnic groups were initially hesitant to send their children.

[57] Interview with clan elders, Community #1, Nanumba North District, 4 July 2019.

[58] Bening (1990, 240).

virtually no paths to wealth via the private sector, these new formal sector workers became the first economic elites, even if their salaries were modest overall.[59] The anthropologist Jack Goody, active in Northern Ghana in this period, recounts how the "first generation of school children grew up and blossomed into school teachers, lawyers, politicians, and civil servants of all descriptions," creating a brand new economic elite linked directly to the expansion of school access.[60]

In turn, new economic elites were able to pass on their advantages within families by providing enhanced educational and employment opportunities to their children and relatives. In the oral histories, one of the main ways respondents explain why some families in their villages are better off today than others is by pointing to whose relatives were the community's pioneers at school, and as a result, now have the most educated family members working in the formal urban economy who both remit income back to their rural relatives and help them secure employment outside the rural North through connections in the city.

The opening quote in the chapter includes such an example: the tendana traced the origins of his community's wealthiest family to its first school graduate, who was able to use his position as a government teacher to support his relatives' own educations, creating opportunities not available to most other families until later on.[61] A respondent in one of the Frafra communities similarly explained that his clan – the chief's clan – has become wealthier than others in his community because,

our fathers were educated. Some were soldiers. Some were police. They had gone to school before, so they tried to send their kids to school. But the others were farmers and hunters ... so they were not having the mind for school at first. So that was why this [clan] was having the 'big people' – they were the first to go to school. That's why we have those people in such numbers from this area.[62]

---

[59] More broadly, see Ricart-Huguet (2021a).

[60] Goody (2004, 8). A particularly striking feature of historical accounts of the early independence era in Northern Ghana is how socially close-knit the new elite was – almost all had done their post-primary education together, whether in the South, at Tamale Secondary School, or at the few teacher training colleges. Goody continues, "[the new elites] all knew each other well and their acquaintances stretched from shopkeepers to sanitary officials, from presidents to councillors, from chiefs to commoners. The whole spectrum of 'literate' employment was there, arising out of the school situation."

[61] Interview with tendana, Community #1, Nadowli District, 27 May 2019.

[62] Interview with chief's interpreter and sons, Community #1, Bolgatanga East District, May 20, 2019.

Young (2013) shows that these types of remittances from urban elites to rural relatives are a common cause of inequality across rural Africa. Another commonly described means by which the early advantages of education transferred across generations within the same families is that once the early pioneers at school reached a civil service position or private sector job in the South, they would then work to secure jobs for other family members in the same agency or firm.[63]

With better early access to school in "invented chiefs" communities than "never recognized" communities (Tables 4.4 and 4.5), more of these new elites emerged in the mid-twentieth century where the colonial state had invented chiefs in the early-twentieth century. And because enrollments were often highly concentrated within these communities in the families of the chief – as described in the previous section – the benefits of education then compounded narrowly within "invented chiefs" communities, producing the inequality observed in Table 4.1.

Similarly, "never recognized" communities have less inequality overall than the "invented chiefs" communities both because (a) they had fewer students enrolled in the early years of the education system who could benefit from this valuable windfall from the state (Tables 4.4 and 4.5); and (b) in the absence of chiefs to dominate enrollment decisions, the first students who did enroll were less likely to be narrowly concentrated in single families within each community, producing less intra-ethnic inequality in access to the economic benefits of early education. This can be seen, for example, in the Konkomba community described above in which local orphans were enrolled in school first in the 1950s. An elder explained that one of those orphans had now become a prominent doctor in the Ghana Health Service, much like the first "pioneers" in the Dagaba and Frafra communities. But because he was an orphan, not the child of a major local family, he does not have close relatives left in the community today that he supports financially, dampening any effect his personal achievements might have had on contemporary intra-communal inequality.[64]

These patterns are demonstrated more systematically by additional tests in Table 4.6. Columns 1 and 2 of Table 4.6 find that the degree of (male) school enrollment in a community by 1960 is strongly associated with greater inequality in 2010. Thus not only does the invention of chieftaincy predict 1960 enrollment (Table 4.4), but enrollment, in turn,

---

[63] Interview with retired teacher, Community #2, Nadowli District, May 27, 2019; Interview with retired teacher, Community #1, Bolgatanga East District, May 20, 2019.
[64] Interview with clan elder, community #3, Saboba District, May 17, 2019.

TABLE 4.6 *Education and inequality: rural "invented chiefs" vs. "never recognized" communities*

Outcome:	1 Inequality (*I*) in 2010 (wealth index)	2 Inequality (*I*) in 2010 (wealth index)	3 Inequality (*I*) in 2010 (wealth index)
	OLS	OLS	OLS
"Invented chiefs" (%) in community		0.043* (0.020)	0.028 (0.019)
Boys enrolled (%) in 1960	0.242*** (0.028)	0.219*** (0.033)	0.097 (0.068)
Average distance (km) to other gov't institutions, by year (1901–1960)	−0.001 (0.001)	−0.001 (0.001)	−0.001 (0.000)
"Invented chiefs" (%) in community* Boys enrolled (%) in 1960			0.176* (0.081)
Community-level controls	Y	Y	Y
N	2763	2763	2763
adj. R^2	0.254	0.255	0.256

† significant at $p < 0.10$; *$p < 0.05$; **$p < 0.01$; ***$p < 0.001$. OLS regressions, with standard errors clustered by plurality ethnic group. All models include the same restricted set of communities as in Table 4.1. For simplicity, I only report results for *I* calculated over all community residents. Results for the more restricted intra-ethnic measure are similar.

predicts inequality, with more inequality today where education from the state was available sooner. These OLS models include the same set of communities and controls as in Tables 4.1 and 4.4. They also add a control for the presence of all other state institutions, operationalized as the average distance (in km) per year from 1901 to 1960 to the nearest non-school state institution, to show that this relationship is specific to schooling, not due to more general proximity to other types of state investment and institutions.[65]

Most crucially, column 3 of Table 4.6 finds an interaction between 1960 enrollment and the population from "invented chiefs" groups: "invented chiefs" communities *only* have significantly higher inequality today than otherwise similar "never recognized" communities if they had early access to school, with at least some students enrolled by 1960.[66]

[65] This test draws on the data from Figure 3.1 (Chapter 3).
[66] Roughly one quarter of communities in Northern Ghana still had zero students enrolled in primary school by 1960.

This interaction suggests that access to education is a key mechanism linking the invention of chieftaincy to contemporary inequality: inequality is greatest where some students were enrolled by 1960 and a small set of families got an economic head start over everyone else; but in communities without access to school by 1960, there is little inequality today – here, the first school graduates only came later, after educated Northerners had become much less scarce and the relative economic advantage from education had fallen (see Figure 2.4).

4.6 ALTERNATIVE MECHANISMS

While the interaction in Table 4.6 is strongly suggestive of education access serving as the key mechanism, I also consider and rule out the most plausible alternatives.

4.6.1 Other Rents from Chieftaincy

Inequality within "invented chiefs" communities could instead be due to other economic advantages also available to chiefs. But the interaction effect in Table 4.6 rules out many plausible alternative sources of rents: any other explanation for the relationship between the invention of chieftaincy and contemporary intra-communal inequality *must be correlated with 1960 school enrollment*. Chiefs' other opportunities for wealth accumulation from their judicial roles or via local tax collection – a responsibility gained in 1935 – were present in communities both with and without school access by 1960, directly inconsistent with Table 4.6. Moreover, a key source of chiefs' wealth in other African cases – land – is not a plausible alternative. Chapter 3 describes that until the 1979 land reforms, chiefs did not exercise significant grassroots authority over land among either the "invented chiefs" or "never recognized" groups. Those reforms then granted more land power to chiefs across communities both with and without school enrollment in 1960, again inconsistent with the interaction in Table 4.6.

Historical sources detail that a few invented chiefs became relatively wealthy from tax collection and other forms of rent-seeking in the colonial period. Lentz (2006, 63–64) quotes a colonial official from the 1920s describing several newly empowered Dagaba chiefs as "living like 'robber barons'," with some able to amass upwards of fifty wives and hundreds of cattle.[67] Grischow (2006, 71) notes that these chiefs were often able to do so by claiming more powers for themselves than the colonial state had actually given them. But as Chapter 3 describes, these were more exceptions than the rule. Many invented chiefs – artificial impositions of an absent state that could not fully defend their authority – struggled to amass substantive power within their communities until many decades into the colonial period, impeding their ability to accumulate significant rents from their positions. Reports of non-compliance with tax collection and other forms of extraction were common.

Qualitative evidence suggests that, at least in the very early years of the public education system, chiefs' advantages in enrolling their children may have counterintuitively resulted from their *lack* of real local power. Many respondents described that when the first schools were built in the colonial period (i.e., in the 1920s–1930s), most Northerners were hesitant to send their children. Male children played an important economic role that families could not afford to do without. Families were also (reasonably) suspicious of what would happen to their children if they were taken; prior to the expansion of community day schools in the 1950s (Figure 3.7), most students attended boarding schools outside their community.[68]

Yet because chiefs were directly reliant on the state for their positions, colonial officials could hold them uniquely accountable for enrollment, forcing them to supply children. If chiefs were too weak to convince other families to do so, they had to fall back to sending their own. In this way, the earliest benefits of education could accumulate narrowly to chiefs' families irrespective of whatever substantive power these artificially imposed leaders had developed. This is unlike potential sources of wealth from other sources, such as tax collection, that depended on chiefs' ability to compel compliance.

For example, in his memoir of childhood in a Dagaba community in the 1930s, Gandah (2004) explains that the District Commissioner forced his father, the chief, to send his sons:

---

[67] Gandah (2009, iiv) provides a similar account of his father's reign as chief of Birifu, a Dagaba community near Lawra.

[68] An MP narrated that, "When they took my father to school [in the early 1930s], the story my father told me was that his mother and the aunties came over ... and they cried the whole day because they were taking him away into the boarding school ... It was a very painful experience to have him taken." Interview with Wala MP from Upper West Region, Accra, 13 July 2019.

The District Commissioner ... approached him and asked if he would like to send more children to school as there were five vacancies to be filled. He intimated that since he [the chief] was the initiator of the building of the school, its failure would reflect on him as having sold a white elephant to his people. (37–38)

The earliest children enrolled from chief's households were not necessarily the "best and brightest" – as would be expected if chiefs immediately saw school as a valuable opportunity – but those who were easiest to send, either because they were least skilled at economic activities or did not have mothers with clout within their polygamous household. A retired school principal from a royal family in a Gurense community near Bolgatanga explained that in many Gurense and Frafra communities:

If somebody who comes from the palace was sent to school, then its because the person's mother was not around – maybe divorced, or dead. And they also sent stubborn children – they would cane them and then send them to the schools [as punishment]. Even chief's palaces, from our house, there were children who didn't have strong mothers to defend them. They were sent.[69]

Similarly, another retired teacher from a Frafra community recounted that initially, his community's chief "only sent the lazy ones – the ones who weren't so into farming. They tried to keep the best children back to farm." It was only decades later, once the first students graduated and the benefits of education became apparent, that demand for schooling increased, as evinced by the example of a chief's appeal for a school in the early 1960s in Figure 4.3. The retired teacher from the Frafra community quoted above described that only once community members saw children that they had perceived as "lazy" receive better economic opportunities than their peers, "people realized there was real value in it."[70]

4.6.2 Economic Geography

Another alternative is that some unobserved feature of economic geography is correlated with group locations – or sides of the pre-1914 border – and explains present-day differences in inequality. For example, irrespective of the environmental controls already included in the regressions above – soil suitability, rainfall, and slope – perhaps communities from ethnic groups in the far west of Northern Ghana grow different crops

---

[69] Interview with retired teacher, Zuarungu, May 20, 2019.
[70] Interview with retired teacher, Community #1, Bolgatanga East District, May 20, 2019.

TABLE 4.7 *Accounting for unobserved differences in economic geography*

Outcome: Inequality (*I*) in wealth index (by EA/community, 2010)	1 OLS	2 OLS	3 OLS	4 OLS	5 OLS
Gold Coast pre-1914 (0,1)	0.013 (0.024)				
"Invented chiefs" % in community		0.064* (0.029)	0.057[†] (0.034)		
Community latitude (WGS84)		0.005 (0.025)		0.040 (0.039)	
Community longitude (WGS84)			−0.004 (0.012)		−0.002 (0.039)
Ethnic group FEs	Y	N	N	Y	Y
Community-level controls	Y	Y	Y	Y	Y
N	2768	2767	2767	946	946
adj. R^2	0.267	0.247	0.248	0.292	0.291
Standard errors	By group	By group	By group	By group	By group

[†] significant at $p < 0.10$; *$p < 0.05$; **$p < 0.01$; ***$p < 0.001$. OLS regressions, with standard errors in parentheses. Standard errors are clustered by ethnic group. Columns 1–3 focus on comparison of "invented chiefs" and "never recognized" communities, as in Table 4.1. Columns 4–5 restrict instead to the "always chiefs" ethnic groups.

than groups to the far east, or are incorporated into different regional trading networks, with independent effects on inequality.

Table 4.7 demonstrates in several ways that this is unlikely through a series of placebo-type tests. First, column 1 of Table 4.7 repeats the reduced form model from column 2 of Table 4.1 after adding ethnic group fixed effects – dummy variables for the largest ethnic group in each community – to restrict all comparisons to be within-group. If something else beyond the invention of chieftaincy across the pre-1914 border explains contemporary inequality, there should still be differences in inequality across the border between villages populated by the same groups (i.e., when holding the history of chieftaincy fixed). But column 1 shows this is not the case.

Second, columns 2 and 3 of Table 4.7 repeat the basic model in column 1 of Table 4.1 after adding controls for the latitude and longitude, respectively, of each community's geographic centroid. Column 2 thus restricts the comparison of "invented chiefs" vs. "never recognized" communities to those within similar horizontal geographic bands, while column 3 does the same for similar vertical geographic bands. Each accounts for any unobserved factors within similar geographic areas that could separately explain inequality. The original result remains and latitude and longitude also do not predict inequality on their own, inconsistent with any explanation that suggests some underlying geographic or economic feature correlated with terrain explains the variation in Table 4.1.

Third, columns 4 and 5 of Table 4.7 combine the intuition behind columns 1–3 by switching focus to the "always chiefs" ethnic groups. Several of these groups – especially the Gonja, Dagomba, and Mamprusi – occupy large stretches of territory that cross much of the region (see Figure 3.1). I again include ethnic group fixed effects to restrict comparisons to communities of the same ethnicity, holding the history of chieftaincy fixed. I then examine whether each community's latitude or longitude predicts its 2010 inequality. If underlying economic geography – rather than the history of chieftaincy – explained intra-community inequality, I should still observe significant variation in inequality within these groups across locations. But I do not: inequality does not change as one moves further away from the pre-1914 border.

A related concern emerges from Herbst's (2000) claims about the effects of geographic distance on the state's ability to project power and reshape society: perhaps the effects above are explained simply by differences in remoteness from centers of state power, with the state more likely to have generated inequality in easier to reach areas. But similar to the null results for other geographic features in Table 4.7, I find no evidence that intra-community or intra-ethnic inequality varies with distance from the national capital, Accra, or the regional capital of the Northern Territories, Tamale. Repeating column 1 of Table 4.1 with these distances added sequentially as controls, the main result remains and distance is not a predictor of inequality.

4.6.3 Other Post-treatment Differences: Migration and Violence

An additional concern is that the patterns in Table 4.1 are due to some other *post-treatment* difference between ethnic groups on different sides of the pre-1914 border that occurred after the invention of chieftaincy, but is spatially correlated with it. Two developments later in the twentieth century are particularly plausible: different rates of internal migration or different experiences of violence.

First, most ethnic groups in Northern Ghana still live overwhelmingly within the same geographic areas as in the early colonial period. But some members of "never recognized" groups migrated across the original

Anglo-German border in the mid-twentieth century. Intra-village inequality might be especially low in migrant "never recognized" communities because they have been settled more recently, with less time for economic stratification to have developed.

The most widely discussed migration has been among the Konkomba, who moved into unpopulated areas in Nanumba and Gonja territories in the late colonial and early post-independence periods. By the late-twentieth century, the Konkomba had come to outnumber the Nanumba and Gonja in the Nanumba North, Nanumba South, and Kpandai districts, as well as form significant populations in three other districts (West Gonja, Central Gonja, and East Gonja) where they had not lived prior to the annexation of Togoland.[71] To show that these migrations cannot explain Table 4.1, I re-estimate the models after dropping all Konkomba-majority communities in the six districts in which large-scale Konkomba in-migration has been described in historical sources, especially Talton (2010). All results remain as in Table 4.1.

Second, since independence, there have been a series of violent conflicts, the focus of Chapter 8. While there has been some violence across all types of ethnic groups, the largest-scale bouts of violence have been overwhelmingly concentrated among "never recognized" and "always chiefs" groups. There could be concern that negative economic shocks of conflict have lowered inequality among some "never recognized" communities relative to "invented chiefs" communities. I again repeat the analyses in Table 4.1 after dropping all communities in the districts most affected by violence that has involved "never recognized" groups.[72] The results again remain the same, inconsistent with the after-effects of conflict accounting for contemporary differences in inequality.

4.6.4 Is the Control Group the Treatment Group?

A final alternative is that the difference in inequality is more a function of the state's denial of independent chiefs to "never recognized" communities than anything it did in "invented chiefs" communities. In practice,

---

[71] These new settlements account for many of the "never recognized" communities visible to the West of the original German border in Figure 3.2. They represent new settlement in virgin land, not Konkomba integration into existing Gonja or Nanumba communities.

[72] Violence in 1981 conflict was concentrated in the Nanumba North and Nanumba South districts. Violence in 1991–1992 was concentrated in the Kpandai District. Violence in 1994–1995 occurred in eight districts: Nanumba North, Nanumba South, Kpandai, Yendi, Zabzugu-Tatale, Saboba, Gushiegu-Karaga, and West Gonja. See Chapter 8 for more details.

the state left pre-existing intra-ethnic institutions in place in most "never recognized" communities, while nominally placing these areas within the official jurisdiction of chiefs from other ethnic groups (mainly, the "always chiefs" groups; see Chapters 3 and 5). However, surrogate chiefs from the "always chiefs" groups were posted into a small subset of "never recognized" communities, with a chief from a different ethnic group, who was not a permanent resident of the community, ruling over the local "never recognized" population. There could be concern that in the subset of communities where it was practiced, surrogate chieftaincy artificially blocked intra-ethnic inequality from emerging over time because the outsider chiefs captured local resources for themselves.

It is not possible to reconstruct a record of every "never recognized" community that experienced surrogate chieftaincy. From historical sources, however, I can identify the key chieftaincy within the "always chiefs" kingdoms from which most surrogate chiefs were dispatched and appointed. For example, among the Konkomba – the largest "never recognized" group – surrogate chiefs primarily reported up to Dagomba divisional chiefs in Sunson and Demon and the Nanumba paramount chief in Bimbila (see Chapter 5).[73] It is reasonable to assume that surrogate chieftaincy was most likely to have occurred in "never recognized" communities that are more geographically proximate to the towns from which their "always chiefs" overlords attempted to project authority. Yet in an additional analysis I find that inequality within the "never recognized" groups is uncorrelated with proximity to the main set of towns from which "always chiefs" groups dispatched surrogate chiefs.[74] This suggests that surrogate chieftaincy is unlikely to serve as an alternative mechanism for Table 4.1.

4.7 CONCLUSION

I demonstrate how the first two actions of Northern Ghana's scarce modern state powerfully and directly reshaped society by producing long-lasting economic inequality within rural communities. In a context with few private sector paths to wealth, early contact with the state through

[73] Tait (1961), Dawson (2000), Talton (2010).
[74] For each majority "never recognized" community, I calculate the distance (in km) to the closest chieftaincy seat within each Traditional Council (Native Authority) jurisdiction from which historical sources describe such surrogate chiefs being appointed. The correlation between this distance and intra-community inequality (as measured in panel (a) of Table 4.1) is $r = 0.02$.

the education system provided valuable windfalls, creating new stratification across generations. This stratification became entrenched over time
because the state has remained so scarce for so long, preventing most
other community members from catching up by extracting similarly valuable windfalls of their own. Over the remainder of the twentieth century,
public education eventually became widely available throughout Northern Ghana. Virtually every community has a primary school today. But
as human capital became less scarce, the marginal advantage provided by
education declined, preventing newly educated families from displacing
the elites launched by early access to schooling.

This chapter suggests that the initial economic benefits of chieftaincy
positions created by the state may have had much less to do with chiefs'
explicit powers – such as collecting taxes and serving as judicial figures
within their communities – than with the other economic opportunities that became available simply because chiefs had privileged contact
with the distant state apparatus. The chapter also shows that the state
provision of education – a key component of state-building in many contexts – is most likely to create lasting inequality in society when states
provide very little of it overall. As a result, in hinterland regions where
the state is most absent, simple actions like building schools can have their
largest effects. Chapter 9 examines the parallel introduction of schooling
in Southern Ghana, a region where the state was both less absent and less
resource-advantaged relative to society, and shows that the much greater
availability of non-state access to human capital (via missionaries) and the
much more rapid expansion of public schooling to a wider cross section
of the population led to very different dynamics of elite formation.

The next chapter complements this focus on the direct societal effects
of the state's isolated actions by pivoting to indirect effects instead. I focus
on the bottom-up responses of those who were left out and left behind –
the "never recognized" communities disadvantaged by the state in the
colonial and early postcolonial periods.

5

Bottom-Up Responses to Scarcity

Because the government endorsed the chieftaincy system, the Konkombas ... were coerced in a way to go in for a chieftaincy system ... Everyone wants to become a chief.

– Konkomba business leader, Saboba, July 2019

During the oral history interviews, I observed a common pattern across several communities. The farmland would still be where it had been for generations. But sometime in the late twentieth century, all of the homes had voluntarily been torn down and rebuilt in a new location, moved several kilometers to the side of the nearest road. There are many possible reasons to do this, including to gain easier access to markets. But when asked why they had moved, community elders gave a consistent answer: they wanted to be *closer to the state*. In a community near Kpalba that moved in 1982, an elder recalled, "We realized it would be better to come to the roadside so we can better get things from the government."[1] The tendana (earth priest) in a community in Mion District similarly recalled why they rebuilt their homes near the road in 1995: "Any time government wanted to bring support, because we were inside [the bush], they just sent the support straight to Sambu [the nearest town]. They didn't know about us ... so they wouldn't come."[2]

Scott (1998) argues that a core aim of many developing states is to make their populations more "legible" – if society becomes more visible to the state, the state's capacity to govern (and extract) increases.[3] In his

[1] Interview with clan elders, Community #1, Saboba District, May 17, 2019.
[2] Interview with tendana and clan elders, Community #1, Mion District, May 16, 2019.
[3] Lee and Zhang (2017), Brambor et al. (2020).

telling, schemes to improve legibility are something that states *do to their societies*. And he and many others argue that societies often respond with resistance and attempts to flee from the state's reach.[4] But Chapter 2 argues that the opposite may be more likely in hinterland regions with scarce, resource-advantaged states. Where the state remains scarce, the losers from earlier state actions – realizing their disadvantages – may instead seek out greater contact with it. Their hope, in the words of Walker (2015), is that increasing their legibility to the state will improve their "eligibility" to benefit from it, enabling them to secure future windfalls of state resources of their own. In doing so, neglected communities may voluntarily mimic the society-changing actions commonly undertaken by states seeking to expand their reach, even without any involvement from state officials.

Increasing legibility was something the two communities above *did to themselves*. There was no state-led resettlement program like what Scott (1998) studies in Tanzania, or as has been a similar state-building tool in other countries. Instead, community members voluntarily rebuilt their homes at significant personal expense. In a subnational region in which they expected the state to be a *net provider* – with little threat of stifling taxation but much to be gained from state-funded local public and private goods – increasing proximity to the state did not appear threatening; the state's scarcity was a problem they hoped to proactively solve.

In a small way, this opening example demonstrates the broader phenomenon examined in this chapter: that scarce states can also reshape hinterland society *indirectly* by incentivizing society to change itself. My main focus is on an even larger bottom-up response to state scarcity in the form of a modern-day attempt to invent chieftaincy institutions from scratch among the largest "never recognized" ethnic group, the Konkomba. While changing where a village is located is a means of literally moving closer to the state, creating new leadership institutions represents a more figurative attempt to achieve a similar goal, making it easier for the distant state to "see" a community by empowering an intermediary recognizable to the state to interface with it.

Windfalls from the first two state actions examined in Chapters 3 and 4 passed over most Konkomba communities. The colonial state did not invent new chiefs and the postcolonial state disadvantaged Konkomba communities in its provision of education. The Konkomba were losers again when the state made its third intervention – the 1979 devolution of

---

[4] For example, Ying (2020).

land to chiefs. Because they lacked independent chiefs, the land reform formally gave away most Konkomba land to the "always chiefs" ethnic groups, whom the state had placed above the Konkomba in the colonial period.

Recognizing their compounding disadvantages, a small set of the initial Konkomba educated by the mid-1970s began a grassroots social movement to improve their group's treatment by the state. After the 1979 land reform, a central focus of their efforts was to do from below what British state-builders had done from above for many other acephalous ethnic groups seven decades earlier: invent chieftaincy. Believing that chiefs are necessary for attracting state resources – especially state-backed land rights – Konkomba communities see themselves as having been essentially "coerced" by the state's neglect, in the words of the activist quoted at the opening of this chapter, into attempting to adapt and incorporate the chieftaincy institutions of neighboring groups into Konkomba culture.

To date, this bottom-up effort has not produced well-functioning chieftaincy institutions throughout Konkomba society. Most new Konkomba chiefs have failed to become fully independent from the "always chiefs" groups and many are still struggling to build legitimacy and substantive authority within their communities.[5] The large majority of Konkomba villages still lack state-recognized chiefs, even as many now (newly) have residents referring to and carrying themselves as a chief.

But despite its incompleteness, this attempt to create chieftaincy represents an important example of the intense societal upheaval that can emerge from hinterland communities' endogenous responses to state scarcity. This "syncretic" institution-building – the reassembling of shards and fragments of different cultural elements into something distinctly new[6] – has become such a fraught site of political competition because it has been caught between two impulses: a public-spirited attempt by the initial activists to change societal institutions in order to improve their group's overall welfare, and the much more private attempts of enterprising community members to co-opt the broader effort in pursuit of the individual rents that they have learned can flow from the state to chiefs.

Sustained contestation over chieftaincy has had major effects on society. On the negative side, the push to create chiefs helped spark two major bouts of inter-ethnic violence that led to thousands of deaths (examined in

---

[5] This restricts these new chiefs' ability to serve as brokers or influence voters in the manner I will examine in Chapter 7.

[6] Galvan (2004). In the study of religion, syncretism refers to the blending of beliefs and practices from separate traditions.

more detail in Chapter 8), and more recently, has fed smaller-scale intra-ethnic conflicts over chieftaincy succession that are undermining the social cohesion of affected communities. More positively, however, the effort has significantly reduced historical discrimination against Konkomba communities by other ethnic groups and has helped establish *de facto* economic independence from the "always chiefs" groups.[7]

The Konkomba are not the only example of a contemporary African ethnic group imposing ostensibly "traditional" leadership on itself long after colonial rule has ended. Within Northern Ghana, Stacey (2014*a*, 2014*b*) has documented a related and even less successful push by the Nawuri – a much smaller "never recognized" group concentrated in the Kpandai District – to also establish independent chiefs of their own. Robinson (2019) richly explores a modern-day effort to create new traditional chiefs among the Lhomwe in Malawi. More broadly, a large body of theory in political science identifies conditions under which collectives – such as the rural communities examined here – may empower new leaders to overcome collective action problems and coordinate the provision of local public goods.[8]

But existing explanations cannot adequately account for Konkomba chieftaincy. Robinson (2019) describes the Lhomwe creation of chieftaincy as one part of a coordinated, politician-led agenda to increase the salience of Lhomwe identity. This echoes a well-studied phenomenon of politicians building electoral coalitions through conscious efforts to construct new ethnic identities.[9] The Konkomba experience does not fit this pattern. Most institutional creation has been *ad hoc* and from below, not initiated top-down by office-seeking politicians. Similarly, there is no evidence that concerns about intra-communal collective action have driven the push for chieftaincy. Instead, Konkomba communities already had functioning, pre-existing institutions of clan leadership. These institutions have been undermined by the push for chieftaincy, which has, if anything, only served to reduce communities' ability to act collectively by creating new internal social fissures.

The remainder of the chapter tracks the creation of Konkomba chieftaincy over time, concluding with a theoretical discussion of how the state's scarcity incentivized Konkomba communities into action. Unlike other empirical chapters that draw on quantitative data, I focus on this

---

[7] Talton (2010).

[8] Ostrom (1990), Baldassarri and Grossman (2011).

[9] Bates (1983), Posner (2005).

in-depth case study of a particularly illustrative example of an endogenous societal response to state scarcity. I employ the six sets of oral histories in Konkomba communities as well as forty elite interviews conducted across 2008, 2018, and 2019 with Konkomba activists, chiefs, and politicians.

5.1 THE SETTING

5.1.1 Konkomba Society in the Early and Mid-twentieth Century

At the outset of the colonial period, Konkomba settlements stretched from the area around Yendi eastward over the Oti River into present-day Togo. This placed the Konkomba at the direct periphery of three precolonially centralized kingdoms – Dagbon (Dagomba), Mamprugu (Mamprusi), and Nanum (Nanumba). Although these groups would later maintain that the Konkomba had been a conquered, subordinate tribe, Tait (1961, 8–10) and Talton (2010, 24–26) suggest there is little evidence that chiefs from other groups had exercised real authority.[10]

Instead, the Konkomba were an acephalous society without leadership beyond individual clans, or extended families. The main authorities were *uninkpel*, clan elders, typically the oldest man in each extended lineage within each village.[11] With multiple clans in most villages, Konkomba communities had multiple uninkpel responsible for their respective families, rather than any overarching community-level authority, as would occur if there were a chief.[12] Similar to most other Northern ethnic groups, Konkomba communities also had religious authorities in the form of tendanas – *utindam* in Likpakpaln, the Konkomba language – earth priests with responsibility for allocating farmland. Utindam are elders from each community's earliest lineage.

The British decision to not impose new chieftaincy institutions among the Konkomba – detailed in Chapters 3 and 4 – was aided by Dagomba, Mamprusi, and Nanumba claims that the Konkomba had already fallen

---

[10] Tait (1961, 9) writes, for example, that "Dagomba 'rule' was limited to sporadic raids to obtain the slaves needed for the annual tribute to Ashanti."

[11] Talton (2010, 16), Tait (1961, 35–36).

[12] Talton (2010, 33) suggests that some clans settled in the closest proximity to the Dagomba also already had a village headman known as an *ubour* (or *biborb*), borrowing the concept of a community leader from their chiefly neighbors. But Tait (1961, 11) suggests this practice was not widespread in the precolonial or colonial periods; my interview subjects consistently referred to the uninkpel system as the previously dominant form of intra-communal governance.

under their jurisdiction prior to German rule. In much the same way the British justified inventing chieftaincy in Dagaba and Sisala communities as restoring an imagined precolonial "natural order,"[13] the British justified placing the Konkomba under the centralized "always chiefs" groups as a means of restoring the ostensible precolonial hierarchy in the recently annexed German territory.[14] In practice, this meant that from the 1920s on, any Konkomba communities near Mamprusi, Dagomba, and Nanumba territory, respectively, were placed under *new* "overlords" from these groups – as chiefs from the "always chiefs" groups came to refer to their role. Overall, the Dagomba took formal control over the largest share of Konkomba settlements.

Cross-ethnic indirect rule took several forms. First, and most commonly, chiefs in nearby communities gained nominal authority over the surrounding Konkomba villages, visiting periodically to pass along dictates from British officials, settle disputes, and collect taxes. In practice, the uninkpel system largely continued as before, with clan elders managing Konkomba communities' own day-to-day affairs. For example, the Sunson Na, the chief of Sunson, a Dagomba village in the present-day Yendi District, became the supervisory chief of Konkomba villages spread across much of what is now the Saboba District.

Second, and elsewhere, rule by the "always chiefs" groups instead took the form of "surrogate chieftaincy," with a chief from one of these other groups posted by his respective paramount chief to live in a Konkomba community and rule over it directly. Demon represents one such example, with a Dagomba chief – the Demon Na – posted there by the Ya Na – the Dagomba paramount – to rule over a largely Konkomba population. By the mid-twentieth century, surrogate chieftaincy was particularly common in the Nanumba Traditional Area, where otherwise homogenous Konkomba communities would be led by a single Nanumba resident – the chief. Under the systems of rotation in chieftaincy appointments practiced by the "always chiefs" groups (see Chapter 7), these surrogate chiefs were not permanent residents of these communities, but outsiders shuffled in and out over time.

Third, in the smallest set of cases, supervisory chiefs from the "always chiefs" groups – such as the Dagomba Sunson Na – appointed Konkomba elders as sub-chiefs, or "liaison chiefs," to serve as their emissaries.[15]

---

[13] Lentz (2006).
[14] Talton (2010).
[15] Dawson (2000, 5).

This was most common in the largest Konkomba towns, such as Saboba and Kpalba, which had liaison chiefs by the 1930s appointed by the Sunson Na and Demon Na, respectively. Tait (1961) emphasizes that liaison chiefs rarely had substantive authority – and thus were not real chiefs – but served as mouthpieces for the "always chiefs" groups. He writes, "These sub-chiefs are of very little importance ... they are of no consequence. A Konkomba chief is known as such only to the Dagomba royal chief in whose chiefdom he holds office" (11).[16] Describing the liaison chief of Saboba, Tait recounts of the 1950s:

When there is something to be done ... he cannot call the clan elders [uninkpel] of his supposed chiefdom to a meeting is his house but must himself walk to each hamlet in turn to discuss matters with the various elders. This would be unthinkable behaviour in a Dagomba chief. Furthermore, agreement or non-agreement lies wholly with the elders and the chief has no authority to command them in anything (11).

Into the 1970s, rule by the "always chiefs" groups resulted in rent extraction from Konkomba communities. Konkomba men were mandated to provide periodic free labor on the farms of Dagomba, Mamprusi, and Nanumba chiefs, as well as to donate a portion of their harvests each year to these chiefs and pay other customary duties. Taxation was coupled with more quotidian forms of discrimination – price discrimination in markets, slurs in public places, even the forced conscription of Konkomba men by Dagomba chiefs to fight in World War II in place of Dagombas.[17] Tait (1961, 9) summarizes the situation at the end of the colonial period: "instances of ... extortion are frequent." As respondents in the oral histories in one community near Kpalba recall, "our parents realized that they were under slavery."[18] Cross-ethnic indirect rule created a state-sanctioned system in which Konkomba – and the other "never recognized" ethnic groups – became second-class citizens.

5.1.2 State Scarcity in Konkomba Territory

The state was especially scarce in Konkomba areas throughout the colonial period. Despite representing the second most populous ethnic group

---

[16] Dawson (2000, 5) similarly notes that "these individuals possessed little authority throughout the colonial period."

[17] Interview with KOYA co-founder, Saboba, July 6, 2019; interview with former KOYA president, Amasaman, Greater Accra, July 15, 2019.

[18] Interview with clan elders, Commuinty #1, Saboba District, May 17, 2019.

in the North,[19] the Konkomba were mostly governed from Yendi – the Dagomba capital – with no permanent civil servants posted into Konkomba communities along the Oti River until the creation of a Saboba Sub-District in 1947. State investment was incredibly limited, with the first primary school only built in 1951, at Saboba.[20] This was eventually followed by two other primary schools at Demon and Wapuli in 1957 and 1958, respectively. At independence, just 29 percent of Konkomba-majority communities were within a 10 km radius of a school, compared to 49 percent of Dagomba-majority communities, and 63 percent of Northern communities overall.

For decades, the main contact between the state and the Konkomba came in the form of British efforts to police Konkomba communities, including to put down violent Konkomba resistance to Dagomba rule. Konkomba rejection of Dagomba chiefs grew by the end of the colonial period, including with the 1940 murder of the Dagomba chief of Jagbel and the 1944 murder of the Dazberi Na.[21] While there was no permanent British officer, a detachment of (African) police was posted in Saboba from 1933.

Konkomba communities remained comparatively distant from the state after independence. Until the late 1980s, administration of most Konkomba communities was still based from the district capitals of the "always chiefs" groups, such as Yendi, Nalerigu, and Bimbilla; officials from those groups, in turn, steered resources away from Konkomba areas.[22] In Ghana's first legislative elections of the 1950s, constituencies were drawn in favor the "always chiefs" groups. Until the 1990s, almost all Konkomba communities were represented by Dagomba, Mamprusi, or Nanumba politicians. Multiple Konkomba-majority districts were not created until the decentralization reforms of 1988.

Given this restrictive districting and the group's delayed access to education, there were virtually no Konkombas among Northern Ghana's post-independence governing class who could lobby for resources. My interview subjects could name only *one* Konkomba politician who

---

[19] The Konkomba population reached 500,000 in Northern Ghana in the 2010 census.

[20] By contrast, Tamale – the largest Dagomba settlement – received its first school in 1909, and Yendi, the Dagomba capital, received a school in 1921. Yendi had a permanent presence of British officers right from 1914.

[21] Talton (2010, 77–78), Tait (1961, 10).

[22] Saboba was briefly its own district in 1963 at the end of Nkrumah's regime (Talton 2010, 128), but was placed back under Yendi in 1966 after Nkrumah was removed; Saboba was only permanently administered separately from 1984 (Bening 2010).

achieved meaningful authority prior to the late 1980s – Isaac (I. B.) Bawa, who was one of the first Konkomba to attend school at Yendi in the 1930s and then served as Saboba's District Commissioner from 1963–1966.[23] One of the first Konkomba District Chief Executives (mayors) appointed after the 1988 decentralization reform recalls of earlier decades, "Because of not going to school early, Konkombas didn't have our people in government after independence ... who could talk on our behalf politically. So a lot injustice was meted to us ... It was the Dagombas who ruled."[24]

Konkomba communities were further disadvantaged in access to state resources by their continued lack of traditional chieftaincy. The colonial hierarchy of chieftaincy continued after independence. The authority to appoint chiefs in Konkomba communities remained with their colonial "overlords" from the "always chiefs" groups and Konkomba communities remained within the Dagomba, Nanumba, Mamprusi, and Gonja Traditional Councils, as shown in Map 5.1. Not only did this deny Konkomba communities intermediaries who could interface with the postcolonial state on their behalf, it also raised difficulties for internal Konkomba efforts at self-provision of resources in the absence of the state, such as through attempts to create informal "wing schools" in communities left without public schools (see Chapter 4). For example, oral history interviews in a village in Mion District detailed how attempts by a church to build the community's first (private) primary school in the 1980s were stalled for years by the Mion Lana – the Dagomba chief of the area – who refused to sign off the necessary permits to put up a proper school, and even called in the police to tear the first structure down.[25]

5.2 LAND REFORM AND THE DEMAND FOR CHIEFTAINCY

State intervention in Northern Ghana – in the form of land reform in the late 1970s (Chapter 3) – pushed Konkomba communities to change their society from within.

5.2.1 The Konkomba Youth Association

By the mid-1970s, a very small Konkomba educated class was emerging, populated by the pioneers of the primary schools in Saboba, Wapuli, and

---

[23] Talton (2010, 114). Talton (2010, 134) notes an additional Konkomba politician – E. S. Yani – who was briefly elected to Parliament from Saboba in 1969.
[24] Interview with former District Chief Executive, Saboba, June 23, 2018.
[25] Interview with retired teacher, Community #1, Mion District, May 16, 2019.

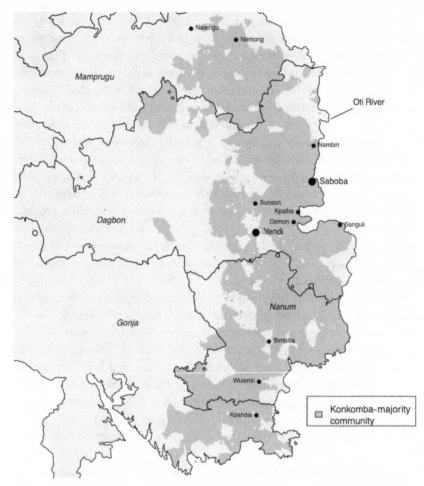

MAP 5.1 Konkomba communities in Northern Ghana. Shaded census Enumeration Areas (EAs) have Konkomba majority populations. The larger polygons demarcate the Mamprusi, Dagomba, Nanumba, and Gonja Traditional Council jurisdictions (see Figure 3.2).

Demon. Upset about injustice faced by their communities, a group came together in 1975 to create the Konkomba Youth Association (KOYA). At the core of KOYA's agenda was an attempt to bring Konkomba communities in closer contact with the state in order to reap more benefits.[26] The organization's second president succinctly described KOYA's

---

[26] The organization also had several other goals, including efforts to end child marriage and encourage girls' school enrollment. Interview with KOYA president, June 23, 2018; interview with KOYA co-founder, Saboba, July 6, 2019. Also see Talton (2010, 153).

mission using a Likpakpaln aphorism: "we say in our language that 'if your mother is not in the funeral house, you will go without food.' Its not that there's no food – there is. But there's no one in the funeral house who will remember that my son has not eaten."[27] In the equivalent American saying, if Konkombas wanted to eat, they would have to gain a seat at the state's table.

This soon became an effort to create their own system of traditional chieftaincy that could equalize their status relative to the "always chiefs" groups. There had been ill-fated earlier attempts to convert clan leadership and the colonial system of liaison chieftaincy (described above) into something more akin to real chieftaincy. In 1945, the liaison chief appointed by the Demon Na in Kpalba sought to free his community from the Demon Na's control by successfully appealing directly to the Ya Na – the Dagomba paramount – to be appointed on equal footing to the Demon Na.[28] Tait (1961, 11) describes how the new Kpalba Na began carrying himself as a Dagomba chief, but claims he still lacked real authority within his community.[29] In the 1960s, I. B. Bawa, the first major Konkomba politician, had advocated that Konkombas create chieftaincy institutions, but this effort went nowhere; at the time, "most Konkomba did not share his view of the necessity of Konkomba chieftaincy."[30]

A key roadblock to efforts like Bawa's – exemplified by the Kpalba Na's need to work through the Ya Na for his appointment – was that one of the only ways for Konkombas to gain the legal status of chiefs was with the approval of existing Dagomba, Nanumba, and Mamprusi chiefs. Chieftaincy appointments in Northern Ghana involve a two-step legal process: first, chiefs are "enskinned" – appointed to a position; second, their appointments are "gazetted" – formally registered with the state – by the National House of Chiefs, a non-partisan state agency that regulates chieftaincy. Crucially, membership in the National House of Chiefs, and its respective Regional Houses of Chiefs, is reserved for already-gazetted chiefs. As of the 1970s, all members of the Northern Region's House of Chiefs were from "always chiefs" groups. Up until 1992, the national government also reserved the authority to unilaterally

---

[27] Interview with former KOYA president, Amasaman, Greater Accra, July 15, 2019.
[28] Talton (2010, 98).
[29] "The present chief of Kpailba [sic] lives to some extent like a Dagomba in that he dresses like one, keeps a horse and wears the types of medicines prepared and sold by Dagomba mallams. But ... he has little authority among his own people: the important men are still the elders [uninkpel]" (Tait 1961, 11).
[30] Talton (2010, 129).

recognize new chiefs, keeping open a slim chance Konkomba chiefs could bypass the House of Chiefs. But successive presidents showed no interest in exercising this power, avoiding backlash from existing chiefs on whom they relied politically.

5.2.2 Divesting Land to Chiefs

The change to land policy in 1979 inspired KOYA to take matters into their own hands. Chapter 3 describes that to this point all land was formally owned by the state. In practice, however, customary land-holding carried on as before. Among the Konkomba, each community's utindam (earth priest) continued allocating plots.[31] For reasons that Chapter 3 explains were exogenous to local developments within Northern Ghana, this changed in the late 1970s. The crumbling military dictatorship of I. K. Acheampong sought the political support of Northern chiefs by creating a state commission to propose constitutional and legal changes that would divest state ownership of Northern land. Reflective of the broader exclusion of Konkombas from the Northern elite at the time, no Konokmbas or members of any other "never recognized" groups were named to the commission, which was dominated by the "always chiefs" groups. KOYA – only recently created – made a formal petition arguing that the customary owners of land in Konkomba communities were the Konkomba themselves. But their appeals were ignored. The Commission's report recommended that all land be vested in chiefs on behalf of their communities. The report specifically argued that the "rightful" owners of Konkomba land were the Dagomba, Nanumba, Mamprusi, or Gonja chiefs in whose jurisdictions Konkomba lived. These recommendations were added to the new 1979 Constitution and then further legislated under the new government of Hilla Limann.[32] They remain in place today.

Chiefs from the "always chiefs" groups now had legal backing to directly tax Konkomba communities for land they had been farming for generations. These new rights were not immediately met with an increase in state enforcement; in the direct aftermath of the land reform, the state's absence meant that *de facto* land allocation in most communities continued as before.[33] But the formal change presented a clear legal path

---

[31] Pul (2003, 67), Jonsson (2009, 510).

[32] Jonsson (2009, 510), Talton (2010, 147–149).

[33] Even to the present, chiefs in some parts of Northern Ghana are still struggling to fully assert their new *de jure* rights (Lund 2008, Yaro 2010).

through which Konkombas could not only attempt to re-assert their formal ownership rights, but free themselves from the control of other ethnic groups and attract more state attention and resources for themselves. KOYA's current president recalls the Konkomba elite's reaction to the 1979 changes: "We know this is our land ... We've always been found here, even before the German times .... This is our area. But somebody says that because you don't have a solidified system of traditional governance, you don't have land."[34] The solution was to try to create that "solidified system" of independent traditional governance.

KOYA leaders active in the aftermath of the 1979 land reform explicitly describe the subsequent push to invent chieftaincy and recast their communities' internal leadership institutions as a publicly-spirited effort in direct response to this change to land policy. As one activist, quoted in the epigraph, described it: "Because the government endorsed the chieftaincy system, the Konkombas and the other acephalous tribes were coerced in a way to go in for a chieftaincy system, rather than keep the uninkpel system."[35] Another similarly explained their motivations, "In Ghana's constitution ... there is [now] a whole thing about chieftaincy. That thing says if you want to be recognized, if you want to do this, if you want to do that, you need chiefs .... It's [*the push for chieftaincy*] because of the legal framework ... if you go outside it, you are nowhere."[36]

5.3 CONFLICT AND CHIEFTAINCY

The resulting push by KOYA to create Konkomba chiefs represented a large rupture with status quo society. Its most immediate, and severe, societal effect was large-scale violence. That violence, in turn, derailed KOYA's initial plans and instead opened up the space for the much more uncoordinated and privately motivated institution-building within Konkomba communities that continues to today.

KOYA's first major effort to establish chieftaincy came in the Nanumba Traditional Area, where surrogate chieftaincy (described above) was most extensive. In 1977, before the land reform, Konkombas living in Bimbilla – the Nanumba capital – had elected their own leader in defiance of the Bimbilla Na – the Nanumba paramount. Konkomba residents began bypassing the Bimbilla Na's court to take disputes directly to this new

---

[34] Interview with KOYA president, Saboba, June 23, 2018.
[35] Interview with Konkomba business leader and KOYA adviser, Saboba, July 6, 2019.
[36] Interview with former KOYA general secretary, Saboba, July 6, 2019.

headman.[37] After 1979, KOYA activists supported the efforts of the new headman and actively urged other Konkomba-majority villages surrounding Bimbilla to similarly elect new leaders. The KOYA president at the time explains KOYA's message:

[W]e can do it in an indirect way. If there's a surrogate chief, we just have our own chief. You can call him whatever you want: we can call him obour [chief], we can call him uninkpel [elder], we can call him utindam [earth priest], and that's who we will go to. Nobody can tell you that your position is not recognized. He is a chief over us if we recognize him. Just ignore the surrogate chief.[38]

But these efforts led to a violent response from the Nanumba, several of whom briefly kidnapped the new Konkomba headman of Bimbilla in April 1981, sparking inter-ethnic clashes in which several hundred people died.[39]

During the violence, Konkomba communities chased off, or killed, many of their Nanumba surrogate chiefs.[40] Afterwards, communities installed their own leaders in the now vacant positions. A Konkomba politician from the Nanumba South district recalls that the selection process for these new chiefs was "just internal to the community, they were not recognized by anybody."[41] The new Konkomba chiefs were not officially enskinned or gazetted, never becoming legally recognized chiefs. But Konkomba elders began carrying themselves as chiefs, taking up the former palaces and duties of the departed Nanumba chiefs.

Villages in the oral history interviews in Nanumba North District narrated similar accounts. In one, the uninkpel of the largest clan appointed himself after the violence to the position of the departed Nanumba chief. Because the chief had also ruled over seven surrounding Konkomba villages, this uninkpel started similarly claiming to be the leader of those seven other settlements, in turn appointing Konkomba uninkpel from the other villages as his "sub-chiefs."[42] *De facto* Nanumba control over land in the area ended, a major improvement in the Konkomba position. Overall, a KOYA leader describes that the events of 1981 meant that the Nanumbas "became afraid to repost chiefs" in many

---

37 Talton (2010, 157–158).
38 Interview with former KOYA president, Amasaman, Greater Accra, July 15, 2019.
39 Pul (2003).
40 Interview with former KOYA president, Amasaman, Greater Accra, July 15, 2019; interview with former KOYA general secretary, Saboba, July 6, 2019; also see Talton (2010, 163).
41 Interview with Konkomba MP from Northern Region, Accra, June 27, 2019.
42 Interview with clan elders in Community # 2, Nanumba North District, July 4, 2019.

villages, which effectively meant that "they had lost their territory," even if they were still formally viewed by the government as the legal owners.[43]

The events of 1981 recurred on a much larger scale in 1994. In the late 1980s, KOYA began petitioning the government to have the existing Konkomba liaison chief in Saboba (the Uchabor-Boro) recognized as an independent paramount chief. Rather than continuing as an emissary of the Dagomba, they envisioned the Saboba chief heading an entirely separate Traditional Council, with no Dagomba involvement. The Saboba chief would then be able to appoint his own hierarchy of chiefs beneath him, guaranteeing unfettered Konkomba land ownership throughout Konkomba settlements along the Oti River. KOYA leaders carefully assembled historical documents attesting to their precolonial independence from Dagbon with the goal of presenting a legal case.[44] But during the 1992 push for democratization, President Rawlings made an additional political concession to chiefs nationwide – for reasons unrelated to the Konkombas' demands – adding a provision to the new 1992 Constitution that removed the government's authority to appoint chiefs directly. Going forward, existing chiefs at the Regional and National Houses of Chiefs had the sole power to approve (gazette) new appointments, which meant the only way KOYA's proposal could succeed was if Dagomba chiefs, including the Ya Na, agreed to relinquish their own power.[45]

KOYA submitted its petition for an independent paramountcy to the National House of Chiefs in 1993. The petition presented a re-imagining of Konkomba precolonial history in which the Konkomba had always had chiefs prior to British rule.[46] KOYA's petition was flatly rejected. In the tense aftermath, a market dispute spiraled into the largest spasm of violence in Ghana's postcolonial history, pitting the Konkomba against the "always chiefs" groups, especially the Dagomba and Nanumba.

---

[43] Interview with former KOYA general secretary, July 6, 2019. This was not universally the case, however. Surrogate chieftaincy continues in a few communities in the Nanumba Traditional Area, including one of the three villages in Nanumba North district included in the oral history interviews, where a Nanumba chief was recently re-installed to oversee an otherwise entirely Konkomba village. Interviews with chief and clan elders in Community #3, Nanumba North District, July 5, 2019.

[44] Interview with former KOYA president, Amasaman, Greater Accra, July 15, 2019.

[45] Pul (2003), Jonsson (2009).

[46] Mahama (2003, 16). This claim appears just as historically dubious as the narrative Dagomba chiefs presented to British officials in the 1920s that they had already conquered the Konkomba prior to colonization.

The fighting stretched throughout much of 1994 into 1995, leaving between 2,000 and 15,000 dead, and as many as 200,000 temporarily displaced.[47]

In the aftermath, the push for chieftaincy took its most significant steps. At the elite level, a coalition of civil society groups and NGOs helped negotiate a peace accord between KOYA and the Dagomba chiefs. The Ya Na agreed to a half measure: instead of allowing for a separate Konkomba Traditional Council, the Ya Na promoted three Konkomba liaison chiefs – in Saboba, Sanguli, and Nambiri – to a higher status within the existing Dagomba Traditional Council, making them equal in rank to the highest level of Dagomba divisional chiefs beneath the Ya Na.

By promoting the three Konkomba chiefs, the Dagomba engaged in a careful re-working of the nomenclature of chieftaincy appointments that would create the outward appearance that the Konkomba now had paramount chiefs, but in practice maintain Dagomba control. Previously, the Ya Na was the Dagomba paramount, with a series of divisional chiefs beneath him. The Ya Na now became the "overlord" of the Dagomba Traditional Council, while each divisional chief was labeled a separate "paramount" chief, even as they were appointed by and still accountable to the Ya Na, who retained ultimate land authority. The three promoted Konkomba chiefs were given an equal rank as these elevated Dagomba "paramounts," and ostensibly would gain the power to now appoint new Konkomba chiefs beneath them within each of their local areas. A Konokmba participant in the negotiations explains, "Our chiefs were elevated to paramount chief status on the same day as Dagomba chiefs. So Saboba chief is now a paramount chief, the Sunson chief is now paramount chief, the Savelugu chief is paramount chief. They are all given paramountcies."[48]

Simultaneously, at the grassroots level, the bottom-up process that occurred in Konkomba communities in the Nanumba Traditional Area spread more widely. Individual Konkomba communities began taking their own initiative to select community leaders and start informally labeling them as "chiefs" to create the appearance of legal legitimacy for their claims to independent land ownership. A former KOYA president recalls that "as a result of the 1994 conflict, so many leaders sprung up all over the place. Chiefs. They were not gazetted, but these are people we refer to as chiefs – ubour ... They were not officially recognized as the chiefs,

[47] Pul (2003), Van der Linde and Naylor (1999). For more information, see Chapter 8.
[48] Interview with former KOYA general secretary, Saboba, July 6, 2019.

but we started calling them chiefs." In addition to existing uninkpel who added a new title, many were simply local people "who showed leadership qualities ... who just came up" and started being referred to as chiefs.[49]

5.4 CHIEFTAINCY IN THE WAKE OF VIOLENCE

The greatest growth in Konkomba chieftaincy has occurred after the 1994–1995 violence. But because the Konokmba continue to lack an independent Traditional Council – without a clear hierarchy of chiefs with well-delineated jurisdictions – the expansion of Konkomba chieftaincy has become a "free-for-all," with communities and aspiring chiefs all improvising in search of legitimacy for these new institutions. A Konkomba leader describes the prevailing system of chieftaincy appointments by noting that "at the moment, we are all living in a vacuum and everybody is trying to do what they want to do" for themselves.[50] Attracting private goods from the state, not securing group-wide recognition and land ownership, is now the principal motivation for most actors creating chieftaincy.

There are now multiple conflicting and legally ambiguous paths available to Konkomba seeking to become chiefs, with prospective chiefs forum shopping in search of the most promising path for their private ambitions. These paths are visualized in Figure 5.1. Figure 5.1 focuses on the Dagbon Traditional Council, but a similar transformation has also happened within the jurisdictions of the other "always chiefs" groups. Prior to the mid-1990s (Panel (a)), only a small handful of Konkomba were appointed as liaison chiefs by supervisory Dagomba chiefs above them in the chieftaincy hierarchy. After the violence (Panel (b)), many new Konkomba chiefs now appoint themselves entirely informally with the consent of their communities, others are appointed by the new Konkomba "paramounts" elevated after the violence, while others continue to seek out formal appointments under the supervisory authority of Dagomba (and Nanumba and Mamprusi) chiefs, at times against the wishes of their own communities.

The free-for-all has had three effects. First, with each passing year there is a growing number of Konkomba communities with someone who refers to himself as "chief." Yet, second, very few wield the social legitimacy and influence of the more established chiefs from other ethnic

---

[49] Interview with former KOYA president, Amasaman, Greater Accra, July 15, 2019.
[50] Interview with business leader and KOYA adviser, Saboba, July 6, 2019.

Panel (a): Before

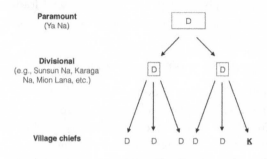

Paramount
(Ya Na)

Divisional
(e.g., Sunsun Na, Karaga
Na, Mion Lana, etc.)

Village chiefs

Panel (b): After

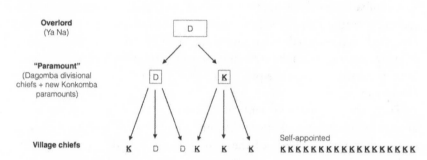

Overlord
(Ya Na)

"Paramount"
(Dagomba divisional
chiefs + new Konkomba
paramounts)

Village chiefs

FIGURE 5.1 Approximate organization of Dagbon Traditional Council, before and after mid-1990s. Panel (a): A mock organizational chart of the chieftaincy hierarchy prior to the violence. The paramount (Ya Na) appointed Dagomba (D) divisional chiefs who, in turn, appointed various Dagomba (D) village-level chiefs. (The chart is simplified; there are more than 2 divisional chiefs and more than 3 villages per division.) At this time, a small set of Konkomba (K̲) "liaison chiefs" were appointed by Dagomba divisional chiefs. Panel (b): After the violence there were now three types of Konkomba chiefs: (i) A few "liaison chiefs" had been elevated to "paramounts" (divisions) under the Ya Na and could appoint Konkomba village chiefs; (ii) Additional village chiefs sought appointments from existing Dagomba divisional chiefs; and (iii) The largest set of new village chiefs were self-appointed, outside the hierarchy altogether.

groups. The large majority of Konkomba communities still do not have chiefs who wield unfettered power over land or act as important electoral brokers (see Chapter 7). Only a small fraction of these chiefs – as few as twenty-five across the over 700 Konkomba-majority communities in Northern Ghana (as per the 2010 census) – have been formally gazetted by the National House of Chiefs.

Third, and most importantly, the scramble for chieftaincy has birthed new internal conflicts, demonstrating that even if this attempt at institution-building has been incomplete, the new chiefs' presence is significantly transforming Konkomba society, with chieftaincy now the site of significant political contestation. Many of the early activists instrumental in the initial push for chieftaincy now express significant reservations about it, worrying that the new conflicts emerging around competing claims to chieftaincy will ultimately undermine any public benefits. Yet the haphazard creation of chieftaincy continues despite their concerns. I outline the conflicting pathways now available to become a Konkomba chief and then describe each of these effects in turn.

5.4.1 The Chieftaincy Free-for-All

There are now many paths to becoming a Konkomba chief. First, some become chiefs solely through the informal consent of their communities. As described above, this was particularly common among the first waves of chiefs installed immediately after the 1981 and 1994–1995 violence. The oral histories in Nanumba North District interviewed what one might term as "aspirational chiefs": uninkpel carrying themselves as chiefs within their communities, despite having no formal appointment. And indeed, some of the other respondents in these same communities denied that these uninkpel were truly their chiefs, indicating that informal consent is often fragile and transient, subject to local rivalries among families within a community.[51]

Second, some chiefs within the territory of the Dagomba Traditional Council are now formally enskinned by one of the three new Konkomba paramounts.[52] KOYA had hoped the elevation of a Konkomba paramount would allow him to appoint a coherent hierarchy of gazetted village-level chiefs beneath him. But the promotion of three co-equal Konkomba chiefs (see above), rather than one, complicated this vision. Appointment authority remains fractured; without agreement about which chief is senior to the others, each paramount's authority does not extend in practice beyond his own extended clan. The Saboba chief (the Uchabor-boro) only enskins chiefs within the Bichaborb

---

[51] Interviews in Community #1, Nanumba North District, July 4, 2019; Interviews in Community #2, Nanumba North District, July 4, 2019.

[52] Most of these new appointments are still yet to be legally gazetted by the National House of Chiefs, however.

clan, the extended lineage group indigenous to Saboba, and does not wield unified appointment authority within any clear territorial jurisdiction; Konkomba communities just a few miles from Saboba have chiefs enskinned by other chiefs.[53] A Konkomba politician laments, "we still don't have a central authority ... Each clan is independent."[54]

Third, some aspiring chiefs have started acquiescing to continued rule by chiefs from other groups by going to them directly for formal appointments. Supervisory chiefs from the "always chiefs" ethnic groups no longer collect rents or demand free labor from Konkomba communities – these practices ended after the violence of the 1980s and 1990s. But many still benefit from Konkomba communities by taking payments directly from aspiring Konkomba leaders in return for appointing them as chiefs under their jurisdiction. Interview subjects narrated multiple situations in which Konkombas have "chopped" – bought – appointments in this manner, seeking out the Dagomba, Nanumba, or Mamprusi chiefs who have historical claims over their villages from the colonial era.[55] As one example, one Konkomba MP openly described how his brother secured an appointment directly from the Nayiri, the Mamprusi paramount chief, by explicitly paying him for it.[56]

Aspiring Konkomba chiefs are turning to Dagomba, Nanumba, and Mamprusi chiefs for appointment for two reasons. First, they place high value on a formal enskinment over simply securing informal consent from community members because they think a formal position is necessary to attract the full attention of politicians – and the lucrative private benefits they believe might come with it (e.g., see Chapter 7). A KOYA leader observed that many Konkomba now "want to become a chief because they think that if you are a chief, you are recognized by the politicians."[57] The "aspirational chiefs" described above from the Nanumba North district both were actively seeking formal enskinment from the Bimbilla Na, the Nanumba paramount, even as they both traced their positions to the violent expulsion of previous Nanumba chiefs by their own communities.[58]

[53] Interview with former KOYA general secretary, Saboba, July 6, 2019; interview with former MP of Saboba, Accra, July 8, 2008.
[54] Interview with former MP of Saboba, Accra, July 8, 2008.
[55] For example, interview with Konkomba educators, Saboba, May 17, 2019.
[56] Interview with Konkomba MP from North East Region, Teshie-Nungua, Greater Accra, July 28, 2019.
[57] Interview with Konkomba business leader and KOYA adviser, Saboba, July 6, 2019.
[58] Interviews in Community #1, Nanumba North District, July 4, 2019; Interviews in Community #2, Nanumba North District, July 4, 2019.

Second, turning to the formal legal authority of the "always chiefs" groups is a means to resolve internal Konkomba succession disputes, as state courts still recognize the appointment authority of Dagomba, Nanumba, and Mamprusi chiefs. In disagreements about which clan should hold the leadership within a Konkomba village, the clan able to "chop" a chieftaincy position from a Dagomba chief will usually win out in the state's eyes. This is part of why the appointment authority of the new Konkomba paramounts remains so limited. Other clans living near the new paramounts often seek out appointments from Dagomba chiefs instead to get out from the control of the clan of the neighboring Konkomba chief.[59] This has even led to cases where there are two rival chiefs claiming to be the official leader of the same community; one enskinned by a Konkomba chief, another by a Dagomba chief, or even two enskinned by different Dagomba chiefs, with rival families forum-shopping in search of higher-level chiefs willing to legitimize their respective claims.[60]

Early KOYA leaders are dismayed at the way in which these actions are unraveling the original goal of creating a unified, hierarchical set of traditional leaders who could help Konkombas secure political independence, and with it, greater state recognition of their communities' needs. "It's a great blow on us .... Unfortunately, we have elements within us who think that there's nothing wrong with working with the Dagombas to create confusion," one argued.[61]

5.4.2 Limits to Legitimacy and Effectiveness

One key result of this free-for-all is that many of the new Konkomba chiefs have been unable to project significant *de facto* authority within their communities, regardless of the legal status of their appointments. Writing of the new chiefs emerging in the 1990s, Dawson (2000, 5) notes that Konkomba chiefs "still wield only illusory power in the contemporary context." Many politicians campaigning in Konkomba areas do not think the new chiefs are important electoral brokers, as examined in Chapter 7; "it's not like other places where the chief can come out openly and decree that this is the person" the community will vote for, one MP

---

[59] Interview with Konkomba educators, Saboba, May 17, 2019.
[60] Interview with KOYA president, Saboba, June 23, 2018; interview with Konkomba business leader and KOYA adviser, Saboba, July 6, 2019.
[61] Interview with Konkomba business leader and KOYA adviser, Saboba, July 6, 2019.

reflects.[62] Some chiefs admit the limits of their influence, such as a sub-chief appointed near Saboba by the Uchabor-boro, who argued, "I don't see any change [in real power]. The new paramountcies have no power, they have no jurisdiction to do anything, they are just empty vessels."[63]

Chiefs' substantive influence is limited for several reasons. First, because the majority are only appointed informally, they do not have the full range of powers of chiefs from other groups. This includes that they cannot defend their land rights in court, for example, and are often not included at formal government and political events that summon the chiefs of a district. This limits their influence over the flow of government benefits to their communities. A KOYA leader complains, "In other strong traditional authority systems, before a government official is appointed from your area, those chiefs are consulted. But Saboba here, it is not done ... They will just go and appoint somebody without consulting the chiefs."[64] Instead, most Konkomba chiefs only have grassroots influence insomuch as their communities voluntarily give it to them. The KOYA business leader narrates, "when you say you are a chief, what does it mean? It doesn't mean much ... [A chief's influence] depends on your personal status. How have you conducted yourself to merit respect?" Chiefs that do not have the internal respect of their communities do not "function as such as real chiefs."[65] An uninkpel interviewed in the oral histories in one community said of his village's self-declared chief, "the people don't regard him as a chief," because he appointed himself without consulting them.[66]

Second, and in turn, chiefs are not afforded this respect when their appointments are seen as illegitimate by community members. Why should this particular person now get the right to lead the community and not someone else? In what had previously been flat, acephalous societies, there can be little agreed-upon means to resolve such disputes. But appointments made by outsiders to the community are especially suspect. A district assemblymember (elected local councilor) in a town near Saboba included in the oral history interviews said of his community's chief, "people don't mind him." In his view, the chief was "imposed" on the community by the Uchabor-boro (the Saboba paramount) against residents' wishes. Several interview respondents claimed that the uninkpel

[62] Interview with Konkomba MP from Northern Region, Accra, July 26, 2019.
[63] Interview with Konkomba sub-chief, Saboba, July 2, 2008.
[64] Interview with KOYA president, Saboba, June 23, 2018.
[65] Interview with Konkomba business leader and KOYA adviser, Saboba, July 6, 2019.
[66] Interview will clan elder in Community #2, Nanumba North district, July 4, 2019.

still were the town's real leaders, not the chief. A retired teacher explained, "[the chief] can't influence anybody. It's the elders. It's all the elders ... Nobody goes to his palace."[67]

Disrespect for chiefs is particularly common if appointments are seen as "chopped" via private arrangements with other ethnic groups' chiefs. One of the co-founders of KOYA laments the role Dagomba chiefs are playing in appointing locally illegitimate Konkomba chiefs, and argues that Dagomba chiefs are exploiting these requests to select Konkomba chiefs who will be most willing to accommodate continued Dagomba claims to power:

[Y]ou've gone to a Dagomba who will agree with you and you come back and say you are now a chief, when we know that we should have the right to choose our own chief. How do you want me to agree with you and to support you? That will not happen ... When our people ... go to Dagombas to pick the title of chief. ... [the Dagomba chiefs] would rather look amongst us and pick somebody they think they can get to be with them. Can use him.[68]

Unsurprisingly, community members often refuse to acknowledge the authority of chiefs they believe were appointed for this reason. The most prominent example is the current Saboba chief himself (the Uchabor-Boro). He turned to the Sunson Na – a Dagomba of nominally equal rank in the Dagomba Traditional Council – for an appointment to back his claim over a rival family in a protracted dispute. In interviews, many educated Konkomba activists were apoplectic that their chief would collaborate with the Sunson Na, as it backtracked on all their work to secure Konkomba independence from Dagomba authority. They claimed many Saboba residents now refused to meet with him or honor any of his requests, although it was clear the chief still enjoyed support from his own local faction.[69]

Third, some respondents argued that chiefs face deeper challenges establishing legitimacy because the trappings of their positions – their styles of dress, their chosen titles, even their palaces – are modeled on "foreign" customs borrowed from other groups and imported into Konkomba society. A Konkomba educator argued that "our chiefs are

---

[67] Interviews with assemblymember, retired teacher, and clan elder in Community #2, Saboba district, May 17, 2019.

[68] Interview with KOYA co-founder, Saboba, July 6, 2019.

[69] One interview subject refused to even call the Uchabor-Boro by his title or name over the course of a two hour interview, referring to him dismissively only as "that boy." Interview with former KOYA general secretary, Saboba, July 6, 2019.

not so influential because chieftaincy is a borrowed tradition."[70] A KOYA leader similarly linked the weakness of Konkomba chiefs to the fact that "our chieftaincy is not tailored on a Konkomba stand."[71] A Konkomba chief himself observed that chiefs struggled for legitimacy because everything is modeled on the "the Dagomba tradition. But we have our own traditions and we should be given the chance and opportunity to practice our own traditions."[72] He argued that as long as Konkomba chiefs remained formally under the Traditional Councils of the other groups it would not be possible to appropriately reimagine chieftaincy customs in a way that is more in line with Konkomba culture.

Yet even if this cultural adaptation reduces internal legitimacy, it is clear that Konkomba chiefs themselves feel pressure to incorporate other groups' traditions as a way of legitimating themselves to external audiences, especially to the government and politicians. Talton (2010, 163) argues that as new Konkomba chiefs began emerging after the 1981 violence, whether they had legitimacy in their communities was somewhat besides the point: "[t]he extent to which they actually exercised political authority within Konkomba society was not as important as what they represented to outsiders." Projecting an image as a powerful chief – which means adopting the cultural referents associated with chieftaincy elsewhere in Northern Ghana – is a means of attempting to leverage chieftaincy into greater recognition from the state – to benefit the community and, especially, to the private benefit of the new chief. In this way, the symbolism associated with chieftaincy in other ethnic groups appears to carry real value for Konkombas seeking chieftaincy positions, even independently of a chief's true substantive authority in a community.[73]

A clear example comes from the oral histories in Nanumba North mentioned above. The two informal Konkomba chiefs in these villages had both recently constructed chief's palaces – circular structures with pointed metal roofs – in front of their homes in the past two years, explicitly mirroring the architectural style of Dagomba and Nanumba palaces.[74] A KOYA leader explains that chiefs like these men often build such palaces both to try to signal to politicians who visit the community that they are important and must be engaged with, and as a means of

---

[70] Interview with Konkomba educators, Saboba, May 17, 2019.
[71] Interview with former KOYA general secretary, Saboba, July 6, 2019.
[72] Interview with Konkomba sub-chief, Saboba, July 2, 2008.
[73] For a similar focus on the symbolic power of chieftaincy, see Lund (2006, 2008).
[74] Interviews in Community #1, Nanumba North district, July 4, 2019; interviews in Community #2, Nanumba North district, July 4, 2019.

staking out their family's claim to hereditary succession. Given the informality and contested nature of their current appointments, they fear the chieftaincy could easily pass to another family upon their death; placing the community's palace at their own home strengthens the succession case of their own children.[75]

5.4.3 Effects on Society

Konkomba chiefs' struggles to project authority and build popular legitimacy do not mean that chieftaincy has been inconsequential, however. Instead, the main consequences come less from the direct effects of chiefs themselves than from the indirect effects the bottom-up scramble for chieftaincy has had on social cohesion and conflict. In this way, the process of institution-building has become more important than the result. The most direct effects on conflict were the two major clashes in 1981 and 1994–1995, described above, that left thousands dead. But the period since the mid-1990s has also seen increasing intra-communal, intra-Konkomba conflict. Resistance to the invention of chieftaincy is actively occurring, but is focused within communities, rather than targeted as a backlash against the state or the state policies that had inspired the effort to create chiefs.

Internal conflicts are now especially common around chieftaincy succession. In groups like the Dagomba, positions rotate among different families ("gates") and chiefs themselves rotate across communities during their careers.[76] In others, including many of the chieftaincies created by the British, positions are hereditary. But with no history of chieftaincy, Konkomba culture offers no template for succession. Most positions are at most a few decades old – if not considerably newer – with few, if any, established precedents. "We don't have any documentation as to how one becomes a chief," a KOYA leader explains.[77]

This poses a recurring problem: whenever a chief dies, succession can be bitterly disputed by different families within a community who employ their own selective reading of the improvisatory history of Konkomba chieftaincy to validate their claims. These conflicts have become particularly challenging in communities that informally installed their own chiefs in the aftermath of the 1981 and 1994–1995 violence. Another former

---

[75] Interview with former KOYA president, Saboba, July 3, 2008.
[76] Staniland (1975). See Chapter 7.
[77] Interview with former KOYA president, Saboba, July 3, 2008.

KOYA leader explains that even when communities were able to agree on who should be their leader immediately after the violence,

> The negative side comes in when those people pass on. Their children want to assume the position, as if it's a family thing. Meanwhile, their sons may not have the same leadership qualities as their fathers ... But there's no way to say this is how we did it in the past, because it's brand new ... It has brought about a lot of conflicts.[78]

As a result, many of these communities briefly had chiefs with social legitimacy, but have seen that fall apart once chieftaincy reaches its second generation. At a higher level, similar intra-family disputes are now ongoing for each of the three new Konkomba paramounts, generating fears of violence as rival factions in Saboba, Sanguli, and Nambiri all make competing claims. For example, as of mid-2019, the Sanguli paramount chief officially enskinned by the Ya Na could not even travel to Sanguli to take up his position in person because of threats on his life from supporters of a rival claimant who had gone ahead and named himself paramount chief instead.[79]

Successive governments are now meddling in these disputes, hoping to secure the loyalty of at least a subset of voters in a particular community by backing their families' factional positions. My interviews included regular discussions of rumors that both of Ghana's major parties were funding the court cases of particular chieftaincy claimants,[80] paying Dagomba chiefs on claimants' behalf for appointments,[81] and even building new palaces for chiefs to legitimate claims to succession.[82]

At the same time that chieftaincy is creating new internal conflicts, it has begun undermining the effectiveness of pre-existing leadership institutions that have been used in the past to manage intra-communal disputes and coordinate collective action. Uninkpel and utindam (tendanas) still exist, but they are losing authority as they face competition from chiefs. This has manifested in conflicts over who really has the authority to allocate land within villages: the utindam – following long-standing custom; or the chiefs – who now claim land ownership under the legal regime adopted after 1979. The current KOYA president narrates,

---

[78] Interview with former KOYA president, Amasaman, Greater Accra, July 15, 2019.
[79] Interview with Konkomba business leader and KOYA adviser, Saboba, July 6, 2019.
[80] For example, interview with former KOYA general secretary, Saboba, July 6, 2019.
[81] For example, oral history interviews, Community #3, Saboba district, May 17, 2019; interview with Konkomba educators, Saboba, May 17, 2019.
[82] Interview with leaders of the Konkomba Students Association, Saboba July 3, 2008; interview with former KOYA president, Saboba, July 3, 2008.

Land ownership has really become a big problem for us [again]. Because now our people are indoctrinated to think that the chiefs own the land. But deep down, they know that the chief doesn't own the land. So when the utindam is coming now, chiefs are now also pushing, saying that we must both benefit from it. So its gotten to the point that even now if the utindam gives you the land, the chief has to stamp on the paper, to legalize that land for you.[83]

Similarly, elder Konkomba activists who have observed the long-run changes occurring since the 1970s lament how the authority of uninkpel has diminished with the rise of chieftaincy. One argues, "the uninkpel system is no more functioning. It's not functioning ... I think the coherent structure of a community as bonded together by the presence of uninkpel ... is falling apart."[84]

Instead of creating new, more powerful leaders within communities, chieftaincy may only be helping Konkomba society become *more acephalous* in practice by resulting in a situation in which chiefs both lack the social legitimacy to govern effectively themselves, but are also now undermining the pre-existing community leadership institutions that had functioned before their emergence.

5.5 ENDOGENOUS INSTITUTION-BUILDING AMID STATE SCARCITY

Chapter 2 argues that the hypothetical ability of the state to provide resources more valuable than otherwise available in society can encourage endogenous societal changes, with societal actors trying to reconfigure local institutions to better access state benefits. The Konkomba effort to create chieftaincy exemplifies this dynamic. Unlike top-down state-building initiatives in which an outside force attempts to impose changes on a society, such as in the examples famously chronicled by Scott (1998),[85] bottom-up changes like those among the Konkomba happen without the presence of a third party enforcer. Communities must take on state-like work on their own.[86] This creates collective action and coordination problems that generate the conflicts witnessed within Konkomba society.

The impetus for bottom-up efforts to become more legible can be rooted in either public or private motives, in pursuit of public or private

---

[83] Interview with KOYA president, Saboba, June 23, 2018.
[84] Interview with Konkmoba business leader and KOYA adviser, Saboba, July 6, 2019.
[85] Similarly, see Hyden (1980).
[86] Bierschenk and Olivier de Sardan (2014).

goods. Public benefits include having a clearly identifiable leader who reduces the state's difficulty in interacting with a community, and, especially after 1979, entitling community members to land ownership. But there are also private stakes: the individuals picked as new chiefs often appear primarily motivated by the potential rent-seeking opportunities, including the ability to collect payoffs from politicians seeking votes (see Chapter 7), or to use control over land to engage in informal taxation. The examples above show that these public and private motives are in direct tension, especially when competition over who, specifically, gets to be a new chief leads those designing new institutions to place private interests above community interests. Aspiring chiefs invest in building would-be palaces in front of their homes, for example, not because it will help attract state resources to the broader community, but because it will both help them attract politicians' attention and secure their family's succession case.

The risk that public and private motives work at cross-purposes is especially acute because there are no widely agreed-upon templates for what these new institutions should look like. British state-builders inventing chieftaincy elsewhere in Northern Ghana largely imposed rigid one-size-fits-all institutions on society. By contrast, the creation of new Konkomba institutions has been more syncretic, or blended, with Konkomba actors innovating their own *ad hoc* system of chieftaincy by reassembling various "shards," in Galvan's (2004) metaphor, of other institutional traditions into a new mosaic, layering leadership systems borrowed from other ethnic groups on top of pre-existing Konkomba social practices.[87] In the examples above, existing Konkomba institutions, such as the uninkpel system, were adapted into something else, fused with cultural ideas about chieftaincy from Dagomba society, with existing Konkomba uninkpel essentially "changing hats," claiming new duties, and styling themselves as Dagomba chiefs. That this cultural borrowing draws heavily on Dagomba and Nanumba culture is not a coincidence – given their physical proximity and the decades-long experience of living under Dagomba and Nanumba rule, these "always chiefs" groups provide a readily accessible "cultural tool kit" on which aspiring Konkomba chiefs can draw.[88]

---

[87] Similarly, this could be referred to as a process of "bricolage" (Hagmann and Peclard 2010).

[88] Firmin-Sellers (2000) similarly documents how the bottom-up reimagining of institutions elsewhere in Ghana (in her case, over land ownership) is constrained by the

Different combinations can be made from among these borrowed institutions, however, exemplified by the multiple paths to a chieftaincy appointment visualized in Figure 5.1. Would-be chiefs search for institutional forms that maximize their private ability to access state resources. This risk is heightened by the fact that aspiring chiefs are building new institutions to appeal to two very separate audiences: their own communities, but also a much more external audience of politicians and state officials. What the state thinks chieftaincy looks like – the symbology that has emerged around Dagomba and Nanumba chiefs, for example – is quite important for what Konkomba chiefs feel they must look like too in order to gain the state's respect. And official enskinments by higher-level Dagomba and Nanumba chiefs are still highly valued because of what they signal to this external audience, even as I document how seeking these appointments clearly undermines new Konkomba chiefs' legitimacy with their own communities.

The result is that these attempts to state-build from below are fraught with potential conflict, but in a very different form than that on which Scott (1998) and other scholars of grassroots resistance in the countryside typically focus. Even as Konkomba activists explicitly view the state as "coercing" them into chieftaincy, resistance to this effort has been more internal to society, pitting the winners and losers of the new institutional forms that are emerging against each other, rather than targeted against the state itself.[89] Building on this analysis, Chapter 8 explores in more detail the implications for political violence of the new internal conflicts created by bottom-up societal changes that attempt to reduce state scarcity.

5.6 CONCLUSION

The bottom-up adoption of Konkomba chieftaincy offers a refracted parallel of the earlier experiences of "invented chiefs" groups. At the outset of the twentieth century, the colonial state forcibly imposed chieftaincy on these other acephalous societies, using the creation of chieftaincy as a central state-building initiative in the hinterland. Initially, these other groups' chiefs faced nearly identical challenges asserting legitimacy as

---

available "tool kit" of easily accessible cultural referents of what new institutions might look like.

[89] Boone (2014) similarly describes how state decisions to empower customary institutions can deflect conflict away from central state leaders towards more local actors.

new Konkomba chiefs today. Chapter 3 describes that colonially imposed chiefs were at times ignored and resisted by their communities, while succession eventually became bitterly disputed in the absence of clear traditions.[90] But whereas the continued backing of state authority allowed colonially invented chiefs to gradually amass power in their communities, Konkomba chiefs face the same challenges today without any unified state support.

Unlike the colonial invention of chieftaincy, Konkomba chieftaincy has emerged *despite* the state's intentions, not because of them. There is no evidence state leaders intended the 1979 reform to produce Konkomba chieftaincy. This was instead a concession to existing chiefs to buy their support, much as Baldwin (2014) documents elsewhere. Rather than facilitate the creation of new chiefs, the main state body regulating chieftaincy – the National House of Chiefs – has been a major impediment, blocking KOYA's petitions for an independent paramountcy and not yet gazetting the large majority of self-declared Konkomba chiefs. But Konkomba activists make clear that what happened after the land reform was still tantamount to the state having invented chieftaincy. State policy unintentionally *forced* Konkomba communities to pursue chieftaincy institutions of their own.

In this way, the Konkomba experience demonstrates the other side of the theory in Chapter 2. Where the state retains substantial resource advantages relative to its society, contact with the state can provide highly prized access to rents. Even if the state remains "weak" in most conventional ways the term is defined – including bureaucratically incapable and limited in its formal presence – these resource advantages allow the state's actions to have powerful indirect effects because the possibility of better accessing state resources creates incentives for societies to *change themselves* in response.

More specifically to the study of traditional leaders in African politics, the Konkomba case also helps show how nominally "traditional" institutions can still be incredibly in flux in the modern period and are not purely descendants of either precolonial systems of governance or the actions of the colonial state. The exact incentives for acephalous societies in hinterland regions to invent their own chiefs from scratch in the modern period may be different in other African countries that have different legal regimes around chieftaincy than Ghana's; the push for chieftaincy

---

[90] Awedoba et al. (2009). See Chapters 7 and 8.

examined in this chapter was a direct response to a particular postcolonial land policy.

But the Konkomba experience still presents useful lessons. It suggests a need for significantly more caution in assuming that precolonial institutions persist across rural Africa – an implicit assumption of most analyses employing data from Murdock (1967), for example. Essentially all of the ethnic groups in Northern Ghana coded in these analyses as acephalous now have some form of chieftaincy and political centralization, even if imperfectly institutionalized. Moreover, in contrast to Mamdani's (1996) claim that chiefs were artificial impositions of the colonial state, the Konkomba experience helps echo Spear (2003), Galvan (2004), and others in showing that "traditional" institution-building could also be a much more modern, postcolonial process, rooted in the agency of indigenous populations.

This concludes Section II. Section III pivots to the political consequences of the social changes – both direct (Chapter 4) and indirect (Chapter 5), colonial and postcolonial – created by Northern Ghana's scarce state.

PART III

POLITICAL EFFECTS

6

Dynasties

'Ah, are you the only people!? Just last time it was your brother, now you too want to come.'
– MP from Upper West Region describing responses to his
first run for office, July 2019

Windfalls from early contact with the state did not create economic inequality alone. They also generated persistent political inequality. Part III turns to the political effects of the state's isolated actions in the hinterland. I begin by focusing on the first major political outcome described in Chapter 2: dynastic politics, a form of elite capture in which the same small set of families dominates politics across generations.

Recent scholarship on political dynasties focuses on how the electoral incumbency advantage – especially within legislatures – sustains families in power in modern democracies by conferring three types of benefits on the descendants of politicians: campaign resources, name recognition, and, at least in some contexts, social leverage over voters.[1] But much deeper sources of advantage – long pre-dating democratization – may also deliver these same benefits and explain which families dominate contemporary elections.[2] This is especially where the state remains scarce over time and the economy underdeveloped, allowing early allocations of advantage to stick.

---

[1] Dal Bo et al. (2009), Chandra (2016), Querubin (2016), Geys and Smith (2017), Smith (2018).
[2] Jensenius (2016).

Dynastic families in Northern Ghana are widespread, extending decades prior to democratic rule into the colonial era, or earlier. These dynasties connect initial colonial-era chiefs – often installed into their positions directly by the state – to modern elected officeholders. Across all elections in Ghana's history, I estimate below that over 41 percent and 47 percent of the Members of Parliament (MPs) ever elected from the "invented chiefs" and "always chiefs" groups, respectively, are from the same families that British officials recognized or elevated as chiefs in the first decades of colonial rule. In some areas of the North, a casual observer might even think that these chiefly families are the "only people" in power, as the MP quoted above described the joking reaction of voters to his first campaign. He ran for office in a constituency in which multiple uncles had held government positions, his cousin had recently been named paramount chief, and his grandfather and great-grandfather had been the paramount chief in the past.[3] The prevalence today of dynastic families like this MP's is even greater than in the core cases of dynastic politics examined in recent literature – such as India, Japan, and the Philippines[4] – even as I show in the following text that the mechanism of persistence is not the modern incumbency advantage, but the much earlier accumulation of advantages through contact with a scarce state.

I link Northern Ghana's dynasties to the first two state interventions described in Chapter 3: the colonial invention of chieftaincy and differential access to education for chiefs' families. The analysis combines archival data on chiefs from the early colonial period, a new dataset of all parliamentary candidates in Northern Ghana from the country's first elections in 1951 to present, and qualitative life history interviews with a random sample of twenty contemporary MPs. I find that the descendants of early colonial chiefs still make up a substantial portion of parliamentary nominees and winners today. The rate of dynastic holding is now highest among the "invented chiefs" ethnic groups, for whom the majority of MPs elected in 2016 were still descended from the specific chiefs installed by the colonial state in the early twentieth century. Dynasties also remain common among the "always chiefs" groups, but are virtually nonexistent among the "never recognized" groups, for whom chieftaincy has only emerged much later, if at all (Chapter 5), and elite families were not elevated through concentrated access to early state windfalls.

---

[3] Interview with Wala MP from Upper West Region, Accra, July 13, 2019. Paternal male first cousins are typically referred to as "brothers."

[4] Chandra (2016), Querubin (2016), Smith (2018).

Classic studies of weak states often take the existence of local political elites as a given and then explore the conditions under which those elites are able to subvert and capture the state. This chapter instead interrogates where those elites come from in the first place. I show that many dynastic elites in Ghana's hinterland are creations of the very state over which they now exercise control. The chapter suggests that the state's few actions in the hinterland can significantly reshape who holds political office over time, even in a context in which many analysts would view the state as lacking autonomy relative to these same elites.

In the next section, I introduce the literature on dynastic politics and explain how early contact with the state provides an alternative form of incumbency advantage that offers long-run political rewards. After a brief overview of elections in Ghana, I introduce the data sources and present descriptive results on patterns of dynastic capture. I then show that early access to education for chiefs' families provides a primary mechanism for these patterns. I end by addressing alternative explanations.

6.1 DYNASTIES AND THE SCARCE STATE

Political dynasties are a form of elite capture. I define a dynasty as when members of the same family hold political power across multiple generations within the same area. While some scholars restrict focus narrowly to dynasties only within the same office – such as when an MP is replaced in the same seat by a descendant – the definition used here reflects the fact that the most relevant local political positions may evolve over time, especially in countries that only recently democratized.

Dynasties exist in both advanced and developing democracies, including in the US.[5] In Japan, Smith (2018) estimates that 28 percent of contemporary legislators are from dynastic families. In the developing world, dynasties have been explored in India – where Smith (2018, 5) estimates 12 percent of legislators are dynastic – and the Philippines – where as many as 41 percent of legislators have family ties to previous generations of politicians.[6]

There is debate about the consequences of dynastic politics.[7] In some contexts, scholars suggest it may be a beneficial means to select for

[5] Dal Bo et al. (2009).
[6] Chandra (2016) and Querubin (2016), respectively.
[7] Chandra (2016), Smith (2018).

politicians with the connections and skills to govern effectively. But others view dynasties as fundamentally at odds with accountability, even a form of oligarchy corrosive to democracy.[8] The latter concern is especially acute where the state is weak.[9] Capture by "neo-feudal" elites is a key indicator in O'Donnell's (1993) characterization of "brown areas" of the state where nominally democratic elections do not survive. In the Africanist literature, state weakness is often explicitly described in terms of a lack of state autonomy, with capture by narrow sets of elites seen as a leading indicator of the state's inability to govern effectively.[10]

What often links studies of dynastic politics across these contexts is the observation that families sustain themselves in power by holding some combination of three similar sets of advantages: access to rents, used to fund campaigns; name recognition, which serves as a valuable political brand; and, especially in contexts with clientelist politics, social influence over voters. Recent literature on dynasties mostly focuses on a single explanation for the origins of all three: the electoral incumbency advantage.[11] Focused specifically on dynasties within legislatures, these studies argue that legislative office begets legislative office, with a candidate more likely to be elected as MP if her parent was also an MP and could accumulate the advantages of office.

Incumbency surely is not the only source of familial political advantages, however.[12] Candidates from families already atop underlying socioeconomic hierarchies will also have better access to campaign financing, including network connections to other elites from which to raise funds, better name recognition, or better leverage over voters lower in the social ladder. In many new democracies, especially in Africa, the ability to self-finance campaigns is particularly important for electoral success, providing a leg up to socioeconomic elites.[13] Moreover, in countries still in their first generation of sustained electoral competition, there may have not been enough time for electoral incumbency advantages to accumulate, potentially privileging elites that pre-date democratization over those only created by modern access to rents from office. For example, in countries

---

[8] Michels (1915).

[9] Smith (2018).

[10] Migdal (1988), Chabal and Daloz (1999), Englebert (2000).

[11] Dal Bo et al. (2009), Querubin (2016), Smith (2018). This overwhelming focus appears motivated, at least in part, by an empirical exigency – the ease of estimating the causal effects of incumbency via regression discontinuity designs.

[12] Indeed, Fiva and Smith (2018) show that even in Norway, incumbency advantages are not a sufficient explanation for dynastic politics.

[13] Koter (2017), Arriola et al. (2021).

that only democratized in the 1990s, the first generation of politicians to reap large rents from elected positions are often still themselves active in politics, without a full opportunity yet for the next generation to attempt to follow them in power. In these contexts, understanding dynastic politics requires broadening focus beyond legislative incumbency.

If not incumbency, where else might dynastic elites come from? One potential answer is the economy: dynastic political elites are those with the largest private fortunes. But this only kicks the question back a step – how did specific families first get their opportunities to amass wealth? An alternative answer is instead society, with dynastic families emerging from long-standing societal hierarchies, even dating to the precolonial period. But the theory in Chapter 2 suggests that in hinterland regions like Northern Ghana neither factor – allocations of advantage from the private economy or societal institutions – can be understood separately from the historical actions of the state. By providing windfalls of resources, the scarce state is the key actor who assigned initial opportunities to amass wealth in the private economy. And even where the state is weak, we cannot assume that underlying societal hierarchies represent an unbroken legacy of the past. Instead, the scarce state's actions have the potential to create new inequality from scratch.

This chapter suggests that modern-day dynastic elites in hinterland regions of new democracies emerge more from predemocratic state-building – the allocation of windfalls to narrow sets of recipients at the outset of society's contact with the state – than from either the benefits of modern incumbency or the accumulated advantages of precolonial social hierarchy. Evaluating this argument means looking at dynasties that connect early office-holding in the initial period of modern-state building with contemporary political power. In the early colonial period, chiefs were the only political position held by the African population. Today, after democratization, chiefs' formal governance role is greatly diminished and elected politicians instead hold the primary power. I thus focus on dynasties that link early colonial chiefs to contemporary elected officials.[14]

6.2 ELECTIONS IN GHANA

Ghana had sporadic early experiences with elections and then became a consolidated democracy from the 1990s. The first elections were in

---

[14] Chapter 7 instead examines family persistence within individual chieftaincy positions themselves.

1951, under colonial rule, after the British allowed for internal elections to the Legislative Assembly. While legislators from the South were directly elected via popular vote, the Northern Territories were initially only allowed to select their nineteen legislators through an electoral college. Delegates handpicked by colonial officials – representatives of each Native Authority – voted in a single constituency, with nineteen votes to spread among thirty-four candidates.[15]

All subsequent elections have instead used first-past-the-post plurality rules in single-member districts. The British granted popular suffrage in the North in the next elections in 1954, dividing the Northern Territories into twenty-six constituencies. Additional elections were held again in 1956, also in twenty-six constituencies, choosing the representatives who would serve in Ghana's first Parliament upon independence. In these early elections, a pan-ethnic Northern-based political party – the Northern People's Party (NPP) – emerged to represent Northern interests and serve in opposition against Kwame Nkrumah and the CPP, which held the national majority. After independence, Nkrumah consolidated authoritarian power, declaring Ghana a one-party state. Over this period, many NPP MPs were coopted into the CPP. Some who resisted were jailed or exiled.[16]

Democracy returned briefly in 1969 and 1979. After the 1966 coup, the new military regime allowed for elections in 1969. The new parliament served until an additional coup in 1972. Democracy returned again in 1979. For the first time, a Northerner, Hilla Limann, a Sisala ("invented chiefs"), was elected President. Limann's government was short-lived, however, overthrown in yet another coup by Jerry Rawlings in late 1981, which ushered in another decade of autocratic rule under the Provisional National Defence Council (PNDC). In 1992, Rawlings acceded to democratization, converting the apparatus of his PNDC regime into one of Ghana's two main contemporary parties – the National Democratic Congress (NDC) – and standing for the presidency as a civilian.[17] Although the 1992 Parliamentary election was uncontested amidst a boycott and allegations of fraud, Ghana has now held competitive elections for President and Parliament every four years since 1996. The other major party is the New Patriotic Party (NPP); although it shares

---

[15] Ladouceur (1979, 79–82).

[16] Ladouceur (1979). Subsequent parliamentary elections in 1965 were undemocratic, with a single hand-picked CPP candidate standing in each constituency.

[17] Riedl (2014) provides a detailed history of this transition.

an acronym with the earlier Northern People's Party, the contemporary NPP's electoral base is broader and based in the South. Today, Northern Ghana elects fifty-seven of the country's 275 MPs.

Across these decades, the most important elected office other than President has been the legislator (MP). MPs become powerful local patrons within their constituencies and, if elected from the President's party, can be selected to serve in the Cabinet, gaining significant power over national policymaking. The only other powerful local political officials – today called District Chief Executives (DCEs), or mayors – continue to be presidential appointees (see Chapter 3). The only other elected positions, from 1988 on, have been to non-partisan District Assemblies and Unit Committees, equivalent to City and Village Councils. But district assembly and unit committee members have very limited substantive authority. As a result, I focus on legislative (MP) elections.

6.3 DATA: MATCHING NAMES

I draw on archival sources to identify the names of all candidates in each legislative election since 1951, as well as the names of the chiefs serving in each community across Northern Ghana in the early colonial period. Figure 6.1 provides examples of the two main archival sources. The data on politicians includes all 761 nominated candidates for Parliament (or Legislative Assembly) in Northern Ghana from 1951 to 2016.[18] I restrict to the major parties in each election, plus any independent or minor party candidates who received more than 10% of the vote, in order to remove a handful of fringe vanity candidates from each election who are unlikely to be real political elites. The overwhelming majority (97.4 percent) of these candidates are men; the analysis below does not have an adequate sample size of female MPs to unpack gender differences in dynastic politics.[19]

The data on chiefs uses colonial-era registers listing the names of all chiefs recognized by the British in each community in the Northern Territories as of three moments in time: 1909, only seven years after the colonial invention of chieftaincy began; 1922; and 1934, just before colonial officials formally empowered the Native Authorities (see Chapter 3)

---

[18] This spans all contested elections across this period: 1951, 1954, 1956, 1969, 1979, 1996, 2000, 2004, 2008, 2012, and 2016.

[19] There are high barriers to women's representation in Northern Ghana, including due to conservative gender norms. Women make up a much smaller proportion of parliamentary candidates and nominees in this region compared with the rest of the country (Ichino and Nathan 2022).

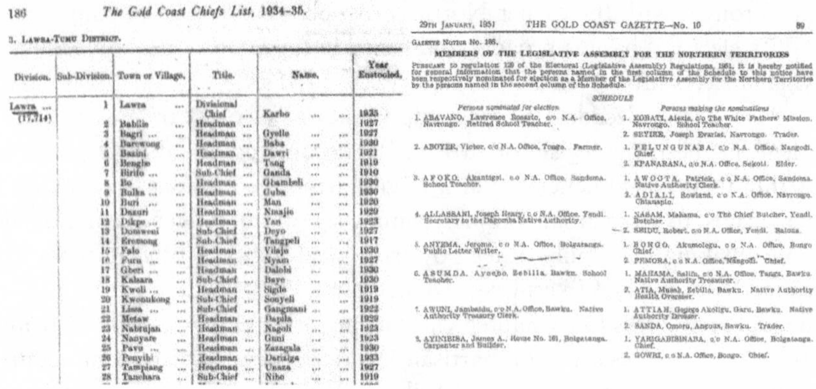

186 *The Gold Coast Chiefs List*, 1934–35.

3. Lawra-Tumu District.

Division.	Sub-Division.	Town or Village.	Title.	Name.	Year Enstooled.
Lawra ... (17,714)	1	Lawra ...	Divisional Chief ...	Karbo	1935
	2	Babilie ...	Headman ...		1927
	3	Bagri	Headman ...	Gyelle	1927
	4	Barewong ...	Headman ...	Baba	1930
	5	Bazini ...	Headman ...	Dawri	1921
	6	Benghe ...	Headman ...	Tang	1919
	7	Birifo	Sub-Chief ...	Ganda	1910
	8	Bo	Headman ...	Gbambeli	1930
	9	Bulka	Headman ...	Guba	1930
	10	Buri	Headman ...	Man	1920
	11	Dazuri ...	Headman ...	Nmajie	1929
	12	Dikpe	Headman ...	Yan	1923
	13	Domweni ...	Sub-Chief ...	Deyo	1927
	14	Eremong ...	Sub-Chief ...	Tangpeli	1917
	15	Falo	Headman ...	Vilaje	1930
	16	Fura	Headman ...	Nyam	1927
	17	Gberi	Headman ...	Dalobi	1930
	18	Kalsara ...	Sub-Chief ...	Baye	1930
	19	Kwoli	Headman ...	Sigde	1919
	20	Kwonukong ...	Sub-Chief ...	Souyeli	1919
	21	Lissa	Sub-Chief ...	Gangmani	1922
	22	Metaw ...	Headman ...	Dapila	1929
	23	Nabrujan ...	Headman ...	Nagoli	1923
	24	Nanyare ...	Headman ...	Guni	1923
	25	Pavu	Headman ...	Zazagala	1930
	26	Penyibi ...	Headman ...	Darizige	1933
	27	Tampiang ...	Headman ...	Unaza	1927
	28	Tanchara ...	Sub-Chief ...	Nibe	1919

29th January, 1951 THE GOLD COAST GAZETTE—No. 10 89

Gazette Notice No. 186.

MEMBERS OF THE LEGISLATIVE ASSEMBLY FOR THE NORTHERN TERRITORIES

Pursuant to regulation 129 of the Electoral (Legislative Assembly) Regulations, 1951, it is hereby notified for general information that the persons named in the first column of the Schedule to this notice have been respectively nominated for election as a Member of the Legislative Assembly for the Northern Territories by the persons named in the second column of the Schedule.

SCHEDULE

Persons nominated for election	*Persons making the nominations*
1. ABAVANO, Lawrence Rosario, c/o N.A. Office, Navrongo. Retired School Teacher.	1. KOBATI, Alexis, c/o The White Fathers' Mission, Navrongo. School Teacher.
	2. SEYIRE, Joseph Evarist, Navrongo. Trader.
2. ABOYER, Victor, c/o N.A. Office, Tongo. Farmer.	1. PELUNGUNABA, c/o N.A. Office, Nangodi. Chief.
	2. KPANARANA, c/o N.A. Office, Sekoti. Elder.
3. AFOKO, Akantigsi, c/o N.A. Office, Sandema. School Teacher.	1. AWOGTA, Patrick, c/o N.A. Office, Sandema. Native Authority Clerk.
	2. ADIALI, Rowland, c/o N.A. Office, Navrongo. Chiasapio.
4. ALLASSANI, Joseph Henry, c/o N.A. Office, Yendi. Secretary to the Dagomba Native Authority.	1. NASAM, Mahama, c/o The Chief Butcher, Yendi. Butcher.
	2. SEIDU, Robert, c/o N.A. Office, Yendi. Balona.
5. ANYEMA, Jerome, c/o N.A. Office, Bolgatanga. Public Letter Writer.	1. BONGO, Akumolegu, c/o N.A. Office, Bongo. Chief.
	2. PEMORA, c/o N.A. Office, Nangodi. Chief.
6. ASUMDA, Ayoebo, Zebilla, Bawku. School Teacher.	1. MAHAMA, Salifu, c/o N.A. Office, Tanga, Bawku. Native Authority Treasurer.
	2. ATIA, Musah, Zebilla, Bawku. Native Authority Health Overseer.
7. AWUNI, Jambaidu, c/o N.A. Office, Bawku. Native Authority Treasury Clerk.	1. ATTIAH, Gegiro Akoligu, Garu, Bawku. Native Authority Dresser.
	2. SANDA, Omoru, Angoua, Bawku. Trader.
8. AYINIBISA, James A., House No. 161, Bolgatanga. Carpenter and Builder.	1. YARIGABISINABA, c/o N.A. Office, Bolgatanga. Chief.
	2. GOWRI, c/o N.A. Office, Bongo. Chief.

FIGURE 6.1 Archival sources for name matching. The Gold Coast Chiefs List (left) provides an official registry of chiefs in each community in the Northern Territories at different moments of time in the colonial period. The indigenous-language given names in this list are often now the surnames of these chiefs' descendants. Historical election returns back to Ghana's first election in 1951 are reconstructed from the official government gazette (right).

to collect taxes and begin constructing schools. These lists thus identify who was placed into chieftaincy positions *before* the main windfalls from chieftaincy – including privileged access to education for chiefs' family members (Chapter 4) – began being realized on a large scale.

I link the legislative contestants to the early chiefs by matching politicians from the same constituencies by name to the chieftaincy registries. Most Northern ethnic groups use similar naming conventions for male children. Most sons have an indigenous-language given name, a religious English (Christian) or Arabic (Muslim) given name, and one (or more) indigenous-language surname(s).[20] Surnames indicate the patriline; typically, a son's surname is either his father's or paternal grandfather's indigenous-language given name. When his paternal grandfather was an important local figure, such as the chief, the grandfather's name is particularly likely to be used. Royal families in Northern Ghana are called "gates," a local term for an extended lineage group. Rather than

[20] The main exception is two overwhelmingly Muslim "always chiefs" groups – the Dagomba and Gonja – in which a substantial portion of the population uses purely Arabic (Muslim) names that make it difficult to infer family ties because they repeat a small set of possibilities (e.g., Mohammed, Adam, Ibrahim). But this is not common among "invented chiefs" (or "never recognized") groups, the main focus here. Both the overall descriptive patterns and the regression analyses that I report below are robust to excluding all Dagomba and Gonja politicians.

the father's or grandfather's name as surname, members of prominent royal gates often instead share a common surname among all male descendants – the given name of the first chief in their family – expressly to signal their chiefly heritage.[21] As a result of these conventions, politicians' names often contain direct information about chiefly ancestry.

I take all name fragments from the politicians and chiefs and remove English or Arabic given names. I also remove any names that match the eight most common indigenous names in the combined set.[22] With these deletions, I am not able to infer family ties for 151 politicians, who I remove from the denominator below. This only significantly affects estimates for the "always chiefs" groups, which account for 89% of these deletions.[23] I narrow the set of possible matches using fuzzy string matching before manually checking each match. Importantly, I only code a politician as matching the same name as an early colonial-era chief if the chief served in a community that is *within the same local constituency in which the politician contested*.[24]

This measure cannot perfectly identify each politician's descent, but is not systematically biased in favor of either over- or under-stating the total number of politicians descended from early colonial chiefs. I validate this with life history interviews with a random sample of current Northern MPs, interviewing twenty from a sample of twenty-seven, stratified to include equal numbers from the three types of ethnic groups ("invented chiefs," "always chiefs," "never recognized").[25] Seventeen of twenty interviews confirmed the coding of their chiefly heritage was

---

[21] For example, the first chief listed in Figure 6.1 is Karbo, the chief of Lawra mentioned in the opening anecdote in Chapter 1. His descendants continue to use Karbo as their surname to signal their membership in the Karbo royal family (gate). Many chieftaincy positions (at least nominally) rotate among gates. Each time a chief dies, all male cousins from the gate whose turn it is to hold the position are potential candidates. Having the gate name as a surname is one way to limit questions about one's eligibility.

[22] These names (e.g., "Mahama") are outliers; too common to reliably signal family ties. Most politicians with one of these names still have other indigenous-language names remaining that can be used to match. Moreover, after removing these few common names, the average chiefs' name fragment appears just 1.2 times, with little chance the same politician could match to multiple chiefs from the same small geographic area.

[23] Only 4% of candidates from "invented chiefs" ethnic groups had names that could not be used to infer family ties.

[24] For the 1951 election there were no constituencies in the North, but the archival documents helpfully list each candidate's hometown (see Figure 6.1, right panel). This is used instead.

[25] Seven MPs declined to participate. More details on these interviews are in the Appendix.

correct, one was ambiguous,[26] and two were incorrect – one false positive and one false negative. These MPs represent a particularly hard test: politicians from 2019 are, by default, the most generationally removed from the colonial era, with the greatest chance an early chief's name is no longer used. Beyond validating my measure of dynasties, I also draw on the interviews to help evaluate potential mechanisms for dynastic office-holding.

6.4 PATTERNS OF DYNASTIC OFFICE-HOLDING

I begin with descriptive evidence before pivoting to qualitative sources that help explain the mechanisms behind these patterns. The key descriptive statistics are in Figures 6.2, 6.3, and 6.4, each organized by the three ethnic categories introduced in Chapter 3. Figure 6.2 shows the prevalence of dynasties in Northern Ghana across all elections dating back to 1951. Figure 6.3 focuses on Ghana's initial colonial-era elections in the 1950s, while Figure 6.4 zooms forward to the two most recent elections in the data (2012 and 2016) to demonstrate the historical persistence of dynasties into the contemporary period.[27]

Among the "invented chiefs" groups, Figure 6.2 shows that a third (34 percent) of politicians who have ever democratically contested for Parliament match to chiefs in their same local areas in 1934 or earlier. This was highest in the independence-era, when 64 percent of candidates were from chiefly families (Figure 6.3), but still includes nearly a third (32 percent) of the candidates from "invented chiefs" ethnic groups contesting in recent elections (Figure 6.4). The representation of descendants of early chiefs is even higher among elected MPs, with candidates related to early chiefs winning disproportionately whenever they contest. Figure 6.2 shows that 41 percent of MPs ever elected from "invented chiefs" ethnic groups have been from the same families installed as chiefs in their constituencies in the early colonial period. This peaked in the 1950s, when 81 percent of elected MPs were from this narrow stratum of families (Figure 6.3). But decades later, Figure 6.4 shows that nearly a majority of recent MPs (45 percent) from these groups were still descended from early colonial chiefs. After the 2016 election, this reached 53 percent (nine of seventeen). This is a high degree of dynastic capture relative to other cases. For example,

---

[26] Due to limited recall of his family history, one MP could not confirm the coding one way or the other.

[27] Ghana's 2020 elections occurred after the data collection for this book.

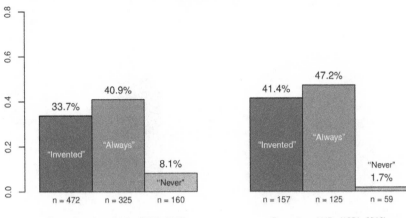

FIGURE 6.2 Proportion of candidates (left) and elected MPs (right) with family ties to early colonial chiefs (in office 1909–1934), across the 1951 through 2016 legislative elections. Proportions are split by ethnic category in Table 3.1.

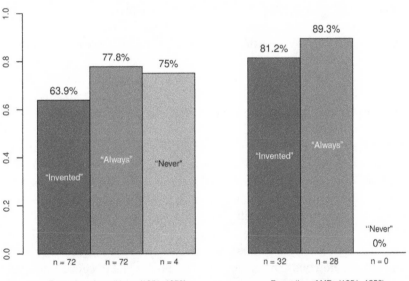

FIGURE 6.3 Proportion of candidates (left) and elected MPs (right) with family ties to early colonial chiefs (in office 1909–1934), during the initial colonial-era 1951, 1954, and 1956 legislative elections. Proportions are split by ethnic category in Table 3.1.

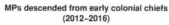

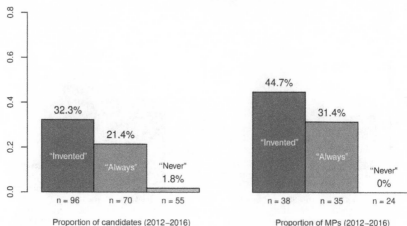

FIGURE 6.4 Proportion of candidates (left) and elected MPs (right) with family ties to early colonial chiefs (in office 1909–1934), during the recent 2012 and 2016 legislative elections. Proportions are split by ethnic category in Table 3.1.

Smith (2018, 5) estimates that 12 percent, 28 percent, and 41 percent of legislators are from dynastic political families in India, Japan, and the Philippines, respectively – three central cases for the recent literature on dynasties.

There is similar evidence of dynasties among the "always chiefs" groups, although my estimates are much noisier for these groups due to the name matching limitations described above. Figure 6.2 shows that 41 percent of candidates and 47 percent of MPs ever elected from these precolonially centralized groups also appear to be from the same families serving as chiefs in their local constituencies in the early colonial period. This similarly peaked in the initial independence era, with 89 percent of elected MPs from these families (Figure 6.3), though the candidates from these chiefly families still make up a significant plurality of all MPs from the "always chiefs" groups in recent elections – 31 percent (Figure 6.4). Notably, however, in these most recent elections Figure 6.4 suggests that there is now *more* dynastic office-holding linked to chiefs among the "invented chiefs" groups, upon whom the state artificially imposed chieftaincy institutions, than in the "always chiefs" groups, which organically developed chieftaincy in the precolonial period.

By contrast to both of these groups, there is little evidence of dynasties linked to early colonial chieftaincy among the "never recognized" groups in any of Figures 6.2, 6.3, or 6.4. This is essentially by definition: this third category largely did not have chiefs in the early colonial period from whom dynasties could begin (Chapters 3 and 5). Just 8 percent of all candidates since 1951 from "never recognized" groups share a name with an early colonial chief. While this includes three of the (just) four candidates who ever ran from these groups in the 1950s (Figure 6.3), no "never recognized" MPs were elected in that period and none of the dozens of MPs elected from these groups since democratization in the 1990s has had a name match to an early chief.[28] In the final section of this chapter, I directly consider and rule out the possibility that there are instead other types of dynasties among the "never recognized" groups rooted in something other than early access to chieftaincy.

Overall, across all ethnic groups, family ties to an early colonial chief are electorally valuable. It is not just that many candidates with chiefly heritage run for office, but they are also more likely to win whenever they do so. In a regression with constituency-year fixed effects, I find that candidates linked to early colonial chiefs are 11.0 percentage points (95 percent CI: 0.2, 21.8) more likely to win than others contesting for the same seat.

Yet while many contemporary MPs have family ties to early colonial chiefs, there is much less evidence for the formation of legislative dynasties. This is inconsistent with the main source of dynastic politics being the legislative incumbency advantage, as examined in other cases. I compare the names of MPs to previous MPs in their same parliamentary constituencies to see if the same family has held the same parliamentary seat over time. Just 9 percent (seven) of the MPs descended from early colonial chiefs also have a name match with a previous MP from their constituency. In total, less than 3 percent of elected MPs have a direct name match to a previous MP from their same constituency.[29] Rather than arising from more recent advantages accumulated via modern incumbency, dynastic families in Northern Ghana instead appear to be drawing on much earlier and longer-standing advantages tied to their relatives' office-holding as chiefs long before independence and democratization.

---

[28] The few matches in Figure 6.3 are Bimobas, an exception consistent with the theory. Representing just 3 percent of the Northern population, the Bimoba are the earliest "never recognized" group to have had multiple "liaison" chiefs appointed in the colonial period under the supervising authority of an "always chief" group (the Mamprusi).

[29] I address why this number is so low in the final section of the chapter.

Finally, while these estimates focus on Parliament, these are not the only positions of power that dynastic families can hold. Thirty-six percent and 41 percent of the cabinet ministers ever appointed from the "invented chiefs" and "always chiefs" groups, respectively, are also linked to early colonial chiefs.[30] Members of chiefly families are also commonly appointed as DCEs (district mayors), although I lack systematic data on DCE appointments over time with which to examine this directly. Finally, many chieftaincy positions in the "invented chiefs" groups are also hereditary within families. In a parliamentary constituency in which a descendant of an early chief serves as MP, it is also likely that a close relative is simultaneously serving as the chief in one of the local communities.

6.5 WHY DID DYNASTIES EMERGE?

The early windfall of resources conferred on chiefs' families by the state provides the most straightforward explanation for the electoral advantages of chiefs' descendants. Chapter 4 shows that the families of colonial-era chiefs benefited from disproportionate early access to education, providing a significant head start into the formal sector economy in a context in which human capital was otherwise very scarce. This opened paths to elected office in several ways. In the initial elections in the 1950s – before students enrolled in the wave of new schools opened in the 1950s (Chapters 3 and 4) had even graduated – there were very few Northerners with the English literacy to launch viable political careers. In many areas of the North, the sons of chiefs simply comprised almost the entire pool of realistic candidates. In later elections, access to human capital has become more widespread. But the compounded economic resources that early contact with the state provided to chiefly families have now given chiefs' descendants a significant advantage in self-financing increasingly expensive campaigns for office. In the remainder of this section, I trace out how state-provided windfalls elevated candidates from chiefly families in both independence-era and modern-day elections, respectively.

At first blush, linking dynasties to the effects of state action may appear inconsistent with the sustained success of candidates with early chiefly heritage among the "always chiefs" groups. Some chiefly families from the "always chiefs" groups have been in socially advantaged positions

---

[30] No (0 percent) "never recognized" cabinet ministers have similar name matches.

since the precolonial period, before the modern state emerged.[31] These families then received the same windfalls from state action as in the "invented chiefs" groups, including preferential early access to education for their children. For the "always chiefs" groups, it is thus difficult to separate out the effects of pre-existing social stratification from the effects of the modern state's actions.

While my data do not allow for a causal test of these two mechanisms, reasoning through a comparison to the "invented chiefs" groups suggests that the colonial state's actions, not precolonial class stratification, comprise the dominant explanation. Separating these two potential sources of advantage is possible among the "invented chiefs" groups, where only one of the two mechanisms is operative: Chapter 3 describes that rather than building on pre-existing hierarchies, the initial selection of chiefs in the "invented chiefs" groups was highly arbitrary, with state officials reordering what were otherwise flat, acephalous societies. Yet Figures 6.2, 6.3, and 6.4 show that the prevalence of dynastic office-holding has been roughly equal across the "always chiefs" and "invented chiefs" groups. In Ghana's most recent elections, there are now even *more* dynasties among the "invented chiefs" groups: in 2016, for example, 32 percent of candidates and 53 percent of elected MPs from "invented chiefs" groups were descended from early colonial chiefs versus 22 percent and 39 percent, respectively, from "always chiefs" groups. This suggests that the advantages produced by state action – present in both sets of groups – are already enough to have produced the level of dynastic office-holding seen in the "always chiefs" groups, even without any further effect from precolonial advantages of chiefs' families.

6.5.1 Dynasties in the Independence Era

The pool of viable candidates was limited in the 1950s, the period reflected in Figure 6.3. One set of possible candidates were the chiefs themselves, already active in local governance through the Native Authorities. A small set of senior chiefs also served on the Northern Territories

---

[31] Unlike in the "invented chiefs" groups, however, chiefs in the "always chiefs" groups often rotate across different communities over their careers, rather than remain fixed as local elites in a single area. In addition, new "royal" families are created each generation, with commoners appointed into entry-level positions. This potentially reduces the overall degree to which precolonial advantages persist in individual families across time. Chapter 7 details these institutions of rotation in more depth.

Council, an advisory body to colonial leadership. But chiefs faced hurdles to seeking positions in the new legislature created in 1951. Few chiefs in this period were educated or literate, having come of age before meaningful school construction. While literacy was not a formal requirement for elected office, this limited their ability to contribute in Assembly meetings, which were in English. Ladouceur (1979, 73) describes that Northern Territories Council meetings in the late 1940s were laborious affairs, with each chief speaking through his own translator, in his own language; "much was lost because of the continuous interpretation between English and the various vernaculars." Moreover, sitting chiefs were often unable to take time away from their communities to travel to Accra to sit in the Assembly.

The second set of potential candidates was the small set of Northern "literates" who had completed school and could better engage as equals with Southern politicians in the Assembly. The main wave of primary school construction in the North discussed in Chapters 3 and 4 only began in the late 1940s, picking up in earnest after 1951. The at most several hundred literate Northerners already old enough to contest for Assembly seats in the early 1950s had attended school a generation earlier at the North's tiny set of selective boarding schools. They largely worked in just two professions – as government teachers and as clerks for the Native Authorities.[32] Among the teachers, training college brought many to the South (the first teachers' college in the North only opened in 1944, in Tamale). While there, trainees were introduced to the emerging Southern political parties and independence movement, providing connections to Southern politicians that would later help their political careers.[33] In addition, given there were still so few Northern schools, many in this generation of literate Northerners had attended school together, forming personal bonds they would draw on when entering politics.[34] Most importantly for the formation of dynasties, because the colonial state gave significant preference to chiefs' families in admission to the North's

[32] Ladouceur (1979, 84).

[33] For example, in the early elections of the 1950s, the CPP partnered with several of these teachers to expand its party organization into the North for the first time (Ladouceur 1979).

[34] Goody (2004). In the archival documents on school admissions examined in Chapter 4, the lists of names read as a virtual "who's-who" of the independence-era Northern political elite. In Gandah's (2004) memoir of his school days in the late 1930s and early 1940s, there are footnotes after his first mention of nearly every schoolmate – and many of his teachers – that describe how that person went on to some important political or state position in the 1950s–1970s.

first boarding schools, the large majority of these men were the sons (or nephews) of chiefs.[35]

In the first election in 1951, multiple chiefs sought office directly; eight of the first nineteen legislators were sitting chiefs, chosen by an electoral college itself largely comprised of chiefs. But by 1954, with the shift to mass suffrage, most chiefs bowed out voluntarily. Only three of the twenty-six Northern MPs elected in both 1954 and 1956 were chiefs.[36] Instead, the chiefs' children stepped up in their place. One of the new MPs elected in 1954, Abayifaa Karbo from Lawra, the son of a chief (and a future chief himself), explained why this happened:

It was impossible for the chiefs to appreciate what was going on in the South; they were isolated and out of touch with the South. They had difficulties in understanding the debates ... so they trusted the literates, who were mostly their own sons. Their educated sons understood much better than they themselves.[37]

The central advantage of these new MPs from chiefly families was less that they were personally very well-resourced to fund a campaign for office – their government salaries as teachers or clerks were high relative to prevailing local wages, but still quite modest – than that they formed nearly the entire available pool of people with the literacy necessary to serve effectively in the legislature. They were also virtually the only Northerners with the knowledge of Southern parties and issues to become effective politicians in a Southern-dominated political system. Ladouceur (1979, 87) describes that so many chiefs' sons who had been trained as teachers went into politics at the same time in this period that it briefly created a shortage in the supply of qualified teachers in the North.[38]

By contrast, no politicians (zero) from the "never recognized" groups were elected in each of 1951, 1954, or 1956.[39] The evidence in Chapters 4 and 5 shows that this was both because there were still many fewer educated people from these groups at the time, and because the first electoral constituencies were drawn in such a way as to dilute the power of "never

---

35 Ladouceur (1979, 84–85).
36 Ladouceur (1979, 84).
37 Quoted in Ladouceur (1979, 85). The Karbo family's dynasty is highlighted in Chapter 1.
38 By 1954, there were only 206 Northerners trained as teachers, of whom just 20 had achieved the certificate qualifying them for leadership positions at schools; twelve of these twenty senior teachers were elected to the Legislative Assembly in 1954 alone (Ladouceur 1979, 87).
39 Only four candidates from these ethnic groups even contested: three in 1954 and one in 1956.

recognized" communities and allow their "overlords" from the "always chiefs" groups to win in their place.

The ability of chiefs' educated sons to dominate initial elections contrasts notably from independence-era elections in non-hinterland regions of Africa. In Southern Ghana, examined closely in Chapter 9, education was much more widespread much earlier. These same initial elections pitted a conservative "old guard" aligned with the interests of prominent chiefs against a more radical set of educated commoners aligned with Nkrumah's CPP. Many CPP leaders, including Nkrumah himself, were not from upper-class chiefly families at all, but had gained access to education through private mission schools, which were much more widely available in the South and allowed more children from non-elite backgrounds to also access human capital. Migdal (1988, 135–137) describes early postcolonial politics in Sierra Leone as defined by a similar dynamic, with traditional chiefs contesting against a new urban educated elite that had emerged separately from the chiefly upper class.

Chapter 2 argues that the key difference between these cases and Ghana's hinterland is the scarcity of human capital, an outcome of differences in the state's presence and resource advantages relative to society. Human capital was less narrowly concentrated in a small set of families where there was either greater state provision of education or greater private provision via missionaries. But in the hinterland, where the state was both relatively absent and the only widespread provider, its decision to prioritize chiefs' children led directly to chiefs' families dominating the first wave of elections.

6.5.2 Dynasties in Contemporary Elections

More striking is the degree to which descendants of early colonial chiefs continue to be substantially overrepresented in more recent elections, even six decades after independence. Since the 1950s, the pool of possible candidates has expanded significantly, with human capital now much more widely available. The dominance of descendants of early colonial chiefs moderately declined relative to the 1950s in Ghana's 1969 and 1979 elections and then bottomed out to its lowest level in 1996.

A flood of new faces entered Northern politics in 1996 eager to participate after a decade and a half of autocratic rule. At the same time, many earlier political elites remained in the diaspora; many elite Ghanaians with the financial and educational ability to be mobile had left Ghana in pursuit of better opportunities during the economic crisis and autocratic repression of the 1970s and 1980s.[40] With the party system still consolidating and candidate nomination procedures *ad hoc* and largely up to the personal discretion of party leaders, the bar to gaining a nomination in 1996 was unusually low, especially for those willing to stand in opposition to the NDC, which dominated the North at the time.[41] For 1996, just 17 percent (seven of forty-two) of candidates from "invented chiefs" groups and 19 percent (four of twenty-one) of candidates from "always chiefs" groups in the data have name matches to early colonial chiefs.

Yet by two decades later, with Ghana's new democratic system solidified, the descendants of early colonial chiefs were able to reassert their previous dominance. Figure 6.4 shows that the near-majority of MPs from the "invented chiefs" groups who have won recent elections are now from the same narrow stratum of chiefly families that dominated Ghana's earliest elections. The return of chiefly dynasties appears due to the financial advantages many of these families have accrued over generations from the economic head start provided by early access to education. The descendants of early colonial chiefs are often among the wealthiest and best-educated elites from their poor, rural constituencies, with the personal resources and elite connections needed to win increasingly expensive modern elections, including fiercely contested primary elections.

Similar to other new democracies in Africa, MPs in Ghana largely self-finance their own campaigns.[42] Since the 1990s, clientelism has been an increasingly widespread feature of electioneering, requiring large war chests to provide favors and benefits to voters.[43] Once in office, MPs are deluged with requests from constituents for patronage and personal assistance that far exceed both their official salaries and the constituency development funds they receive from the government. MPs regularly draw on private funds to meet voter requests.[44]

Surveys of candidates suggest that campaign costs have risen in recent decades, especially since the mid-2000s.[45] A central reason is a shift in how the major parties nominate parliamentary candidates. From the 1950s through the 2000 elections, candidates were mostly handpicked

[40] Akyeampong (2000).
[41] Riedl (2014), Ichino and Nathan (2018).
[42] Koter (2017), Arriola et al. (2021).
[43] Lindberg (2003), Asante and Kunnath (2018), Nathan (2019), Brierley and Kramon (2020).
[44] Lindberg (2003), Lindberg (2010).
[45] Asante and Kunnath (2018).

by party leaders. Since 2004, both parties have instead introduced competitive primaries, while only handpicking candidates in special circumstances. These primaries are dominated by vote buying and have come to serve as a form of auction that screens for the highest-bidding aspirants who can best fund the local campaign apparatus on the party's behalf. Simply being nominated can now cost many tens of thousands of US dollars, dramatically more than in 1996.[46]

This system biases in favor of wealthier candidates who have worked in the formal sector outside the rural North, especially those who have lived abroad, where the most lucrative private employment opportunities often lie.[47] It also biases in favor of candidates with personal connections to other elites in the capital or diaspora that can be used for fundraising. Notably, this shift in candidate selection mechanisms also coincided with the significant repatriation of elite Ghanaians from abroad in the early 2000s as the economy improved and the opposition NPP took power, reducing the risk of repression to previous PNDC (NDC) opponents.[48] In combination, the increased supply of elite candidates and higher bar to nominations has raised the barrier to entry for prospective candidates significantly, advantaging the historical chiefly elite.

In the life history interviews, many current MPs from the "invented chiefs" and "always chiefs" ethnic groups described how they were able to parlay their families' preferential early access to education from the state into elite professional opportunities in urban areas or abroad, and now have returned (often from abroad) to their ancestral Northern constituencies to convert that financial success into political careers. In line with the argument in Chapter 2 and the related account in Wantchekon et al. (2015), a central feature in their narratives of their own political success is that their families were educated *early* – before most others in their home communities – when the relative return to education was higher than it would become once most other Northerners also gained access to it.

A typical example from the interviews is a Dagaba ("invented chiefs") MP from the Upper West Region. The MP's grandfather was appointed in the early colonial period to the invented chieftaincy in a village within his constituency, and was then succeeded as chief by the MP's father, who as a chief's son was also among the first Dagaba to ever attend school in

---

[46] Ichino and Nathan (2012, 2018).
[47] Pinkston (2016), Ichino and Nathan (2022).
[48] Hamidu (2015).

the late 1920s and then be hired into the colonial civil service. Because of his father's government job, the MP grew up in a wealthier town outside his constituency where there were better schools. After graduating, he attended university abroad, ultimately receiving a PhD in the UK. After decades abroad, he moved back to Ghana in 2008 explicitly to run for office. He could draw on income from business in the UK to privately bankroll his campaigns; in fact, he had already been quietly funding his party's previous MP in the constituency while still living abroad.[49]

Another MP from Upper West Region similarly described how his father – the son of a chief – was also among the very first people from his ethnic group to attend school and be hired into the civil service. He explained that this meant his family was already wealthier than others in the constituency from childhood. He and his siblings "were brought up ... to feel that you are the best in the place. There was no need for money. I didn't need money to be able to go to school." He added that his father's education and government position "gave me a lot of confidence that I was better than others," inspiring the MP to seek a political career after his education was finished.[50]

Coming from an educated family with chiefly heritage also eases paths to private campaign fundraising. When a candidate comes from a long-standing royal family, another MP explained, "obviously they have political godfathers" inside the family, "which comes with resources." Their relatives often "are able to marshal a lot of resources to assist such a person." This is in part because these candidates are more likely to have relatives hired into well-compensated positions in the private sector due to the family having an early foothold in the urban economy in the South.[51] Another MP described that the fact that his father and grandfather were chiefs meant "that you already have allies, allies that were created by my father, allies that were created by my [other relatives]. We make use of all those alliances" when raising money and other forms of support for campaigns.[52]

Access to funding and "godfathers" who can help bankroll a run for office also come from MPs' personal experiences working in the private sector outside the North. An MP from Upper East Region with degrees

[49] Interview with Dagaba MP from Upper West Region, Accra, June 27, 2019.
[50] Interview with Wala MP from Upper West Region, Accra, July 13, 2019.
[51] Interview with Konkomba MP from Northern Region, Accra, June 26, 2019.
[52] Interview with Kasena MP from Upper East Region, Accra, June 25, 2019.

from UK and US universities explained that while working in a well-compensated job at an international agency in Accra,

I had people who really admired me and wanted me to go into politics ... people in the business community that I had interfaced over the course of my job, who felt that they could share my vision ... I was able to mobilize a lot of resources from that group to allow me to be able to do my campaign.[53]

Like many of his colleagues, this MP reached such a high position in Accra in part because he had highly educated parents who supported his own education after being among the very first in each of their home communities to be educated.[54]

Similar to the example above, multiple other MPs from the "invented chiefs" and "always chiefs" groups also described returning from well-paying jobs in Accra or abroad to run for office in rural constituencies in which they had never actually lived before. To be legally eligible to contest, a candidate must either reside in a constituency or "hail from" it – have ancestral ties to the area. Most MPs from the "invented chiefs" and "always chiefs" groups fall into the latter category. A Dagomba MP in Northern Region who had spent most of his career in Accra noted, "My biggest hurdle that I had to cross in my campaign was to convince people that I was not an outsider ... [My opponents] made me seem like I was an Accra boy who had just come to take the seat." He argued he was able to overcome this challenge by appealing to his chiefly ancestry – his great-grandfather and grandfather had been well-known chiefs in the area.[55] Another MP similarly described, "when ... I declared my intention to contest, there were a lot of people who did not actually know I came from [the constituency] ... I never schooled there ... I had left the constituency and was ... in Accra and in England." When it came to his primary for his party's nomination, the "people who were to take the decisions – the delegates – they didn't know me."[56] But in a system in which nominations can now be effectively bought by the highest bidder, it has become common for well-financed "outsiders" like this MP to be able to overcome a lack of local connections. Other respondents explained that party leaders actively recruit well-connected candidates from "big families" – even if

---

[53] Interview with Frafra (Gurense) MP from Upper East Region, Accra, July 19, 2019.

[54] His father became a senior military officer, while his mother was a government education official and constituency-level political party leader. Interview with Frafra (Gurense) MP from Upper East Region, Accra, July 19, 2019.

[55] Interview with Dagomba MP from Northern Region, Accra, June 26, 2019.

[56] Interview with Frafra (Gurense) MP from Upper East Region, Accra, July 19, 2019.

they live in urban areas or the diaspora – because they know they will have the resources to be competitive.[57] And as shown in Chapter 4, these "big families" are disproportionately the descendants of early colonial chiefs.

Table 6.1 uses the interview data to show overall descriptive patterns in the life histories of MPs from the different categories of ethnic groups.[58] The key theme running through interviews with the MPs from chiefly ethnic groups – the "invented chiefs" and "always chiefs" groups – was that they began their political careers with significant economic advantages from their families. The typical MP from these groups has parents or grandparents who were educated and already worked in government or the civil service when the MP was a child. Given that most MPs are in their fifties and sixties, this means their families gained access to education in the colonial period, when they would have been among the first small set of Northerners to graduate. Benefitting from the better schooling that can then be provided by well-employed parents, these MPs all attended elite universities, either in Ghana (64 percent) or abroad (36 percent). A majority lived abroad before entering Parliament, exemplifying the many Ghanaian elites who entered the diaspora in the 1980s through late 1990s. The large majority had also already worked in government in some capacity. Pinkston (2016) documents that professional experiences abroad and in government are two major paths Ghanaian politicians use to amass the private resources needed to support a political career. Only one MP from these ethnic groups was living and working in his rural constituency before taking office.

Notably, this same overall pattern of background characteristics holds among the respondents from these ethnic groups who both were and were not descended from early colonial chiefs. While chiefs' relatives were those by far most likely to gain early access to education and formal sector employment, the MPs in the sample from nonchiefly backgrounds largely came from families lucky enough to have also received similarly early access to human capital for some other reason.

---

[57] Describing a previous opponent, one MP said, "[The opposing party] brought a former [government official] ... because he had money. He had went and worked in the UK, so he had resources! ... He had lived so long outside. When he came he was doing things [in the campaign] that showed that he was really rich," which made it very difficult for the MP to retain his seat. Interview with Birifor MP from Upper West Region, Accra, July 22, 2019.

[58] The questionnaire for these interviews is the Appendix.

TABLE 6.1 *Trajectories to office: MP interviews by ethnic category*

	Chiefly groups ("Invented" + ("always" groups)	Non-chiefly groups ("Never recognized" groups)
Family background:		
Royal family since early colonial period	45% (5)	0% (0)
Parent in civil service or government position	64% (7)	33% (3)
First generation in family to attend school:		
Grandparents	9% (1)	0% (0)
Parents	55% (6)	11% (1)
Own	36% (4)	88% (88)
Early life:		
Grew up in their rural constituency	64% (7)	88% (8)
Attended an elite university:		
In Ghana (e.g., Legon, KNUST, UCC)	64% (7)	33% (3)
Abroad (e.g., UK, US)	36% (4)	11% (1)
Adult life (before Parliament):		
Worked primarily in their constituency before running	9% (1)	66% (6)
Worked as a public school teacher (GES)	18% (2)	77% (7)
Worked abroad (e.g., UK, US) for extended period	55% (6)	11% (1)
Held a government position before running (e.g., DCE)	73% (8)	22% (2)
Describes self as mostly "self-made" financially	45% (5)	88% (8)
N	11	9

Descriptive statistics from MP life history interviews ($N = 20$). These MPs were serving as of 2019.

These patterns contrast starkly with the "never recognized" ethnic groups, among whom the colonial state did not elevate particular families early in the colonial period and access to education often only came significantly later. Table 6.1 shows instead that the typical "never recognized" MP today is self-made and not from a family that benefitted from early access to state resources. Only 1 (11 percent) of these MPs had parents who were already educated in the colonial period. Almost all of them grew up in their rural constituencies and the majority still lived and worked there upon taking office. Few attended elite universities, lived abroad, or had worked in government.

Instead, the most common professional background of a "never recognized" MP is a public school teacher. Teaching was historically (in the 1950s) a common background for MPs from the chiefly groups when it was still one of the only formal professions available to Northerners that could launch families on a better economic trajectory. But in the modern period, teaching is a far less lucrative and lower-status career than the private sector experiences as businessmen and lawyers (extremely rare in the 1950s) now available to many of the MPs descended from the families of early teachers. Indeed, following the logic in Chapter 2, especially Figure 2.4, simply receiving the same economic opportunity later is often insufficient to close the gap that has emerged with those who received it early if initial advantages compound.

Unlike the MPs described above who funneled private or family fortunes into their campaigns, many of the MPs from the "never recognized" groups described that they only were able to win because they had outside financing from party leaders. While party financing is rare overall, party leaders do interfere in primaries and target resources to candidates in particular constituencies when it is strategically useful. A Konkomba MP who had been working as a public school teacher described how he was initially recruited into politics,

Haruna Iddrisu [the NDC leader in Parliament] had heard of me. I didn't know him, but someone spoke well about me. So he called me. He invited me to his house in Tamale and said he wanted to help me to go politically. So he sent for me, and he supported me, both resource wise – he gave me a car, a pickup – and he also gave me money for the campaign.[59]

Senior party leaders reached out to this MP because they were looking for a locally popular Konkomba to nominate. Recognizing the high rates of ethnic voting among many Northern ethnic groups in parliamentary contests, the parties at times intervene in primary elections to strategically seek out candidates from particular ethnic groups even when there are not well-funded elites from those groups stepping forward on their own to contest.[60]

---

[59] Interview with Konkomba MP from Northern Region, Accra, June 21, 2019.
[60] Ichino and Nathan (2012, 2018) describe similar interventions in primaries to handpick nominees from strategically preferred ethnic groups.

Along these lines, an MP who was a teacher from a very small "never recognized" group in the Upper West Region – the Chakali, which make up the plurality in just one constituency – also recounts that he was initially recruited to contest by national party leaders desperate to find a viable candidate from his ethnic group that could run against the Wala ("always chiefs") incumbent,

> They ran into difficulty getting a candidate for our constituency ... They contacted almost every educated [Chakali] person within the constituency and they all declined. Then they even came and traveled ... to Accra to scout for any possible person from our constituency residing in Accra who might want to go back and stand. They tried and didn't get anybody ... But somewhere September 1999, this letter was brought from Accra to me, out of nowhere, saying I should contest for NPP. I was directed to the Regional Chairman to go see him and confirm whether I would contest or not.[61]

Although he lost his first election in 2000, he went on to serve three terms in Parliament, winning based on strong bloc voting from his co-ethnic constituents. Not descended from colonial-era chiefs, these MPs from "never recognized" groups needed these forms of outside support to overcome their lower class backgrounds.

Consistent with this interview evidence, it is also possible to quantitatively (albeit roughly) connect the early provision of education by the state to the later presence of dynastic candidates and MPs. In Chapter 4, I use village-level 1960 census data to measure male school enrollment after the first decade of widespread school construction in the North. I show that this significantly predicts present-day within-village economic inequality. The areas with the greatest school enrollments as of 1960 are those that had received the earliest access to education. And because within-village enrollments were still quite low by 1960 and one quarter of communities still had no access to schooling at all, this census data helps identify the local areas in which some families had already begun to receive a head start in access to human capital. Figure 6.5 aggregates the 1960 census data to the parliamentary constituency level and regresses the presence of a candidate (left panel) or winning MP (right panel) with early chiefly heritage in each election after 1960 on the proportion of boys enrolled by 1960. These descriptive models include election year fixed effects to control for time trends.

In line with my argument, the predicted probabilities in Figure 6.5 show that larger numbers of dynastic candidates and MPs emerged in

---

[61] Interview with Chakali MP from Upper West Region, Accra, June 27, 2019.

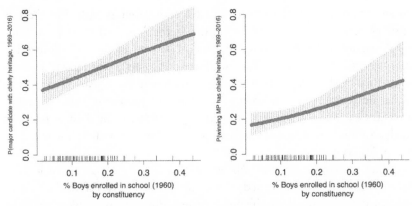

FIGURE 6.5 Probability of candidates and elected MPs with family ties to early colonial chiefs. Predicted probability that a major party candidate with family ties to an early colonial chief (1902–1934) runs (left) or wins (right) in each Parliamentary constituency in Northern Ghana in each election from 1969 to 2016, by the proportion of boys enrolled in school in that constituency as of 1960 (as calculated in Chapter 4). The models are logistic regressions with election year fixed effects.

areas that had earlier access to education from the state. Simulating from these models, moving from 10th to 90th percentile in constituency-level proportion of boys enrolled in 1960 (from 6.1 percent to 21.9 percent) results in a 12.6-percentage point increase in the probability of having a candidate (95 percent CI: 1.5, 22.6) and a 8.5-percentage point increase in probability of having an elected MP (95 percent CI: $-0.2, 17.0, p = 0.06$) descended from an early colonial chief.

6.6 ALTERNATIVE MECHANISMS

I argue that politicians descended from colonial-era chiefs continue to win modern elections because early access to human capital – a valuable windfall provided by contact with an otherwise scarce state – created a persistent economic advantage for their families. But there are also plausible alternative mechanisms. I consider and find limited support for five possibilities, providing further suggestive evidence that the early actions of the state form the clearest explanation for Figures 6.2 and 6.4.

First, perhaps the analysis above mistakes an effect of chiefly heritage for a simpler legislative incumbency advantage. This would be the case if chiefs' sons were first elected in the 1950s because they were the only plausible candidates, but then their own sons were elected in modern elections not because of their descent from colonial-era chiefs, but because of newer advantages their fathers had accumulated as MPs. But there is little evidence that office-holding in the 1950s launched subsequent family dynasties; I describe above that just 9 percent of the MPs descended from early colonial chiefs are *also* descended from an earlier MP in their constituency. In a regression model with constituency-year fixed effects, being descended from an earlier MP does not predict winning a parliamentary election over other candidates ($p = 0.71$), while descent from an early colonial chief still strongly predicts victory ($p = 0.04$). These two variables do not interact ($p = 0.66$).

Ghana's democracy may still be too recent for a broad set of legislative dynasties to have formed, especially in the North. With the British still ultimately controlling the purse strings, the rents available from positions in the colonial Legislative Assembly in the 1950s were likely too small to create persistent family advantages, especially compared to the rents available to MPs today. After independence under the CPP dictatorship, only the small handful of Northerners who reached Nkrumah's inner circle likely consolidated enough rents to launch political careers for their children.[62] Moreover, until the last several decades, the number of Northerners at the highest echelons of the state – where opportunities to accumulate rents from incumbency would be greatest – was tiny, consistent with the North's historical underrepresentation relative to the South. For example, just thirteen politicians from Northern Ghana in my dataset served as cabinet ministers at some point between 1951 and democratization in 1992.

Since the 1990s, opportunities to amass rents from parliamentary and ministerial positions have become more common, and it remains possible legislative dynasties could form in the future as the current generation of politicians retires. But many of the Northern politicians who began to dominate since the 1990s are still active in politics today, not yet having fully stepped aside for their children's generation to contest for their seats. For now, dynastic politics remains much better explained by the earlier accumulation of advantages among families descended from colonial-era chiefs.

Second, there could be concern that colonial-era chiefs simply had so many more children than other families that the pool of constituency

---

[62] One of these exceptions – an MP descended from colonial-era chiefs who is also linked to an earlier MP – is John Dramani Mahama, Ghana's president from 2012–2017 (previously an MP from 1997–2009). His father, Emmanuel Adama (E. A.) Mahama, was the first MP from the West Gonja constituency and became a minister under Nkrumah (Mahama 2012).

residents is so heavily comprised of their descendants that the appearance of dynasties is spurious. Polygamy was common across the North in the colonial period, and some particularly wealthy chiefs had dozens of children.[63] But polygamy was common among other families too; many other households also had large numbers of children. Overall, the large majority of Northerners do not claim direct descent from chiefs. The high proportions of elected MPs with chiefly heritage in Figures 6.2 and 6.4 – with over 40 percent of MPs descended from early chiefs – imply that there must be some effect of chiefly heritage on candidate success.

The evidence is more mixed for the third and fourth alternatives, but both still are not sufficient on their own to explain the patterns above. The third possibility is that candidates with chiefly heritage benefit more from name recognition than from the economic benefits of early access to human capital. The fourth alternative is that candidates with chiefly heritage benefit instead from the explicit electoral influence of contemporary chiefs who are their relatives.

A small set of respondents agreed that name recognition may aide candidates on the margins. The Wala MP quoted at the opening of the chapter argued that his royal surname has "helped me a lot. That one I have to admit. Because my family ... is highly respected. My grandfather has done a lot of good [as chief]. People have benefitted a lot from my forbearers, and they have told their children about it."[64] Others without chiefly heritage speculated that it might have helped them in this fashion. A Frafra MP argued, "I think that to have had come from a family with a quote, unquote 'address' – where you mention [the name] and people say 'oh yes, that family,' of course I think that it could have" helped.[65] Similarly, a few respondents argued that being related to present-day chiefs – quite common among the candidates descended from early colonial chiefs – can be directly beneficial through their influence over voters. A Kasena MP described that "being from a royal family means my own hometown, they are like subjects, my family's subjects. They are available to support me."[66] Along these lines, Ladouceur (1979, 118–119) argues

---

[63] Lentz (2006) and Gandah (2009) note several extreme examples of chiefs in the Upper West Region. Importantly, however, only a small subset of these children were typically sent to school, concentrating the windfall from human capital much more narrowly in the chief's family tree (Gandah 2004).

[64] Interview with Wala MP from Upper West Region, Accra, July 13, 2019.

[65] Interview with Frafra (Gurense) MP from Upper East Region, Accra, July 19, 2019.

[66] Interview with Kasena MP from Upper East Region, Accra, June 25, 2019.

that chiefs' explicit endorsements could be particularly beneficial to the election of chiefs' sons in the 1950s.

But both factors are unlikely to account fully for the patterns above. Most interviewed MPs were instead very skeptical that a royal surname would be so explicitly beneficial, arguing that candidates with chiefly heritage often had to win *in spite* of their name recognition. As will be examined in Chapters 7 and 8, chieftaincy succession is often bitterly disputed in Northern Ghana, with protracted legal cases (and at times violence) between families. Being from one faction can hold a candidate back because voters associated with rival factions would never support them, while a non-royal candidate can win from all sides. Nine of the interviewed MPs – including all but one from the "invented chiefs" groups – made a variant of this same point. For example, one argued, "chieftaincy conflict has put most of the people at a crossroads whereby you cannot get universal love" if you are linked to one side.[67] Another similarly claimed, "[C]oming from a royal family ... you are quite constrained ... Even within the [local community], you might have an opposing house that wanted to be chiefs who might be natural opponents."[68] A third noted that "when you get yourself so bogged down by the royal family ... [some] tend not to vote for you. Because they think that you must diversify the leadership because you can't have both" the chieftaincy and MP position in one family.[69] One MP described actively going out of his way to play down his father's family ties to chiefs in his campaign because he was linked to the numerically smaller side in the local chieftaincy dispute.[70]

Explicit influence from related chiefs is also an insufficient alternative explanation. While chiefs often serve as electoral brokers, as will be examined in Chapter 7, candidates are usually only personally linked to the chief in a single community comprising a small overall share of their constituency's electorate. This limits the plausible scope of any direct influence from a relative serving as chief. Only one of the twenty interviewed MPs is directly related to a sitting paramount chief (as opposed to lower-level village or divisional chief) whose direct influence over voters could plausibly reach throughout his full constituency. More common are examples like the Dagaba MP from Upper West Region profiled above

---

[67] Interview with Gonja MP from Northern Region, Accra, June 25, 2019.
[68] Interview with Dagaba MP from Upper West Region, Accra, June 27, 2019.
[69] Interview with Frafra (Gurense) MP from Upper East Region, Accra, July 19, 2019.
[70] Interview with Dagomba MP from Northern Region, Accra, July 25, 2019.

who had lived in the UK. His first cousin is the chief today in his ancestral home village, where the MP's father and grandfather had both also been chiefs in the past. But the position was formally vacant amidst a protracted succession dispute during each of the MP's three successful elections. And even if inherited social influence allowed for 100 percent support in this village, it accounts for just 2 percent of his constituency's electorate (807 of 41,132 registered voters in 2016).[71]

Finally, there could be concern that the lack of dynasties in the "never recognized" groups is overstated. While, by definition, MPs from the "never recognized" groups are unlikely to be related to early colonial chiefs, perhaps there are still other forms of dynastic politics active instead. Alternatively, given the "never recognized" groups' delayed access to education, it may simply be that dynasties are only forming now with this current generation of politicians and similar patterns as in the "invented chiefs" and "always chiefs" groups will emerge in the future.

I find little evidence for either possibility. Chapter 5 and the discussion above already describe that few members of the "never recognized" groups reached any elite political positions in the North until the 1980s or later, with little opportunity for other types of dynasties not linked to chieftaincy to have formed instead. For example, no MPs from any "never recognized" group were elected throughout the 1950s; only one Konkomba MP – the largest "never recognized" group – was elected before 1979. Just three of the over forty MPs ever elected from the "never recognized" groups by 2016 have a family name match to a previous MP from their constituency. Moreover, drawing on Talton (2010) and the interviews in Chapter 5, I can identify fifteen of the most influential nonelected Konkomba leaders active in politics in the 1950s through 1970s, such as in the founding of the Konkomba Youth Association (KOYA).[72] If there were other dynasties forming among "never recognized" groups not linked to chiefs, these would be the most plausible types of people to have started them. Although four of these early Konkomba activists later ran themselves as parliamentary candidates, none appear related to any of the Konkomba MPs elected in the modern period (1996–2016), which would have indicated a possible dynasty.

---

[71] Interview with Dagaba MP from Upper West Region, Accra, June 27, 2019.

[72] Talton (2010, 151) identifies the ten most important leaders in KOYA's founding and its predecessor activist movements by name. From my interviews, I can also identify five other early senior Konkomba activists, including multiple subsequent KOYA Presidents and General Secretaries.

Indeed, when asked directly whether there were dynastic Konkomba political families, the interview respondents in Chapter 5 reported that they did not believe there were any.[73]

The reason other forms of dynastic politics have not emerged among "never recognized" groups is likely directly related to the findings on economic inequality in Chapter 4. With wealth less narrowly concentrated in a small set of elite families, there are fewer potential candidates with a clear financial advantage over the others, creating a more even playing field in access to local political power. For example, while many of the current MPs from the "never recognized" groups describe themselves as among the first in their communities to have become educated (Table 6.1), they were educated a generation (or more) later than the parents or grandparents of the MPs from the "invented chiefs" and "always chiefs" groups, at a time when the relative economic returns to education were much lower because it was much more widely available across the North. One Konkomba interview respondent explained the lack of dynasties among his group in these terms, noting that while the early pioneers at school among groups like the Dagaba became wealthy elites, launching their descendants into high positions, delayed access to education in Konkomba communities means that something similar "will never be so among the Konkombas. We have a very elastic and wider" access to education, rather than concentrated advantages in a few families.[74]

Moreover, although chieftaincy is now beginning to emerge among the Konkomba and several other "never recognized" groups, it is so far only doing so in the haphazard fashion described in Chapter 5. With most chiefs still struggling to project real authority, it is not clear that the new chieftaincy positions provide sufficiently sustained access to economic rents to replicate the creation of elites from the earlier wave of chieftaincy invention by the colonial state.

6.7 CONCLUSION

This chapter documents high levels of dynastic office holding in Northern Ghana. Among the "invented chiefs" groups, a substantial plurality of candidates and elected legislators since the late colonial period are descended from early colonial-era chiefs appointed by the state. This is

---

[73] Interview with former KOYA general secretary, Saboba, July 6, 2019; interview with Konkomba business leader and KOYA adviser, Saboba, July 6, 2019.
[74] Interview with Konkomba business leader and KOYA adviser, Saboba, July 6, 2019.

consistent with significant elite capture of political power in this hinter-land region. Building on the analysis of economic inequality in Chapter 4, I suggest that the key mechanism for elite persistence is that early con-tact with a scarce state provided valuable economic windfalls through the selective provision of human capital, creating long-run advantages for a small set of families.

Scholars such as Migdal (1988) famously posit that a major gov-ernance challenge in many rural areas of developing countries is that "strong societies" dominate and pervert the rule of weak states; that is, the state lacks sufficient autonomy from societal elites to govern effec-tively.[75] Yet I illustrate that the strong societal actors who have captured sustained power are themselves direct creations of the state that they are capturing. State weakness defined along one dimension – a lack of state autonomy from society – does not imply state weakness along another – the implicit power of the state to transform and remake society.

Where this chapter is silent, however, is on the effects of dynastic politics and elite capture. The next chapter pivots to the distributional consequences of elite persistence. I examine the closely-related persis-tence of these same elite families in another domain – their control over village-level chieftaincy institutions – and show how capture at the vil-lage level facilities clientelist politics and alters the ability of hinterland communities to extract benefits from state leaders.

---

[75] O'Donnell (1993), Chabal and Daloz (1999), Englebert (2000).

7

Invented Chiefs and Distributive Politics

They enjoy the privilege of non-competitive choice and they also enjoy the privilege of an inability to dismiss them. So they are more inclined to being very corrupt.

– Civil society activist and Dagaba royal family member, Bolgatanga, June 2018

The scarce state's actions – especially the invention of chieftaincy – have had lasting implications for distributive politics. Long after independence, chiefs continued to serve as important links between hinterland communities and the state. In Ghana's initial autocratic periods, state leaders relied on chiefs in the North as allies who could help ensure acquiescence from the local population while the state turned its attention elsewhere.[1] In the absence of a significant local bureaucracy, chiefs also helped implement state policies, such as organizing to construct and maintain schools (Chapter 4). With democratization, however, what state leaders needed from chiefs in the North changed. Rather than tacit acceptance, state leaders wanted votes in competitive national elections. In this new institutional environment, many chiefs pivoted to becoming community-level brokers, a role common among traditional leaders in African democracies with clientelist politics.[2] Chiefs serving as brokers help bargain with politicians on their communities' behalf, offering politicians explicit or implicit assistance in mobilizing votes in return for state benefits.

---

[1] Bates (1981), Chazan (1982), Boone (2003).
[2] Baldwin (2015), Koter (2016), Gottlieb (2017), de Kadt and Larreguy (2018), Kramon (2019).

Under autocracy, chiefs' role as intermediaries and policy implementers helped communities access benefits from a scarce and neglectful state that otherwise largely ignored areas without chiefs. Chapter 4 shows, for example, that communities with chiefs were much more likely to receive schools, the main local public good that the state delivered to the North in the post-independence period. Since democratization, however, the welfare implications of chiefs have become more ambiguous. In electoral periods, the ability of chiefs to serve as community-level brokers makes clientelism more viable for politicians, allowing them to secure votes from coordinated blocs without having to reach individual voters.[3] But this may not benefit voters themselves. Chiefs acting as community-level brokers can produce gains for their voters by helping collectively bargain to extract more resources from politicians than voters would be able to on their own. Yet chiefs can also exploit intermediary positions for private rent-seeking, taking advantage of their voters and leaving voters worse off than they would be if interacting with politicians directly.

Where there is elite capture and chiefs are not beholden to their followers to continue in their positions, chiefs are more free to trade away votes for deals in their own, not voters', best interest. Unaccountable brokers who have captured community-level power may then strike worse deals for their clients than voters could achieve on their own without a broker, or than voters would receive if under the influence of a more accountable broker.

Accountability between community-level brokers and their clients in Northern Ghana is shaped by institutional rules for the selection of chiefs.[4] The *ad hoc* nature of the colonial state's imposition of chieftaincy in the "invented chiefs" groups (see Chapter 3) left behind institutions prone to capture, in two ways. First, moving down a level from the analyses in Chapter 6, there is also significant dynastic persistence within villages, with the same families elevated by the state at the outset of colonial rule continuing to control chieftaincy across generations. In the words of the civil society activist quoted at the opening of the chapter, dynastic chiefs often both "enjoy the privilege of non-competitive choice," preventing community members from screening for better chiefs, and "the privilege of an inability to dismiss them," preventing community

---

[3] Holland and Palmer-Rubin (2015), Rueda (2016), Kramon (2019).
[4] More broadly, see Acemoglu et al. (2014), Baldwin and Mvukiyehe (2015), Baldwin and Holzinger (2019).

members from sanctioning poor performers.[5] This impunity generates opportunities for rent-seeking and undermines bottom-up accountability.[6] Second, in cases where the control of single families is less secure, poorly codified succession rules have created openings for another form of capture – by politicians – with successive ruling parties using their influence over the legal apparatus to ensure the appointment of compliant co-partisans who are more accountable to the politicians who have installed them as chiefs than to community members. Similar to *hereditary capture*, *partisan capture* also undermines communities' ability to both screen for better brokers and sanction poor performance.

By contrast, there appears to be less capture overall among chiefs in the "always chiefs" groups. Though rules for chieftaincy succession among these precolonial kingdoms evolved under British rule, succession still largely follows power-sharing practices that emerged organically in the precolonial period. In all but one of these groups, positions rotate across families, are not hereditary, and are not held for life. Instead, chiefs pursue careers across multiple jurisdictions, seeking promotions up the hierarchy of chiefs. Although there are still prominent succession disputes, these rules allow for greater accountability of chiefs to their subjects. And crucially, there still are not chiefs who can effectively act as community-level brokers at all in the large majority of "never recognized" communities, even as there have been nascent attempts at creating chieftaincy.

These different histories of traditional chieftaincy across the "invented chiefs," "always chiefs," and "never recognized" groups allow for comparisons of the ability of rural communities with and without chiefs who serve as community-level brokers to extract state resources in return for their votes, as well as comparisons among communities in which chiefs have very different accountability relationships with their subjects. This chapter explores the effects of these differences on the distribution of state resources – including electricity, running water, secondary schools, and public sector jobs – in Ghana's modern democratic period.

I use archival data on chieftaincy succession, combined with multiple waves of village-level census data, polling station-level election results, geo-coded Afrobarometer surveys, and the oral history and elite interviews. My comparisons of state resource provision in "invented

---

[5] Interview with civil society activist and Dagaba royal family member, Bolgatanga, June 28, 2018.

[6] For a summary of theories of accountability focused on screening vs. sanctioning, see Fearon (1999).

chiefs" versus "never recognized" communities leverage the same natural experiment examined in Chapter 4, with the pre-1914 Anglo-German colonial border exogenously assigning communities to having a community-level broker today. This creates an unusual empirical opportunity to study the selection of voters into chieftaincy (and brokerage more generally).[7]

I begin with suggestive evidence that chiefs in colonially invented positions are more prone to capture and are perceived as less accountable by their subjects. Next, I show that these chiefs are nonetheless important community-level intermediaries in contemporary elections. I find that ethnic groups with chiefs cluster their votes more at the community level, consistent with traditional leaders serving as vote-coordinating community-level brokers, and demonstrate that chiefs also appear to substitute for more direct, individual-level voter mobilization by party organizations.

I then examine the implications of chiefs for distributive politics since democratization. The chieftaincy institutions most susceptible to capture – those invented during colonial rule – reduce voters' ability to extract a series of state-provided benefits during modern electoral competition compared both to communities without formal chiefs and to communities with more accountable chieftaincy institutions dating to the precolonial period. I provide descriptive evidence for this claim and then present similar results when instrumenting for the presence of colonially invented chieftaincy using the original Gold Coast-Togoland border.

This chapter connects clientelism to the scarce state's actions, showing that one particularly large effect of the state on political competition has been through the creation of the community-level brokers that allow parties to engage in clientelism at scale. Clientelism in this hinterland is facilitated most effectively by the chiefs that the state itself created. In turn, the largest distortions in the provision of state development resources in the modern electoral period are produced by these same chiefs. By contrast, voters in "never recognized" communities – in which

---

[7] Existing analyses of traditional chiefs are typically not able to use communities that lack chiefs as a comparison for estimating the effects of chieftaincy on resource distribution. Baldwin (2015, 2019) proxies for a comparison group by examining vacancies created by chiefs' deaths in Zambia. But the effect of a short-term absence in an equilibrium in which politicians and voters otherwise rely on chiefs may be a fundamentally different quantity of interest from the effect of never having a chief. De Kadt and Larreguy (2018) instead compare voters of the same ethnicities living just inside or outside the borders of chiefs' jurisdictions in South Africa, but do not explore effects on resource distribution.

the state did not directly generate new social hierarchies – are better able to extract state service provision in the modern electoral period because their votes are not similarly captured by state-created elites.

With this latter finding, the chapter also serves as an important addendum to Chapter 5's analysis of modern efforts to invent chieftaincy from scratch among the Konkomba. The Konkomba push for chieftaincy emerged in the late 1970s, prior to democratization, under the strong belief that having independent chiefs would allow for better treatment by the state. This belief was accurate under autocratic rule, with "invented chiefs" groups favored with schools and other benefits while "never recognized" groups were largely ignored.

But after democratization, shifts in the incentives of state leaders changed the potential impact of chiefs. With state leaders now actively needing votes from "never recognized" groups – regardless of whether they had chiefs – creating new middlemen who could exploit their positions to extract private rents may only hurt "never recognized" communities relative to a situation in which parties are forced to compete much more directly for their individual votes. Since democratization, Konkomba communities are, ironically, benefitting from the limited initial success of their effort to create chieftaincy; remaining acephalous means their votes remain uncaptured. Viewed in this context, it should be less surprising that in Chapter 5, key Konkomba activists instrumental in the initial push for chieftaincy in the 1970s and 1980s now express significant reservations about the continued wisdom of such a move, especially amidst widespread attempts by those seeking chieftaincy appointments today to engage in exactly the types of private rent-seeking described in this chapter.[8]

The next section begins by explaining how the accountability of community-level brokers to their clients should affect the likelihood they secure state resources for their communities. I then explore the brokerage roles played by chiefs in Northern Ghana across regime types and describe how differences in succession and appointment institutions – rooted in the actions of the early colonial state – produce variation in the bottom-up accountability of chiefs. The remainder of the chapter introduces the data sources before presenting analyses that, first, establish empirically that chiefs serve as community-level brokers in modern elections, and second,

---

[8] The shift towards more private motivations for creating chieftaincy is detailed in Chapter 5.

show their implications for distributive politics. I conclude by considering alternative explanations.

7.1 THE DISTRIBUTIVE EFFECTS OF COMMUNITY-LEVEL BROKERS

In electoral contexts, traditional chiefs are well-positioned to serve as community-level brokers. Chiefs in many African countries are said to leverage their socioeconomic power – including their control over land, their role as mediators in disputes, and their ability to compel communal labor – to become "king makers" who coordinate community votes and facilitate patronage exchanges.[9] By coordinating bloc voting on a party's behalf, community-level brokers allow parties to win support wholesale.[10] This lets parties substitute away from costly individual-level engagements with voters, including much more complex efforts to initiate (and potentially monitor) direct party-to-voter interactions.[11] Where community-level brokers are active and effective, there should be more bloc voting and less direct individual-level resource distribution by, or voter contact with, parties and politicians themselves.

Where community-level brokers are instead absent, politicians may turn to other types of intermediaries,[12] but they are comparatively less efficient. A particularly common alternative would be to campaign through local party organizations, a widespread approach elsewhere in Ghana.[13] Without chiefs' land-owning, judicial, or labor-organizing powers, local party agents will typically have less community-wide influence than chiefs, making them relatively less able to coordinate bloc voting and strike wholesale community-level deals with politicians. For example, Nathan (2019) suggests that politicians' reliance on party brokers – of whom there are often multiple competing with each other per community, with followings among only a fraction of the local electorate[14] – is most common where chiefs are not effective enough to help politicians.

Even if they are efficiency-enhancing for politicians, the implications for voters of community-level brokers like chiefs remain unclear. Some

---

[9] Lemarchand (1972), Koter (2013), Baldwin (2015), Koter (2016), Gottlieb (2017), de Kadt and Larreguy (2018).
[10] Kramon (2019), Gottlieb and Larreguy (2020).
[11] Stokes et al. (2013), Rueda (2016).
[12] Holland and Palmer-Rubin (2015)
[13] Brierley and Nathan (2021*a*).
[14] Brierley and Nathan (2021*a*) shows that typical party agents in Ghana only even know less than a quarter of residents at their polling station by name, let alone have authority to influence behavior across full rural communities.

studies expect that community-level brokers strike beneficial deals for their followers, producing gains from collective bargaining. If brokers are "free agents" – non-partisans able to drive a hard bargain between competing parties – they can create an auction for a community's votes, more effectively extracting resources than voters can individually.[15] Politicians may also target more resources to communities where they know a strong broker is capable of coordinating support because they can be more certain of the electoral returns from doing so.[16] The vote-coordinating of intermediaries should also be beneficial if they are simply pointing voters to candidates with whom they will best cooperate in co-producing local resources.[17]

Yet brokers also often exploit intermediary positions for rent-seeking, skimming from benefits passed down by politicians or coordinating votes in return for side-payments that never reach voters.[18] Rent-seeking is a bigger risk when there is capture and brokers are not accountable to voters.[19] Brokers will also strike worse deals for voters when they themselves are accountable to a party or political patron for their position, not to voters, and thus cannot drive hard bargains for voters between parties.[20] This suggests that chiefs who are particularly unaccountable to their subjects are those least likely to act in voters' best interest.[21]

This relationship between chiefs' bottom-up accountability and the gains they produce for their followers should hold regardless of how exactly these brokers coordinate votes, a key focus of other research on chiefs. It is often assumed that chiefs' vote coordination is implicitly coercive – for example, through threats over access to land.[22] If there is coercion, unaccountable chiefs should be the most effective brokers. But vote coordination could also be achieved more through persuasion and

---

[15] Novaes (2018).

[16] Gottlieb and Larreguy (2020).

[17] Baldwin (2015).

[18] Holland and Palmer-Rubin (2015), Auerbach (2016), Brierley and Nathan (2021*b*).

[19] Auerbach (2016), Corstange (2016), Shami (2017).

[20] de Kadt and Larreguy (2018).

[21] Baldwin (2015) predicts more consistently positive effects of chiefs on their communities. This emerges in part from focusing on different outcomes. Baldwin (2015, 109) examines *co-producible resources* that communities help provide to themselves, while I focus on *state resources* directly provided by politicians. Co-production depends as much on the ability of chiefs to solve intra-community collective action problems as on politicians' distribution. Unaccountable chiefs may still be quite effective at compelling communal self-provision (Acemoglu et al. 2014, Baldwin and Mvukiyehe 2015), as I find for the Northern Ghanaian case below.

[22] Boone (2003), Ntsebeza (2005). Conroy-Krutz (2018) shows that communities vote more as blocs in rural Uganda where voters depend on local elites for land tenure.

social respect,[23] or because voters draw informational value from chiefs' candidate endorsements.[24]

Coercion also provides the most direct explanation for why unaccountable chiefs continue successfully coordinating votes even as they extract fewer state resources for voters. But underperforming chiefs could also retain their influence even if coercion is limited. For example, chiefs can take advantage of the respect of isolated rural voters who cannot easily observe the relative extent to which they are disfavored in allocations of state resources.[25] Voters may also still benefit in other ways from voting with the chief. If unaccountable chiefs are effective at the co-production of smaller-scale resources, as discussed above, voters may still support chiefs' preferred candidates in expectation of more cooperative co-production.[26] Short-run defections from voting with the chief may only compound a community's disadvantages, leading to fewer co-produced resources in addition to fewer resources directly from politicians.

7.2 CHIEFS AS BROKERS IN NORTHERN GHANA

Chiefs act as the primary community-level brokers in Northern Ghana. While chiefs have served as intermediaries in some form since the colonial period, chiefs' current role differs from both the colonial period and Ghana's several decades as an autocracy prior to the 1990s. With this shift in roles over time, the potential benefits to a community from having a chief have changed as well. This section describes how chiefs linked communities and the state in both the autocratic era and since democratization, and then details how variation in succession and appointment institutions across the major categories of Northern ethnic groups explain differences in the bottom-up accountability of chiefs to community members.

7.2.1 The Authoritarian Period

Under authoritarianism, chiefs were important grassroots intermediaries, but did not act as electoral brokers in the manner conceptualized above. Instead, chiefs served two other purposes for state leaders: they used their

---

[23] Gottlieb (2017)

[24] Baldwin (2015).

[25] Conroy-Krutz (2018). Posner (2005) and Carlson (2016) demonstrate that rural African voters often have very limited information about what other communities are receiving instead.

[26] Baldwin (2015). Also see Brierley and Ofosu (2022).

local authority to create local acquiescence to autocratic rule by foregoing collective action against the state; and, with a scarce formal state, they served as channels through which policies could be implemented on the ground.

Under colonial rule and the additional autocratic regimes that followed, central state leaders did not need chiefs to provide their communities' votes or actively generate popular support for the regime. Instead, following the theory in Bates (1981), state leaders' primary political demand of the rural hinterland was that local populations not revolt. Chiefs were the local authority figures in these areas best positioned to coordinate collective action against the regime.

Much as colonial regimes turned to indirect rule as a means to ensure social control, a common strategy among many post-independence autocrats across Africa was to prevent popular resistance in rural areas by buying off the main societal elites, such as chiefs, who had the local influence necessary to mobilize mass rural resistance.[27] This is what happened in Northern Ghana: starting from Nkrumah, post-independence autocrats entered into alliances with Northern chiefs, buying their personal acquiescence by targeting them with private benefits and agreeing not to undermine their authority.[28] The modern state's third major action outlined in Chapter 3 – the 1979 devolution of land rights to chiefs – is an example of exactly such a strategy: state leaders gave up authority over land in an effort to buy chiefs' support, and with it forestall any threat from the countryside at a time when state leaders' main focus was instead on urban areas.[29]

Moreover, because the state bureaucracy was kept incredibly scarce throughout the colonial and authoritarian periods in the North, chiefs were also useful to state leaders as agents of local policy implementation, blurring the boundary between state and society.[30] Chapter 3 describes how chiefs maintained formal positions in the local government system deep into the post-independence period. In lieu of local bureaucrats, chiefs were involved in implementing the few state actions that central state leaders undertook. This included the construction of new schools – the second major intervention outlined in Chapter 3. Chapter 4 shows that

---

[27] Riedl (2014), Koter (2016).

[28] This strategy is richly documented by Boone (2003). Also see Ladouceur (1979). This contrasts notably from Nkrumah's attempts to suppress chiefs in Southern Ghana (Rathbone 2000).

[29] Chazan and LeVine (1979).

[30] Lund (2006), Hagmann and Peclard (2010), Bierschenk and Olivier de Sardan (2014).

initial post-independence school construction was heavily concentrated in communities with chiefs because chiefs were roped into the construction process.

In this context, having a chief was likely strictly positive in terms of the state resources a community could access compared to not having one. Acephalous "never recognized" groups lacked similar centralized local authority figures who could credibly threaten to coordinate collective action against the state. Because they thus posed an even more limited political threat than neighboring ethnic groups, "never recognized" communities could safely be ignored by state leaders. And without chiefs who could implement state policy in their communities – such as overseeing the construction of schools – they were differentially passed over in access to local public goods, as detailed in Chapters 4 and 5. It is not a coincidence that the bottom-up demands for chieftaincy in Konkomba communities examined in Chapter 5 emerged directly from these experiences of extended state neglect under authoritarian rule in the 1970s and 1980s.

7.2.2 The Modern Democratic Period

But the value of a chief to a community became more ambiguous with twin shifts in political context in the early 1990s. Democratization – which occurred for reasons completely exogenous to the internal politics of the North[31] – shifted what state leaders wanted from hinterland communities, and, by extension, from hinterland chiefs. In the highly competitive national electoral environment that soon emerged, especially starting with the 2000 election, both major parties (the NDC and NPP) had new incentives to aggressively pursue Northern votes. To ensure political survival in a context of razor thin margins in presidential elections, state leaders actively needed to mobilize support in the North – even among the "never recognized" groups – not merely ensure compliance.

Meanwhile, decentralization reforms beginning from 1988 (see Chapter 3) meaningfully deconcentrated the state bureaucracy to the local level in the North for the first time, displacing the state's need to rely on chiefs as policy implementers.[32] Chiefs no longer held any responsibilities as state agents at the local level. Instead of defaulting

---

[31] The developments behind Ghana's democratization are summarized well in Riedl (2014).
[32] Like democratization, decentralization was implemented nationally due to external pressures on the regime exogenous to the politics of the North itself (Ayee 1993).

to having influence into state resource distribution in the absence of bureaucrats, chiefs increasingly were only able to deliver resources to their communities if they could act as effective community-level brokers who could bargain with politicians.

My elite interview respondents were nearly universal in describing chiefs as becoming key electoral brokers since democratization.[33] While most respondents stressed that chiefs typically do not have the power to simply compel subjects to vote a certain way, there was widespread agreement both that chiefs are influential and that politicians rely on chiefs as a central means of campaigning. For example, a senior leader of the NDC in Upper East Region described, "In this area, it isn't that when you go and see a chief, they can just command the people. No. But it adds. It adds to your chances."[34] A civil society activist, while noting that chiefs are ostensibly supposed to remain politically neutral under Ghana's constitution, argued, "they say that chiefs are not involved in politics, but that is just in writing. In practice, [the chief] sends word around that this is my preferred party. And most will vote like that."[35] A scholar from Upper West Region described the prevailing view of chiefs' electoral influence using an aphorism: "if the chief sneezes, the MP catches cold ... They are very strong."[36]

While most exchanges between politicians and chiefs are unobservable, chiefs are thought to extract a range of private rents from politicians in return for mobilizing votes. In addition to standard forms of patronage – cash, job opportunities for relatives – this includes other benefits like renovated palaces or even motorbikes and cars. Of the benefits passed to chiefs by politicians, one respondent described, "They can, for instance, buy you a car. Build a house for you. Give you clothing that you can wear and look like a chief. They make sure that you have stipends, regular stipends coming in. So it becomes difficult for you to say no to somebody" seeking political support.[37] A particularly central private benefit is state influence in succession. Where succession is contested, chiefs benefit directly from politicians exerting leverage over the courts and police to ward off rival claimants.

---

[33] Ladouceur (1979) describes Northern chiefs briefly serving a similar role in Ghana's initial elections as well.

[34] Interview with NDC regional executive, Zuarungu, June 29, 2018.

[35] Interview with civil society activist and Dagaba royal family member, Bolgatanga, June 28, 2018.

[36] Interview with scholar and Sisala royal family member, Tamale, June 27, 2018.

[37] Interview with Dagaba civil society activist, Tamale, June 30, 2018.

In return, chiefs are claimed to influence voters' behavior in multiple ways. Similar to Baldwin's (2015) evidence from Zambia, many interview respondents argued that voters trust and take valuable information from chiefs' candidate endorsements because they signal which politicians are likely to act in the best interest of their community. These endorsements draw on the social respect chiefs are afforded as elders and spiritual leaders. A district assemblymember (local councilor) in Upper West Region described that "politicians make a lot of promises and we go, 'who will deliver?' That's what we need the chief for. He's the coordinator to bring everyone together" with the most insight into who will perform best.[38] An MP from Upper East Region described, "they are the opinion leaders and their endorsement really matters. Once they demonstrate that they are with you, their people turn to support you."[39] Some endorsements are only made quietly within communities, as chiefs seek to avoid public scrutiny for violating the constitutional provision against partisan activity. But increasingly, other chiefs are comfortable making open endorsements at public durbars and campaign rallies.[40]

Chiefs also have more direct sources of leverage. In communities where chiefs have been able to successfully consolidate ownership over land after the 1979 reforms, the ability to control the most important resource in the agrarian economy creates opportunities for coercion.[41] Along these lines, a Dagaba civil society activist pointed to land ownership as a key source of influence: "if the chief has economic power, then the tendency of that chief to influence the people [in elections] is high."[42] Other respondents stressed that chiefs gain coercive leverage from their quasi-judicial role as arbiters of local disputes.[43] Another civil society activist described, "most of all, they are arbiters. They handle conflict situations in the local community. So if you decide to be recalcitrant, they'll just wait. When there's another issue involving you and somebody, they'll rule in favor of the person. So you keep losing and losing" if you do not comply with their

[38] Interview with District assemblymember, oral history community #2, Nadowli District, May 28, 2019.

[39] Interview with Kasena MP from Upper East Region, Accra, June 25, 2019.

[40] Public endorsements are widely covered in the Ghanaian press each election cycle. Brierley and Ofosu (2022) find that these endorsements have significant effects on voter behavior.

[41] Goldstein and Udry (2008) document how chiefs' land ownership produces local political power in similar legal contexts in Southern Ghana.

[42] Interview with Dagaba civil society activist, Tamale, June 30, 2018.

[43] In most ethnic groups, chiefs operate as an important informal nonstate judicial system, handling most lower-level civil and criminal issues.

requests.[44] In addition, similar to other types of brokers,[45] respondents also described chiefs gaining leverage through their role as key "problem solvers" that community members rely on to access social assistance in times of need. One respondent described,

Those of us who are educated, you'll sit there and listen [to the chief's endorsement] but not be convinced. But a big chunk of people will follow and listen to the chief and actually do what he has asked them to do. Because they also go to the chief's house occasionally to ask for handouts, in order to survive ... in order to address all manner of societal problems. So it makes the chief hold a lot of authority ... He has leverage.[46]

Chiefs' problem-solving ability itself often relies on the fact that they come from the better-educated and wealthier extended families within their communities, for the same reasons explored in Chapter 4. This gives many chiefs privileged social connections to relatives outside the community who can be used to help residents with nonstate forms of assistance. The NDC party leader quoted above argued that this is a particular source of influence within rural communities:

If there's one guy who is economically sound and he's even outside the country ... in UK or USA ... and he solves family problems, they will rely on him to remit, If there's hunger, they rely on him to remit. When it comes to decision-making, anybody who's got him to his side has the chance of controlling the place.[47]

7.2.3 Accountability and the Origins of Chieftaincy

As chiefs' political role has shifted towards serving as community-level brokers, the accountability relationship between chiefs and their subjects becomes more important in determining whether chiefs primarily use their intermediary positions to help the community or to take advantage of their influence for more private ends. Under autocracy, even if chiefs also engaged in rent-seeking, their role as policy implementers meant that not having a chief could mean simply being cut out of access to some state benefits entirely. This is no longer the case. In competitive elections,

---

[44] Interview with civil society activist and Dagaba royal family member, Bolgatanga, June 28, 2018. The scholar from Upper West Region confirmed "if you rely on them for dispute resolution, you need to respect them." Interview with scholar and Sisala royal family member, Tamale, June 27, 2018.

[45] Auyero (2000), Zarazaga (2014), Brierley and Nathan (2021a).

[46] Interview with scholar and Sisala royal family member, Tamale, June 27, 2018.

[47] Interview with NDC regional executive, Zuarungu, June 29, 2018.

"never recognized" communities without chiefs cannot safely be ignored by state leaders. If a chief is not available as a broker, parties must find other, more direct, means to engage these voters. It now becomes possible that voters could extract more benefits from a party directly than if their contact with that party were instead mediated through an unaccountable rent-seeking broker.

The different institutional histories of ethnic groups in Northern Ghana create variation in the accountability of community-level brokers.[48] In particular, colonially invented chiefs are especially unlikely to be accountable to their subjects. As Chapter 3 describes, colonial invention was deeply arbitrary. Appointment procedures varied widely within ethnic groups and clear succession institutions were rarely codified. This has heightened present-day risks of two types of capture: *hereditary capture*, with permanent control by single families, and *partisan capture*, the political imposition of partisan chiefs. Formal models of political accountability argue that it can operate through two channels: voters either induce politicians to behave well by prospectively screening for "good types," those most likely to perform in a community's interest, as they initially select leaders; alternatively, voters retrospectively sanction poor performers by removing them from office.[49] Extending these models to chieftaincy, each form of capture facilitated by colonial invention limits accountability by reducing communities' ability both to screen for more altruistic chiefs when appointments are made and then to sanction rent-seeking chiefs once they are appointed.

In terms of hereditary capture, the original families empowered by the colonial state have in some cases used the economic advantages they accrued over time (see Chapter 4) to capture effectively permanent control.[50] An illustrative case is Lawra, the Dagaba town highlighted at the opening of Chapter 1, where the British introduced chieftaincy in 1903. Starting from their first appointment to the position in 1927, the Karbo family has been able to sustain dynastic local power in the absence of clear succession rules. The second Karbo chief's son, Abayifaa Karbo, was among the first Dagaba to receive higher education and was elected

---

[48] Baldwin and Holzinger (2019) provide broader cross-national evidence of variation in forms of bottom-up accountability between chiefs and community members across Africa.

[49] Fearon (1999).

[50] Hereditary positions mostly do not employ primogeniture. Instead, positions pass within the broader patriline: a dying chief's brothers and patrilineal first cousins, as well as all of their sons, are potentially eligible.

as the area's first MP, benefitting from the support of his father, who he eventually succeeded as chief.[51] Upon Abayifaa Karbo's death in 2004, the wealth and educational advantages that the Karbos had accumulated allowed them to "ride rough-shod" over other claimants, interpreting ambiguous rules in their own favor and installing Abayifaa's nephew as the new chief.[52] Like his grandfather once did for his uncle, this chief now uses his influence to campaign openly for his son, who became the area's MP.[53]

Lawra exemplifies a pattern among "invented chiefs" groups. I measure hereditary capture using contemporary registers from the National House of Chiefs, the official agency that registers chiefs, combined with the British archival documents listing all chiefs in the Northern Territories in 1909, 1922, and 1934 (see Chapter 6). This data suggests that the sustained capture of chieftaincy positions by single families is especially common among groups with invented chiefs. While not a full list of all chiefs, the contemporary registers list any changes in chieftaincy appointments dating back to the 1980s. For the 485 rural communities with documented changes, I code that 44 percent of positions passed between chiefs sharing the same surname in "invented chiefs" groups compared to only 19 percent for "always chiefs" groups.[54] In addition, I match the two sets of lists to code whether contemporary chiefs share a surname with colonial-era chiefs from the same community, indicative that the same family has likely held power for decades. Across the 534 rural communities in the contemporary records that I can match to colonial-era records, there are three times as many cases in which a family from the early colonial period still occupies the chieftaincy among "invented chiefs" (30 percent) than "always chiefs" groups (10 percent).

Alternatively, where single families have not captured indefinite hereditary control, succession disputes are common, creating opportunities for Ghana's ruling parties to install captured partisan chiefs. MacGaffey (2013, 162) describes that partisan interference in chieftaincy has become so common that "litigation and political alliance with the party in power" are now major mechanisms for appointing chiefs. When a new ruling

[51] Bening (1990, 133), Lentz (2006, 205–209).
[52] Awedoba et al. (2009, 53).
[53] Brankopowers (2017).
[54] As in Chapter 6, I first remove all Christian and Muslim name fragments that do not indicate family ties.

party takes power, they often seek to intervene in on-going succession disputes to install allied chiefs. "It's musical chairs: get this person who does not support our cause out and get another person in there," one respondent describes.[55] This creates another avenue to capture: many chiefs are popularly known to be "NDC men" or "NPP men," partisans whose continued power depends on their ties to a specific party.[56] When making endorsements in their communities, these chiefs "are looking at ... [who] contributed to my being where I am today ... It's time to pay them back."[57]

Succession disputes that allow for partisan interference are also far more common in the "invented chiefs" groups. Awedoba et al. (2009) comprehensively document all active succession disputes in the first decade of the 21st century, the same period examined below. Among thirty-one disputes, 68 percent (21) involved invented chieftaincies, including five of the seven "invented chiefs" groups.[58] Awedoba et al. (2009) trace most of these disputes to ambiguities left behind by haphazard colonial institution-building.

Both dynamics contrast with groups that have always had chiefs. These groups rotate positions among "gates," or sub-group clans. At any one time the paramount is from one gate, while divisional and village-level chiefs are from others. Rather than allowing for capture by a single family, positions are not hereditary and offices are typically not held for life. Instead, in a system locally labeled "itinerant chiefship,"[59] chiefs start their careers at the lowest levels and are gradually promoted or rotated to other positions. Among the Dagomba – for whom chieftaincy dates to the 15th century – there are usually multiple candidates, each representing different families, lobbying for each position. Although "pecuniary considerations" clearly matter and some appointments are "chopped" (bought) in the manner described in Chapter 5, higher-level chiefs are

---

[55] Interview with Dagaba civil society activist, Tamale, June 30, 2018. Similarly, Lund (2008, 23) observes that in the mixed Kusasi and Mamprusi communities around Bawku, in Upper East Region, "chiefs have been put in and out of office with government changes to such an extent that most villages around Bawku have a current as well as a former (and possibly future) chief."

[56] "We have NPP chiefs and NDC chiefs. We know them. You don't need a soothsayer to tell you that this man is here and this man is there." Interview with scholar and Sisala royal family member, Tamale, June 27, 2018.

[57] Interview with Dagaba civil society activist, Tamale, June 30, 2018.

[58] The only "invented chiefs" groups without documented succession disputes are tiny: the Mo and Namnam, each less than 1% of the northern population.

[59] Interview with registrar of the Dagbon Traditional Council, Tamale, May 24, 2019.

said to consider local preferences when making appointments. An official in the Dagbon Traditional Council observes that "you must already show the community that you have them at heart." While the appointing chief makes the ultimate decisions, "the community can even say that ... we prefer this one. If the [appointing] chief is ok with that, he'll listen."[60] In turn, ordinary Dagomba have informal veto powers that create avenues for bottom-up accountability; for example, "the people may refuse to allow [a new chief] to occupy the palace if they do not like him."[61] Similarly, some positions are also set aside for "commoners," creating an institutionalized means for new, previously nonroyal families to enter traditional leadership.[62]

Instead of dynastic capture, chiefs in this context are often outsiders to the communities they oversee and hope to maintain good relations with residents in order to rise in the future. Protests to higher-level chiefs can block future promotion. To the extent itinerant chiefs want respect and compliance from local residents, they often have to work to earn it; in such a context, the official in the Traditional Council reports, "once there's dissatisfaction, you have a difficulty in working there. Even as a chief when you give orders, people are very reluctant in following that order."[63] Returning to the accountability framework summarized in Fearon (1999), this set of institutions creates opportunities to screen for better chiefs at the outset, by considering a wider range of candidates beyond a single family, while the possibility of promotion and rotation creates an implicit threat of sanction for ambitious chiefs that may help deter some abuses.

Similar institutions exist among all but one of the other "always chiefs" groups.[64] For example, the Gonja system "allows a person ... to rise from being a relative nobody to the paramountcy."[65] Tonah (2004) documents similar forms of bottom-up accountability in a Mamprusi community in which residents rejected an unpopular appointment and forced a candidate from another family to be chosen. These similar institutions co-evolved alongside each other – with significant borrowing

---

[60] Interview with registrar of the Dagbon Traditional Council, Tamale, May 24, 2019.
[61] MacGaffey (2013, 95).
[62] Staniland (1975, 26), Awedoba et al. (2009, 205).
[63] Interview with registrar of the Dagbon Traditional Council, Tamale, May 24, 2019.
[64] The exception is the Kasena, the smallest "always chiefs" group, among whom many positions are instead hereditary.
[65] Awedoba et al. (2009, 139). On Gonja appointment institutions, also see Wilks et al. (1986, 8–16) and Goody (1967).

across groups – in the nineteenth century and earlier. They are not pure precolonial legacies, however. Some of the similarity also dates to concurrent British efforts to codify institutions for each of these kingdoms in the early 1930s as the colonial state implemented the Native Authority system – a step taken among the "always chiefs" groups, but notably not among the "invented chiefs" groups.[66]

There are still succession disputes at the highest levels in some of these kingdoms, most notably a long-running feud among gates seeking the Dagomba paramountcy (see Chapter 8). But at lower levels – especially among divisional and village chiefs – power is decentralized across a complex, ever shifting assortment of families. Tellingly, Awedoba et al. (2009) document succession disputes at the sub-paramount level in only one "always chief" group – the Gonja – but do so for every "invented chiefs" group for which there are disputes.

More quantitatively, Afrobarometer surveys show that these differences in institutions are reflected in contemporary perceptions of chiefs' accountability. Respondents in Northern Ghana from ethnic groups with invented chiefs are less likely to report that their chiefs listen to their concerns than respondents from groups that have always had chiefs (75 percent "always chiefs" vs. 60 percent "invented chiefs," $N = 183$, $p = 0.06$).[67] Respondents from groups with invented chiefs are also 10 percentage points less likely to report trusting their chiefs than respondents from groups that have always had chiefs ($p < 0.01$, $N = 528$).[68]

Combined with the presence of the "never recognized" groups, these differences in accountability allow for two main comparisons below. First, by comparing "invented chiefs" and "never recognized" communities, I can examine the resource extraction of community-level

---

[66] These efforts are described in Lund (2008, 33). Also see *Northern Territories Annual Report for 1930–1931* (1931) and *Northern Territories Annual Report for 1933–1934* (1934). In the process of codifying succession rules, the British also changed them, using precolonial practices as a template, while interrupting existing lines of succession to ensure the appointment of chiefs preferred by colonial leaders. For example, on the Wala case, see Wilks (1989, 148). The implications of these changes for future conflicts are discussed in Chapter 8.

[67] I introduce the Afrobarometer data below. Question Q54C (Round 4).

[68] Questions Q49I (Round 4) and Q52K (Round 6). However, respondents from groups with invented chiefs report personally interacting with chiefs during the past year at the same rate as respondents from groups that have always had chiefs (31 percent vs. 32 percent), indicative of the similar formal roles played by both types of chiefs. Questions Q27B (Round 4) and Q29F (Round 6).

brokers who are likely to be unaccountable to their voters versus a reference category of communities that largely lack these brokers at the community level. Chapter 5 describes the incomplete and still on-going efforts by some "never recognized" communities to invent chiefs for themselves in the modern period, but notes that in the large majority of communities any newly created chiefs are still not widely accepted by community members or gazetted by the state, limiting the degree to which they can act as influential community-level brokers. As a result, for most areas dominated by "never recognized" groups, the parties must engage voters through other means than chiefs.[69] Second, by comparing "invented chiefs" and "always chiefs" communities, I can examine the differential effectiveness of community-level brokers who are relatively more or less accountable. The argument above predicts a clear direction for both main comparisons: *communities with colonially invented chiefs should fare worse at securing state resources.*

The argument above is agnostic about the third possible comparison – between "never recognized" and "always chiefs" communities. While the differences in selection institutions documented here indicate that "always chiefs" communities have less capture than "invented chiefs" communities, chiefs whose positions date to the precolonial period are still unelected and bottom-up accountability mechanisms remain informal. It is not clear whether chiefs in "always chiefs" groups will be sufficiently accountable overall that the benefits of collective bargaining through a community-level broker outweigh the risks of rent-seeking.

7.3 DATA SOURCES

The analysis employs three data sources. First, I examine bloc voting at the community (village) level using geo-coded polling station results from the 2012 and 2016 presidential elections for all rural areas in the North.[70] As of 2012, polling stations in the rural north had 491 registered voters on average, mostly corresponding to a single community or section of a town. Polling stations are joined with the same

---

[69] The main exceptions are the small set of cases where a chief from a "never recognized" group has been formally enskinned and gazetted within the hierarchy of a neighboring "always chief" groups (e.g., the Uchabor-Boro, the chief of Saboba, is an official appointee within the Dagbon Traditional Council, as described in Chapter 5). In a robustness test, I find that all results below are robust to dropping any communities in which the official chieftaincy registries from the National House of Chiefs indicate that a cross-ethnic appointment has been made.

[70] 2012 results are only available for forty-eight of fifty-seven constituencies.

enumeration area-level 2010 census data examined in the earlier chapters to calculate demographic characteristics. I approximate demographics of each polling station by taking spatially weighted averages of census characteristics in the vicinity (two kilometer radius). Second, I examine individual-level contact with parties using Afrobarometer data, subsetting to rural respondents in Northern Ghana. I rely on the Round 5 (2012; $N = 424$ in the north) and Round 6 (2015, $N = 376$) surveys. Both are representative samples of each Northern region (province). I calculate demographic characteristics of the communities in which each respondent resides by linking respondents to their census enumeration areas. Third, I estimate the contemporary provision of state resources by examining changes in enumeration area-level census data between the 2000 and 2010 censuses.[71]

7.4 QUANTIFYING CHIEFS' INFLUENCE AS BROKERS

The first set of analyses confirm quantitatively that chiefs in Northern Ghana serve as community-level brokers. In line with the discussion above, I show that having chiefs predicts vote coordination at the polling station (community) level and that chiefs allow parties to substitute away from direct individual-level mobilization through the party organization itself. Each result is strongest for groups with chiefs invented by the state.

7.4.1 Bloc Voting by Community

I first examine the clustering of votes in the 2012 and 2016 presidential election by rural polling station. Clustering indicates bloc voting, a key component of a broker's ability to engage in an exchange with a party.[72] The outcome is a Herfindahl index of vote shares at each polling station; scaled from 0 to 1, this is the probability that two randomly selected voters supported the same party.[73]

---

[71] Slightly different enumeration areas boundaries were used in each census. I calculate a weighted average of the 2000 data within each 2010 enumeration area boundary, weighting by the proportion of the area of each 2000 enumeration area within the 2010 enumeration area. To account for measurement error, I construct a Herfindahl index of the extent to which the surface area of each 2010 enumeration area is concentrated within in a single 2000 enumeration area. I use this as a control below; the results are also robust to dropping matches in the bottom 25th percentile on this index.

[72] Conroy-Krutz (2018).

[73] I focus on the presidential election both because it is by far the most important office for the distribution of state resources, and because it holds fixed the candidates across locations. There is also much more missingness in the parliamentary results.

I estimate two sets of OLS models in Table 7.1. First, to ease interpretation of ecological data, I restrict columns 1 and 2 to communities
where the large majority of the population ($\geq$ 75 percent) is from a single
ethnic group.[74] The predictor in column 1 is an indicator for whether the
polling station is dominated by a group that has never had recognized
chiefs. Communities with chiefs ("invented chiefs" or "always chiefs")
are the omitted category. Column 2 flips this: the predictors are communities that always had chiefs or have invented chiefs. In columns 3 and
4, I instead examine marginal differences in the population proportion
of each type of ethnic group, using the full sample. All models include
parliamentary constituency fixed effects.[75] All models also control for
underlying demographic characteristics that could affect vote coordination.[76] Standard errors are clustered by the plurality ethnic group in each
community.

In column 1, I find that communities that do not have recognized chiefs
score 2.8 percentage points ($p = 0.02$) lower on the index of vote clustering than communities with chiefs. Column 2 shows that, by contrast,
communities dominated by groups with invented chiefs score 5.1 percentage points higher ($p < 0.01$) than communities of groups without
chiefs. This is substantively large: 5.1 percentage points on the Herfindahl
index is equivalent to the difference between a polling station in which the
NDC and NPP both received 50% of the vote and a station in which one
received 65.9 percent and the other 34.1%. In addition, column 2 shows
that communities of groups that have always had chiefs are also more
likely to cluster their votes than those without chiefs, although $p = 0.08$.
Columns 3–4 show that similar results hold for marginal differences in
population proportions in the full sample.[77]

7.4.2 Party Contact and Individual-Level Engagement

Next, I examine whether ethnic groups that engage in more bloc voting
are also less exposed to individual-level contact with parties, indicative

---

[74] This applies to 74 percent of stations.

[75] Ghana's parties organize campaign strategies by constituency. This also controls for
possible spillover from concurrent parliamentary elections.

[76] These are: ethnic fractionalization, electricity access, the extent of secondary education,
and the proportion with formal or public sector employment. The latter three collectively
indicate whether a polling station is situated in a more developed town or a small village.

[77] Variation in bloc voting cannot be explained by direct ethnic voting. These results are
robust to dropping polling stations with majorities from either group with candidates
contesting the elections. In both elections, the NDC presidential candidate was Gonja
and the NPP vice presidential candidate was Mamprusi.

TABLE 7.1 *Voter coordination by polling station, 2012 and 2016 presidential elections*

Outcome: Herfindahl index of vote coordination by polling station (PS)	1	2	3	4
PS of "never recognized" group (0,1)	−0.028* (0.012)			
PS of "always chief" group (0,1)		0.020 † (0.011)		
PS of "invented chief" group (0,1)		0.051** (0.017)		
Pop. % from "never recognized" groups			−0.037** (0.013)	
Pop. % from "always chief" groups				0.000 (0.018)
Pop. % from "invented chief" groups				0.049* (0.022)
Ethnic fractionalization	−0.031* (0.016)	−0.032* (0.015)	−0.014 (0.010)	−0.011 (0.010)
Electricity access %	−0.045*** (0.012)	−0.042*** (0.012)	−0.046*** (0.012)	−0.040*** (0.012)
Secondary education %	0.139 (0.101)	0.149 (0.098)	0.103 (0.077)	0.130† (0.070)
Formal sector employment %	−0.010 (0.051)	−0.011 (0.051)	0.006 (0.048)	−0.002 (0.045)
2016 election (0,1)	−0.022** (0.008)	−0.022** (0.008)	−0.021** (0.007)	−0.021** (0.007)
Parliamentary const. fixed effects	Y	Y	Y	Y
N	5,500	5,500	7,410	7,410
adj. R^2	0.191	0.193	0.192	0.192

† significant at $p < 0.10$; *$p < 0.05$; **$p < 0.01$; ***$p < 0.001$. All models are OLS, with parliamentary constituency fixed effects. Columns 1 and 2 are restricted to polling stations in which one type of ethnic group makes up 75 percent or more of the surrounding population. Columns 3 and 4 include all polling stations. Standard errors clustered by the plurality ethnic group at each polling station.

that brokerage via traditional leaders substitutes for more direct mobilization. The unit of analysis shifts to the individual voter. Table 7.2 focuses on two outcomes: whether Afrobarometer respondents report being offered gifts for their votes and whether respondents report direct personal interactions with party agents.[78] The first is a standard measure of exposure to individual-level electoral clientelism.[79] The second proxies for connections to party agents – the primary actor through which Ghana's parties engage in individual-level, house-to-house campaigns within communities when not using chiefs as community-level brokers.[80] These are linear probability models (OLS) with standard errors clustered by ethnic group. I include individual- and community-level controls that could also affect campaign attention, including the margin of the previous presidential election in each respondent's parliamentary constituency to rule out differences between core vs. swing areas.

Colonially invented chiefs appear to substitute the most for direct campaigning by parties. Column 1 of Table 7.2 shows that respondents from "never recognized" groups are 7.5 percentage points ($p = 0.02$) more likely to receive direct offers of vote buying than respondents from groups with invented chiefs (the omitted category). Column 2 shows that respondents from "never recognized" groups are 8.7 percentage points ($p < 0.001$) more likely to have contact with party organizations. This more than doubles the baseline level of contact (8.2 percent) in groups with invented chiefs. Column 2 also shows significantly greater partisan contact for respondents from the "always chiefs" groups compared to those with invented chiefs. This is consistent the result above: groups that have always had chiefs both coordinate their votes to a lesser degree and receive more direct mobilization.

Column 3 introduces an indicator for whether a respondent is from the same ethnic group as their Traditional Council jurisdiction. Respondents of the same ethnicity as the state-recognized local chiefs in their area – and thus those most likely to have social ties to these chiefs – are 5.4 percentage points ($p = 0.001$) less likely to have contact with party agents. Column 4 finds that contact with party agents increases in distance from the seat of a powerful paramount or divisional chief – the higher-level chiefs in the hierarchy of each Traditional Council (see Chapter 3). A

[78] The questions are: "During the last national election in 2008, how often, if ever did a candidate or someone from a political party offer you something, like food or a gift or money, in return for your vote?"; "During the past year, how often have you contacted any of the following persons about some important problem or to give them your views: A political party official?"

[79] Kramon (2019).

[80] Nathan (2019), Brierley and Kramon (2020), Brierley and Nathan (2021a).

TABLE 7.2 *Party contact by chieftaincy type, Afrobarometer respondents*

Outcome:	1 Campaign gift	2 Party agent contact	3 Party agent contact	4 Party agent contact
"Never recognized" group (0,1)	0.075* (0.032)	0.087*** (0.022)		
"Always chief" group (0,1)	0.016 (0.014)	0.101*** (0.021)		
Same group as local Traditional Area (0,1)			−0.054*** (0.016)	
Distance (km) to Closest Major Chieftaincy				0.003* (0.001)
Age (years)	−0.010 (0.006)	0.000 (0.006)	0.001 (0.006)	0.000 (0.006)
Age * Age	0.000 (0.000)	0.000 (0.000)	0.000 (0.000)	0.000 (0.000)
Female (0,1)	−0.001 (0.020)	−0.101*** (0.021)	−0.102*** (0.021)	−0.101*** (0.021)
Secondary education (0,1)	−0.033 (0.035)	−0.019 (0.022)	−0.024 (0.021)	−0.017 (0.022)
Assets index	0.032 (0.017)	0.069*** (0.016)	0.072*** (0.017)	0.072*** (0.017)
Community electricity access %	−0.037 (0.037)	0.051 (0.065)	0.065 (0.069)	0.070 (0.063)
Community secondary education %	0.046 (0.149)	−0.547* (0.264)	−0.654* (0.286)	−0.702** (0.265)
Community formal sector employ. %	−0.245 (0.232)	0.190 (0.385)	0.128 (0.387)	0.275 (0.399)
ln(Community population)	0.004 (0.009)	0.001 (0.015)	0.009 (0.016)	0.012 (0.015)
Margin of previous presidential election (parl. constituency level)	0.095 (0.089)	0.010 (0.084)	−0.068 (0.093)	−0.028 (0.084)
Afrobarometer round 6 (0,1)		0.087** (0.024)	0.100*** (0.026)	0.088** (0.027)
Constant	0.181 (0.117)	0.037 (0.161)	0.095 (0.173)	0.008 (0.164)
N	379	664	664	664

(continued)

TABLE 7.2 *(continued)*

Outcome:	1 Campaign gift	2 Party agent contact	3 Party agent contact	4 Party agent contact
Mean of the outcome variable	0.061	0.149	0.149	0.149
Afrobarometer survey clusters	49	90	90	90
Afrobarometer round(s)	R5	R5, R6	R5, R6	R5, R6

[†] significant at $p < 0.10$; [*]$p < 0.05$; [**]$p < 0.01$; [***]$p < 0.001$. OLS coefficients with robust standard errors clustered by ethnic group. To ease interpretation, I drop the small minority of respondents living in the north who are from southern ethnic groups.

respondent twenty kilometers further away from a community where a major chief sits is 6.0 percentage points ($p = 0.01$) more likely to have contact with party agents.

These patterns closely match interview evidence on how parties campaign. For example, a very common claim among party elites was, in the words of an NDC constituency leader, that when seeking votes from communities where chiefs are available as effective brokers, "we don't go for each house to house from one person to another. We just go to the community."[81] In this way, chiefs are efficiency enhancing for parties. But in "never recognized" communities without chiefs who can act as community-level brokers, direct contact between the parties and voters becomes more common, as the party works for each individual vote.

In the oral history interviews, respondents were asked who in the community serves as their main point of contact with politicians. In all six Dagaba and Frafra communities ("invented chiefs"), respondents mentioned the chief as being among the key intermediaries. For example, in one Frafra community, elders described that the chief has a close relationship with the MP, who visits him regularly, and hosts campaign events at his palace in pursuit of his endorsement.[82] But the chief was not identified as the key link to politicians in any of the six Konkomba communities ("never recognized"); instead respondents in four of the six communities identified local party branch executives as their main

[81] Interview with NDC constituency executive, Northern Region, Tamale, May 13, 2019.
[82] Interview with chiefs' relatives and tendana, Community #1, Bolgatanga East District, May 20, 2019.

point of contact with politicians, suggesting there is much more direct engagement with the party organization. In one Konkomba community, one elder reported that they "don't have anybody to lead them to [politicians] for help.. it's all just individuals for themselves" interacting with politicians on their own.[83]

7.5 IMPLICATIONS FOR STATE RESOURCE DISTRIBUTION

I now turn to the key estimates of interest: whether the brokerage role of chiefs helps voters extract valuable resources from the state. For each of the two main comparisons outlined above – "invented chiefs" vs. "never recognized," "invented chiefs" vs. "always chiefs" – I find that communities of groups with invented chiefs – the areas most directly reshaped by the state's interventions into society – benefit less from the contemporary distribution of state resources. I begin with descriptive analyses of these comparisons and then use the pre-1914 colonial border for a better-identified examination of the comparison between the "invented chiefs" and "never recognized" communities.

The unit of analysis shifts back to the community, now proxied by the 2010 census enumeration area, as in Chapter 4. I focus on resources that can only be provided by the state to isolate provision by state leaders from the potentially separate ability of communities to self-provide or co-produce their own smaller-scale resources, as examined instead by Baldwin (2015, 2019).[84] I include multiple resources to avoid over-interpreting patterns for any specific good.[85] I examine five measures of state distribution: (i) the percentage of residents with electricity; (ii) the percentage of adults with some secondary education, indicative of both government provision of secondary schools, scarce in the North, and provision of scholarships, a common private patronage good; (iii) the percentage with access to piped water, which is increasingly available in Northern towns; (iv) the percentage with public sector employment, indicative of access to patronage jobs; and (v) whether each enumeration area was included in one of the new administrative districts

---

[83] Interview with uninkpel (elder), Community #1, Mion District, May 16, 2019.

[84] Public sector jobs and new districts are out of the control of local communities. Expansions to electricity and piped water, as well as construction of new secondary schools, are very capital intensive, requiring direct state involvement.

[85] Kramon and Posner (2013).

created between 2000 and 2010.[86] Because they divide local government resources over a smaller group of people, new districts direct a bundle of valuable benefits to recipient communities and are highly valued by residents.[87]

The analyses all focus on contemporary flows of resources, examining the 2010 level of each resource controlling for the 2000 level, to isolate changes in resource provision that happened within an electoral period when chiefs could serve as community-level brokers.[88] These analyses thus explicitly compare communities with the same historically accumulated level of each resource, such that aggregate differences in initial levels across groups cannot account for the results. There are longer-run inequities in levels, or stocks, of these resources. As described above, in the autocratic periods preceding democratization both sets of groups with chiefs – the "always chiefs" *and* "invented chiefs" groups – received more initial state investments than the "never recognized" communities, leaving them with greater stocks upon democratization.

Figure 7.1 presents head-to-head comparisons of each category of ethnic groups. The x-axis is the coefficient from separate OLS regressions of each outcome variable (y-axis) on the population proportion in each community from either the "invented chiefs" (top two panels) or "never recognized" groups (bottom panel). The top panel of Figure 7.1 drops all communities with majority "always chiefs" populations to compare communities with invented chiefs and those that never have had chiefs. The middle panel instead drops communities with majority populations from the "never recognized" groups to compare groups with invented chiefs and those that always have had chiefs. The bottom panel drop communities with majority "invented chiefs" populations to compare the "never recognized" and "always chiefs" groups. The first four outcomes in each plot are the 2010 level of each variable, controlling for the 2000 level in the same community. The fifth outcome is an indicator for an enumeration area being included in a new district between 2000 and 2010.

---

[86] The number of districts went from twenty-four to fifty in the north between 2000 and 2010. I code any enumeration area as being in a "new" district if its original district was split.

[87] Grossman and Lewis (2014), Hassan (2016).

[88] The over time changes in the percentages of residents with access to each resource are not always positive at the community level. For example, the mean proportion with water access over time is flat. But in the face of population growth, maintaining the same percentage with access still reflects increased provision (i.e., larger absolute number of connections).

To account for variation in both demand and the marginal cost of extending services, I control for the distance to the nearest electrified or piped enumeration area as of 2000 in the analyses for electrification and running water, and the 2000 rate of completed middle school education in the analyses of secondary school access. To account for partisan favoritism, I control for 2000 NDC vote share by parliamentary constituency. To account for community wealth, I control for each community's level of development as of 2000, measured as electrification and formal sector employment. Other controls include: community size (logged 2000 population); each community's distance to its district capital (the largest town in the area) as of 2000; the index of the overlap between the census maps; and each community's distance to the hometown of its MP.[89]

The first four models in each plot of Figure 7.1 also include fixed effects for the 2000 district, to examine distribution within districts. After decentralization, districts in Ghana have received formula-based allocations of funds from the national government, which are then allocated within districts by local officials of the national ruling party.[90] Most opportunities for political targeting of local public goods and public sector patronage jobs are thus *within district*.[91] Traditional Council jurisdictions and administrative districts can cross-cut, such that most districts contain a mix of groups with different types of chieftaincy. I instead include region fixed effects for the final outcome, as the government assigned the number of new districts to each region proportional to population and then made within-region decisions about boundaries. Standard errors for the first four outcome variables are clustered by the community's plurality ethnic group.[92]

The key result across Figure 7.1 is that communities with larger populations from groups with invented chiefs do significantly worse in

---

[89] MPs can affect distribution separately through a constituency development fund (CDF). This measures the average distance to the hometown of each MP, weighted by years in office.

[90] Banful (2011), Williams (2017).

[91] Nathan (2019). The main possible exception is electricity; some electrification projects are instead decided nationally by the electrical utility. The results for electricity are robust to dropping the fixed effects.

[92] A large literature establishes that new districts in Africa, including in Ghana, are often targeted as patronage to specific spatially clustered ethnic groups (e.g., Grossman and Lewis 2014, Hassan 2016). I do not cluster errors by ethnic group when the outcome is new district, because new districts are largely targeted at the ethnic group level, with limited within-cluster variation in the outcome.

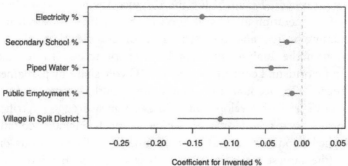

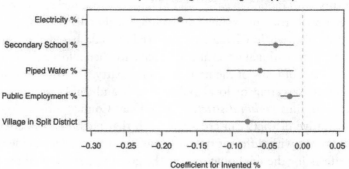

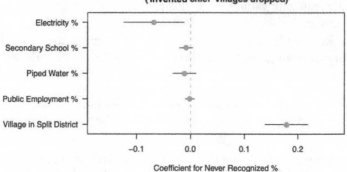

FIGURE 7.1 Distribution between 2000 and 2010, head-to-head comparisons. OLS coefficients with 95 percent confidence intervals. Coefficients are not standardized – the range on the x-axis varies with the range of each outcome.

contemporary access to each type of resource, when compared both to "never recognized" communities and "always chiefs" communities. These disadvantages are substantively large: the average community dominated by an ethnic group with invented chiefs saw a 14-percentage point smaller increase ($p = 0.004$) in the percentage of its residents with access to electricity than an otherwise similar "never recognized" community without a formal chief (top panel); this difference is even larger for the comparison to "always chiefs" communities, with potentially more accountable chiefs (17 p.p., $p < 0.001$). Similarly, "invented chiefs" communities were eleven ($p < 0.001$) and eight ($p = 0.01$) percentage points less likely to be included in new districts compared to "never recognized' and "always chiefs" communities, respectively.

By contrast, there is no consistent pattern in the third head-to-head comparison in the bottom panel of Figure 7.1, comparing communities dominated by groups that have always had chiefs and have never had recognized chiefs. "Never recognized" communities receive less electricity than "always chiefs" communities, but are more likely to be included in new districts. There are no differences for the other outcomes.

The comparisons in Figure 7.1 are observational. But the control variables rule out most plausible sources of potential confounding, even in the "invented chiefs" and "always chiefs" comparison (middle panel), in which chieftaincy is definitely not exogenously assigned. By focusing on contemporary changes in access, these models compare communities of the same size and level of development that had otherwise similar resource access as of 2000; any historical differences across ethnic groups that could also explain differences in resource provision up to that point will already drop out.

I can also turn to a better identified approach for the comparison of the "invented chiefs" and "never recognized" communities (top panel of Figure 7.1). As detailed in Chapter 4, the pre–World War I (1899–1914) Anglo-German colonial border creates plausibly exogenous variation in the colonial invention of chieftaincy compared to the "never recognized" groups. In Figure 7.2, I leverage this exogeneity to repeat the analysis for the comparison of the "invented chiefs" and "never recognized" groups in Figure 7.1 above, again dropping all communities with majority "always chief" populations. Figure 7.2 contains the same OLS estimates from above for the coefficients on the proportion of the population in each enumeration area from an "invented chiefs" group. It then compares these estimates to coefficients from (a) a new analysis that instruments

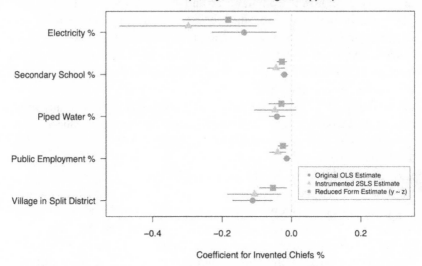

FIGURE 7.2 Comparison of OLS, 2SLS, and reduced form estimates for head-to-head comparison of "invented chiefs" and "never recognized" groups, with 95% confidence intervals.

for each community's population proportion from "invented chiefs" ethnic groups using two-stage least squares (2SLS) and (b) reduced form ("intent-to-treat") models, which are OLS regressions of each outcome on the instrument. The analysis remains at the community level with district fixed effects and includes the same controls as above.[93] Standard errors remain clustered as in Figure 7.1.

The treatment in the 2SLS models is each community's population share from ethnic groups with invented chiefs. The instrument is the community's population share from ethnic groups that had both (a) been precolonially acephalous and (b) initially lived entirely on the British side of the Anglo-German border. Given that the British invented chiefs among almost all precolonially acephalous groups on their side of the border and none on the other side, the first stage relationship between this instrument and the treatment is very strong. The 2SLS models estimate a Local Average Treatment Effect (LATE) among "compliers," which in this case are communities that have larger populations from "invented chiefs" groups

---

[93] Because the controls are all "post-treatment," I also conduct similar analyses without the controls and find that all results are robust to excluding them.

because they have larger populations from ethnic groups that were once acephalous and had initially lived on the British side of the pre-1914 border. The reduced form estimates instead provide an overall comparison of precolonially acephalous ethnic groups that initially lived on each side of the pre-1914 Anglo-German border.

Figure 7.2 confirms the descriptive result from above: communities with larger populations from groups with invented chiefs are disadvantaged in their ability to extract all five types of state resources relative to communities populated by groups that largely lack traditional leaders who could serve as effective community-level brokers. This is consistent with invented chiefs reducing the benefits voters can extract from politicians relative to not having chiefs. All estimated effects are similar across the OLS, 2SLS, and reduced form models, although some estimates for water are now only significant at the $p < 0.1$ level.

7.6 ALTERNATIVE EXPLANATIONS

Additional analyses rule out potential alternative explanations. First, I address several possible concerns with using changes on the census as a measure of resource distribution. In addition to the fact that I control for the 2000 level of each resource, there is little risk of ceiling effects: despite baseline inequities, all groups entered 2000 with significant need for each resource. Moreover, differences between the separate comparisons of "invented chiefs" vs. "never recognized" communities and "always chiefs" vs. "never recognized" communities clearly rule out that the results could be due to a simple "catch up" effect, in which ethnic groups that have lower initial stocks on average in 2000 receive more between 2000 and 2010 because of greater need.[94] In addition, all results are robust to controlling for changes in total population and are not artefacts of differential population growth.[95]

Second, the evidence above is not simply the incumbent (2001–2008) NPP government directing resources away from NDC supporters.

---

[94] Both the "invented chiefs" and "always chiefs" communities have greater stocks of each resource on average in 2000 than the "never recognized" communities. But while I find more contemporary flows to "never recognized" communities than "invented chiefs" communities, there are no clear differences between "never recognized" vs. "always chiefs" communities.

[95] Where appropriate, the results are also robust to examining dichotomous shifts in access – that is, whether a community has any electricity or not – not just percentage changes in levels.

Although some parts of the North historically favor the NDC,[96] the "invented chiefs" groups are not homogeneously pro-NDC and all models already control for NDC vote share at the parliamentary constituency level. They are also robust to controlling for constituency-level competitiveness. I cannot measure community-level partisanship in the same time window as the census data because polling station results are not available before 2012. But I use the 2012 and 2016 results to identify communities most likely to have been core NDC strongholds across time as enumeration areas containing polling stations with NDC vote share above the 75th percentile across both elections. All results hold when dropping these most consistent NDC strongholds, suggesting the results hold when subsetting primarily to swing and pro-government (NPP) communities.

Third, even though I restrict to state-provided resources, there could be concern that these differences are still an outcome of each group's propensity for self-provision via collective action. I measure collective action through two indicators from the Afrobarometer for how often respondents come together with their community to solve problems.[97] The first is an indicator for whether a respondent ever joined with others in his/her community to act collectively on an issue.[98] The second indicator collapses two questions measuring participating in community-level civic associations or other civil society groups – the types of organizations that could oversee a community's self-provision of local public goods – into a binary variable for any associational membership.[99] In Table 7.3 I regress these indicators on each respondent's group type, plus the same covariates as Table 7.2. The models are logistic regressions with standard errors clustered by ethnic group. In the opposite of what would need to hold if this alternative were true, groups with invented chiefs are *most*

---

[96] Bob-Milliar (2011).

[97] These questions come from Rounds 4-6.

[98] Q: "Here is a list of actions that people sometimes take as citizens. For each of these, please tell me whether you, personally, have done any of these things during the past year. If not, would you do this if you had the chance: Got together with others to raise an issue?"

[99] Q1: "Let's turn to your role in the community. Now I am going to read out a list of groups that people join or attend. For each one, could you tell me whether you are an official leader, an active member, an inactive member, or not a member: A religious group that meets outside of regular worship services?"; Q2: "Let's turn to your role in the community. Now I am going to read out a list of groups that people join or attend. For each one, could you tell me whether you are an official leader, an active member, an inactive member, or not a member: Some other voluntary association or community group?"

TABLE 7.3 *Collective action by chieftaincy type, Afrobarometer respondents*

Outcome:	1 Joins with others for action	2 Joins with others for action	3 Joins with others for action	4 Civic association member	5 Civic association member	6 Civic association member
"Always chief" group (0,1)	−0.521** (0.195)			−0.338† (0.192)		
"Invented chief" group (0,1)		0.780*** (0.178)			0.543* (0.218)	
"Never recognized" group (0,1)			−0.249 (0.275)			−0.224 (0.217)
Individual-level controls	Y	Y	Y	Y	Y	Y
Community-level controls	Y	Y	Y	Y	Y	Y
N	836	836	836	848	848	848
Afrobarometer round(s)	R4, R5, R6	R4, R5, R6	R4, R5, R6	R4, R5, R6	R4, R5, R6	R4, R5, R6

† significant at $p < 0.10$; * $p < 0.05$; ** $p < 0.01$; *** $p < 0.001$. Logistic regression coefficients with robust standard errors clustered by ethnic group. All controls as in Table 2.

likely to act collectively – consistent with evidence that unaccountable chiefs can be quite effective at compelling collective behavior[100] – even as they extract the fewest state resources for their communities during modern elections.

Moreover, I conduct placebo tests for access to less capital-intensive goods that can be produced by communities on their own, without state involvement: boreholes, which Baldwin (2015) identifies as a resource that local rural communities can produce themselves,[101] and whether household trash is collected, a low-cost activity some communities coordinate on their own. Repeating the analyses above for these new outcomes, communities dominated by groups with invented chiefs are not disadvantaged in boreholes or trash collection, consistent with the results above being distinct from self-provision. It also is not credible that "invented chiefs" groups extract fewer resources because chieftaincy succession disputes leave them internally divided: this is inconsistent with the Afrobarometer result for collective action and with the finding that these groups cluster their votes the most.

Fourth, the observed disadvantages of communities populated by "invented chiefs" groups are robust to controlling for indicators of other cultural differences: religion (Islam), patrilineal versus other types of inheritance systems, a cultural attribute shown to predict political behavior,[102] and whether groups traditionally live in compact villages or scattered homesteads,[103] which may be correlated with elements of local social structure. The results are also robust to sequentially dropping communities dominated by each individual ethnic group, such that no particular cultural or other feature of a specific group is driving the results.

Fifth, in similar robustness tests as in Chapter 4, I also rule out the effects of Northern Ghana's sporadic, localized ethnic conflicts, using the geo-located conflict event data examined in more detail in Chapter 8 to

---

[100] Acemoglu et al. (2014), Baldwin and Mvukiyehe (2015), Gottlieb (2017).

[101] Boreholes could of course also be provided by local politicians (Ejdemyr et al. 2018). But unlike the resources above, digging a borehole does not *require* major state investment. Indeed, in the oral history interviews, multiple respondents identified boreholes, specifically, as a good provided through nonstate channels, including as a private donation by elite residents living in the city. For example, interview with chief, Community #2, Bolgatanga District, May 21, 2019.

[102] Robinson and Gottlieb (2021).

[103] Murdock (1967). This robustness test requires dropping the communities from groups not included in the Murdock (1967) data, however.

drop any communities most affected by conflicts that might have prevented state resource delivery. Sixth, these differences in goods provision cannot be attributed to variation in the ease of the state reaching these communities, as would be proxied by distance from the capital or other centers of state power.[104] The controls in my main specifications above already include the distance to the nearest similar good (e.g., distance to nearest electrified community as of 2000) and distance to the district capital, holding the fixed the marginal cost of reaching communities. Moreover, the district fixed effects restrict all comparisons to communities with similar distances to the capital.

Finally, many possible concerns about violations of the exclusion restriction in the 2SLS estimates above are already ruled out by the discussion of the exogeneity of the colonial border treatment in Chapter 4.[105] Moreover, because the new analyses in this chapter all control for the historically-accumulated levels of reach resource as of 2000, the exclusion restriction only must hold once conditioning on 2000 levels. An exclusion restriction violation would have to influence the 2010 levels of resources independently from the 2000 stocks in each community. But the effects on resource distribution of any unaccounted-for historical difference between groups on different sides of the 1899-1914 border are very likely to already be captured in the differences in 2000 stocks of resources.

7.7 CONCLUSION

This chapter joins Chapter 6 in demonstrating the downstream political effects of the societal changes created by the scarce state. I show that in Ghana's modern electoral period, rural communities led by chiefs invented by the state cluster their votes more – indicative that chiefs are facilitating brokered clientelism – and yet are less able to extract highly valued and scarce state resources from politicians in return for these votes. I argue that these patterns are rooted in the greater degree of capture of chieftaincy positions in these ethnic groups, which complements the similar capture in elected office-holding examined in Chapter 6. Chiefs serving in positions created by the early actions of the modern state are

---

[104] Herbst (2000).

[105] For example, the results above are robust to controlling for pre-existing geographic differences, including using localized measures of rainfall, soil quality, and slope (ruggedness) from FAO (2012).

particularly unaccountable to local residents, with dynastic families able to monopolize succession and ruling parties also able to manipulate the vague rules the state left behind to install co-partisans who do not drive hard bargains for community members when acting as brokers.

The next chapter concludes Section III by considering a final political outcome also shaped by the scarce state's actions: the onset of intra- and inter-ethnic violence. The chieftaincy succession disputes described in this chapter are one key cause of that violence, joined by the conflicts over land that emerged from the state's devolution of land rights to chiefs.

8

Nonstate Violence as a State Effect

Official or governmental intervention seems to be the genesis of the conflict.
– Awedoba et al. (2009, 53)

Ghana has been among the most peaceful countries in sub-Saharan Africa since independence. Yet its northern hinterland is the one subnational region in which this peaceful reputation is not especially accurate. Over the last four decades, Northern politics has been characterized by repeated flare-ups of violence. The largest, in 1994, killed as many as 15,000 people by some reports. None of these incidents represented a civil war or rebel insurgency. Instead, rather than targeting the state, the violence has emerged from what existing literature terms "communal" or "nonstate" conflicts. While civil wars have long been the disproportionate focus of research on conflict in Africa, nonstate communal violence has been more frequent in recent decades.[1]

The literature on conflict would not find it surprising that Ghana's most violent subnational region is a hinterland in which the state is particularly absent. Consistent with central claims in Herbst (2000) and the seminal work of Fearon and Laitin (2003), a large body of research on civil war predicts that sustaining violent mobilization is most feasible where the state is least able to police against it, especially in remote regions with terrain that is hard for the central state to penetrate.[2] A smaller and more recent literature on nonstate communal violence makes

---

[1] Sundberg et al. (2012), Cunningham and Lemke (2014), Palik et al. (2020).
[2] Buhaug and Rod (2006), Tollefsen and Buhaug (2015), Muller-Crepon et al. (2020), Lewis (2020).

nearly identical predictions – that competition between local actors "often takes a violent turn where the state is incapable of enforcing the peace."[3] Across forms of violence, the conventional wisdom is that hinterlands are especially violent because the state's absence creates a security vacuum.

Yet the main through-line connecting violence across Northern Ghana's post-independence history is that nearly every underlying conflict appears to have been caused by the state's actions – not its inaction. The Northern Ghanaian scholars contributing to Awedoba et al.'s (2009) survey of recent conflicts observe repeatedly, for conflict after conflict, a clear theme, exemplified by the opening quote: the state itself is "the genesis of conflict."[4] This chapter concludes Part III by arguing that nonstate communal violence can be another political outcome of an absent, resource-advantaged state's isolated interventions in hinterland regions. Because the state's actions have such outsize effects on society, the state's few steps into society generate waves of societal upheaval that create conflict. Even though the resulting violence is targeted at other societal actors, not the state, this "nonstate" violence still is a clear state effect. Pointing to weak state capacity is not sufficient to understand why hinterland violence occurs. Similar to Boone's (2014) characterization of violence over land elsewhere in Africa, communal violence in Northern Ghana is "as much a *result* of state-building as a reflection of the absence or failure thereof."[5] State scarcity causes violence by creating grievances in society, not through the state's inability to police.

A scarce state can generate nonstate violence in hinterlands through two channels. First, and most broadly, violence may emerge as an unintentional, unplanned side effect of state interventions into society made to address other goals. Because efforts to delegate local authority, distribute local public goods, or allocate property rights – the three main state actions introduced in Chapter 3 – provide windfalls that create new forms of inequality within or across ethnic groups, these actions also generate the underlying inter- or intra-ethnic grievances behind violent mobilization. As Chapter 5 argues, the losers of these state actions – excluded from initial windfalls – see themselves falling behind relative to the winners and mobilize in response. But rather than resisting the state's actions, as in Scott (2009), their goal is instead to get closer to the state

---

[3] Muller-Crepon et al. (2020, 8). Also see Elfversson (2015), Rudolfsen (2017).

[4] Awedoba et al. (2009, 53). This quote refers to a specific chieftaincy dispute (in Upper West Region), but similar claims are made of most conflicts in their volume.

[5] Boone (2014, 4). Emphasis in the original.

and extract windfalls of their own. Instead of civil war, the contestation that emerges becomes communal conflict in which societal actors jockey with each other for the state's attention and recognition, turning to violence as a means to remake local societal institutions in order to better position themselves to benefit from the state.

Second, in a smaller set of cases, violence may also be an intentional outcome of state action. Recognizing that the state has the potential for such outsize effects on society in these regions, state leaders may also make the state intervene selectively for the very purpose of generating new grievances that are strategically useful for their political survival. Studying communal nonstate violence in India, Wilkinson (2004) observes that inflaming ethnic conflict can be a powerful tool for polarizing a local electorate and winning votes. When state leaders face similar political incentives in hinterland regions, nonstate violence may be purposefully stoked.

I illustrate how these two channels connect state actions to hinterland violence using an original dataset of all documented violent conflict events in Northern Ghana from 1960 through early 2020. By expanding and updating existing datasets with new material from historical sources, I code the location, date, magnitude, and issues of contention in each event with one or more fatalities. Almost all of the ninety events in the data share a similar overall motivation, emerging from competition for the state's attention amidst the widespread belief that being recognized by the scarce state as the legitimate customary traditional authority in a given domain is a means to access valuable, but scarce resources. Almost all inter-ethnic violence in Northern Ghana has been about competition over which groups' set of traditional leaders will be recognized by the state, while almost all intra-ethnic violence has emerged from succession disputes over which aspiring chief will receive the state's blessing.[6]

While underlying grievances often initially emerged from the first two major state actions described in Chapter 3 – the invention of chieftaincy and differential provision of early access to education – the state's third major action – the 1979 land reform – had the most direct effect on violence. With only one exception, there is no evidence of large-scale inter- or intra-ethnic violence from independence until the 1979 change in land policy. This is even though the post-independence

---

[6] Chapters 5 and 7, respectively, have already given examples of each type of dispute.

state was relatively scarcest and most incapable of policing against violence in the 1960s and 1970s compared to the much more violent decades since. But immediately after 1979, with the new land policy raising the economic stakes of receiving the state's recognition, violence exploded.

The chapter begins by developing the argument for why nonstate communal conflict in the hinterland is better viewed as a downstream outcome of state actions, not state inaction. After introducing the data and showing how over time variation in violence is directly tied to the 1979 land reform, I then turn to descriptive regression analyses to explore community-level predictors of violence. I find little evidence that violence is predicted by standard variables suggested by the "security vacuum" explanation, such as remoteness from administrative centers or the ruggedness of terrain. Instead, inter-ethnic conflicts are most likely after 1979 in more fertile communities, where the benefits of land ownership are greater, and those populated by "never recognized" ethnic groups, the populations most threatened by the state's change in land policy. Intra-ethnic conflict is most likely where the state's differential provision of education generated more intra-ethnic, intra-communal economic inequality, a key source of capture of chieftaincy positions by privileged families (see Chapter 7). To provide more direct evidence that state actions caused this violence, I end by drawing on qualitative case studies of key examples of inter- and intra-ethnic violence.

8.1 WHY IS THERE SO MUCH VIOLENCE IN HINTERLANDS?

Economic inequality is a key predictor of nonstate communal violence in Africa.[7] It is an especially strong predictor of violence in contexts of weak state capacity, with the state least able to prevent economic grievances from flaring into violence.[8] Consistent with this interaction, other studies find that nonstate violence is more common in remote areas of African countries with limited road connectivity to the national capital.[9] Similarly, in an overview of cross-national trends in nonstate violence, Palik

[7] Fjelde and Ostby (2014). Similarly, it is also a key predictor of civil war (Ostby et al. 2009, Cederman et al. 2011, Cederman et al. 2013, Huber and Mayoral 2019). Cunningham and Lemke (2014) show that many predictors of civil war also extend to other forms of violence.

[8] Rudolfsen (2017).

[9] Muller-Crepon et al. (2020).

et al. (2020, 29) argue that many violent nonstate events "occur in the periphery" and are "a sign of lack of control or lack of interest by the state."[10]

But Chapter 2 suggests that the inequality that creates grievances and the state scarcity that constrains efforts to police against any violence that might grow from those grievances are not independent of each other. Economic inequality comes from somewhere. And an explanation of hinterland violence focused only on the direct effects of the state's inability to police is incomplete. A central claim of this book is that if the state has resource advantages relative to society, the state's very absence in hinterlands gives the few actions it does still take outsize weight, with the ability to create significant inequality within society. The state scarcity that limits state leaders' power to prevent violent mobilization may also have caused the original grievances that inspire that mobilization.[11]

This need not be intentional. Even if state leaders wished that the hinterland remained peaceful so they could focus on other more politically important subnational regions,[12] isolated state actions intended to keep the state scarce in the hinterland can generate grievances that lead to communal conflict by providing valuable economic windfalls to narrow sets of societal actors. In the absence of future state actions to offset them, or a robust private sector, the state's allocations of advantage can be expected to stick, raising the stakes for the losers of those actions to respond – regardless of whether these losers are families excluded from private benefits, or whole ethnic groups disadvantaged by uneven state investments in local public goods. As argued in Chapter 5, where the state is a net provider of highly demanded resources, the losers' bottom-up responses often taken the form of attempts to reimagine and redefine societal institutions in ways that improve their ability – or eligibility[13] – to access new state windfalls for themselves. The initial winners of state action have similar incentives to organize to prevent these changes and preserve their newfound advantages.

Where the state delegates significant grassroots authority through traditional or customary institutions at the local level, as is common in many

---

[10] Also see Elfversson (2015).

[11] Ying (2020) provides a useful parallel to these claims for the study of civil war, finding that sudden increases in state activity in areas where the state had previously been absent, not the steady state of state absence itself, is most correlated with civil war onset.

[12] Boone (2003), Slater and Kim (2015).

[13] Walker (2015).

cases in Africa and elsewhere,[14] conflicts between the winners and losers of earlier state actions become conflicts about whose version of "tradition" will be recognized by the state going forward. As Galvan (2004) shows for Senegal, customary institutions are not necessarily stagnant precolonial or colonial inheritances, but fluid and actively contested institutions that evolve through ongoing processes of institutional syncretism, with societal actors blending elements of different possible institutions into new forms that best fit their circumstances. The prospect of windfalls from the state gives members of hinterland societies incentives to reimagine traditional institutions in new ways that would benefit them. This could be inventing new forms of chieftaincy to claim state recognition, as in the Konkomba example from Chapter 5. Alternatively, it could be reinterpreting poorly codified succession rules by selectively drawing on different possible historical precedents from neighboring communities to claim that you, not a rival from another family, deserve to become the next chief, as in the chieftaincy disputes described in Chapter 7. Rather than seeking to replace the state – as among rebels in civil wars – the conflicts that emerge from these forms of bottom-up institution-building are targeted more locally, aimed at changing the status quo within society to better position oneself to be seen by the state.

This builds on Boone (2014), who observes that land-related conflicts are often highly localized in African countries with "neocustomary" land regimes, in which the state delegates control to local actors such as chiefs. In these settings, conflict is targeted at local traditional institutions, not the state itself, in contrast to a smaller set of cases with "statist" land institutions – in which access to land is distributed centrally – where land conflicts instead metastasize up into national politics.[15] But this claim that disputes over customary institutions localize conflict away from the state can apply much more broadly than to land disputes, potentially extending to any domain where state recognition of local societal institutions would confer valuable access to economic or political power. And even in heavily "neocustomary" institutional environments, the state is still a very central, albeit indirect, party to these localized conflicts. As a reserve of highly demanded resources, the state becomes the key arbiter of societal disputes, whose attention the conflicting parties actively seek. Lund (2008) observes that receiving the imprimatur of state recognition

---

[14] Gerring et al. (2011), Boone (2014), Baldwin (2015), Slater and Kim (2015), Matsuzaki (2019).

[15] In the latter case, violence is more likely to become a civil war, rather than nonstate communal conflict (Boone 2014).

and legitimacy for one's side is incredibly valuable in what are ostensibly nonstate communal conflicts because it helps signal whose competing interpretation and (re)imagining of societal institutions will be more likely to be rewarded.

In turn, high demand for the state's recognition also creates opportunities for state leaders to much more intentionally instigate nonstate conflicts. Localized conflicts are not as threatening to the political survival of state leaders. In some cases, these leaders may even have perverse incentives to encourage conflict. They can do so by selectively leveraging state recognition of one of the competing sides in a dispute, or even by merely publicly dangling the possibility that they might do so in the future. Especially during electoral periods, fomenting localized conflict can be a valuable political tool if it polarizes voters into supporting a political party or candidate seen as most likely to protect the interests of their group.[16] Moreover, to the extent that local traditional leaders serve as politically valuable electoral brokers, as described in Chapter 7, politicians have incentives to intervene in internal disputes to install favored intermediaries. When state leaders generate conflict, it is especially inaccurate to argue that low state capacity is the explanation for violence; these are cases in which state leaders intentionally withhold state coercive authority to allow violence, not situations in which the state's absence is a binding constraint on preventing violence.[17]

An important qualification to this argument is that the internal societal conflicts sparked by the state – intentionally or otherwise – will not automatically lead directly to violence, especially to large-scale violence. Violence is just one tactic for resolving a conflict.[18] Many nonstate conflicts over the nature of societal institutions – such as the chieftaincy succession disputes in Chapter 7 – end up in state courts or are resolved through other mediation.[19] When violence does emerge, the most proximate spark might seem unplanned;[20] the largest violence described below began as spontaneous fistfights in markets or bars against a background of underlying grievance.[21] And even where violence is intentionally

---

[16] Wilkinson (2004).

[17] Choosing not intervene to stop violence can be tantamount to choosing that violence occurs (Wilkinson 2004).

[18] Lawrence and Chenowith (2010).

[19] Awedoba et al. (2009).

[20] Fearon and Laitin (1996).

[21] The 1994 Konkomba-Dagmoba "Guinea Fowl War" famously began as a fight in a market over the price of a guinea fowl (Awedoba et al. 2009, 202). The 1981 Konkomba-Nanumba conflict is at times labeled the "Pito War" because one of the

sparked, it will stop after one incident if the broader community does not feel compelled to join in. A key issue for explaining when particularly large-scale violence occurs is to understand when initial sparks are more likely to spiral into sustained fighting.[22]

Large-scale communal violence is a collective behavior that requires solving collective action problems to mobilize participation. Conditional on the state having created an underlying conflict, major violence should be more likely when the organizational infrastructure needed to help facilitate collective action is already in place within society prior to a spark. In the cases below, two common forms of pre-existing social organization served this role, helping to translate isolated incidents into broader violence. First, in situations where state leaders and other political elites sought to directly foment conflict, grassroots political party organizations often provided a ready-made structure for collective action. Second, the social movement organizations (SMOs) that emerged out of the bottom-up institution-building efforts described in Chapter 5, such as the Konkomba Youth Association (KOYA), also played a similar role.[23]

Both types of organization provide an existing social network structure linking across individual families and communities over which information and social pressure can flow. Before violence breaks out, these networks provide a channel for political or social movement elites to build collective identities and spread narratives of grievance that broaden the pool of people who see themselves as party to the conflict, even among those who are not direct participants in the original dispute (e.g., the particular families litigating a chieftaincy case).[24] Once violence begins, these networks provide a means to sustain mobilization.

8.2 COUNTING VIOLENT EVENTS

I attempt to catalogue the location, size, participants, and other details of every fatal incident of political violence in Northern Ghana from

---

first incidents occurred in a bar where pito (a local beer) was served (Brukum 2001, 8). See Table 8.2.

[22] Fearon and Laitin (1996), Klaus (2020).

[23] KOYA is just one example of a broader phenomenon in the region; similar SMOs, also typically called "youth associations," formed to advocate for the interests of other ethnic communities around the same time. Lentz (1995) notes that several then became participants in the violence of the 1980s and early 1990s.

[24] Klaus (2020).

1960 to mid-2020.[25] While it would be ideal to code the universe of underlying conflicts and then study which flare into violence, this is not possible. Chieftaincy succession disputes, in particular, are very common, but because many involve only a few families and never see any violence, they are never recorded in the media or historical sources.[26] By focusing instead on violent incidents with at least one fatality – those most likely to be discoverable in the historical record – I can be more confident of systematically observing the full set of cases.[27] Moreover, by comparing more and less fatal events I can still explore why some violence sparks broader conflagrations while other events remain one-off incidents.

I begin with two existing subnational datasets: the Armed Conflict Location & Event Data project (ACLED) and the Social Conflict Analysis Database (SCAD).[28] Both are based on aggregating media reporting. For Northern Ghana, ACLED covers 1997–2020, while SCAD covers 1991–2017, but both datasets are incomplete and can be imprecise about conflict locations. I thus supplement them with additional conflict events coded from a wide range of historical sources, as well as update existing ACLED and SCAD entries for any events in which the reporting in historical sources differs.[29]

The final data includes ninety fatal events between 1960 and 2020 across thirty-nine separate underlying conflicts;[30] forty-six violent events

---

[25] Following the standard conflict datasets, I exclude quotidian crime (e.g., ordinary murders) and focus on incidents in which there was a clear political dispute between societal groups.

[26] Awedoba et al. (2009) attempt to document all active chieftaincy disputes across the region for a single decade – creating a data source used in the analysis in Chapter 7 – but no similarly comprehensive data is available for other time periods.

[27] Of course, some violence does not result in any fatalities. Bob-Milliar (2014) catalogues such "low-intensity" violence in the context of several recent Ghanaian elections, for example. But because nonfatal incidents typically attract much less attention from media and historical accounts, it is simply impossible to systematically observe them across time.

[28] ACLED (2016) and Salehyan et al. (2012), respectively.

[29] Overall, 16 events (18%) were missing in both ACLED and SCAD, while I had to correct the coding for another six (7%). The main additional sources are Awedoba et al. (2009), described above, and an internal memorandum from Ghana's National Peace Council that attempted to map out the full set of Northern conflicts through 2017 (National Peace Council 2017). Additional conflict event information is drawn from Drucker-Brown (1989), Pul (2003), Lund (2008), Talton (2010), MacGaffey (2006, 2013), and Issifu (2017).

[30] Some conflicts had fatalities in multiple separate flare-ups over time. I define a conflict event as any period of sustained fighting (including taking place across multiple locations) preceded and followed by clear periods of sustained peace.

across sixteen distinct inter-ethnic conflicts and forty-four incidents across twenty-three distinct intra-ethnic conflicts. Of the ninety events, nineteen are coded as high fatality, with ten or more estimated deaths. Violence of this size typically indicates the presence of sustained mobilization, including across multiple days or locations. The other seventy-one events were low fatality, coded as those with fewer than ten estimated deaths, mostly corresponding to violence on one day at a single location that never spiraled further. Because each of the nineteen high-fatality events can be confirmed across many different sources, I am confident that this is the universe of large-scale violence since at least 1960. However, it is possible that some smaller-scale events – isolated incidents that never recurred – may have happened in the initial decades after independence, when media coverage was sparsest, and never been recorded. For this reason, I am only confident in the coding of small-scale violence after 1980.

8.3 PATTERNS AND PREDICTORS OF VIOLENCE

Figure 8.1 plots the frequency and severity of violence over time. A striking pattern is immediately evident: with the exception of a single riot in Yendi in 1969, there was no large-scale violence in Northern Ghana for more than two decades after independence. Chapter 3 describes that amidst a decade of negative growth, state capacity bottomed out during the 1970s, with the state becoming even scarcer than before independence.[31] To whatever extent Northern Ghana has had a security vacuum, with the state simply incapable of enforcing peace, it would have been greatest in these initial decades, especially the 1970s. Yet inconsistent with conventional wisdom about why hinterlands are so violent, there was not major violence. Moreover, most of the deaths in the one large-scale incident that did occur – in 1969 in Yendi – were caused by state security forces explicitly attempting to police against violence; they fired into the crowd to stop the riot.[32] This was not a case of violence happening beyond the watchful eye of the state.

But immediately after 1979, when the state officially delegated land ownership across the North to chiefs (see Chapter 3), large-scale violence abruptly exploded, as indicated by comparing the periods before and after the dashed vertical line in Figure 8.1. This pattern is strongly consistent

---

[31] Chazan (1982), Drucker-Brown (1989).
[32] Awedoba et al. (2009, 209), MacGaffey (2006, 84).

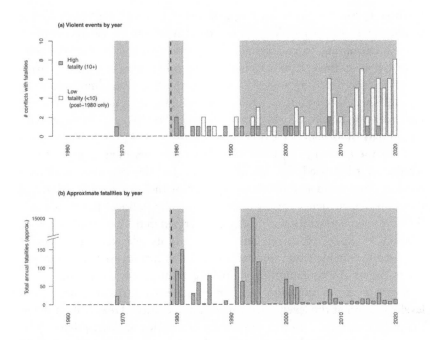

FIGURE 8.1 Frequency and scale of ethnic violence (1960–2020). Panel (a) displays the number of violent events per year in Northern Ghana, split into high fatality (10+) events, for which data is available from 1960, and low fatality (<10) events, for which the time series on reliably begins in 1980. Panel (b) displays approximate fatalities by year. The dashed vertical line in each panel indicates the 1979 land reform. The shaded time periods are when Ghana was a democracy.

with state intervention, not the state's absence, being the more important cause of violence. In early 1980, fighting broke out between Vagala communities, a "never recognized" group without independent chiefs, and their historical Gonja ("always chiefs") overlords, killing approximately fifty people.[33] At nearly the same time, a chieftaincy dispute in Wa over the appointment of the Wala ("always chiefs") paramount chief led to a riot in which an estimated forty people died.[34] A year later, Konkomba ("never recognized") communities rebelled against the supervisory control of Nanumba ("always chiefs") chiefs, as described in

[33] Awedoba et al. (2009, 175–176).
[34] Wilks (1989, 194–201).

Chapter 5, resulting in at least 150 deaths.[35] Just like the Vagala-Gonja conflict in 1980, this violence was explicitly about "never recognized" groups attempting to re-assert *de facto* land ownership after the state formally gave their land to chiefs from other ethnic groups. Large-scale violence flared up somewhere in Northern Ghana almost annually through the 1980s into the early 1990s, culminating in the largest bout of violence – the Konkomba-Dagomba "Guinea Fowl War" – in 1994, with an estimate of as many as 15,000 deaths.

Since the early 1990s, these high fatality events have comparatively receded. But localized, low fatality violence remains common, with four or more fatal incidents almost every year of the past decade. Many of these smaller incidents appear to be inflamed by political party competition after democratization in 1992, as described in the case studies below. Notably, by 2020, Northern Ghana both had its relatively most present and locally capable state apparatus ever in its history to that point and yet its largest absolute number of violent communal conflicts (Figure 8.1).

Switching from variation over time, Table 8.1 turns to community-level variation at the level of the census Enumeration Areas (EAs) used in the prior chapters. I present the results of a series of descriptive regressions which suggest that the state's other two major interventions into society in Chapter 3 – variation in the colonial invention of chieftaincy and the uneven early provision of education – also help explain the underlying grievances in many conflicts even if they only were sparked after the 1979 land reform. Because the specific types of grievances that animate inter-ethnic and intra-ethnic conflicts can differ, I split the analysis; columns 1 through 3 focus on predictors of inter-ethnic violence, while columns 4 through 6 focus on intra-ethnic violence. In columns 1 and 4, the outcome variable is a binary indicator of any fatal event in that community at some point between 1960 and 2020. These models are logistic regressions.[36] In columns 2 and 5, the outcome is instead a count variable – total years with a fatal event in each community – to give more explanatory weight to communities with repeated violence. The count models are negative binomial regressions.[37] Columns 3 and 6 repeat columns 2 and 5 restricting to high fatality (10+) events.

---

[35] Awedoba et al. (2009, 202) suggest the true count may have been as high as 2,000 deaths.

[36] These results are robust to instead using rare events logit (King and Zeng 2001).

[37] There is overdispersion in the counts. Columns 2 and 5 are also robust to instead using Poisson or quasi-Poisson regressions.

TABLE 8.1 Predictors of fatal inter- and intra-ethnic violence, by community

Outcome:	1 Inter-ethnic violence (0,1)	2 Years with inter-ethnic violence	3 Years with high fatality inter-ethnic violence	4 Intra-ethnic violence (0,1)	5 Years with intra-ethnic violence	6 Years with high fatality intra-ethnic violence
Slope index (ruggedness)	−0.348 † (0.192)	0.210 * (0.104)	0.280 ** (0.107)	−0.110 (0.814)	0.196 (1.080)	−2.651 (2.266)
Distance to Accra (km)	−0.021 *** (0.001)	−0.012 *** (0.000)	−0.012 *** (0.000)	−0.004 (0.003)	−0.007 * (0.003)	−0.033 * (0.016)
Distance to closest Northern city (km)	−0.008 *** (0.002)	−0.001 (0.001)	−0.001 (0.001)	−0.001 (0.006)	−0.004 (0.008)	−0.031 (0.025)
Boys enrolled (%) in 1960	−1.317 * (0.622)	−0.722 ** (0.271)	−1.069 *** (0.282)	6.089 *** (1.041)	10.714 *** (1.866)	14.983 *** (4.354)
Soil quality index	0.291 *** (0.045)	0.057 *** (0.017)	0.052 ** (0.017)	0.059 (0.151)	−0.153 (0.191)	0.824 (0.508)
"Never recognized" (%)	3.242 *** (0.163)	1.489 *** (0.079)	1.489 *** (0.080)	0.364 (0.709)	0.058 (0.913)	−6.309 (5.454)
Intercept	9.084 *** (1.940)	1.335 (1.033)	0.882 (1.068)	−3.825 (8.258)	−3.841 (10.882)	27.022 (25.756)
N	3,906	3,906	3,906	3,906	3,906	3,906
Model	Logit	Neg. Binom.	Neg. Binom.	Logit	Neg. Binom.	Neg. Binom.

† significant at $p < 0.10$; * $p < 0.05$; ** $p < 0.01$; *** $p < 0.001$. Observations are 2010 census enumeration areas (communities). The outcome in columns 1 and 4 are binary indicators for a fatal event in any year and the models are logistic regressions. The outcomes in Columns 2–3 and 5–6 are the count of years (1960–2020) with fatal events per community and the models are negative binomial regressions. The results for the logistic regressions are robust to using rare events adjustments (King and Chen 2001). The negative binomial regressions are generally robust to using Poisson or quasi-Poisson regressions instead. Slope and soil quality are measured from FAO (2012), dividing each index by 1,000 to ease readability of the table.

To more systematically test standard claims that violence in hinterland regions is a function of the inability of the state to project its authority, I include two sets of predictors. First is a measure of the slope, or ruggedness, of the terrain in each community, drawn from FAO (2012).[38] This index is scaled here from 0 (fully vertical) to 10 (flat). While Northern Ghana is mostly flat savannah – it has mean 9.48 on the slope index, with standard deviation 0.296 – there are pockets of rugged terrain that could facilitate violence beyond the state's reach.[39] Second, I include two standard measures of remoteness from state power centers: distance (in km) to the national capital, Accra; and distance (in km) to the nearest Northern city – Tamale, Wa, or Bolgatanga. From 1983 to 2018, these were Northern Ghana's three regional (provincial) capitals, where troops were stationed and from which state forces could be dispatched to put down violence.[40]

The models in Table 8.1 also include a series of other predictors that instead help capture the ways in which historical state actions might predict violence. First, I include the measure of village-level boys' school enrollment from the 1960 census data, introduced in Chapter 4. This measures which communities were winners overall in the state's initial independence era provision of local public goods and thus had small sets of students gain a head start in human capital accumulation prior to the rest of the region, generating greater intra-communal, intra-ethnic inequality (Chapter 4).[41] Second, I include a soil quality index, also from FAO (2012); scaled from 0 (least) to 10 (most), it estimates suitability for staple crops, proxying for communities in which agricultural land is more productive and thus more is at stake in decisions over who owns land. This has mean 6.88 and standard deviation 1.25. Third, I include the population proportion from "never recognized" ethnic groups, to identify

---

[38] The FAO data and process for merging raster grid cells to the census EA map are introduced in Chapter 4.

[39] In the colonial period a small separatist religious group successfully operated from the Tongo (Tong) Hills, a particularly rugged area in the Talensi District, and violently resisted colonial officers' attempts to disperse them (Allman and Parker 2005). The slope index reaches as low as 8.50 in the Tongo Hills, three standard deviations below the region's mean. The North's hilliest area is near Tatale, along the border with Togo (6.44 on the slope index).

[40] Prior to 1983, there were just two regions (provinces), headquartered in Tamale and Bolgatanga.

[41] I do not include the inequality measure from Chapter 4 itself as a predictor in Table 8.1 because it is measured after most of the violent events, and, as Chapter 4 describes, may potentially be an endogenous outcome of the violence.

communities both overlooked by the colonial state's invention of chieftaincy and those then most likely to have been formally dispossessed by
the state's 1979 reform.[42]

The patterns in Table 8.1 are inconsistent with violence being
explained by a security vacuum. Across models, the ruggedness of terrain
is not consistently associated with more violence. While flatter terrain
predicts less inter-ethnic violence in column 1 at the $p < 0.1$ level, the sign
flips in columns 2 and 3, and there is no association with intra-ethnic
violence across columns 4–6. Moreover, remoteness from the capital is
negatively associated with each type of violence, in the opposite direction
of the conventional account, while distance from regional power centers
is mostly uncorrelated with violence. Taking Table 8.1 together, violence,
if anything, appears more likely in communities that should be relatively
easier, not harder, for the central state to reach.

By contrast, the measure of state provision of education by 1960 is
strongly associated with both types of violence. Across columns 1–3,
communities that were disfavored in the early state provision of local
public goods (lower school enrollment) – the losers in emerging state-
generated inter-communal, inter-ethnic inequality – are significantly more
likely to have experienced inter-ethnic violence. These are communities
where bottom-up mobilization seeking out the state should be most likely
according to the theory in Chapter 2. In columns 4–6, greater early school
enrollment, and its associated higher levels of intra-community, intra-
ethnic inequality, instead strongly predicts more intra-ethnic violence.
Simulating from column 4, the probability of intra-ethnic violence in a
given community increases by 77.7 percent (0.19 percentage points) when
comparing one of the one quarter of Northern communities with no boys
yet enrolled in school by 1960 with a community with the mean number
of boys enrolled (10 percent). While there are likely also other differences
between communities that received different initial school access, this correlation is consistent with communities where some local families gained
a significant economic head start over others from early contact with the
scarce state then experiencing more violent intra-ethnic contestation for
local power.

---

[42] There could be concern that ethnicity measures from the 2010 census are endogenous,
but this is the only census with disaggregated ethnicity data. The relationships for the
other predictors in Table 8.1 are robust to excluding this final predictor. Moreover, even
in cases where groups were temporarily displaced by major violence, most people were
eventually able to return, such that 2010 ethnic composition should still be a broadly
accurate indicator of settlement prior to each incident.

Moreover, the final two predictors are associated with inter-ethnic violence in a manner that suggests grievances over land ownership can help explain inter-ethnic violence. There is significantly more inter-ethnic violence in communities with larger populations from the "never recognized" groups – those with the largest state-generated grievances over land after the 1979 reforms. Simulating from column 1, a community with 80% of its population from a "never recognized" group is 23.1 percentage points (95 percent CI: 21.3, 24.8) more likely to have had at least one fatal inter-ethnic event than a community with no residents from these groups. This is an over 350 percent increase in the probability of violence. In addition, inter-ethnic conflict is consistently significantly more likely in communities with more valuable soil, where there would have been a stronger underlying incentive to fight over land once pre-existing tenure regimes were abruptly thrown into doubt by the 1979 reform.

8.4 CASE STUDIES

The relationships in Table 8.1 are descriptive associations, not causal evidence. But by digging into the qualitative histories of individual conflicts, I reinforce that this violence has very clearly been instigated by state actions, rather than emerging from a vacuum left by the state's absence.

In Tables 8.2 and 8.3 I provide more detailed information on the largest twenty conflicts in terms of fatalities, listing ten inter-ethnic and intra-ethnic conflicts, respectively.[43] Tables 8.2 and 8.3 show two clear patterns, borne out in the case studies below. First, almost all conflicts are rooted in the pursuit of state recognition, with societal actors turning to violence as part of an attempt to better position their preferred interpretation of traditional institutions as the one that will be rewarded and accepted by the state. In Table 8.2, seven of the ten largest inter-ethnic conflicts share this motivation. Six of these are examples of the same dynamic introduced in Chapter 5: attempts by "never recognized" ethnic groups to assert independent chieftaincy and seek state recognition so they could control their own land after 1979.[44] In Table 8.3, all ten

---

[43] For some of the remaining very small conflicts – those with just one or two fatalities – there is often too little in the historical record to reliably code the last two columns in Tables 8.2 and 8.3.

[44] The three not about seeking state recognition were instead unrelated tensions between farming communities and Fulani pastoralists, but these other conflicts represent only

conflicts were also about seeking state recognition, with eight involving chieftaincy succession disputes. The remaining two were disputes between tendanas (earth priests) and chiefs, arising from ambiguities in the state's implementation of the 1979 land reform.[45]

Second, a comparison of the conflicts in Tables 8.2 and 8.3 with and without high fatality events is also consistent with the claim above that a key reason some blew up into more sustained violence while others quickly petered out is the pre-existing presence of organizational infrastructure through which narratives of grievance could spread more widely and collective violent mobilization could then be facilitated. In Table 8.2, all six inter-ethnic conflicts with sustained, high fatality violence occurred in contexts in which social movement organizations (SMOs), such as KOYA or other ethnic youth associations,[46] were already drumming up narratives of grievance among the broader ethnic group and creating network connections across communities that could be tapped to sustain mobilization. In one of these cases – the conflict in Bawku – party leaders also actively fanned tensions and party organizations provided an additional structure through which participation could be mobilized. By contrast, similar organizations were active prior to violence in only one of the low fatality conflicts. Similarly, in Table 8.3, all three intra-ethnic conflicts that featured high fatality violence had active SMOs and/or political party involvement leading into violence, compared to just one of the seven that saw low fatality violence.[47]

In the remainder of this section, I focus on several illustrative examples to demonstrate these two patterns more directly. Among the inter-ethnic conflicts in Table 8.2, I first zoom in on the history of the 1994–1995 Konkomba-Dagomba War ("Guinea Fowl War"), the very similar 1991–1992 Nawuri-Gonja conflict in Kpandai, and the long-running Kusasi-Mamprusi conflict in Bawku. Viewed together, these three cases

a tiny fraction of the overall violence. This type of conflict is broadly common across Sahelian West Africa as Fulani herders migrate transnationally in search of range land. Although Tonah (2002) also attributes the recent rise of farmer-herder conflict in Northern Ghana to state land policy, these conflicts are exceptions that follow different patterns than all of the other inter-ethnic conflicts.

[45] Lund (2008).

[46] Lentz (1995).

[47] In the one exception – the intra-Bimoba conflict in Najong – an MP and government minister is alleged to have instigated the violence, but it is unclear if he is involved purely in a personal capacity (his own family is party to the underlying land dispute) or if he has drawn on his party's local organization to mobilize collective action. See GhanaWeb (2017), Savannah News (2018).

TABLE 8.2 *Largest inter-ethnic conflicts, 1960–2020*

Conflict	Events in dataset	Year(s)	Location(s)	Main groups participating	Total fatalities (approx.)	Main contention	Organizational involvement
Konkomba-Dagomba War ("Guinea Fowl War")	3	1994, 1995	Bimbilla, Saboba, Yendi, Tamale and many surrounding districts	Konkomba (never) vs. Dagomba (always)+ Nanumba (always)	Up to 15,000	State recognition: which group has the legitimate chiefs?	Active SMOs
Bawku Conflict	17	1983, 1985, 2000, 2001, 2003, 2004, 2007, 2008, 2009, 2010	Bawku	Mamprusi (always) vs. Kusasi (invented)	Over 200	State recognition: which group has the legitimate chiefs?	Active SMOs + Pols. or party orgs.
Nawuri-Gonja Conflict	2	1991, 1992	Kpandai and surrounding communities	Nawuri (never) vs. Gonja (always)	Over 160	State recognition: which group has the legitimate chiefs?	Active SMOs

Conflict		Years	Communities	Groups		State recognition	Active SMOs
Nakpanduri Conflict	9	1984, 1985, 1986, 1989, 2012, 2013, 2014, 2017	Nakpanduri, Bimbagu, Kpemale	Konkomba (never) vs. Bimoba (never)	Over 160	**State recognition:** which group has the legitimate chiefs?	Active SMOs
Konkomba-Nanumba War	1	1981	Bimbilla, Wulensi, Kpandai and surrounding communities	Konkomba (never) vs. Nanumba (always)	At least 150[†]	**State recognition:** which group has the legitimate chiefs?	Active SMOs
Vagala-Gonja Conflict	1	1980	Tuna and surrounding communities	Vagala (never) vs. Gonja (always)	At least 50	**State recognition:** which group has the legitimate chiefs?	Active SMOs
Konkomba-Chokosi Dispute	3	2018, 2019	Naaduni, Nazawni, Garinkuka, and surrounding communities	Konkomba (never) vs. Chokosi (never)	6	**State recognition:** official boundaries between communities' land	Active SMOs

(continued)

TABLE 8.2 (*continued*)

Conflict	Events in dataset	Year(s)	Location(s)	Main groups participating	Total fatalities (approx.)	Main contention	Organizational involvement
Farmer-herder tensions	2	2020	Abrumase	Fulani (never) vs. Gonja (always)	5	Vigilante killings targeting local ethnic minority (Fulani herders) after a murder	No
Farmer-herder tensions	1	2020	Charia	Fulani (never) vs. Dagaba (invented)	2	Vigilante killings targeting local ethnic minority (Fulani herders) after crime wave	No
Farmer-herder tensions	1	2019	Nangon (Karaga)	Fulani (never) vs. Dagomba (always)	2	Vigilante killings targeting local ethnic minority (Fulani herders)	No

Conflicts that include violent events in the high fatality category (see Figure 8.1) are in **bold**. †: the official death count for this conflict is disputed; some sources put it as high as 2,000 (Awedoba et al. 2009, 202).

TABLE 8.3 *Largest intra-ethnic conflicts, 1960–2020*

Conflict	Events in dataset	Year(s)	Location(s)	Main groups participating	Total fatalities (approx.)	Main contention	Organizational involvement
Andani-Abudu Conflict	10	1969, 1987, 2002, 2003, 2006, 2008, 2014, 2019	Yendi, Tamale	Dagomba (always)	84	**State recognition:** which family (gate) is the legitimate successor to chieftaincy?	**Active SMOs +** **Pols. or party orgs.**
Wa Chieftaincy Dispute	2	1980, 1997	Wa	Wala (always)	41	**State recognition:** which family (gate) is the legitimate successor to chieftaincy?	**Active SMOs**
Bimbilla Crisis	5	2014, 2015, 2017, 2018	Bimbilla	Nanumba (always)	33	**State recognition:** which family (gate) member is the legitimate successor to chieftaincy?	**Pols. or party orgs.**

(continued)

TABLE 8.3 *(continued)*

Conflict	Events in dataset	Year(s)	Location(s)	Main groups participating	Total fatalities (approx.)	Main contention	Organizational involvement
Bunkpurugu Chieftaincy Dispute	3	2015, 2016	Bunkpurugu	Bimoba (never)	7	**State recognition:** which family (gate) is the legitimate successor to chieftaincy?	No
Kafaba Chieftaincy Dispute	2	2016, 2017	Kafaba, Kalampo	Gonja (always)	7	**State recognition:** which family (gate) is the legitimate successor to chieftaincy?	No
Daboya Chieftaincy Dispute	2	1994, 1995	Daboya (Wasipe), Yazori	Gonja (always)	6	**State recognition:** which family (gate) member is the legitimate successor to chieftaincy?	No
Namoligo-Tindongo Land Dispute	1	2012	Namoligo, Tingondo	Frafra (invented)	4	**State recognition:** is the chief or the tendana the legitimate land owner?	No

Najong Land Dispute	1	2017	Najong	Bimoba (never)	4	State recognition: is the chief or the tendana the legitimate land owner?	
Zaare Chieftaincy Dispute	1	2002	Zaare	Frafra (invented)	3	State recognition: which family (gate) is the legitimate successor to chieftaincy?	No
Temaa Chieftaincy Dispute	1	2010	Temaa (Jegori)	Konkomba (never)	3	State recognition: which family (gate) is the legitimate successor to chieftaincy?	No

Conflicts that include violent events in the high fatality category (see Figure 8.1) are in **bold**.

both show how state interventions, both unintentionally and at times quite intentionally, created the underlying grievances that led to violence and then how large-scale violence drew on pre-existing organizations to spread beyond initial incidents. I then turn four intra-ethnic conflicts in Table 8.3: the Andani-Abudu chieftaincy dispute among the Dagomba, the intra-Nanumba succession dispute in Bimbilla, and smaller, more iso-lated intra-ethnic conflicts in Daboya and Namoligo-Tindongo. These latter four cases again reinforce that underlying disputes were generated by a mix of the unintentional and intentional impacts of specific state actions. The two cases with high fatality violence also had clear evi-dence of elite-led partisan mobilization, unlike the two cases that did not expand.

8.4.1 Inter-ethnic Conflicts

The Konkmoba-Dagomba War
The largest conflict in Northern Ghana's history pitted Konkomba com-munities against residents of the surrounding "always chiefs" groups, especially the Dagomba, in 1994 and 1995. Estimates by NGOs involved in post-conflict reconstruction put the death toll as high as 15,000, with over 200,000 temporarily displaced.[48] As initially detailed in Chapter 5, the underlying grievances in this conflict emerged very explicitly in response to state actions: the 1979 land reform, as well as a more minor decision in the 1992 constitution to remove the government's ability to bypass the National House of Chiefs and directly enskin and gazette chiefs.

Konkomba communities were long neglected by the state, facing a sustained lack of access to valuable state benefits. Their grievances were significantly heightened when the 1979 land reform gave chiefs from the "always chiefs" groups legal ownership over all Konkomba land. This new state intervention became the "defining moment for the articulation and mobilization of pan-Konkomba militancy,"[49] sparking the bottom-up social movement aimed at developing new chieftaincy institutions, described at length in Chapter 5. Indeed, the activist quoted in Chapter 5 suggests that this single state action effectively "coerced" the Konkomba into mobilizing to create their own chiefs.

[48] Van der Linde and Naylor (1999).
[49] Pul (2003, 71).

The grassroots movement – spearheaded by KOYA – that expanded across Konkomba territory throughout the 1980s created an intra-ethnic organizational structure that made large-scale violence more feasible. Alongside its effort to encourage communities to invent their own chiefs, one of KOYA's missions was to construct a widely shared sense of pan-Konkomba identity across previously disparate villages and clans.[50] At the heart of this new identity was a narrative of grievance over a lack of state recognition. Moreover, KOYA's organizational efforts also created new social networks, including by organizing an annual "Easter Convention" in Saboba, in which residents from hundreds of separate Konkomba villages would assemble, forming personal links and ties that could then be activated to facilitate broader collective action.

The spark for violence came from a second state policy change that occurred alongside democratization. The new constitution stripped the government of its power to appoint chiefs, vesting this exclusively in existing chiefs. This gave Dagomba chiefs "absolute discretion as to the status" of the Konkombas' claims to independent chieftaincy and land ownership.[51] In 1993, KOYA leaders petitioned the Ya Na (Dagomba paramount) for the recognition of a co-equal Konkomba paramount. In a decision delivered in October 1993, the claim was openly rejected, making clear that there was no legal path to independent Konkomba chieftaincy under current state policy. In the aftermath, informal Konkomba militias began to form. Although it is unclear whether the militias had explicit support from top KOYA leaders, they could draw on bonds forged among grassroots KOYA activists. After a market dispute on February 1, 1994, fighting quickly spread. After a ten-day delay, the army belatedly intervened as a peacekeeping force. Violence flared again in March 1995 before finally subsiding.

Nawuri-Gonja conflict

The Nawuri-Gonja conflict followed an almost identical logic of the state's actions instigating violence, albeit from a much smaller "never recognized" ethnic group. Since the colonial creation of Native Authority jurisdictions in the early 1930s, the town of Kpandai and its surrounding villages have been placed within the Gonja kingdom, under the supervision of Gonja chiefs, despite having few Gonja residents. Since independence, most of the population have been Konkombas. But

---

[50] Talton (2010).
[51] Pul (2003, 51).

Kpandai town itself is dominated by the Nawuri. Since the 1950s, Nawuri activists have attempted a nearly identical social transformation to that examined in Chapter 5, petitioning the state to recognize newly invented and independent Nawuri chiefs.[52]

After the 1979 land reform, these efforts took on new urgency, with the state now officially legitimating Gonja chiefs' claims to ownership of all land in Kpandai.[53] By the mid-1980s, just as with the Konkomba, Nawuri activists were coordinating their campaign for independent state recognition through an ethnic youth association, while Gonja activists worked through the Gonjaland Youth Association to similarly lobby the state to retain its recognition of the supremacy of Gonja chiefs.[54] Both organizations meant pre-existing structures for collective action were in place prior to the violence.

Fighting began in early 1991. The Gonjaland Youth Association announced it would hold its annual convention in Kpandai, seen as an intentional provocation to the Nawuri majority. At roughly the same time, the self-styled Nawuri chief of Kpandai – not state recognized, but enjoying the informal support of many Nawuri residents, just like many of the self-styled Konkomba chiefs in Chapter 5 – attempted to act as the owner of local land, ignoring the Gonja Kpandaiwura (chief of Kpandai). Each chief sold the same plot to different buyers.[55] The resulting disputes sparked riots that resulted in over 100 deaths, with Nawuris driving most Gonja residents out of Kpandai. Violence flared again in 1992, with approximately sixty more deaths. There is still a Kpandaiwura appointed by the Gonja paramount chief, but he now lives in exile, fifty kilometers away, and "has limited influence over local affairs,"[56] allowing self-appointed Nawuri leaders to reassert *de facto* control over local land. As in the Konkomba-Dagomba war two years later, the state's decision to continue recognizing Gonja chiefs' "overlordship" of Nawuri communities in the aftermath of land reform set the course for conflict.

The Bawku Conflict
Repeated Mamprusi-Kusasi violence in Bawku has a different background, but is still directly rooted in grievances created by state intervention. Recurring violence in Bawku also provides an example of a

---

[52] Stacey (2014b).
[53] Awedoba et al. (2009, 183).
[54] Lentz (1995).
[55] Awedoba et al. (2009, 182).
[56] Stacey (2014a, 35).

conflict seemingly purposefully fanned by state leaders and in which party organizations helped provide the basis for mobilization.

The Kusasi, a precolonially acephalous group, comprise the majority in villages around Bawku, but there has been a significant Mamprusi ("always chiefs") population in Bawku itself since before colonial rule. The British invented chiefs among the Kusasi as described in Chapter 3. But from 1931, while setting up the Native Authority system, the British made the paramount chief of Kusasi territory, to whom all village chiefs owed their appointments, a Mamprusi, stationed in Bawku. In turn the Bawkunaba (chief of Bawku) was appointed by the Nayiri, the Mamprusi paramount. The last colonial-era Mamprusi Bawkunaba died in 1957, just as Ghana gained independence. Succession quickly became caught up in electoral politics. The Nayiri was one of the main backers of the Northern People's Party (NPP), an opposition party contesting Nkrumah's CPP. Seeking to undercut his opposition and consolidate support among the more numerous Kusasi, Nkrumah installed a Kusasi as Bawkunaba in 1958, breaking the colonial-era chieftaincy system and elevating the Bawkunaba into a co-equal Kusasi paramount chief independent of Mamprusi control.

This direct state interference into Bawku society generated reprisals from Mamprusis, culminating in Nkrumah's attempted assassination near Bawku in 1962. In response, Nkrumah's regime repressed Mamprusi leaders, jailing many and sending others into exile.[57] But immediately after their 1966 coup, Ghana's new military leaders, who had received backing from Mamprusi elites, vacated the 1958 Kusasi appointment and re-installed a Mamprusi. This began a cycle in which successive state leaders would attempt to change out the Bawkunaba after taking power. Bawku has become one of the most prominent examples of state leaders intentionally intervening in chieftaincy succession to install co-partisans for political gain.

The stakes of the existing Bawku conflict increased after the state's 1979 land reform because control over the chieftaincy position now, for the first time, also came with a state-backed claim to land. In 1981, the Mamprusi Bawkunaba installed after the 1966 coup died. The new PNDC military regime enjoyed support at the local level from Kusasi activists with ties to Nkrumah's CPP regime and quickly worked to reinstall a Kusasi. PNDC leaders organized a large public rally in Bawku in

[57] Lund (2008, 114–116).

December 1983 to celebrate the Kusasi return to power, seen as an open provocation to violence. Riots ensued in which as many as thirty people were killed. Mamprusi leaders directly accused Kusasi PNDC politicians of acting as ethnic entrepreneurs, using the rally to incite ethnic riots that would consolidate Kusasi support.[58] Further violence occurred in 1984 and 1985; following the Kusasi Bawkunaba's appointment, Kusasi village chiefs in the surrounding communities began seizing Mamprusi farmland, arguing that under the state's new land policies after 1979, Kusasi chiefs were now the rightful owners.[59]

After democratization in 1992, the Bawku conflict remained enmeshed in electoral politics, with the NDC (successor party to the PNDC) receiving near universal support of Kusasi voters and the NPP (New Patriotic Party) receiving overwhelming support of local Mamprusis.[60] In this context, elements of the grassroots party organizations in Bawku – already active in mobilizing voters to participate in electoral politics – have come to double at times as virtual ethnic militias. Major violence emerged again in the immediate aftermath of the 2000 election, when the NPP won power for the first time, and with it, raised the prospect that they might reinstall a Mamprusi. A first violent riot between political party activists broke out after a dispute over vote counting in the 2000 election. A second partisan-tinged riot occurred in 2001, after the new NPP Vice President paid a courtesy call on the Mamprusi claimant to the paramountcy, interpreted by Kusasis and NDC supporters as another provocation meant to purposefully inflame violence.[61] Violence recurred again in 2008 and 2009, amidst further efforts by local politicians to drum up tensions around the 2008 election.

8.4.2 Intra-ethnic Conflicts

The Andani-Abudu Chieftaincy Dispute

The protracted chieftaincy dispute over the Dagomba paramountcy is another example of a conflict generated very explicitly by state action, not inaction. Two extended royal families – the Andani and Abudu – lay competing claims to the position of Ya Na, the paramount chief of

---

[58] Lund (2008, 119–120).

[59] Lund (2008, 121).

[60] The NPP (New Patriotic Party) that emerged in 1992 is a different party than the NPP (Northern People's Party) active in the North in the 1950s, though the later-day NPP built on strong ties to prior leaders of the earlier NPP.

[61] Lund (2008, 128).

Dagbon, sitting at Yendi. These families are "gates," patrilineal clans originally descended from different sons of the same earlier Ya Na. Violence between supporters of the Andani and Abudu factions first emerged in 1969 before taking off in a more sustained fashion in the early twenty-first century. Most violence has occurred in Yendi, though the resulting dispute has affected local politics throughout all of Dagbon, leading in particular to additional violence in Tamale as well.

That Tamale – the North's largest city, administrative capital, and home to a large military base – and Yendi – a large, easily accessible town – would be the site of so much violence sits directly at odds with security vacuum-focused explanations of hinterland violence. If there were anywhere that the modern state should have been especially capable of suppressing violence, this would be it. Instead, the underlying dispute was created by state attempts to rewrite internal Dagomba institutions. Violence then flared when state leaders acted as ethnic entrepreneurs in pursuit of political support. And the conflict has been repeatedly egged on by wealthy educated elites living outside the North – the very types of urban elites elevated by state action in the manner examined in Chapter 4 – who have pursued their private political ambitions by intervening in and prolonging the dispute.[62]

The position of Ya Na dates as far back as the fifteenth century. Prior to the colonial rule, as described in Chapter 7, the Dagomba had evolved complex rules of succession and power-sharing among lineages.[63] The British attempted to codify these rules in 1930, drafting a formal constitution for Dagbon. MacGaffey (2006) observes that "this document has been regarded in Dagbon ever since as a sacred record of tradition, though in fact it was largely shaped by British preconceptions" and changed key details of how succession operated.[64] Moreover, colonial state officials subsequently ignored their own new provisions when making future appointments.[65]

---

[62] Pellow (2012).

[63] Staniland (1975).

[64] MacGaffey (2006, 82).

[65] MacGaffey (2006, 82) continues: "the [colonial] administration made whatever decisions it found convenient, without much regard for the 'rules'" it itself had written. The Dagomba are just one example of the colonial state's interventions into the institutions of the "always chiefs" groups. Key institutions in each of these groups changed from contact with the colonial state and do not simply persist in the same form as they had in the precolonial period. The succession conflicts in Wa – source of the second largest intra-ethnic violence in Table 8.2 – similarly originally stem from *ad hoc* British attempts to change precolonial institutions (Awedoba et al. 2009, 49, Wilks 1989).

This state meddling directly generated the original Andabi-Abudu dispute. In 1948, the Ya Na – from the Andani family – died, and was replaced by an Abudu, following an establish system of rotation. But when the new Abudu Ya Na unexpectedly died soon afterwards, colonial officials helped replace him in 1954 with another Abudu, giving the Abudu a second turn in a row. The Andani protested that they had been cheated out of their turn, while the Abudu insisted it was correct to appoint a replacement from their family because their own turn had been unnaturally short.

This initial dispute was then prolonged and exacerbated by repeated politically motivated state interventions.[66] Similar to the Bawku conflict above, the allegiances of the two families in independence-era electoral politics became a key factor. Like many Northern chiefs, the new Abudu Ya Na had initially thrown his support behind Nkrumah's opposition. Andani elites responded by rallying to the CPP. Nkrumah rewarded the Andani for their support by issuing a decree in 1960 stipulating that the next Ya Na must be Andani. In 1967, the Abudu appointed in 1954 died and an Andani took the position under the terms of Nkrumah's order. But in 1969, the new United Party (UP) government of Kofi Busia, courting the support of Abudu elites opposed to Nkrumah, withdrew the 1960 decree, vacated the new Andani Ya Na's appointment and installed an Abudu instead. This sparked violent riots in which twenty-three people were killed, the North's only large-scale violence before 1979.

In 1972, Busia's government was dispatched in yet another coup, supported locally by Andani leaders. The new military government immediately revoked Busia's 1969 decision, vacated the new Abudu Ya Na's appointment and re-installed an Andani. The PNDC (then NDC) government of Jerry Rawlings (1982–2000), styled as a quasi-successor to Nkrumah's CPP, also enjoyed strong Andani support and kept the 1972 Andani Ya Na in place.

After the 2000 election, the anti-Nkrumah opposition returned to national power for the first time, now in the form of the NPP (New Patriotic Party). During the 2000 campaign, local NPP operatives seeking ethnic votes had promised they would replace the Andani Ya Na with an Abudu.[67] The NPP Vice Presidential candidate, Aliu Mahama, was also a senior member of the Abudu family, and after winning, the party

---

[66] Tonah (2012, 2) summarizes that the "conflict ... resurfac[ed] with every change of government, with the conflicting parties jockeying for [Dagomba] support."

[67] MacGaffey (2006, 87), Pellow (2012, 55), Tonah (2012, 10).

appointed another Abudu elite as the mayor (District Chief Executive) of Yendi. This emboldened Abudus, who began organizing parallel celebrations of Dagomba festivals and even informally attempting to appoint their own local chiefs, forming a sort of "shadow cabinet" within Dagbon.[68] During a major festival in March 2002, violence broke out. An Abudu-aligned mob stormed the Ya Na's palace, assassinating him and killing dozens of family members. The mob paraded the Ya Na's body through the streets of Yendi. As many as forty people were killed.

Andani loyalists immediately accused the NPP government of direct complicity. As evidence, they note that the security agencies delayed for three days in responding, even though it was taking place in a major town where forces were already stationed. Much like Wilkinson's (2004) evidence of police forces standing aside to let ethnic riots happen in India when they served the interests of political leaders, "many residents ... believed that fighting could not have continued for three days in Yendi without complicity on the part of some top government and security officials at the regional and national levels."[69] Rumors also spread that electricity and phone services to Yendi were cut immediately before the assassination, preventing the Ya Na from calling for help.[70]

An official investigation resulted in murder charges against seven NPP party officials, suggesting direct complicity by the local party organization in coordinating the violence and allowing it to escalate into high fatality events. However, all seven were acquitted in a proceeding that Andanis decried as biased by influence from the NPP government.[71] Several even more prominent officials, including the Interior Minister and Northern Regional Minister, were also implicated, but the government declined to prosecute.[72]

Even if the evidence of state complicity was circumstantial, it is clear that educated Dagomba elites on both sides – the types of people who benefitted most from the state windfall of early access to education – have attempted to fan and profit from the conflict. This is suggestive of the link between intra-ethnic inequality and intra-ethnic violence in

---

[68] Tonah (2012, 8).

[69] Tonah (2012, 11).

[70] Pellow (2012, 55).

[71] Tonah (2012, 9–10).

[72] After the NDC won national power again in 2008, fifteen politicians were rearrested and tried again for the Ya Na's murder, but all were acquitted in 2011. Tonah (2012, 10) explains that "the security agencies were accused of doing a shoddy investigation ... making it difficult for the accused persons to be convicted in court."

Table 8.1. Subsequent fatal skirmishes – including the three other violent events listed in Table 8.3 – were instigated by inflammatory rhetoric and actions of these elites. Pellow (2012) observes that educated Dagomba elites in Accra "engage in ... leadership by remote control, pulling strings from afar to manipulate politics at home."[73] This includes by funding litigation, arming informal militias aligned to the local party organizations, and stoking grievances using inflammatory public rhetoric, especially on local talk radio, often in the interest of building private followings in pursuit of elected office. MacGaffey (2006) quotes a local observer of Dagomba politics that "the whole confusion ... is being fomented by the enlightened members of the Dagbon community, who benefit ... financially and politically."[74] Similarly, Pellow (2012) describes that, in their own words, many Dagombas share "universal agreement ... [that] everything happening ... is political ... the fault of ... modern patrons or party politicians" intentionally stoking tensions.[75] An activist closely involved in peacebuilding efforts explained,

There are elites ... who profit from conflict ... Conflict is what makes them who they are. If there is no conflict, then they are nobody. They will never want to see the end of the conflict .... Sometimes it's very surprising that you come across a very lettered individual within these families that you think should have been the one who would quell the tensions. But he's rather the one who is fueling.[76]

This strategy appears to work at producing loyal voter support, with narratives of deep-seated grievance now successfully expanded by elite mobilization far beyond the families directly party to the dispute. Elections have become heavily polarized between supporters of the Andani (NDC) and Abudu (NPP) gates, with the conflict now the dominant means by which parties win votes in Dagomba communities, even above and beyond clientelism or performance at delivering local public goods. Dagomba participants in a focus group said they saw party preference as an "inheritance" from their clans and that members of the wrong party could not even safely campaign in Dagomba villages or neighborhoods in which they did not have support of the dominant clan.[77] One Dagomba

---

73 Pellow (2012, 44).
74 Quoted in MacGaffey (2006, 90). He continues, "such people ... furthered political party ambitions by exploiting their ready access to the news media."
75 Pellow (2012, 57).
76 Interview with civil society activist, Tamale, June 30, 2018.
77 Focus group with Dagomba voters, Tamale, June 28, 2008.

activist explained: "We feel that we are voting for the party that can support our chief. A party that ... can de-skin our chief or kill like what happened, we can never follow it."[78]

The Bimbilla Chieftaincy Dispute

Violence over the position of Bimbilla Na, the paramount of the Nanumba, a smaller "always chiefs" group, echoes similar themes, including both the role of state-generated intra-ethnic inequality in fanning conflict, with urban elites returning home to reimagine local customary institutions to their private benefit, and the role of parties in helping initial sparks grow into protracted violence.

As in Yendi, the Nanumba paramountcy traditionally rotates between two gates. But the conflict has occurred within a single gate, with a dispute over which relative would be put forward to take the family's turn after the previous Bimbilla Na died in 1999. Nanumba chiefs traditionally reach the paramountcy after being promoted up their group's hierarchy over a career as a chief. In the early 2000s, one claimant for the Bimbilla chieftaincy had worked his way up as a chief and was serving in the senior-most position that was commonly the final step before promotion to Bimbilla Na. The other was an elite member of the same family who was the son of a former Bimbilla Na, but had never been a chief. This second candidate attempted to use his influence in the family to essentially cut in line.[79] The "kingmakers" – a council of lower chiefs responsible for selecting the new paramount – divided between the two claimants, producing allegations that the non-chief had paid for support. By 2005, both claimants organized rival enskinmment ceremonies and began carrying themselves as Bimbilla Na. This resulted in protracted litigation over the next decade, during which local Nanumba politics remained suspended in an uneasy limbo with two self-proclaimed chiefs issuing separate orders.[80] Violence broke out in 2014 when one of the two claimants died and his family attempted to bury him in the official funeral ground reserved for paramount chiefs. This sparked reprisals from the other side and then, in further response, supporters of the deceased claimant assassinated the other claimant in his home. Violence between these factions flared again in 2015 and 2017.

---

[78] Interview with Dagomba Youth Association leader, Yendi, June 30, 2008.
[79] He claimed that the senior divisional chief was not eligible because he was not the son of a former paramount chief (Awedoba et al. 2009, 193).
[80] Awedoba et al. (2009, 190–197), Anamzoya and Tonah (2016).

This violence shares its origin with other chieftaincy disputes in a way that illustrates the likely mechanism for the relationship between early education access and conflict in Table 8.1. A common pattern to these disputes is that a wealthy member of an extended royal family who has benefitted from early access to education attempts to leverage his advantages into skipping ahead of other family members. One interview respondent explained that in many such disputes, similar to Bimbilla, "somebody suddenly realizes that he has money ... and that he tangentially relates to a [position] ... And then he starts the trouble ... A fourth cousin or a fifth something will just appear and say 'I also belong to the family ... now I want the chieftaincy.'" If the new claimant has the means to pay off the chief(s) with appointing authority, he can be selected outside the established order of succession.[81] Another respondent described, "the thing is that it's [ultimately] the enskinning authority who decides" and they can be paid to break the rules. "You go and complain and say 'this man is not qualified' ... but he ignores it and goes ahead. That brings conflict."[82]

Moreover, similar to the Yendi and Bawku violence, the conflict in Bimbilla has also become closely tied to electoral politics, with the rival parties aligning locally with each faction and fanning tensions in an attempt to win loyal support. Voting among Nanumbas in Bimbilla is now highly polarized based on allegiances to the deceased rival chiefs. And as in other conflicts with large-scale violence, the local party organizations provide a means of creating broader collective action around the dispute.[83] Kwansa (2020) describes how NDC and NPP factions in Bimbilla have come to operate as rival pseudo-gangs, including with their own marking colors ("whites" vs. "blacks"), polarizing town life around the conflict.

The Daboya and Namoligo-Tindongo Conflicts

Other intra-ethnic conflicts in Table 8.3 have not flared up into high fatality violence, however. While the origins of these conflicts can still be traced to state actions and policy changes, they have remained more

---

[81] Interview with civil society activist and Dagaba royal family member, Bolgatanga, June 28, 2018. Tonah (2004) vividly documents the degree to which pecuniary considerations sway these types of appointment decisions.

[82] Interview with retired teacher, Zuarungu, May 20, 2019.

[83] Kwansa (2020).

narrowly contested by specific families in the absence of social movement or party organizations active at creating broader collective grievances.

One such example is violence in 1994 in the Gonja town of Daboya over who the Wasipewura (chief of Daboya) would appoint as the Yazori-wura, chief of Yazori, a smaller town nearby. The roots of the conflict are very similar to Bimbilla's. Two brothers from the same family came forward for the Yazori position, which is a stepping stone within the Gonja hierarchy toward more valuable higher appointments. One was an educated elite living in an urban area and the other, his uneducated brother. Awedoba et al. (2009, 158–161) report that many residents supported the uneducated brother, fearing the elite candidate wanted to use the position as a launching pad for his career and would be an absentee chief remaining in the city. But the elite claimant was able to negotiate directly with the appointing chief (the Wasipewura) in private for the position, spurring allegations that money changed hands. Shortly after being enskinned at the Wasipewura's palace in Daboya in July 1994, the elite claimant was shot dead along with four of his supporters by a gang aligned with his brother. As a reprisal, the brother was murdered a year later, likely by family members of the first claimant.[84] But because this conflict was internal to a single family in a small community of limited electoral importance, it took on no partisan valence and the active social movement organizations in the surrounding area – such as the Gonjaland Youth Association – had no particular stake in the outcome. Violence stopped with the deaths of the claimants.

A second example of a violent intra-ethnic conflict that did not explode into larger violence is the land dispute between Namoligo and Tindongo, neighboring Talensi (Frafra) communities in the Upper East Region. This conflict is representative of a series of similar disputes studied by Lund (2008), who observes that the state's 1979 devolution of land rights "opened a hornet's nest of potential conflict over land" by being ambiguous as to who the "original owners" were in contexts in which tendanas (earth priests) and chiefs were both active.[85] In many "invented chiefs" communities – as well as "never recognized" communities to the extent they later added chiefs – ambiguous wording in the legal statutes adopted in 1979 generated conflicts between chiefs – the Alhassan Commission's intended beneficiaries[86] – and tendanas, the pre-existing actors who had

---

[84] Awedoba et al. (2009, 160).
[85] Lund (2008, 2).
[86] Talton (2010).

been controlling land informally until 1979.[87] One interview respondent observed that "all because of this constitutional provision ... [now] there is duality in who is the final authority in natural resource management ... The point of conflict is emerging when chiefs want to usurp the tendanas" by acting on their new state-granted rights.[88]

Violence between residents of Namoligo and Tindongo in 2012 killed four people, pitting family members of a tendana against a chief. A report by the National Peace Council describes that the tendana in Tindongo claimed traditional ownership of all land in both communities, while the chief in Namoligo "attempted to sever these relationships and to seek control over the land" for himself by claiming superseding legal authority. Although the conflict connects back to legal changes from 1979, it only came to a head in the early 2010s because these communities had recently become peri-urban, on the outskirts of rapidly growing Bolgatanga, where land is increasingly "attracting high prices ... for home construction by residents in Bolgatanga."[89] But again, without any clear partisan valence to the conflict or any activity by local youth associations or other grassroots movements, the violence stayed localized to residents of these two communities.

8.5 CONCLUSION

This chapter concludes Part III by showing that violent communal conflict in the hinterland is a third political effect of the scarce's state interventions into society. In contrast to common arguments that there is heightened violence in the rural periphery because of the state's difficulty in projecting coercive power across far-flung territory, I suggest that it is instead the very actions that the state still takes that generate conflict in the first place. A combination of state absence and state resource advantages allows isolated state actions to have large effects on society, generating new grievances and forms of grassroots social mobilization that lead to violence.

Moreover, the chapter shows in particular how the state's actions generate violence that is not necessarily targeted back at the state, but instead

---

[87] Intra-ethnic land conflicts after 1979 were more muted in the "always chiefs" groups because chiefs had already consolidated *de facto* control over land vis-a-vis the tendanas before colonial rule.

[88] Interview with civil society activist and Dagaba royal family member, Bolgatanga, June 28, 2018.

[89] National Peace Council (2017).

becomes localized within society, echoing Boone's (2014) broader study of land conflicts in regions in which the state empowers customary institutions. Rather than anti-state resistance, the violence in this chapter all takes the form of nonstate conflict, a numerically more common form of violence across Africa in recent years than civil war.[90] And yet, despite being nonstate conflict, this violence is also not purely internal to customary institutions; the key contention in almost every instance is over whose competing version of the customary will win out in the eyes of the state and earn its recognition. Thus even if fighting is not targeted at state forces, the state is still a near universal target of combatants' attention. In combination with Chapter 5, this helps suggest the need for a broader corrective away from making anti-state resistance a dominant frame in the study of hinterland politics.[91] Where the state is absent but resource-advantaged, societal actors may have even stronger incentives to compete – including violently – for its attention than to resist and push back against its incursions.

The book's final section moves beyond Northern Ghana. Chapter 9 extends the argument to three shadow cases to consider how similar state interventions are likely to have more muted effects on society and politics in settings with other combinations of the two key variables in Chapter 2: the state's presence and resource advantages.

---

[90] Palik et al. (2020).
[91] Scott (2009).

PART IV

EXTENDING THE ARGUMENT

9

Shadow Cases

Northern Ghana is typical of hinterlands in the developing world along the two variables at the heart of the theory in Chapter 2: the state's *presence* has been persistently limited, with a minimal formal footprint, and yet the state also has been *resource advantaged* relative to society, allocating targeted benefits more valuable than those otherwise available.

Other combinations of these variables are also possible. Returning to the comparative argument in Chapter 2, this chapter explores the other three subnational regions defined by the interaction of state presence and resource advantages (Figures 1.1, 2.5). I examine three shadow cases – Southern Ghana, rural Peru, and the early postcolonial rural Philippines. By matching to each of the other combinations of state presence and resource advantages, as shown in Figure 9.1, the shadow cases illustrate Chapter 2's claim that specific interventions by the state into society are likely to be comparatively less impactful in regions in which the state is more present, less resource advantaged, or both. This suggests that state presence and resource advantages comprise the main scope conditions for the empirical patterns in Parts II and III of the book.

At the same time, two of the shadow cases – Peru and the Philippines – also help demonstrate the external validity of the prior chapters' findings beyond Ghana, providing examples of how subnational regions can shift across the cells of Figure 9.1 (Figures 1.1, 2.5) over time. During their respective colonial periods, hinterlands in each of these countries were initially in the same cell as Northern Ghana, with absent, but resource-advantaged states. During these periods of state scarcity, very similar dynamics to what I document for Northern Ghana occurred in each country, with isolated state actions conferring windfalls on society

State's Relative Resource Advantage

		Low (non-advantaged)	High (advantaged)
State's Presence	Low (absent)	Lower impact, short and long term **Case: Philippines**	Highest impact, short and long term **Case: Northern Ghana**
	High (present)	Lower impact in short term New actions offset past actions in long term **Case: Southern Ghana**	High impact in short term New actions offset past actions in long term **Case: Peru**

FIGURE 9.1 Figure 2.5 repeated, with shadow cases. Predicted impact of an isolated state action, holding the size and scale of the action fixed.

that generated new socioeconomic inequality and changed the allocation of political power. But over time, in response to changes in state leaders' political incentives to leave the hinterland be or instead shifts to the balance of economic resources between state and society, both cases subsequently transitioned out of the {absent, advantaged} (or {low, high}) cell in a way that Northern Ghana still has not.[1]

In Peru, postcolonial state leaders chose to substantially increase the state's presence by expropriating and reallocating rural land, pushing former hinterlands into the {present, advantaged} ({high, high}) cell of Figure 9.1 instead. In the Philippines, a combination of a change in colonial regimes and several other external events, including World War II and shifts in the global economy, opened up new opportunities for hinterland elites to amass resources independently of the state, shifting rural regions into the {absent, non-advantaged} ({low, low}) cell of Figure 9.1. As these cases moved away from the {absent, advantaged} cell, their parallels to Northern Ghana stopped. They suggest possible future trajectories for Northern Ghana if the region were to also undergo similar shifts.

---

[1] In the examples below, these shifts mainly occur due to exogenous events, such as major international wars. But they need not be in other cases: subnational regions could also shift cells of Figure 9.1 endogenously, such as if state leaders start investing significantly more heavily in a region, and in doing so, spark sufficiently large economic growth to alter the resource balance between state and society.

Moreover, the inclusion of these non-African cases helps demonstrate the broader applicability of the theory beyond the specific context of former British Africa. The historical parallels between Northern Ghana and Peru and the Philippines suggest that as long as the theory's two key scope conditions are met – with the state absent and resource-advantaged relative to society – the state can have similarly outsize effects on hinterland society even in non-British colonies, countries without traditional chiefs or formal policies of indirect rule, and in world regions far beyond Africa.

The chapter begins with Southern Ghana, an economic and political core region that represents the polar opposite of the Northern hinterland in Figures 1.1, 2.5, and 9.1. Southern Ghana provides the most direct possible comparison to Northern Ghana from the {present, non-advantaged} cell: a region governed by the same modern state and state leaders, in the same institutional environment, and yet in which that state was both always much more present and in which a more robust private sector reduced the state's relative resource advantages. I then turn to the two off-diagonal cells: Peru ({present, advantaged}) and the Philippines ({absent, non-advantaged}).

9.1 THE {PRESENT, NON-ADVANTAGED} CELL: SOUTHERN GHANA

Southern Ghana's parallel colonial and post-independence history provides a stark contrast to the North. Although the modern state inarguably still has had large effects on Southern society, it is much more difficult to draw any straight lines connecting discrete state actions to contemporary socioeconomic inequality or political outcomes. Contrary to assumptions that hinterlands are where the state matters least, comparing Ghana's North and South demonstrates that the effects of the state are far more visible in the periphery.

Consistent with Chapter 2, the specific state actions at the center of the book's analysis, such as empowering chiefs and building schools, have been less impactful at reordering society in Southern Ghana, for two reasons. First, the modern state was consistently more present and active in Southern Ghana than in the North, allocating resources to a far wider spectrum of society over time, rather than concentrating windfalls narrowly in a few hands. In line with the theoretical intuition represented by Figure 2.1, a less concentrated distribution of resources was less able to produce explicitly state-generated forms of inequality compared to the more concentrated, albeit smaller, distribution in the North.

Second, dating back to well before the modern state even came into being at the outset of colonial rule, there have been vastly more opportunities to accumulate resources through private and nonstate channels in the South, leaving the state comparatively much less resource advantaged. Society was already substantially more unequal at baseline, reducing the ability of the same state-provided benefits to reorder society (Figure 2.2). And the losers of individual state actions then had many more outside opportunities to catch up to the winners. This means both that there has been less chance for any state-created advantages to compound, as in Figure 2.3, and that the relative advantages over one's peers provided by specific state benefits, such as education, have been comparatively lower because those benefits have been much less scarce in society, as suggested by Figure 2.4.

In the colonial period, Southern Ghana was split across three historically distinct administrative regions. The original Gold Coast colony was centered on the Atlantic Coast, expanding outwards from Cape Coast, Accra, and the other European trading forts established in the precolonial period. The forts operated as trading outposts, not colonies, with no effort to govern surrounding populations; many were managed by chartered companies, not states directly. In 1821, the British state took over the forts themselves, but it was only in 1874 that they created a formal colonial state with the sustained goal of governing the interior. Separately, throughout the nineteenth century, much of Ghana's central forest belt remained part of the Ashanti Empire, the largest precolonial state in the region. The British only conquered the kingdom and incorporated it into the colony from 1896. The third administrative region, Southern Togoland (Ghana's modern-day Volta and Oti Regions), was joined to the colony after World War I, seized from Germany. To simplify and streamline the discussion, I focus on the first two (and largest) of these regions – the coast and Ashanti.[2]

---

[2] Most territory in these regions falls firmly in the {present, non-advantaged} cell of my typology (Figure 9.1). But there are small peripheral pockets that could be classified instead as hinterlands, such as several remote districts along Southern Ghana's interior border with Cote d'Ivoire. However, because these areas were often still incorporated into the cocoa cash crop economy and had much more active missionary education (described in the following text), they are not as representative of the {absent, advantaged} cell as Northern Ghana, limiting the degree to which they can be used as additional cases to test the book's claims about hinterlands.

9.1.1 Precolonial stratification

Both the coast and Ashanti were heavily incorporated into the global economy long before colonialism and the creation of the modern state. The result was significantly greater baseline socioeconomic stratification than in the North. Maritime trade with Europe began in the fifteenth century. Originally focused on gold, it soon became dominated by the export of slaves. Precolonial political authorities along the coast and in Ashanti were in a privileged position to profit; able to project military force, the leaders of local kingdoms "possessed the means of capture, and chiefs were often big [slave] traders."[3] Wealth from the slave trade helped the precolonial kingdoms, especially Ashanti, grow more powerful, and stratified their societies economically.[4]

After the Transatlantic slave trade was banned at the beginning of the nineteenth century, a new export economy – often dubbed the period of "legitimate commerce" – quickly emerged in its place, focused on palm oil, rubber, gold, and ivory. With the introduction of regular steamship service to Europe in the 1850s, new private sector opportunities opened for African merchants to cut out European firms and export commodities directly to European markets.[5] A new indigenous economic elite of "merchant princes" developed in coastal towns like Cape Coast, Ada, and Axim.[6] Many were from pre-existing chiefly families, able to take economic advantages gained during the slave trade and reinvest them in new activities as market incentives changed.[7]

As trade with Europe developed, European merchant companies and missionary societies also funded the nonstate provision of Western education. The first school opened in 1694 at Cape Coast Castle, initially focused on the children that British slave traders fathered with local women. By the mid-1700s, several dozen children had been sent to Europe for higher education, giving Southern Ghana its first university graduates.[8] Some returned to launch private schools outside the forts, targeted at the broader local population.[9] The first missionary school opened in 1752 in Cape Coast and missionaries began significantly expanding

[3] Akyeampong (2014, 238).
[4] Wilks (1975).
[5] Akyeampong (2014).
[6] Arhin (1983).
[7] Akyeampong (2014).
[8] As of independence in 1957, two centuries later, Northern Ghana still had just one university graduate (Bening 1990).
[9] Graham (1971, 3–10).

education provision into the interior from the 1830s, reaching Ashanti by the 1870s – before the modern state itself had gotten there.[10] The new commercial opportunities and missionary education reinforced each other; many of the "merchant princes" of the mid-nineteenth century coastal economy had attended the early mission schools, parlaying Western education into jobs as clerks for European firms, where they then developed connections to Europe that they could use to launch their own businesses.[11] In turn, these merchants would use their new wealth to provide for the education of their own children.[12]

The combined result of these nonstate opportunities was an increasingly stratified socioeconomic class system already in place when colonialism began on a scale wholly beyond anything in the precolonial North. Along the coast, a new Western-educated elite came to dominate local politics within the Fante, and to a lesser extent, Ga-Dangme ethnic groups.[13] In Ashanti, an even more hierarchical class system emerged around the institution of chieftaincy, conferring significant economic advantages on the kingdom's officeholders.[14] While these new forms of inequality were sparked by contact with Europe, they were very explicitly not creations of the modern state, unlike the examples in Chapters 4 and 6; instead, they resulted from compounding advantages in the private market before colonial rule.

9.1.2 The Colonial Period

Not only was the South already much more stratified at baseline, but the region's greater economic potential meant that it then received substantially more attention from colonial state leaders. Even though the British eventually also turned to indirect rule in the South, governing through traditional chiefs, they still dispatched an order of magnitude more state officials to the region than to the North.[15] For example, by 1921 – one of the few years in which these statistics were directly reported for both

---

[10] Graham (1971, 13, 53–55).

[11] Arhin (1983, 17), Akyeampong (2014).

[12] Graham (1971, 99).

[13] Graham (1971), Arhin (1983).

[14] Wilks (1975), Arhin (1983).

[15] In addition, unlike indirect rule in the North, the British state did not invent new chieftaincies because there were virtually no acephalous societies; all major Southern groups were already politically centralized prior to colonialism. It is thus not possible to replicate the main statistical analyses from Chapter 4 or 7 in the South because there is no similar variation in chieftaincy history.

regions – there were 768 British officers posted to Southern Ghana compared to just 27 to the Northern Territories. Adjusting for population counts in the 1921 census, this meant there were 2,226 residents for every officer in Southern Ghana versus 23,375 per officer in the North.[16] After independence, Nkrumah and other early post-independence leaders continued heavily concentrating state-building efforts in the South, where both their greatest threats and the country's greatest resources lay.[17]

With more state activity on the ground, there were correspondingly more opportunities for a wider range of people to benefit from state resources much earlier. For example, similar to the North, building schools became one of the state's principal outlays to society. But while the British sharply restricted missionaries' access to the North, missionaries were already widespread in the South before colonial rule. Rather than attempt to cut back or establish a rival network of government-run schools, the British instead initially partnered with these pre-existing nonstate providers, offering state resources to help them continue to expand – a common approach in many British colonies.[18] While the British prioritized chiefs' sons for enrollments in the few state-run schools in the South for similar reasons as in the North,[19] missionary schools enrolled a broader cross section of society. Their motivation was not to train compliant state intermediaries, but to spread the Gospel, which meant spreading Western education more widely long before it became similarly available beyond chiefs' families in the North.

Table 9.1 draws on colonial annual reports to track the number of schools of different types in Southern versus Northern Ghana over time. By 1910, the year of the first census, there were just two schools in the North – the government school in Tamale and the White Fathers' school in Navrongo. But building on the region's head start in school-building throughout the nineteenth century, there were already 377 schools in the South, 142 of which were state-supported missionary schools. This disparity between North and South remained enormous over time, even adjusting for the South's larger population. By 1948, Table 9.1 indicates

---

[16] Colonial censuses were often inaccurate undercounts, and errors should have been more severe in regions of more limited state capacity (Brambor et al. 2020). If anything, the figures quoted here understate the true North–South disparity if the undercount was worse where there were fewer officers to oversee the census.

[17] Chazan (1982), Boone (2003).

[18] Frankema (2012). The widespread creation of state-run schools only came in the 1930s, with the introduction of Native Authority day schools similar to those described in Chapter 3.

[19] Graham (1971, 43).

TABLE 9.1 *Schools in colonial period, by type and region*

	1910		1921		1931		1948	
	No. schools	Pop. per school	No. schools	Pop. per school	No. schools	Pop. per school	No. schools	Pop. per school
Southern Ghana:								
Government or Native Authority (public)	8		16		19		872	
Missionary (private, state-supported)	142		214		328		587	
"Unassisted" (private, independent)	227		250		241		1,572	
Total	377	3,025	480	3,469	588	3,869	3,031	1,001
Northern Ghana:								
Government or Native Authority (public)	1		5		6		40	
Missionary (private, state-supported)	1		1		5		7	
"Unassisted" (private, independent)	0		0		0		0	
Total	2	180,903	6	126,228	11	80,492	47	22,904

School (primary, middle, secondary) counts by category for Southern Ghana, comprised of the "Colony," Ashanti, Southern Togoland (after 1914), and Northern Ghana, combining the Northern Territories and Northern Togoland (after 1914), during the year of each colonial census. Population estimates are from the closest colonial census. School counts are from a combination of annual Education Yearbooks and Northern Territories Annual Reports. Where overall figures conflict, I defer to the coding from Northern Territories Annual Report, also used in Chapters 3 and 4.

that there was one school for every 1,001 residents of Southern Ghana compared to one for every 22,904 residents of the North.[20]

---

[20] Moreover, as noted above, this likely understates the true gap because weaker state capacity in the North should have been responsible for a larger population undercount on the census.

Geographically, the larger number of state-sponsored schools in the South allowed the state to project its resources much more widely. Using a list of all state-supported schools in 1921, I geocode the location of every Southern school in a similar manner to the analyses in Figures 3.2 and 3.4. As of 1921, the median community in Southern Ghana, proxied by 2010 census Enumeration Area (EA), was 6.0 km from a state-funded school; overall, 66.7 percent of Southern communities were already within 10 km of such a school.[21] By contrast, the data from Figure 3.4 indicates that the North only had begun to approach similar levels of school penetration by 1960, four decades later. In 1921, the median Northern EA was instead 40.2 km from a school and only 3.8 percent were within 10 km. In 1960, these figures had reached 7.1 km and 65.7 percent, respectively.

However, by restricting to state-funded schools, these statistics understate the degree to which education was more widely available across the South. The most common type of school in colonial Southern Ghana was instead fully private, outside the state's purview completely. "Unassisted" schools – the majority across the South at three of four years in Table 9.1 – were created and operated independently of both the state and the Western missions; their locations are not recorded in the list I geocode above. Most were created by graduates of the mission schools who then set up private schools on their own to evangelize further.[22] These schools penetrated deeper into the Southern countryside away from where Western missions and state-run schools were located.[23] The "unassisted" schools offered additional opportunities across the South for families passed over in the state provision of education to still gain access to human capital. No similar opportunities existed for those passed over by the state in the North.

Under colonial rule, the South's agricultural export economy also continued to provide private paths to wealth outside of state control. Rather than formal sector employment facilitated by access to human capital providing the only real path to elite status, as in the North, cash crop agriculture also provided additional nonstate opportunities to rise. Between 1890 and 1910, the Gold Coast went from exporting

---

[21] Ten kilometers is the estimated catchment area used in Chapter 4.

[22] Frankema (2012).

[23] "Vernacular schools, conducted by catechists of some of the missionary bodies ... [were] generally established in villages remote from a regular school centre ... with a view to furthering the spread of religious education among those who were unable to attend ordinary primary schools" (Graham 1971, 166).

no cocoa to being the world's leading producer.[24] While this dramatic transformation occurred after the colonial state was formed, it was not a state project. Instead, summarizing the research of Hill (1963), Austin (1997, ix) explains that "Ghana's cocoa farmers *put themselves* on the world economic map;"[25] similar to cash crop economies in other non-settler colonies in Africa, the growth of cocoa farming "was [a story] of African enterprise rather than colonial coercion."[26] Private producers, acting independently of colonial officials, realized the export potential of cocoa and responded by organizing themselves into new forms of indigenous business corporations to pool resources to buy land and invest in production at scale.[27] Initial investments in the cocoa economy came from wealth already earned in Southern Ghana's earlier export economy in the mid-nineteenth century, especially from palm oil production, with cocoa representing a continuation of precolonial developments in the private economy, not a sharp economic discontinuity caused by the colonial state.[28]

After initially taking off in the present-day Eastern Region, the cocoa industry increased dramatically when it spread into Ashanti from the 1910s. As with the initial Akwapim and Krobo farmers studied by Hill (1963), Austin (1988, 65) stresses that the expansion of cocoa was "an achievement of [Ashanti farmers] themselves: the colonial government's contribution was largely confined to the provision of a railway (from motives not directly related to cocoa)."[29] Rather than actively facilitate cocoa's growth, the state maintained an often antagonist relationship with producers. To rein in the potentially politically threatening socioeconomic changes this private economy was unleashing, the state tried at various times to restrict export permits to handpicked chiefs or even to ban new cocoa farms (in Ashanti) outright.[30] Efforts to tax farmers and impose price controls resulted in repeated grassroots protests, most famously a series of "hold ups" between 1908 and the late 1930s in which private producers refused to sell their crops unless they received better terms.[31]

[24] Northern Ghana's drier savannah is not suitable for cocoa; all production is in the South.

[25] Emphasis added.

[26] Austin (2014, 311).

[27] Hill (1963).

[28] Hill (1963, 17).

[29] The railway was built to bring gold from mines also in Ashanti to ports at the coast. The farming regions it passed through happened to be well suited for cocoa.

[30] Akyeampong (2014, 260), Austin (2014, 311), respectively.

[31] Austin (1988), Austin (2014).

It was only as an emergency measure during World War II that the state was successfully able to impose a monopsonist buying scheme on the industry that allowed for significant state control and rent extraction.[32]

With this belated state intervention into the private market, cocoa's profitability diminished.[33] But this only came decades after further non-state changes to socioeconomic inequality within Southern Ghana had begun to take hold. While the region's precolonial elite, including the chiefs, were active in cocoa farming, they did not exclusively domi-nate the industry, and it also provided new paths for others to rise in socioeconomic status.[34] In particular, just as with Southern Ghana's mid-nineteenth century "merchant princes," successful farmers used earn-ings from cocoa to ensure the education of their children at private and mission schools, helping accelerate their families' gains.[35]

9.1.3 Postcolonial Politics

Ultimately, with a more active state and many more nonstate paths to wealth and education, postcolonial politics deviated significantly from the North as well. Chapter 6 shows that the North had a single dominant path to independence-era political power: the sons of chiefs, themselves often arbitrarily elevated by the state in the early twentieth century, were privileged in education and formal sector employment, becoming vir-tually the only viable candidates. By contrast, in the South there were multiple paths into Ghana's initial political elite, both rooted, at least in part, in nonstate sources of advantage. First, the precolonial elites – both chiefly families and the merchant families of the coast – already in place prior to the modern state were then further reinforced by state policies. Chiefs, in particular, benefitted from indirect rule. But second, a separate series of entirely new elites also emerged from among previously non-chiefly families through access to nonstate education and/or wealth earned in private business, including cocoa farming.

Whereas early Northern politics is best understood as a case of capture by the chiefly class, Southern politics was instead fundamentally defined by conflict between two very separate sets of elites. The leaders of Ghana's independence movement, Nkrumah and the CPP, were drawn heavily

---

[32] Alence (2001).
[33] Bates (1981).
[34] Austin (1988, 68).
[35] Hill (1963, 17).

from the second group above – educated commoners without chiefly heritage – and saw the chiefly elite as anachronistic colonial collaborators standing in the way of Ghana's modernization. In turn, the opposition to the CPP, initially centered around the rival United Gold Coast Convention (UGCC) party, drew heavily on support from the chiefly elite. Nkrumah actively sought to undermine Southern chiefs once in office, viewing them as his main source of opposition.[36] In Ashanti, chiefs provided significant support for the National Liberation Movement (NLM), a grassroots social movement opposed to the CPP that flirted with violent revolt.[37] Chiefs supported the coup that removed Nkrumah in 1966, and then backed the UGCC's conservative chiefly "old guard" under Kofi Busia, an Akan royal, in the Progress Party government in office between 1969–1972.[38] Post-independence politics also featured similar intra-elite conflict at a more local scale; within Ashanti, for example, independence-era contestation pitted chiefs against the *nkwankwaa* ("young men"), educated businessmen and civil servants who lacked a path to traditional power through chieftaincy.[39]

Due to differences in colonial record keeping and naming conventions, it is impossible to repeat the quantitative analysis of dynasties in Chapter 6 for the South.[40] Yet anecdotally, dynasties dating to the early colonial period appear much rarer. There are prominent exceptions, including Nana Akufo-Addo, Ghana's current president (NPP), and Ken Ofori-Atta, Akufo-Addo's cousin and finance minister; they are descended from precolonial and colonial-era Akyem (Akan) paramount chiefs, as well as from the founders of the UGCC. But right from the outset, the majority in Ghana's first post-independence legislature – dominated by the CPP – did not have chiefly heritage.[41] Over time, many Southern

---

[36] Rathbone (2000), Boone (2003).

[37] Allman (1990).

[38] Ghana's present-day national party system, emerging after 1992, still mirrors this initial cleavage in Southern politics. The NPP traces its political lineage to the anti-Nkrumah opposition, while the NDC sees itself as an extension of elements of the CPP. (They do not share the CPP's animosity towards chiefs, however.)

[39] Allman (1990). Also see Arhin (1983).

[40] In Southern Ghana, the colonial-era chieftaincy registers list chiefs by given name, not surname. Among the Akan, the majority in Southern Ghana, men typically take one of just seven given names, assigned based on the weekday of their birth. And unlike the North, given names do not then become the surname for a father's children (see Chapter 6). This makes it impossible to match chiefs and politicians across generations.

[41] Rathbone (2000, 21–22, 28). Rathbone (2000, 28) notes how markedly different this was from the North, where chiefs or their sons held almost every position in the 1950s.

politicians from "the social margins" – lower-class, non-chiefly backgrounds – have risen to the top of Ghanaian politics after gaining access to education.[42] Nkrumah, educated in a mission school, was an example, as was Jerry Rawlings, president from 1981 to 2000.[43] Moreover, to whatever extent there is a correlation today between elected-office holding and being related to chiefs, the causality may be reversed from Chapter 6. Rather than chiefs benefitting from their appointments to become wealthy elites and then funneling that wealth into campaigns, Austin (1988, 76) observes that cocoa also allowed the relationship to move the other way; wealth earned in farming enabled commoners subsequently to buy chieftaincy appointments and become "royals."

Finally, there are also divergences from the North in the two political outcomes in Chapters 7 and 8. While Southern chiefs retain similar roles as electoral brokers in some rural communities, in part due to their similar influence over land ownership,[44] there are also broad swaths of the South, especially urban areas, where chieftaincy has become quite marginal to electoral politics and chiefs hold little sway relative to local party organizations.[45] Moreover, while there are still many chieftaincy disputes among competing claimants across the South, they remain localized within the specific families party to them; there has never been large-scale communal violence emerging from these conflicts. Across the full range of the ACLED (2016) data from which the data collection in Chapter 8 begins, there are just two total incidents of nonstate communal violence in Southern Ghana in the high fatality (10+) category, with twelve and twenty-five fatalities, respectively. Both occurred in 2017 and were farmer-herder conflicts related to the migration of Fulani pastoralists, not chieftaincy disputes or demands for the state recognition of new traditional authorities. Because the private economy provides more outside opportunity in the South, the community-wide stakes over control over particular chieftaincy institutions are often simply much lower.

---

[42] Nugent (2010, 8).

[43] Nugent (2010a). Both then subsequently started new dynasties of their own after leaving the Presidency – each has a daughter who became a prominent MP – but their families' initial path to prominence diverges widely from Chapter 6.

[44] Goldstein and Udry (2008).

[45] Focusing on Ghana's largest metropolitan area, Greater Accra, Nathan (2019) documents how chiefs only retain electoral influence among some segments of the indigenous Ga minority, with little impact on politics in the city at large.

9.2 THE {PRESENT, ADVANTAGED} CELL: RURAL PERU

Well beyond Africa, rural Peru presents another useful contrast, with sub-national regions that have moved back and forth multiple times between two cells in Figure 9.1: the same {absent, advantaged} cell as Northern Ghana and the {present, advantaged} cell, in which the state retains significant resource advantages relative to society, but is much more active and present, intervening in society to a greater degree. Since the onset of Spanish colonial rule in the mid-sixteenth century, there have been extended periods in which the state was very scarce and remarkably similar dynamics unfolded as in Northern Ghana. Specific, isolated state actions reordered society by providing windfalls that elevated new elites, while the state's prolonged absence otherwise allowed these elites to capture dynastic political power and compound their advantages. But in several other periods, the incentives of state leaders changed: political threats from the rural elite became too challenging, and the state switched strategies and chose to intervene much more extensively in the country-side to reassert dominance. As it did, new state actions offset old state actions. The state wiped out the previous inequality and political elites it had created, expropriating their wealth and giving out new windfalls to new recipients.

In Chapter 2, I argue that because initial advantages compound over time, individual state actions that provide targeted windfalls can have large and sustained long-run effects if there are few new actions that allocate (or expropriate) resources to offset them. As visualized in Figure 2.3, as more time passes and increasing advantages accrue to the early winners of state action, the amount of new state activity needed to allow the initial losers to catch up increases.

Peru demonstrates both that this process of compounding advantages from early state intervention has played out in other hinterlands around the world, and yet also shows what happens when, by significantly reducing its scarcity, the state subsequently intervenes at a sufficiently high level to erode the effects of its earlier actions. In particular, as the state's presence increases, the state becomes less likely to be a net provider, as I argue is common in hinterlands, and instead has the capacity to extract from society in a way that can wipe away earlier distributions of advantage. Rather than sustained elite persistence, with early state actions having long afterlives, subnational regions in the {present, advantaged} cell of Figure 9.1 are more likely instead to feature waves of state-led inequality and elite creation over time, with the state giving, taking away, and giving again. This comparatively reduces the long-run impact of any individual state action relative to cases that remain in the {absent, advantaged} cell.

9.2.1 Elites under Colonial Rule

Spanish explorers seized present-day Peru in the 1530s and the colonial state was established in 1542. While Spain's primary interest was in mining in the interior mountains, agriculture soon dominated the economy of the countryside beyond the mines, especially along the coast. The two most important resources for the emerging agricultural economy – land and the forced labor of the native population – were formally controlled by the state. Isolated distributions of these resources to individual Spanish soldiers and settlers allowed early state leaders to create a brand new elite "by fiat."[46]

Two sets of actors received valuable state windfalls. First, Francisco Pizarro, Peru's initial conquerer (*conquistador*) rewarded his most loyal soldiers by granting them *encomiendas*, which provided tribute payments from and control over the labor of a specific set of conquered native communities. Benefitting from the wealth they could now extract, a small set of recipients (*encomenderos*) quickly rose to "the pinnacle of conquest society."[47] Second, as agriculture took on increased economic importance, the state gave out vast land grants (*mercedes*) to individual settlers that allowed them to start plantations (*haciendas*). Many *encomenderos* also used their new wealth to create *haciendas*.[48] The recipients of both *encomiendas* and *mercedes* were typically not pre-existing elites in Spanish society; instead, "most were drawn from families of commoners," coming to Peru because they had few paths to economic success in Spain and then, essentially by virtue of being in Peru early enough, lucking into state windfalls that allowed them to at times become wealthier than many nobles back in Spain.[49]

Outside major towns, the colonial state remained very absent throughout the sixteenth and seventeenth centuries, allowing these advantages to compound amidst dynastic capture by a narrow set of elite families. In the initial decades of Spanish rule, the *encomenderos* were virtually the state unto themselves; "in the frontier atmosphere of the ... coast, there

---

[46] Ramirez (1986, 33).
[47] Ramirez (1986, 33). Also see Davies (1984).
[48] Ramirez (1986, 35–49; 63–67; 81–93), Davies (1984).
[49] Davies (1984, 15).

were hardly any individual or institutional checks on the *encomendero's* action. The few government bureaucrats in Peru lived in Lima, where they did not witness" what was happening in the countryside.[50] Common to many hinterlands, the attention of colonial state leaders was focused on "more pressing matters elsewhere," such as the cities and mines.[51] Over time, amid backlash to extreme abuses that *encomenderos* exacted on the native population, the state attempted to rein them in by limiting how much labor they could request and appointing colonial officials (*corregidores*), akin to the British colonial state's District Commissioners, into rural districts.[52] However, without a meaningful bureaucracy under their control, individual *corregidores* were forced to rely on an informal analog of indirect rule, partnering with and governing through the very local elites they were nominally meant to oversee; *corregidores* "routinely delegate[d] their authority to lieutenants," often chosen from among the *encomenderos* and other Spanish settlers, allowing the new colonial elite to "co-opt royal bureaucrats and gain their cooperation."[53]

Moreover, with little direct policy interests in the periphery, the colonial state sold off many appointments as *corregidor* as a means of raising revenue, allowing wealthy *hacienda* owners to at times purchase these positions for themselves.[54] In turn, through capture of the local state, elites were able to reward additional windfalls of state resources to themselves, compounding their advantages. This included favored access to further grants of land and indentured native labor.[55] By the end of the seventeenth century, much of rural Peru was dominated by a dynastic *hacienda* elite, whose hereditary advantages had passed across generations since the initial state windfalls of the mid-sixteenth century.[56]

The rural Peruvian experience up to this point bore broad theoretical similarities with Northern Ghana: isolated state actions had arbitrarily elevated a new elite that was then entrenched further through forms of indirect rule adopted as an exigency of state absence. But the parallels were interrupted in the mid-eighteenth century. An exogenous event – war in Europe, followed by a new regime taking the crown in

---

[50] Ramirez (1986, 29).
[51] Ramirez (1986, 97).
[52] Davies (1984, 53).
[53] Ramirez (1986, 50–51).
[54] Guardado (2018), Ramirez (1986, 97).
[55] Ramirez (1986, 142–147), Davies (1984, 31–33).
[56] Elite closure over time was maintained through extensive intermarriage within the narrow elite class. Ramirez (1986), Davies (1984).

Spain – led the Spanish state to adopt administrative changes – the Bourbon reforms – that sought to wrest control over colonial revenues back from local elites. These reforms reduced state scarcity across rural Peru (and other colonies), enabling state officials to intervene more directly into the *hacienda* economy.

The state sharply increased the tax burden on plantations, stopped allowing offices to be sold and instead imported more independent bureaucrats from Spain, and expanded and professionalized the militia, limiting landowners' capture of the coercive apparatus.[57] Coinciding with several acute natural disasters, the increased taxes bankrupted many *haciendas*. In response, the newly empowered state began expropriating land on behalf of creditors. Many long-dominant elite families were wiped out.[58] In response, a newer generation of settlers from Spain who had taken up positions in the bureaucracy and militia "in connection with the implementation of the Bourbon reforms," was able to buy up the *haciendas* on the cheap.[59] By the end of the eighteenth century, increased state presence had replaced one set of elites with another, undoing the long-run effects of earlier state actions.

9.2.2 Postcolonial Windfalls and Redistribution

This process of state-led elite creation followed by state-led elite destruction then repeated itself across rural Peru's postcolonial history, further in line with the theory's predictions for the {present, advantaged} cell. The nineteenth century opened with two decades of near-continuous war, culminating in Peru's independence. War and independence again reduced the presence and capacity of the formal state, allowing the new landowning elite that consolidated in the late eighteenth century free rein to once again engage in capture and raid the state for private benefit. In the 1820s and 1830s, "much of country was reduced to semi-feudal enclaves, in which large landowners expanded their empires" and controlled "private armies" that they used to compete with each other over political power and state spoils.[60]

In the 1840s, a natural resource boom provided yet another opportunity for isolated state action to allocate windfalls to society. Islands

---

[57] Ramirez (1986, 211–220; 254–257), Guardado (2018, 973).
[58] Ramirez (1986, 221–223).
[59] Ramirez (1986, 254–257).
[60] Gilbert (1977, 22–23).

along the coast were discovered to contain large accumulations of guano (bird feces), highly valued on international markets as a fertilizer. Central state leaders controlled the islands and allocated concessions to businesses to export deposits. After initially working with foreign firms, state leaders switched in the 1850s to favoring "friends of the regime," mostly urban merchants not from the landowning elite.[61] The result was another reordering of society, with the state once more essentially creating an elite from thin air "by fiat." Tracing out the family histories of the elites who subsequently dominated Peru in the first half of the twentieth century, Gilbert (1977, 24–25) observes that "[m]any important family fortunes ... have grown directly out of the guano trade," with the state's mid-nineteenth century provision of export licenses directly creating "a new class of extremely wealthy individuals." The urban merchants who received these concessions soon diversified into agriculture, buying up *haciendas* from the independence-era landowners.[62] Over time, as the new elites' economic advantages accumulated, landownership became increasing concentrated nationwide.[63]

In turn, this new wave of state-created elites became yet another dynastic oligarchy, with even more extensive elite capture and clientelism than seen in Northern Ghana in Chapters 6 and 7. By the late nineteenth century, and continuing deep into the twentieth century, a small set of families that had benefitted from the guano boom held most political power. Historians refer to this period as the era of the "forty families."[64] Members of these families both ran for office themselves, with several reaching the presidency, and became patrons to politician clients who ruled in their interest.[65]

Outside of cities, the formal state again remained scarce, allowing the landowning elite to dominate. Basic public service provision in *hacienda* communities was often delegated to landowners themselves.[66] In turn, landowners served as electoral brokers to a much more extreme degree than in Northern Ghana, with significant control over how their tenants and employees voted due to a combination of concentrated economic

---

[61] Gilbert (1977, 24).

[62] Gilbert (1977, 33). The pre-existing landowners also scrambled to marry their families "into the new wealth," allowing the new guano elite to appropriate through inheritance the remaining vestiges of the colonial elite (Gilbert 1977, 25).

[63] Crabtree and Durand (2017, 38).

[64] Gilbert (1977), Crabtree and Durand (2017), McClintock (2019).

[65] Gilbert (1977), Albertus (2015, 37–38).

[66] Albertus (2015, 41–42).

power and very limited bottom-up accountability.[67] Even in *haciendas* not directly controlled by the "forty families," local landowners operated as "ward bosses," linked to national-level planter elites through a "chain of clientelistic relations" and delivering votes to the party preferred by the national elite in return for the state's acquiescence to their local dominance.[68] With clientelism and patronage widespread, state officials in rural areas were often captured clients of landowning patrons. Miller (1982, 113) quotes a local observer in 1910 that rural "government is like an *hacienda*." As in earlier periods in Peruvian history, capture of the local state allowed elites to allocate even more windfalls of state resources to themselves, including new "vast concessions" of land.[69]

In 1968, state leaders' incentives to leave the periphery alone changed again. A military junta led by leftist officers under Juan Velasco seized power in a coup. Reaching power independently of the planter elite, Velasco saw the landowners as a threat, not ally, and attempted to break the oligarchy by transforming the countryside through state-led land reform. While Northern Ghana's poorly-implemented land reform at a similar time further reinforced the advantages of the local elite, the Peruvian version broke them. What ensued was a massive state-led effort that dramatically increased the state's presence in the rural periphery and very explicitly attempted to wipe out the compounded inequality that had emerged from the state's actions in the nineteenth century.[70]

With a substantial increase in state presence, new state actions once again offset the long-run effects of prior actions. By the early 1960s, just 1.4 percent of landowners held 63 percent of the country's arable land. On the coast, the main zone for commercial agriculture, 180 individuals held 56 percent of all farms. In the highlands, 95 percent of the population owned no land.[71] But after 1968, the state set about expropriating 45 percent of all agricultural land, working farm by farm in areas where its presence had previously been limited. In total, approximately 15,000 farms were seized.[72] Long-dominant families were economically devastated; land reform "quickly and effectively broke the power of the

---

[67] Albertus (2015, 42). For a very similar example of clientelist brokerage by *hacienda* owners at this time in neighboring Chile, see Baland and Robinson (2008).

[68] Gilbert (1977, 27).

[69] Crabtree and Durand (2017, 38).

[70] Albertus (2015).

[71] Gilbert (1977, 3).

[72] Albertus (2015, 192–210).

country's old landed oligarchy."[73] Economic inequality fell abruptly,[74] as the state subdivided *haciendas* and redistributed them among the previously landless.

After the land reform ended in 1980 and Peru pivoted to neoliberal economic policies, a new economic elite has emerged again. But it is once more a distinct group of people from the earlier elites, drawn from new segments of society, with greater state presence allowing one wave of elites to be replaced by another. Crabtree and Durand (2017) argue that the post-land reform economy has allowed for a broad "restructuring of the business class" (107) and "democratisation of capitalism" (113) in which new socio-economic elites have emerged from social groups "that were previously poor and excluded" (106).

9.3 THE {ABSENT, NON-ADVANTAGED} CELL: THE POST-WAR PHILIPPINES

The final cell in Figure 9.1 (and Figures 1.1, 2.5) – {absent, non-advantaged} – represents regions where the state is both absent and not resource advantaged relative to society. These latter regions include relatively extreme cases in which well-resourced warlords, cartels, or rebel groups have become so locally dominant that they can effectively resist state efforts to intervene in society. In Chapter 1, I draw on data from ACLED (2016) to suggest that rural regions in the {absent, non-advantaged} cell are rare compared to regions like Northern Ghana in the {absent, advantaged} cell; in sub-Saharan Africa, for example, the overwhelmingly majority of the rural periphery is not dominated by rebel militias or warlords, even within the minority of countries with active civil wars.[75]

But where these regions exist, the effects of similar state actions to those studied in Northern Ghana are likely to be more limited. Because inequality is already very high, with local resources concentrated narrowly in the warlord, cartel or other local elite, isolated allocations of a fixed amount of state resources no longer have the same potential for short- or long-term societal change compared to regions in the {absent, advantaged} cell with more limited initial inequality (Figure 2.2).

---

[73] Crabtree and Durand (2017, 54).

[74] McClintock (2019).

[75] In the subset of African countries with observed rebel activity between 2015 and 2020, rebels were only recorded on average in 17 percent of second-tier administrative units, with most of the rural countryside still unaffected.

In the first decades after independence in 1946, the rural Philippines offers a clear example of the {absent, non-advantaged} cell, with the formal state "impotent" and unable to impose its will in the countryside in the face of well-resourced warlords.[76] Like Peru, this case also provides a particularly useful comparison to Northern Ghana because it suggests another way in which conditions may evolve if the underlying scope conditions in the theory change. The rural Philippines similarly moved from one cell of Figure 9.1 to another over time.

This case began in the same {absent, advantaged} cell as Northern Ghana throughout most of the colonial period, with relatively similar dynamics playing out: a new elite emerged in response to isolated state actions, reordering the pre-existing socioeconomic hierarchy and allowing for political capture and clientelism. But then, unlike Northern Ghana, a series of shocks dramatically increased the resources available to these new elites. These shocks were a mix of exogenous events – World War II and changes in the global economy – and endogenous responses to new state policies after an abrupt shift from Spanish to US colonial rule. As a result, hinterland elites began to rival the central state and challenge its basic sovereignty, pushing many rural communities into the {absent, non-advantaged} cell instead. In this way, the Philippines helps show that many examples of the {absent, non-advantaged} cell in the rural periphery may be downstream outcomes of the same dynamics I study in the preceding chapters. In these cases, isolated state actions do not merely have long and powerful afterlives, as in Northern Ghana, but have such long and powerful afterlives that they drown out the ability of most future state interventions to reorder society.

9.3.1 Initial Elite Formation under Spanish Rule

For centuries after Spanish colonial rule began in 1565, state leaders in the Philippines had little economic interest in pushing into the interior. Unlike Peru and other Spanish colonies in the Americas, but very similar to Northern Ghana, a major plantation or cash crop economy did not initially develop and there were few settlers from the colonial metropole. As a result, the formal state remained absent beyond Manila and several other large towns. To govern the countryside, state leaders relied on cooperation with Catholic missionaries. Friars became the "de facto administrators."[77] They also became the largest landowners, amassing

[76] Anderson (1988), Slater (2010).
[77] Maurer and Iyer (2008, 5), Dulay (2022).

vast tracts. In the areas where they operated, these priests came to exercise "quasi-judicial authority" over the native population, in practice holding a role similar to Britain's District Commissioners, even as they remained outside the formal bureaucracy.[78]

In concert with the friars, the actions of the scarce colonial state also helped create two sets of indigenous elites. First, in a system very similar to British indirect rule in Africa centuries later, the Spanish worked through local headmen from the native population, termed *principales* or *caciques* ("chiefs"), who "acted as intermediaries between the [native population] and their colonial overlords – collecting taxes, directing labor gangs, and leading native troop contingents."[79] These intermediaries were often selected directly by the friars.[80] In return for their assistance, the *principales* received state resources and rents, including "tax exemptions ... and the privilege of exploiting [local] labor for their own purposes."[81]

Second, and ultimately more importantly, Spanish policies also helped generate a new commercial elite who grew to rival and displace the friars as the principal landowners in interior regions of state scarcity. In the seventeenth and early eighteenth centuries, a significant population of Chinese merchants settled in and around the Spanish towns in the Philippines, becoming commercial middlemen linking interior regions of the colony both to these port cities and then on to Chinese markets.[82] In an effort to exert more political control over this rising population, "intermarriage between Chinese immigrant men ... and native women ... was actively encouraged and formally institutionalized by the Catholic Church and colonial authorities."[83] In the racialized caste system that the Spanish state codified, the children of these state-sanctioned marriages became a legally distinct category, the *mestizos*, with the ability to pass between native communities and Spanish settlements in a way that other racial groups were barred from doing.[84]

Over the remainder of the eighteenth and nineteenth centuries, the Chinese-Filipino *mestizos* rose in socioeconomic status in response to a series of additional state actions. In 1762 Britain invaded and briefly held

---

[78] Matsuzaki (2019, 18), Dulay (2022).
[79] Larkin (1982, 601).
[80] Matsuzaki (2019, 18).
[81] Larkin (1982, 601).
[82] Wickberg (1964, 67).
[83] Sidel (2008, 131), Wickberg (1964, 68).
[84] Wickberg (1964), Anderson (1988), Sidel (2008, 131).

Manila. The Chinese merchant population was seen as supportive of the occupation. When Spain regained control, they expelled the large majority of Chinese merchants. The Catholic *mestizo* population, instead seen as loyal to Spain, was allowed to remain. By intervening in the market to provide protection against external competition, this state action created an economic "vacuum" in which *mestizo* businesses were able to flourish.[85] By the mid-nineteenth century, *mestizo* traders and money-lenders dominated commercial activity in the rural Philippines, which historians argue was a direct result of the state's deportation of the prior Chinese commercial class.[86] And in 1844, *mestizo* merchants were protected from competition by state intervention again when the state banned Spanish colonial bureaucrats from participating in internal trade on their own, further clearing the market of potential rivals.[87]

As they grew more prosperous, *mestizo* merchants diversified into agriculture. This transition was aided by both the friars and the state. In the mid- to late 18th century, the friars began to commercially develop their holdings for the first time. Lacking labor, however, they leased out properties to local agents, who in turn arranged the labor of native sharecroppers in what became known as the *inquilino* system. *Mestizo* merchants were the main agents chosen by the friars. Their profits were then reinvested in buying up new land of their own.[88] Moreover, in 1767, the Spanish banned the Jesuits, one of the key groups of friars, from the Philippines (for reasons unrelated to local events); the state expropriated their estates and gradually sold them off; by 1800, many had been bought by *mestizos*.[89] And in the 1880s, a major reform of state land laws attempted to facilitate greater private ownership and stimulate economic growth. *Mestizo* businessmen were again the main beneficiaries, finding loopholes in the new legal system to register lands in their own name that they did not actually control, "claim[ing] extensive areas occupied by their smallholder neighbors."[90] By making land available at "giveaway prices," the new land policies also "reduced the risks of taming the frontier," allowing *mestizo* landowners to extend their holdings deeper into the rural periphery.[91] By the end of the nineteenth century, the *mestizos*

---

[85] McLennan (1969, 69).
[86] For example, Wickberg (1964, 86).
[87] Wickberg (1964, 90).
[88] McLennan (1969, 659), Murray (1972, 153).
[89] McLennan (1969, 653).
[90] McLennan (1969, 673). Also see Wickberg (1964, 92), Matsuzaki (2019, 20).
[91] Larkin (1982, 620).

had surpassed the friars as the largest landholder; by one estimate they now owned half of all land under agricultural production.[92]

As the *mestizos* grew in wealth, they both overtook the *principales* and *caciques* – the native headmen empowered under colonial indirect rule – in socioeconomic status and even subsumed many of them into their own ranks. Intermarriage among these two sets of local elites became widespread in the nineteenth century, allowing the *mestizos* and *principales* to eventually become "amalgamated" into a common cultural grouping that "possessed the lion's share of wealth and, increasingly, all of the political power" in rural areas by the end of Spanish rule.[93] In particular, *mestizo* landholders benefitted economically from these intermarriages because it allowed them to weld their land ownership with the *principales'* control over the indigenous labor needed to farm that land.[94]

9.3.2 Shocks to Elite Resources

Elevated into a new landholding elite, *mestizo* families were put in a privileged position to capitalize on a series of shocks that further increased their resource base to the point that some became more powerful than the state that had first helped birth them. Three external developments were particularly important.

First, just as the *mestizos* transitioned into land-holding in the nineteenth century, the economic value of that land was rising due to changes in the global economy. The Spanish finally opened the Philippines broadly to international trade in the early nineteenth century. This was a response to events exogenous to the colony, including Spain's weakening position in the Americas. By the mid-nineteenth century, Western business interests began operating at scale, seeking to export sugar and other cash crops.[95] As "world commerce arrived,"[96] and markets opened that had never previously existed, *mestizos* were able to convert their new holdings into cash crop plantations. They now became the Philippines' first "*hacendados*" in the model of Spanish settlers elsewhere centuries earlier.[97]

Second, Spanish rule abruptly ended in 1898 due to the Spanish-American War, which occurred for reasons completely exogenous to the

[92] Wickberg (1964, 92).
[93] Larkin (1982, 617–618). Also see McLennan (1969).
[94] Fradera (2004, 310).
[95] Larkin (1982), Anderson (1988).
[96] Larkin (1982, 612).
[97] Anderson (1988).

Philippines. The new American colonial state provided substantial new windfalls to *mestizo* elites, even more directly elevating them than the Spanish state had.[98] The result was elite capture, clientelism, and the private provision of violence – the key outcomes in Part III of the book – on an even grander scale than Northern Ghana.

Rather than centralize state power or invest in a strong local bureaucracy, American officials sought to delegate authority as locally as possible, while also introducing elections for many local positions. Elite *mestizo* families used their advantages in rural areas to dominate these elections and capture the new positions, including through the widespread use of clientelism. In turn, they raided state positions for rents. They also gained new control over local police forces, and with it, a growing ability to convert the state's coercive resources into private militias.[99] American officials largely let this capture continue as long as these elites cooperated with the colonial project.[100] Ultimately, "the American regime provided the perfect opportunity for provincial elites to build upon their previously constructed local economic base, consolidate a powerful local political bailiwick, and proceed to emerge as a national oligarchy."[101]

In addition to allowing these elites to capture local state resources, the American state allowed them to further expand their landholdings. The remaining land controlled by the Spanish friars passed to the state after the US took control and was sold to local buyers. The US also implemented a homestead policy, in which additional state-owned land in the rural periphery was granted to farmers.[102] The weak and captured bureaucracy administering these land programs was subject to significant elite influence, allowing *mestizo* plantation owners to engage in "blatant landgrabbing."[103] As much of the newly distributed state land "feel into [the mesitzos'] hands,"[104] economic inequality increased even more.[105]

The third shock came with World War II, another exogenous event, during which the Philippines were invaded and occupied by Japan. During the occupation, the US armed guerrilla resistance forces in rural areas.

---

[98] Anderson (1988), Sidel (1999), Hutchcroft (2000).
[99] Hutchcroft (2000, 293).
[100] Matsuzaki (2019, 127–128).
[101] Hutchcroft (2000, 295).
[102] Maurer and Iyer (2008).
[103] McLennan (1969, 673).
[104] Anderson (1988).
[105] Maurer and Iyer (2008).

Many arms ended up in the possession of rural elites who had been US allies before the war. They then kept them after the Japanese defeat. This infusion of armaments had the effect of ending any pretense that the central state could reestablish a monopoly on force in the countryside.[106] Immediately after the war, seeking local cooperation against a new threat posed by a leftist insurgency, the American and then Philippine governments (from 1946) let former guerrilla fighters "melt into the elites' 'civilian guards'," while also "channeling firearms to the municipal police forces that these local bosses controlled."[107] The police forces still controlled by the central state were left to atrophy as a concession to gain the cooperation of the rural elites.[108]

By the late 1940s, the combined result of these additional infusions of resources was a clear example of the {absent, non-advantaged} cell of Figure 9.1. The rural countryside was now dominated by an oligarchy of *mestizo* landowners with private armies, able to control private fiefdoms independently of central authority, including through violence and crime. "[T]he Philippine central government effectively lost control over the countryside to regional politicians, some so powerful that they became known as warlords."[109] These elites, still called by the inherited colonial term "*caciques*," used their economic power and ability to wield nonstate violence to dominate elections and consolidate national political power for several decades.[110] Into the twenty-first century, oligarchic *mestizo* families have retained significant power, and it is not a coincidence that the Philippines still have one of the most dynastic political systems in the world.[111] But rather than simply a case of a "strong society" dominating a "weak state," as per Migdal (1988), this is a rural elite that still ultimately traces its rise back to state actions in earlier periods.[112]

9.4 CONCLUSION

Drawing on three shadow cases, this chapter explores the other combinations of the two variables that serve as central scope conditions for the book's theory – the state's presence and resource advantages. The chapter

---

[106] McCoy (1993, 14).
[107] Slater (2010, 97).
[108] McCoy (1993, 14), Slater (2010, 97).
[109] McCoy (1993, 7).
[110] Anderson (1988), Sidel (1999), Slater (2010).
[111] Anderson (1988), Querubin (2016).
[112] Sidel (1999) highlights that the Philippines contradicts Migdal (1988) in this way.

also demonstrates the external validity of the broad patterns from the Northern Ghanaian experience outside of the African context.

Using the Southern Ghanaian case, I suggest that in regions where the state is much more present and the private economy more developed, individual state actions have comparatively lower effects both because there are more other state actions to offset them and because there are more private paths to wealth that can close any state-generated advantages. Using the example of Peru, I argue that in regions in which the state becomes more present over time, but remains resource-advantaged relative to society, waves of new state actions will offset the effects of prior actions, comparatively reducing the long-term impact of any individual action. Finally, using the example of the Philippines, I suggest that in regions in which the state remains absent, but has fewer resource-advantages relative to society, individual state actions will have lower short- and long-run effects than in hinterlands with more resource-advantaged states. But I also suggest that these latter cases may have only emerged in the first place as a long-run outcome of the substantial power of the scarce state, as documented across the previous chapters.

The Paradox of State Weakness

Parts II and III of the book demonstrate a scarce state's ability to have sustained and outsize effects on society and politics in the hinterland despite that state's clear incapacity. This evidence has implications for scholars of state-building and rural politics, as well as for policymakers concerned with improving state effectiveness in the developing world. I conclude by highlighting three of these implications.

First, the book's findings suggest a paradox confronts many analyses of developing states: common indicators for measuring state weakness may be *outcomes* of the changes to society that the state itself has wrought, with the state still powerful enough to have created the very political conditions that render it so seemingly weak.[1] Existing literature risks conflating fixed, relatively time-invariant features of the state that constrain state leaders' decisions with the results of contingent, and potentially reversible, policy choices those leaders have made. Second, this paradox shows a need to reconsider how we think about the state's role in the study of both rural politics and historical persistence. Third, it also suggests reevaluating the possible effects of policy interventions that attempt to expand the state's local presence.

10.1 FIXED CONDITIONS VS. ENDOGENOUS OUTCOMES?

Existing literature uses many different measures to label states weak.[2] To Migdal (1988) and others in a similar tradition, weak states are

---

[1] For a related critique of literature on state strength, see Lindvall and Teorell (2016).
[2] Berwick and Christia (2018).

captured and dominated by societal elites, lacking autonomy from society.[3] To Herbst (2000) and Mann (1988), they are characterized by minimally present, incapable bureaucracies.[4] To Fearon and Laitin (2003) and the World Bank (1997), they are states unable to deliver economic prosperity and high quality public services, from development goods to the rule of law. To the many analyses building from Weber (1946 [1919]), they are defined by an inability to sustain monopolies on the use of force.[5] More recently, Hanson and Sigman (2021) suggest measuring state weakness as a weighted bundle of many of these indicators at once.

Under any of these approaches, Northern Ghana – and, historically, rural Peru and the rural Philippines – would easily be labeled cases of state weakness. And yet, exemplifying the paradox above, many of the indicators that would be used to identify this weakness, such as elite capture, clientelism, and the private use of violence, are outcomes of impactful state actions. The state's characteristics in any one time period are deeply endogenous to the effects of earlier state policy.

For example, autonomy from societal elites has been low in Northern Ghana – and was similarly low for long periods in the Peru and the Philippines – as a result of explicit state actions that created and empowered those elites to the point that they were able to establish dynastic capture and steer the local state apparatus in their interest. In turn, state leaders often chose to undermine local state capacity and keep the state's bureaucratic presence purposefully low – lower than they hypothetically could have – as a means of striking expedient alliances with these very elites.[6] As in many postcolonial African states,[7] state leaders in Ghana gave up their landowning authority to local elites in search of votes; both American officials and early post-independence Philippine leaders stood back and allowed state security forces to come under the *de facto* command of *caciques* in an explicit bargain for political support.[8]

Similarly, state leaders' political bargains with these elites allowed clientelism to thrive, directly undermining the quality of state service provision. It is notable that state-imposed chiefs, not those who emerged organically from society, most widely enable clientelism across Northern

---

[3] Also see Weber (1946 [1919]), Bayart (1993), O'Donnell (1993), Chabal and Daloz (1999).

[4] Also see Acemoglu et al. (2015), Soifer (2015).

[5] For example, Jackson and Rosberg (1982).

[6] Boone (2003).

[7] Baldwin (2014).

[8] McCoy (1993), Slater (2010).

Ghana. And politicians elected into office primarily through clientelist campaigns, such as the dynastic elites of Northern Ghana, have strong and well-documented incentives to resist and scuttle future bureaucratic reforms that would improve the state's capacity and block their ability to distribute patronage.[9] Moreover, if nonstate violence occurs because state leaders intentionally stoke it, as in some conflicts in Northern Ghana, or even actively arm the societal elites who engage in it, as in the Philippines, the state is foregoing its monopoly over the use of force through its own doing, not failing to maintain its sovereignty as a mechanical manifestation of inherent weakness.

When viewed in this light, it becomes unclear what is a fixed trait of a state and what is a downstream outcome of that state's contingent decisions. We often view state weakness as a result of long-run historical processes;[10] in the near term, it becomes a fixed background condition, a starting point for theories of other outcomes, not something that changes meaningfully in response to those outcomes. And yet a growing literature now shows that even within ostensibly weak states in the developing world, contemporary state leaders purposefully toggle on and off their state's capacity in the short run at a local level as they respond to shifting political imperatives.[11] This implies a greater degree of agency in state weakness than most historical accounts consider.

The evidence in this book joins this latter work in suggesting that some common indicators of state weakness could have turned out differently if state leaders had faced different political incentives to allocate their resources. Moreover, as long as the state remains resource-advantaged relative to society, they still could turn out differently in the future if leaders face incentives to engage in new state interventions that offset the accumulated effects of past state actions.

In Chapter 9, Peru serves as an example of a case where long-run state absence was not an inevitable constraint on leaders' autonomy. With shifts to state leaders' political incentives in both the mid-eighteenth and, especially, mid-twentieth centuries, what had been heavily captured and absent states were able to engage in new actions, such as land reform, that essentially wiped out the elites who had been dominating to that point,

---

[9] Shefter (1977), Cruz and Keefer (2015), Nathan (2019).

[10] Tilly (1990), Acemoglu et al. (2001), Besley and Persson (2009), Dincecco (2018). For a review, see Berwick and Christia (2018).

[11] Hassan (2020), Suryanarayan and White (2021). Moreover, there are still meaningful pockets of bureaucratic effectiveness within otherwise incapable states in the agencies or regions where leaders have incentives to cultivate it (Williams 2019, McDonnell 2020).

setting society off on new trajectories.[12] State absence had persisted for so long beforehand not solely because state leaders were constrained, but because they had not previously had sufficient political need to deviate from the status quo. Limits to state presence create political incentives that become self-reinforcing: state leaders who reach power in the context of an absent and captured state often benefit politically from keeping it absent and captured, with little incentive to try to deviate, creating a feedback loop.[13]

In Northern Ghana, both colonial and post-independence state leaders were not forced to be unimpactful in the face of a "strong society," as in Migdal (1988), but instead voluntarily kept the state scarcer than they could have through explicit, contingent political choices in response to short-term political and economic exigencies. As the effects of the actions they did take demonstrate, however, these state leaders still had the latent power to have had major impacts on society, even if at times unintentionally. And as Chapter 7 shows, to the extent previously neglected populations, like the Konkomba and other "never recognized" groups, subsequently did receive better state service provision, it is because democratization changed Ghana's leaders' private incentives for political survival and made them newly sensitive to what (at least some) hinterland voters wanted.[14]

In light of this type of evidence, labeling any state "weak" (or "strong") becomes practically meaningless as an analytic device. If weak states can have as big effects on society as Northern Ghana's, and if their outward appearance of weakness can shift in response to new incentives for their leaders, these states were not so weak to begin with. The literature should move on from this term entirely – it obscures more than it elucidates.

State power is a fluid variable that shifts across subnational regions and different policy domains, not a fixed background characteristic. History is deeply important for informing it, but the relationship is not deterministic. To understand the state's implications for society, we need more nuanced theories of the interplay between underlying state capacity in a given subnational region or policy domain, state leaders' political incentives to actually deploy that capacity, and the characteristics of the

---

[12] Ramirez (1986), Albertus (2015).
[13] For an extension of the claim that limited state capacity can become a self-reinforcing trap, see Nathan (2019). Also see Shefter (1977), Acemoglu and Robinson (2008).
[14] More broadly on the effects of democratization, see Stasavage (2005).

society into which the state seeks to intervene, including the distribution of resources in society relative to what the state can distribute (or extract). Changes to any three of these factors change the apparent power of the state. In particularly resource-poor societies, even minor actions by plainly incapable states can have very powerful effects.

10.2 LESS STATE, MORE EFFECT?

Recognizing this distinction has scholarly and policy implications. For academics, it shows the danger in writing off the state in the study of the rural periphery. Just because the state appears to have been relatively absent in a peripheral region over time, it does not follow that state leaders remained unable to change society along the way. Less state does not equal a less impactful state.

The book argues that regions of limited historical state presence are where the state may be especially able to remake society. In comparison to areas such as Southern Ghana in which more robust private sectors created greater baseline societal stratification before the modern state emerged, society is *less* likely to have been able to preserve itself over time in hinterlands like Northern Ghana because even small shifts to the status quo could have such big impacts there. Going forward, a safer *ex ante* assumption for analysts beginning a study of a given hinterland region in the developing world is that it probably has been extensively marked and reshaped by state contact. Few of the "ungoverned" and "stateless" regions often described in the literature on the developing world are likely to be nearly as ungoverned and pristine from the state's effects as more romantic portrayals of state absence imply.

There is also danger in overlooking state actions as a potential mechanism for any connections between historical variables and contemporary conditions, as has been in common in studies of historical persistence that skip from precolonial or colonial institutions to the present.[15] Correlations between past and present are unlikely to be direct effects of undisturbed pre-existing institutions, but outcomes of the changes the state wrought in between. In particular, the Murdock (1967) data on precolonial centralization, so central to the literature on precolonial persistence in Africa, should not be interpreted nearly as literally as it often is. Modern states have acted and intervened. Societies have changed. Central

---

[15] Austin (2008). For a clear exception, see Wilfahrt (2018, 2021).

to this book's analysis is that many of Northern Ghana's acephalous societies are not acephalous at all anymore, and, as Chapter 5 shows, some of these institutions are still actively evolving today through the bottom-up initiative of local actors responding to the state's absence. Precolonial institutions certainly have had important path-dependent legacies for contemporary economic and political outcomes in many settings, but it is unlikely that those legacies are due to institutions that still exist in the same form that Murdock coded them.

Moreover, hinterlands do not offer a static control group against which to evaluate more dynamic state actions elsewhere. By creating the conditions of state scarcity that magnify the impact of any interventions they do still take, state leaders' decisions to differentially withdrawal from peripheral regions have treatment effects of their own that likely create non-monotonic relationships between the degree of historical state intervention into a region and the effects of that activity on society. We cannot simply compare regions with high treatment "doses" of historical state action to peripheral regions with lower doses, as is very common in the growing empirical literature on historical political economy, and assume that our outcome variables respond linearly to the amount of treatment. This book implies that some of the biggest overall effects of the treatments examined in these studies may have occurred in the regions with the lowest doses, suggesting that a potentially significant inferential challenge confronts this emerging literature.

10.3 POLICY RESPONSES

Finally, although this is not a primary goal of the book, the paradox above offers insight for policymaking. A central challenge for development practitioners in the twenty-first century has been to devise means of making states more effective.[16] Because it remains unknown how to successfully build state institutions on a grand scale in the short term,[17] many initiatives have focused on relatively small interventions that use external resources to prop up new grassroots state, or quasi-state, institutions in areas of state scarcity. In one particularly common example, this involves creating new community councils or local deliberative bodies that oversee new tranches of resources.[18]

---

[16] Fukuyama (2004).
[17] Fukuyama (2004), Berwick and Christia (2018).
[18] Casey (2018).

The argument in this book anticipates that by making narrow infusions of new windfalls into areas where similar resources are otherwise scarce, these interventions may backfire amidst elite capture and rent-seeking, potentially reinforcing pre-existing societal and political hierarchies (or generating new ones), while seeding grievances behind local conflicts that may feedback and undermine the quality of local governance, not improve it. And indeed, many such interventions have struggled along these lines.[19] Small interventions do not imply small effects.

But at the same time, the paradox of state weakness above also suggests that existing state leaders may have more ability to change underlying societal conditions than outside policymakers often assume. In the many developing states that are resource-advantaged relative to hinterland society, more donor aid is not the key constraint for changing the local governance equilibrium and ending elite capture, clientelism, and corruption; these states likely *already* have sufficient resources to have meaningful impacts on society in subnational regions of state scarcity. Infusions of new resources could simply become captured by existing elites, repurposed in the prevailing clientelist equilibrium.[20] Similarly, for policymakers concerned with improving state sovereignty in peripheral regions, more external funding and training for state security forces may also not be a key constraint to reducing nonstate violence. Chapter 8 shows that hinterland violence in Northern Ghana regularly erupted in accessible locations where state forces were already stationed and capable of stopping it.

Instead, because they benefit from the status quo, or are at least not actively threatened by conditions in the periphery,[21] many central state leaders have limited incentives to *want* to use their resources to try to increase local state presence, police against nonstate violence, or change hinterland society. Rather than failing to control the hinterland in the face of costly societal resistance, this book suggests it will often be elements within society itself that strongly demand the increased presence and assistance of the state. State leaders and their local elite allies are the ones who are instead intentionally withholding the state, allowing inequality, elite capture, and clientelism to continue. At the extreme, they at times even let nonstate violence happen because it is politically useful.

[19] Bardhan and Mookherjee (2006), Humphreys et al. (2019), Casey (2018).
[20] van de Walle (2001), Jablonski (2014).
[21] Boone (2003), Slater and Kim (2015).

In contexts where the state is relatively resource-advantaged, if state leaders did significantly increase state presence, Chapter 9 suggests that their actions could create new winners and losers in society, reshaping how local governance unfolds. But encouraging state leaders to do so, and especially to do so in a way that is intentionally egalitarian and does not simply create a new wave of state-generated elites to capture local power or generate new grievances that motivate violence, is not a technocratic problem that can be solved by external policymakers. It is a fundamentally internal and political one, dependent on changes in how the central state views its relationship with its periphery. The path to more effective and incentive-compatible development policy in the rural periphery comes through developing a deeper understanding of hinterland politics, including how local social hierarchies have emerged, how local elites wield influence and sustain their advantages, how communities respond, and the opportunities and challenges that these rural political economies create for state leaders focused on political survival.

Appendix: Qualitative Interviews

1 SELECTING RESPONDENTS

Qualitative interviews occurred in four waves, with respondents selected for different reasons in each wave. First, in 2008, twenty-six elite interviews were conducted with Konkomba and Dagomba civil society leaders, chiefs, and politicians, as well as NGO workers involved in the post-conflict peace process, spanning Tamale, Yendi, Saboba, and surrounding communities. Respondents were selected purposefully, as well as via snowball sampling starting from the initial respondents. Second, larger-scale fieldwork in 2018 and 2019 included an additional twenty-one elite interviews with civil society leaders, political party officials, and public educators across Accra (where many Northern elites are based), Bolgatanga, Damongo, Kumbungu, Saboba, Tamale, Wa, and Zuarungu. Respondents were again selected purposefully.

Third, I conducted oral history interviews in twelve rural communities in 2019. Ethnic groups were selected purposefully: the Dagaba and Frafra are the two largest "invented chiefs" groups (Table 3.1) and span the two main administrative regions where the "invented chiefs" groups live – Upper West (Dagaba) and Upper East (Frafra); the Konkomba were selected because they comprise the majority of the "never recognized" population (Table 3.1) and also to ensure that these interviews could be used for Chapter 5. Once groups were selected, I subset to census Enumeration Areas (EAs) in administrative districts with majority populations from each group and further subset to EAs that had greater than 85 percent population from the group (to ensure the selected community was dominated by that group) and fell within the 10th and 90th percentile of community size (to weed out small hamlets and the largest towns). Communities were then randomly selected after stratifying EAs within groups on the inequality variable (I) in Chapter 4, to ensure a mix of relatively high and low inequality communities from each group.

Within communities, interviews were conducted separately with: the chief or senior-most elder (in Konkomba communities with no chief), or the chief's representative (in one case, the chief had traveled); the tendana (earth priest); clan elders of the largest resident clan other than the chief's clan; the District Assemblymember (elected local government councilor); and a teacher in the community's primary school (if available), as they tend to be very knowledgeable about community affairs but are outsiders without a stake in local disputes.[1] On average, there were four interviews per community. These interviews were semi-structured, based from a common questionnaire (see the following section), with a conscious effort to ask the same questions to different actors to compare responses. All interviews were conducted by the author with assistance of a translator.

Fourth, life history interviews were conducted in 2019 with sitting MPs. I drew a random sample of twenty-seven Northern MPs, of which twenty agreed to participate. The sample was stratified by category of ethnic group in Table 3.1. All interviews took place in Accra while Parliament was in session; thirteen were conducted by the author and seven by a senior research assistant. These semi-structured interviews also followed a common questionnaire; see the following section.

2 QUESTIONNAIRES

The main template for the semi-structured oral history interviews was as follows:

1. Please describe the origins of this community. When was it founded? By whom? Why?
2. How many separate clans (extended family lineages) live in this community? What are they? Who are the indigenes and who are the settlers? When did the settlers come and why?

---

[1] In practice, some of these interviews turned into group events, more akin to focus groups, with, for example, a group of elders from the chief's clan gathering around the chief at his palace and participating in the interview jointly, then a separate group of members of the tendana's family joining the tendana in a separate interview, and so on.

3. Which family/clan is the chief (if applicable) from? Which family/clan is the tendana from?
4. What criteria determine eligibility for each of these positions?
5. What is the origin story of chieftaincy in this community (if applicable)? Who was the first chief? How was he selected?
6. Can you give the list of chiefs from the first chief to the present (if applicable). (Followup questions about the dates and family/clan of each chief, as necessary.)
7. What is the process for selecting the chief here? Who is the enskinning authority?
8. Have there been any issues or disputes around the chieftaincy in this community in the past? What were they?
9. Who allocates land among families in this community? If I wanted to buy land, who would I speak to? Has this changed over time?
10. In your opinion, who is the most influential leader in this community? Why?
11. When did schools first come to this area? Where was the first school? When was the first school built directly in this community?
12. Who were the first students to enroll? Why were they able to go first?
13. Who were the first students to complete secondary school (SHS)? What has happened to them? What do they (did they) do for work? Roughly how many secondary graduates have there been over time?
14. Are there any "elites" who hail from this community and now live outside? For example, this is people who are working in Accra or Tamale, or living abroad, and have "big" jobs – for the government, in politics, in business – and send money back to their families. Who are they? What do they do?
15. What influence do these elites have in the community? For example, do they have influence in local politics? In what ways?
16. Which families do most of these elites come from? Why do they come from these particular families and not other families in the community?
17. Do you think this community is being supported well by the District Assembly compared to what other communities in this area receive? Why or why not?
18. Do you think this community is being supported well by the MP compared to what other communities in this area receive? Why or why not?

19. Does the MP visit the community often? Does he have a personal relationship with the chief?
20. If community members need to contact the MP or the government to ask for assistance, who do they work through? Who here has the ability to get in touch with the MP or DCE?

Respondents in the Konkomba communities were also asked additional questions:

21. What is the current relationship between this community and the Dagomba [Nanumba] chiefs? How has that changed over time? What was the relationship like before the 1981 and 1994 conflicts?
22. Is the obour (headman) here formally enskinned as a chief? If yes, when did that happen? If no, why hasn't that happened? Does he want to be enskinned? Why or why not?
23. How was this community affected by the violence in 1981 and 1994?

The MP life history interviews used the following questionnaire:

1. What is your hometown? Where did you live during your child-hood – there or somewhere else?
2. Where did you go to school? [Answers recorded for each level of education]
3. What work were you doing before you became an MP? Where were you mainly living prior to becoming an MP?
4. Have you ever lived outside Ghana for an extended period? If yes, where? What were you doing there?
5. When you were growing up, what did your parents do for work?
6. How would you describe your family's economic situation during your childhood: was your family wealthier than most others from your hometown, about the same, or facing more economic hard-ships than others in your hometown? Can you give examples of what this was like?
7. What is the highest level of education your parents each received? If applicable, where did they attend school?
8. Who was the first person in your family to attend school? Approx-imately when and at which school? Why/how did this person get the initial opportunity to attend school?
9. Do you come from a political family? That is, were (or are) any of your close family members also politicians?

10. Do you come from a royal family? If yes, which of your relatives have been chiefs? What positions did each person hold? If you were not serving as an MP, would you yourself eligible to be considered for a chieftaincy position should there be a vacancy?

11. (If applicable) Who was your first relative or ancestor to have been a chief? Approximately when was this? What is the story of how he was initially selected as a chief?

12. Are you related to the tendana from your home community?

13. When did you first become active in politics and why?

14. Were you serving in any formal party positions or working in government early in your political career?

15. When did you first contest for elected office? Why then? What specifically motivated you to run?

16. Have you had any important mentors in politics who helped launch your political career?

17. How important have your relationships with traditional leaders in your constituency been to your electoral success? In what ways?

18. How often do you travel back to your constituency? Do you have a house there? Do your wife/children (if any) still live there or here in Accra?

19. (If applicable) Has being from a political family helped your career in elected politics in any way? Or has it made politics more difficult for you? Can you give specific examples of how it has helped or hurt you?

20. (If applicable) Has being from a royal family helped your career in elected politics in any way? Or has it made politics more difficult for you? Can you give specific examples of how it has helped or hurt you?

21. (If applicable) Do you think you would have had an easier time winning elected office if you had been from a political family? Why?

22. (If applicable) Do you think you would have had an easier time winning elected office if you had been from a royal family? Why?

References

Abdulai, Abdul-Gafaru and Sam Hickey. 2016. "The Politics of Development under Competitive Clientelism: Insights from Ghana's Education Sector." *African Affairs* 115(458):44–72.

Acemoglu, Daron, Camilo Garcia-Jimeno and James A. Robinson. 2015. "State Capacity and Economic Development: A Network Approach." *American Economic Review* 105(8):2364–2409.

Acemoglu, Daron and James A. Robinson. 2008. "Persistence of Power, Elites, and Institutions." *American Economic Review* 98(1):267–293.

Acemoglu, Daron, Simon Johnson and James A. Robinson. 2001. "The Colonial Origins of Comparative Development: An Empirical Investigation." *American Economic Review* 91(5):1369–1401.

Acemoglu, Daron, Tristan Reed and James A. Robinson. 2014. "Chiefs: Economic Development and Elite Control of Civil Society in Sierra Leone." *Journal of Political Economy* 122(2):319–368.

Ackah, Charles and Denis Medvedev. 2010. "Internal Migration in Ghana: Determinants and Welfare Impacts." The World Bank, Policy Research Working Paper No. 5273.

ACLED. 2016. "ACLED Version 6 (1997–2015) Africa Data." Armed Conflict Location and Event Data Project, www.acleddata.com/data/.

Afigbo, Adiele Eberechukwu. 1972. *The Warrant Chiefs: Indirect Rule in Southeastern Nigeria, 1891–1929*. London: Longman Publishers.

Akyeampong, Emmanuel. 2000. "Africans in the Diaspora: The Diaspora and Africa." *Affrican Affairs* 99(395):183–215.

Akyeampong, Emmanuel. 2014. "Commerce, Credit, and Mobility in Late Nineteenth-Century Gold Coast: Changing Dynamics in Euro-African Trade." In *Africa's Development in Historical Perspective*, ed. Emmanuel Akyeampong, Robert H. Bates, Nathan Nunn and James A. Robinson. New York: Cambridge University Press, pp. 231–263.

Albertus, Michael. 2015. *Autocracy and Redistribution: The Politics of Land Reform*. New York: Cambridge University Press.

Albertus, Michael. 2021. *Property without Rights: Origins and Consequences of the Property Rights Gap*. New York: Cambridge University Press.

Alence, Rod. 2001. "Colonial Government, Social Conflict, and State Involvement in Africa's Open Economies: The Origins of the Ghana Cocoa Marketing Board, 1939–1946." *Journal of African History* 42:397–416.

Alesina, Alberto, Sebastian Hohmann, Stelios Michalopoulos and Elias Papaioannou. 2019. "Intergenerational Mobility in Africa." NBER Working Paper No. 25534.

Allman, Jean M. 1990. "The Youngmen and the Porcupine: Class, Nationalism and Asante's Struggle for Self-Determination, 1954–57." *The Journal of African History* 31(2):263–279.

Allman, Jean Marie and John Parker. 2005. *Tongnaab : The History of a West African God*. Bloomington: Indiana University Press.

Anamzoya, Alhassan Sulemana and Steve Tonah. 2016. "Multiple Plasters Don't Heal a Wound: An Assessment of the Management of the Bimbilla Chieftaincy Dispute, Northern Ghana." In *Managing Chieftaincy and Ethnic Conflicts in Ghana*, ed. Steve Tonah and Alhassan Sulemana Anamzoya. Accra: Woeli Publishing Services, pp. 139–166.

Anderson, Benedict. 1988. "Cacique Democracy and the Philippines: Origins and Dreams." *New Left Review* I(169).

Archibong, Belinda. 2018. "Historial Origins of Persistent Inequality in Nigeria." *Oxford Development Studies* 46(3):325–347.

Archibong, Belinda. 2019. "Explaining Divergence in the Long-Term Effects of Precolonial Centralization on Access to Public Infrastructure Services in Nigeria." *World Development* 121:123–140.

Arhin, Kwame. 1983. "Rank and Class among the Asante and Fante in the Nineteenth Century." *Africa: Journal of the International African Institute* 53(1):2–22.

Arhin, Kwame, ed. 1974. *The Papers of George Ekem Ferguson: A Fanti Official of the Government of the Gold Coast, 1890–1897*. Cambridge, UK: African Studies Center.

Arriola, Leonardo R., Donghyun Danny Choi, Justine M Davis, Melanie L. Phillips and Lise Rakner. 2021. "Paying to Party: Candidate Resources and Party Switching in New Democracies." *Party Politics*.

Aryeetey, Ernest. 1996. *Structural Adjustment and Aid in Ghana*. Accra: Friedrich Ebert Stiftung.

Asante, Kojo and George Kunnath. 2018. "The Cost of Politics in Ghana." Westminister Foundation for Democracy, www.wfd.org/wp-content/uploads/2018/03/Cost_Of_Politics_Ghana.pdf.

Auerbach, Adam M. 2016. "Clients and Communities." *World Politics* 68(1):111–148.

Austin, Gareth. 1988. "Capitalists and Chiefs in the Cocoa Hold-Ups in South Asante, 1927–1938." *The International Journal of African Historical Studies* 21(1):63–95.

Austin, Gareth. 1997. "Introduction." In *The Migrant Cocoa-Farmers of Southern Ghana*. 2nd ed. Suffolk, UK: James Curry Publishers.

Austin, Gareth. 2008. "The 'Reversal of Fortune' Thesis and the Compression of History: Perspectives from African and Comparative Economic History." *Journal of International Development* 20:996–1027.

Austin, Gareth. 2014. "Explaining and Evaluating the Cash Crop Revolution in the 'Peasant' Colonies of Tropical Africa, ca. 1890 – ca. 1930: Beyond 'Vent for Surplus'." In *Africa's Development in Historical Perspective*, ed. Emmanuel Akyeampong, Robert H. Bates, Nathan Nunn and James A. Robinson. New York: Cambridge University Press, pp. 295–320.

Auyero, Javier. 2000. "The Logic of Clientelism in Argentina: An Ethnographic Account." *Latin American Research Review* 35(3):55–81.

Awedoba, A.K. 2006. "The Peoples of Northern Ghana." lagim.blogs.brynmawr .edu/files/2015/03/The-Peoples-of-Northern-Ghana.pdf.

Awedoba, A. K., Edward Salifu Mahama, Sylvanus M. A. Kuuire and Felix Longi. 2009. *An Ethnographic Study of Northern Ghanaian Conflicts: Towards a Sustainable Peace*. Accra: Sub-Saharan Publishers.

Ayee, Joseph R. A. 1993. "Decentralisation and Local Government under the PNDC." In *Ghana under PNDC Rule*, ed. Emmanuel Gyimah-Boadi. Dakar, Senegal: CODESRIA.

Baland, Jean-Marie and James A. Robinson. 2008. "Land and Power: Theory and Evidence from Chile." *American Economic Review* 98(5):1737–1765.

Baldassarri, Delia and Guy Grossman. 2011. "Centralized Sanctioning and Legitimate Authority Promote Cooperation in Humans." *PNAS* 108(27):11023–11027.

Baldwin, Kate. 2014. "Chiefs, Land, and Coalition-Building in Africa." *Comparative Politics* 46(3):253–271.

Baldwin, Kate. 2015. *The Paradox of Traditional Chiefs in Democratic Africa*. New York: Cambridge University Press.

Baldwin, Kate. 2019. "Elected MPs, Traditional Chiefs, and Local Public Goods: Evidence on the Role of Leaders in Co-Production from Rural Zambia." *Comparative Political Studies* 52(12):1925–1956.

Baldwin, Kate and Eric Mvukiyehe. 2015. "Elections and Collective Action: Evidence from Changes in Traditional Institutions in Liberia." *World Politics* 67(4):690–725.

Baldwin, Kate and Katharina Holzinger. 2019. "Traditional Political Institutions and Democracy: Reassessing their Compatibility and Accountability." *Comparative Political Studies* 52(2):1747–1774.

Ballve, Teo. 2020. *The Frontier Effect: State Formation and Violence in Colombia*. Ithaca, NY: Cornell University Press.

Banful, Afua. 2011. "Do Formula-Based Intergovernmental Transfer Mechanisms Eliminate Politically Motivated Targeting? Evidence from Ghana." *Journal of Development Economics* 96(2):380–390.

Bardhan, Pranab and Dilip Mookherjee. 2006. "Decentralisation and Accountability in Infrastructure Delivery in Developing Countries." *The Economic Journal* 116(508):101–127.

Bates, Robert H. 1981. *Markets and States in Tropical Africa*. Berkeley: University of California Press.

Bates, Robert H. 1983. "Modernization, Ethnic Competition, and the Rationality of Politics in Contemporary Africa." In *State Versus Ethnic Claims: African Policy Dilemmas*, ed. Donald Rothchild and Victor A. Olorunsola. Boulder, CO: Westview Press, pp.152–171.

Bates, Robert H. 1989. *Beyond the Miracle of the Market: The Political Economy of Agrarian Development in Kenya*. New York: Cambridge University Press.

Bates, Robert H. 2008. *When Things Fell Apart: State Failure in Late-Century Africa*. New York: Cambridge University Press.

Bawumia, Alhaji Mumuni. 2004. *A Life in the Political History of Ghana: Memoirs of Alhaji Mumuni Bawumia*. Accra, Ghana: Ghana Universities Press.

Bayart, Jean-Francois. 1993. *The State in Africa: The Politics of the Belly*. London: Longman Publishers.

Bening, R. Bagulo. 1983. "The Ghana-Togo Boundary 1914–1982." *Africa Spectrum* 18(2):191–209.

Bening, R. Bagulo. 1990. *A History of Education in Northern Ghana: 1907–1976*. Accra: Ghana Universities Press.

Bening, R. Bagulo. 2010. *Ghana: Administrative Areas and Boundaries 1874–2009*. Accra: Ghana Universities Press.

Berwick, Elissa and Fotini Christia. 2018. "State Capacity Redux: Intergrating Classical and Experimental Contributions to an Enduring Debate." *Annual Review of Political Science* 21(1):71–91.

Besley, Timothy and Torsten Persson. 2009. "The Origins of State Capacity: Property Rights, Taxation, and Politics." *American Economic Review* 99(4):1218–1244.

Bierschenk, Thomas and Jean-Pierre Olivier de Sardan. 2014. "Studying the Dynamics of African Bureaucracies: An Introduction to States at Work." In *States at Work*, ed. Thomas Bierschenk and Jean-Pierre Olivier de Sardan. Leiden: Brill Publishers, pp. 3–34.

Blundo, Giorgio and Pierre-Yves Le Meur. 2009. "An Anthropology of Everyday Governance: Collective Service Delivery and Subject-Making." In *The Governance of Daily Life in Africa*, ed. Giorgio Blundo and Pierre-Yves Le Meur. Leiden: Brill Publishers, pp. 1–38.

Bob-Milliar, George M. 2011. "'Te Nyogeyeng Gbengbenoe!' ('We Are Holding the Umbrella Very Tight!'): Explaining the Popularity of the NDC in the Upper West Region of Ghana." *Africa: Journal of the International African Institute* 81(3):455–473.

Bob-Milliar, George M. 2014. "Party Youth Activists and Low-Intensity Electoral Violence in Ghana: A Qualitative Study of Party Foot Soldiers' Activism." *African Studies Quarterly* 15(1):125–152.

Boix, Carles. 2015. *Political Order and Inequality: Their Foundations and their Consequences for Human Welfare*. New York: Cambridge University Press.

Boone, Catherine. 2003. *Political Topographies of the African State: Territorial Authority and Institutional Choice*. New York: Cambridge University Press.

Boone, Catherine. 2014. *Property and Political Order in Africa: Land Rights and the Structure of Politics*. New York: Cambridge University Press.

Brambor, Thomas, Agustin Goenaga, Johannes Lindvall and Jan Teorell. 2020. "The Lay of the Land: Information Capacity and the Modern State." *Comparative Political Studies* 53(2):175–213.

Brankopowers, Austin. 2017. "'Lawra seat will forever be NPP's' – Lawra Paramount Chief Assures." *My Joy Online*, 3 October.

Brierley, Sarah and Eric Kramon. 2020. "Party Campaign Strategies in Ghana: Rallies, Canvassing and Handouts." *African Affairs.*

Brierley, Sarah and George K. Ofosu. 2022. "The Effects of Political Endorsements: Experimental Evidence from Ghana." Working Paper.

Brierley, Sarah and Noah L. Nathan. 2021*a*. "The Connections of Party Brokers." *Journal of Politics* 83(3):884–901.

Brierley, Sarah and Noah L. Nathan. 2021*b*. "Motivating the Machine: Which Brokers Do Parties Pay?" Forthcoming, *Journal of Politics.*

Brinkerhoff, Derick W., Anna Wetterberg and Erik Wibbels. 2018. "Distance, Services, and Citizen Perceptions of the State in Rural Africa." *Governance* 31(1):103–124.

Brukum, Nana J.K. 2001. *Guinea Fowl, Mango, and Pito Wars: Episodes in the History of Northern Ghana, 1980–1999.* Accra: Ghana Universities Press.

Buhaug, Halvard and Jan Ketil Rod. 2006. "Local Determinants of African Civil Wars, 1970–2001." *Political Geography* 25(3):315–335.

Cagé, Julia and Valeria Rueda. 2016. "The Long-Term Effects of the Printing Press in Sub-Saharan Africa." *American Economic Journal: Applied Economics* 8(3).

Cammett, Melani and Lauren M. Maclean, eds. 2014. *The Politics of Non-State Social Welfare Provision.* Ithaca, NY: Cornell University Press.

Caplan, Gerald L. 1970. *The Elites of Barotseland, 1878–1969: A Political History of Zambia's Western Province.* Berkeley: University of California Press.

Carlson, Elizabeth. 2016. "Finding Partisanship where We Least Expect It: Evidence of Partisan Bias in a New Democracy." *Political Behavior* 38(1):129–154.

Casey, Katherine. 2018. "Radical Decentralization: Does Community-Driven Development Work?" *Annual Review of Economics* 10(1):139–163.

Cederman, Lars-Erik, Kristian Skrede Gleditsch and Halvard Buhaug. 2013. *Inequality, Grievances, and Civil War.* New York: Cambridge University Press.

Cederman, Lars-Erik, Nils B. Weidman and Kristian Skrede Gleditsch. 2011. "Horizontal Inequalities and Ethnonationalist Civil War: A Global Comparison." *American Political Science Review* 105(3):478–495.

Chabal, Patrick and Jean-Pascal Daloz. 1999. *Africa Works: Disorder as Political Instrument.* Bloomington: Indiana University Press.

Chandra, Kanchan. 2016. Introduction. In *Democratic Dynasties: State, Party, and Family in Contemporary Indian Politics,* ed. Kanchan Chandra. New York: Cambridge University Press.

Chazan, Naomi H. 1982. "Development, Underdevelopment, and the State in Ghana." Boston University African Studies Center Working Paper Series.

Chazan, Naomi H. and Victor T. LeVine. 1979. "Politics in a 'Non-Political' System: The March 30, 1978 Referendum in Ghana." *African Studies Review* 22(1):177–207.

Conroy-Krutz, Jeffrey. 2018. "Individual Autonomy and Local-Level Solidarity in Africa." *Political Behavior* 40(3):593–627.

Corstange, Daniel. 2016. *The Price of a Vote in the Middle East.* New York: Cambridge University Press.

Crabtree, John and Francisco Durand. 2017. *Peru: Elite Power and Political Capture.* London: Zed Books.

Cruz, Cesi and Philip Keefer. 2015. "Political Parties, Clientelism, and Bureaucratic Reform." *Comparative Political Studies* 48(14):1942–1973.

Cunningham, David E. and Douglas Lemke. 2014. "Beyond Civil War: A Quantitative Examination of the Causes of Violence within Countries." *Civil Wars* 16(3):328–345.

Dahl, Robert A. 1957. "The Concept of Power." *Behavioral Sciences* 2(3): 201–215.

Dal Bo, Ernesto, Pedro Dal Bo, and Jason Snyder. 2009. "Political Dynasties." *The Review of Economic Studies* 76:115–142.

Davies, Keith A. 1984. *Landowners in Colonial Peru.* Austin: University of Texas Press.

Dawson, Allan C. 2000. Becoming Konkomba: Recent Transformations in a Gur Society of Northern Ghana PhD Thesis, University of Calgary.

de Kadt, Daniel and Horacio Larreguy. 2018. "Agents of the Regime? Traditional Leaders and Electoral Behavior in South Africa." *Journal of Politics* 80(2):382–399.

Dell, Melissa. 2010. "The Persistent Effects of Peru's Mining Mita." *Econometrica* 78(6):1863–1903.

Dincecco, Mark. 2018. *State Capacity and Economic Development: Present and Past.* New York: Cambridge University Press.

Drucker-Brown, Susan. 1989. "Local Wars in Northern Ghana." *Cambridge Journal of Anthropology* 13(2):86–106.

Dulay, Dean. 2022. "The Search for Spices and Souls: Catholic Missions as Colonial State in the Philippines." Forthcoming, *Comparative Political Studies*.

Ejdemyr, Simon, Eric Kramon and Amanda Lea Robinson. 2018. "Segregation, Ethnic Favoritism, and the Strategic Targeting of Local Public Goods." *Comparative Political Studies* 51(9):1111–1143.

Ekeh, Peter P. 1975. "Colonialism and the Two Publics in Africa: A Theoretical Statement." *Comparative Studies in Society and History* 17(1):91–112.

Elfversson, Emma. 2015. "Providing Security or Protecting Interests: Government Interventions in Violent Communal Conflicts in Africa." *Journal of Peace Research* 52(6):791–805.

Englebert, Pierre. 2000. *State Legitimacy and Development in Africa.* Boulder, CO: Lynne Riener Publishers.

Evans, Peter B., Dietrich Rueschemeyer, and Theda Skocpol, eds. 1985. *Bringing the State Back In.* New York: Cambridge University Press.

FAO. 2012. "Global Agro-Ecological Zones Dataset, Version 3.0." United Nations Food and Agriculture Organization, www.fao.org/nr/gaez/en/.

Fearon, James D. 1999. "Electoral Accountability and the Control of Politicians: Selecting Good Types versus Sanctioning Poor Performance." In *Democracy, Accountability, and Representation*, ed. Adam Przeworski, Susan C. Stokes, and Bernard Manin. New York: Cambridge University Press, pp. 55–97.

Fearon, James D. and David D. Laitin. 1996. "Explaining Interethnic Cooperation." *American Political Science Review* 90(4):715–735.

Fearon, James D. and David D. Laitin. 2003. "Ethnicity, Insurgency, and Civil War." *American Political Science Review* 97(1):75–90.

Filmer, Deon and Kinnon Scott. 2012. "Assessing Asset Indices." *Demography* 49(1):359–392.

Filmer, Deon and Lant Pritchett. 2001. "Estimating Wealth Effects without Expenditure Data – or Tears: An Application to Educational Enrollments in States of India." *Demography* 38(1):115–132.

Firmin-Sellers, Kathryn. 2000. "Custom, Capitalism, and the State: The Origins of Insecure Land Tenure in West Africa." *Journal of Institutional and Theoretical Economics* 156(3):513–530.

Fiva, Jon H. and Daniel M. Smith. 2018. "Political Dynasties and the Incumbency Advantage in Party-Centered Environments." *American Political Science Review* 112(3):706–712.

Fjelde, Hanne and Gudron Ostby. 2014. "Socioeconomic Inequality and Communal Conflict: A Disaggregated Analysis of Sub-Saharan Africa." *International Interactions* 40(5):737–762.

Fradera, Josep M. 2004. "The Historical Origins of the Philippine Economy: A Survey of Recent Research of the Spanish Colonial Era." *Australian Economic History Review* 44(3):307–320.

Frankema, Ewout H. P. 2012. "The Origins of Formal Education in Sub-Saharan Africa: Was British Rule More Benign?" *European Review of Economic History* 16:335–355.

Frimpong-Ansah, Jonathan H. 1991. *The Vampire State in Africa: The Political Economy of Decline in Ghana.* London: James Currey.

Fukuyama, Francis. 2004. *State Building: A New Agenda.* Ithaca, NY: Cornell University Press.

Galvan, Dennis C. 2004. *The State Must Be Our Master of Fire: How Peasants Craft Culturally Sustainable Development in Senegal.* Berkeley: University of California Press.

Gandah, S. W. D. K. 2004. *The Silent Rebel.* Accra, Ghana; Sub-Saharan Publishers.

Gandah, S. W. D. K. 2009. *Gandah-Yir: The House of the Brave.* Legon, Ghana: Institute for African Studies.

Gennaioli, Nicola and Ilia Rainer. 2007. "The Modern Impact of Pre-colonial Centralization in Africa." *Journal of Economic Growth* 12(3): 185–234.

Gerring, John, Daniel Ziblatt, Johan van Gorp, and Julian Arevalo. 2011. "An Institutional Theory of Direct and Indirect Rule." *World Politics* 63(3): 377–433.

Geys, Benny and Daniel M. Smith. 2017. "Political Dynasties in Democracies: Causes, Consequences, and Remaining Puzzles." *The Economic Journal* 127(4):F446–F454.

Ghana Web. 2017. "Minister Fingered in Najong killings." *GhanaWeb*, 24 December.

Gilbert, Dennis. 1977. The Oligarchy and the Old Regime in Peru PhD Thesis, Cornell University.

Goldstein, Markus and Christopher Udry. 2008. "The Profits of Power: Land Rights and Agricultural Investment in Ghana." *Journal of Political Economy* 116(6):981–1022.

Goody, Jack. 1967. The Over-Kingdom of Gonja. In *West African Kingdoms in the Nineteenth Century*, ed. Cyril D. Forde and Phyllis M. Kaberry. London: Oxford University Press.

Goody, Jack. 2004. Editor's Introduction. In *The Silent Rebel*. Accra, Ghana: Sub-Saharan Publishers.

Gottlieb, Jessica. 2017. "Explaining Variation in Broker Strategies: A Lab-in-the-Field Experiment in Senegal." *Comparative Political Studies* 50(11): 1556–1592.

Gottlieb, Jessica and Horacio Larreguy. 2020. "An Informational Theory of Electoral Targeting in Young Clientelistic Democracies: Evidence from Senegal." *Quarterly Journal of Political Science* 15(1):73–104.

Graham, C. K. 1971. *The History of Education in Ghana: From the Earliest Times to the Declaration of Independence*. London: Frank Cass and Co.

Grischow, Jeff D. 2006. *Shaping Tradition: Civil Society, Community and Development in Colonial Northern Ghana, 1899–1957*. Boston, MA: Brill.

Grossman, Guy. 2014. "Do Selection Rules Affect Leader Responsiveness? Evidence from Rural Uganda." *Quarterly Journal of Political Science* 9(1):1–44.

Grossman, Guy and Janet I. Lewis. 2014. "Administrative Unit Proliferation." *American Political Science Review* 108(1):196–217.

Guardado, Jenny. 2018. "Office-Selling, Corruption, and Long-Term Development in Peru." *American Political Science Review* 112(4):971–995.

Habyarimana, James, Macartan Humphreys, Daniel N. Posner and Jeremy M. Weinstein. 2007. "Why Does Ethnic Diversity Undermine Public Goods Provision?" *American Political Science Review* 101(4):709–725.

Habyarimana, James, Macartan Humphreys, Daniel N. Posner and Jeremy M. Weinstein. 2009. *Coethnicity: Diversity and the Dilemmas of Collective Action*. Russell Sage Foundation.

Hagmann, Tobias and Didier Peclard. 2010. "Negotiating Statehood: Dynamics of Power and Domination in Africa." *Development and Change* 41(4): 539–562.

Hamidu, Jamilla. 2015. "Are Ghanaian Diaspora Middle Class? Linking Middle Class to Political Participation and Stability in Ghana." *Africa Development* 40(1):139–157.

Hanson, Jonathan K. and Rachel Sigman. 2021. "Leviathan's Latent Dimensions: Measuring State Capacity for Comparative Political Research." Forthcoming, *Journal of Politics*.

Hassan, Mai. 2016. "A State of Change: District Creation in Kenya after Multi-Party Elections." *Political Research Quarterly* 69(3):510–521.

Hassan, Mai. 2020. *Regime Threats and State Solutions: Bureaucratic Loyalty and Embeddedness in Kenya*. New York: Cambridge University Press.

Hassan, Mai, Daniel Mattingly and Elizabeth Nugent. 2022. "Political Control." Forthcoming, *Annual Review of Political Science*.

Hassan, Mai and Kathleen Klaus. 2020. "Closing the Gap: The Politics of Property Rights in Kenya." Working Paper.

Hassan, Mai and Ryan Sheely. 2017. "Executive-Legislative Relations, Party Defections, and Lower Level Administrative Unit Proliferation: Evidence from Kenya." *Comparative Political Studies* 50(12):1595–1631.

Herbst, Jeffrey. 1993. *The Politics of Reform in Ghana, 1982–1991.* Berkeley: University of California Press.

Herbst, Jeffrey. 2000. *States and Power in Africa: Comparative Lessons in Authority and Control.* Princeton, NJ: Princeton University Press.

Hicken, Allen. 2011. "Clientelism." *Annual Review of Political Science* 14(1):289–310.

Hill, Polly. 1963. *The Migrant Cocoa Farmers of Southern Ghana: A Study in Rural Capitalism.* Cambridge, UK: Cambridge University Press.

Holland, Alisha C. and Brian Palmer-Rubin. 2015. "Beyond the Machine: Clientelist Brokers and Interest Organizations in Latin America." *Comparative Political Science* 48(9):1186–1223.

Houle, Christian, Paul D. Kenny and Nicolas Bichay. 2019. "The Origins of Inequality in Sub-Saharan Africa." Working Paper http://pauldkenny.com/HKB_Inequality%20Africa.pdf.

Huber, John D. and Laura Mayoral. 2019. "Group Inequality and the Severity of Civil Conflict." *Journal of Economic Growth* 24:1–41.

Huillery, Elise. 2009. "History Matters: The Long-Term Impact of Colonial Public Investments in French West Africa." *American Economic Journal: Applied Economics* 1(2):176–215.

Humphreys, Macartan, Raul Sanchez de la Sierra and Peter van der Windt. 2019. "Exporting Democratic Practices: Evidence from a Village Governance Intervention in Eastern Congo." *Journal of Development Economics* 140: 279–301.

Hutchcroft, Paul D. 2000. "Colonial Masters, National Politicos, and Provincial Lords: Central Authority and Local Autonomy in the American Philippines, 1900–1913." *Journal of Asian Studies* 59(2):277–306.

Hyden, Goran. 1980. *Beyond Ujamaa in Tanzania: Underdevelopment and an Uncaptured Peasantry.* Berkeley: University of California Press.

Ichino, Nahomi and Noah L. Nathan. 2012. "Primaries on Demand? Intra-Party Politics and Nominations in Ghana." *British Journal of Political Science* 42(4):769–791.

Ichino, Nahomi and Noah L. Nathan. 2018. Primary Elections in New Democracies. In *Routledge Handbook of Primary Elections*, ed. Robert G. Boatright. New York: Routledge Press.

Ichino, Nahomi and Noah L. Nathan. 2022. "Democratizing the Party: The Effects of Primary Election Reforms in Ghana." *British Journal of Political Science* 52(3):1168–1185.

Issifu, Abdul Karim. 2017. "From 'Bloody Land' to 'Cleansed Land': The Cola Peace Broker in the Nakpanduri War in Northern Ghana." *modernghana.com.*

Jablonski, Ryan S. 2014. "How Aid Targets Votes: The Impact of Electoral Incentives on Foreign Aid Distribution." *World Politics* 66(2): 293–330.

Jackson, Robert H. and Carl G. Rosberg. 1982. "Why Africa's Weak States Persist: The Empirical and Juridical in Statehood." *World Politics* 35(1):1–24.

Jedwab, Remi and Alexander Moradi. 2016. "The Permanent Effects of Transportation Revolutions in Poor Countries: Evidence from Africa." *Review of Economics and Statistics* 98(2):268–284.

Jensenius, Francesca R. 2016. "A Sign of Backwardness? Where Dyanstic Leaders are Elected in India." In *Democratic Dynasties: State, Party, and Family in Contemporary Indian Politics*, ed. Kanchan Chandra. New York: Cambridge University Press.

Jonsson, Julia. 2009. "The Overwhelming Minority: Inter-Ethnic Conflicts in Ghana's Northern Region." *Journal of International Development* 21:507–519.

Kashwan, Prakash, Lauren M. MacLean, and Gustavo A. Garcia-Lopez. 2019. "Rethinking Power and Institutitons in the Shadows of Neoliberalism." *World Development* 120:133–149.

Kennedy, Paul M. 1974. *The Samoan Tangle: A Study in Anglo-German Relations*. Dublin: Irish University Press.

King, Gary and Langche Zeng. 2001. "Logistic Regression in Rare Events Data." *Political Analysis* 9(2):137–163.

Klaus, Kathleen. 2020. *Political Violence in Kenya: Land, Elections, and Claim-Making*. New York: Cambridge University Press.

Knoll, Arthur J. 1978. *Togo under Imperial Germany: 1884–1914*. Stanford, CA: Hoover Institution Press.

Koren, Ore and Anoop K. Sarbahi. 2017. "State Capacity, Insurgency, and Civil War: A Disaggregated Analysis." *International Studies Quarterly* 62: 274–288.

Koter, Dominika. 2013. "King Makers: Local Leaders and Ethnic Politics in Africa." *World Politics* 65(2):187–232.

Koter, Dominika. 2016. *Beyond Ethnic Politics in Africa*. New York: Cambridge University Press.

Koter, Dominika. 2017. "Costly Electoral Campiagns and the Changing Composition and Quality of Parliament: Evidence from Benin." *African Affairs* 116(465):573–596.

Kramon, Eric. 2019. "Ethnic Group Institutions and Electoral Clientelism." *Party Politics* 25(3):435–447.

Kramon, Eric and Daniel N. Posner. 2013. "Who Benefits from Distributive Politics? How the Outcome One Studies Affects the Answer One Gets." *Perspectives on Politics* 11(2):461–472.

Kwansa, Benjamin Kobina. 2020. "Understanding the Intra-Ethnic Conflict in Bimbilla." Danish Institute for International Studies (blog), www.diis.dk/en/node/24350.

Ladouceur, Paul Andre. 1979. *Chiefs and Politicians: The Politics of Regionalism in Northern Ghana*. London: Longman Publishers.

Larkin, John A. 1982. "Philippine History Reconsidered: A Socioeconomic Perspective." *American Historical Review* 87(3):595–628.

Larson, Jennifer M. and Janet I. Lewis. 2017. "Ethnic Networks." *American Journal of Political Science* 61(2):350–364.

Lawrence, Adria and Erica Chenowith. 2010. Introduction. In *Rethinking Violence: States and Non-State Actors in Conflict*. Cambridge, MA: MIT Press.

Lee, Melissa M. 2020. *Crippling Leviathan: How Foreign Subversion Weakens the State*. Ithaca, NY: Cornell University Press.

Lee, Melissa M. and Nan Zhang. 2017. "Legibility and the Informational Foundations of State Capacity." *Journal of Politics* 79(1):118–132.

Lemarchand, Rene. 1972. "Political Clientelism and Ethnicity in Tropical Africa: Competing Solidarities in Nation-Building." *American Political Science Review* 66(1):68–90.

Lentz, Carola. 1995. "'Unity for Development': Youth Associations in North-Western Ghana." *Africa: Journal of the International African Institute* 65(3):395–429.

Lentz, Carola. 2006. *Ethnicity and the Making of History in Northern Ghana.* Edinburgh University Press.

Lentz, Carola. 2009. "'A Man of Great Foresight': SWDK Gandah's History of Birifu Naa Gandah." In *Gandah-Yir: The House of the Brave*, ed. Carola Lentz. Legon, Ghana: Institute for African Studies.

Levi, Margaret. 1988. *Of Rule and Revenue.* Berkeley, CA: Berkeley University Press.

Lewis, Janet I. 2020. *How Insurgency Begins: Rebel Group Formation in Uganda and Beyond.* New York: Cambridge University Press.

Lindberg, Staffan I. 2003. "'It's Our Time to "Chop":' Do Elections in Africa Feed Neo-Patrimonialism Rather Than Counteract It?" *Democratization* 10(2): 121–140.

Lindberg, Staffan I. 2010. "What Accountability Pressures do MPs in Africa Face and How Do They Respond? Evidence from Ghana." *Journal of Modern African Studies* 48(1):117–142.

Lindvall, Johannes and Jan Teorell. 2016. "State Capacity as Power: A Conceptual Framework." Working Paper.

Lowes, Sara and Eduardo Montero. 2018. "Concessions, Violence, and Indirect Rule: Evidence from the Congo Free State." Working Paper https://scholar.harvard.edu/files/lowes_montero_rubber.pdf.

Lund, Christian. 2006. "Twilight Institutions: Public Authority and Local Politics in Africa." *Development and Change* 37(4):685–705.

Lund, Christian. 2008. *Local Politics and the Dyanmics of Property in Africa.* New York: Cambridge University Press.

MacGaffey, Wyatt. 2006. "Death of a King, Death of a Kingdom? Social Pluralism and Succession to High Office in Dagbon, Northern Ghana." *Journal of Modern African Studies* 44(1):79–99.

MacGaffey, Wyatt. 2013. *Chiefs, Priests, and Praise-Singers: History, Politics, and Land Ownership in Northern Ghana.* Charlottesville: University of Virginia Press.

Maclean, Lauren M. 2010. *Informal Institutions and Citizenship in Rural Africa: Risk and Reciprocity in Ghana and Cote d'Ivoire.* New York: Cambridge University Press.

Mahama, Ibrahim. 2003. *Ethnic Conflicts in Northern Ghana.* Tamale, Ghana: Cyber Systems Press.

Mahama, John Dramani. 2012. *My First Coup D'etat: and other True Stories from the Lost Decades of Africa.* New York: Bloomsbury.

Mamdani, Mahmood. 1996. *Citizen and Subject: Contemporary Africa and the Legacy of Late Colonialism.* Princeton, NJ: Princeton University Press.

Mann, Michael. 1988. "The Autonomous Power of the State." In *States, War, and Capitalism.* Oxford: Blackwell Publishers.

Mares, Isabela and Lauren Young. 2016. "Buying, Expropriating, and Stealing Votes." *Annual Review of Political Science* 19:267–288.

Matsuzaki, Reo. 2019. *Statebuilding by Imposition: Resistance and Control in Colonial Taiwan and the Philippines*. Ithaca, NY: Cornell University Press.

Maurer, Noel and Lakshmi Iyer. 2008. "The Cost of Property Rights: Establishing Institutions on the Philippine Frontier Under American Rule, 1898–1918." NBER Working Paper No. 14298.

McCauley, John F. and Daniel N. Posner. 2015. "African Borders as Sources of Natural Experiments: Promise and Pitfalls." *Political Science Research and Methods* 3(2):409–418.

McClintock, Cynthia. 2019. "Peru's Cleavages, Conflict, and Precarious Democracy." In *Oxford Research Encylocpedias Politics*. New York: Oxford University Press.

McCoy, Alfred W. 1993. "'An Anarchy of Families': The Historiography of State and Family in the Philippines." In *An Anarchy or Families: State and Family in the Philippines*, ed. Alfred W. McCoy. Madison: University of Wisconsin Press.

McDonnell, Erin Metz. 2020. *Patchwork Leviathan: Pockets of Bureaucratic Effectiveness in Developing States*. Princeton, NJ: Princeton University Press.

McKenzie, David J. 2005. "Measuring Inequality with Asset Indicators." *Journal of Population Economics* 18(2):229–260.

McLennan, Marshall S. 1969. "Land and Tenancy in the Central Luzon Plain." *Philippine Studies* 17(4):651–682.

Medel, Monica and Francisco E. Thoumi. 2014. "Mexican Drug 'Cartels'." In *Oxford Handbook of Organized Crime*, ed. Leitizia Paoli. New York: Oxford University Press.

Meier Zu Selhausen, Felix, Marco H. D. van Leeuwen and Jacob L. Weisdorf. 2018. "Social Mobility among Christian Africans: Evidence from Anglican Marriage Registers in Uganda, 1895–2011." *The Economic History Review* 71(4):1291–1321.

Michalopoulos, Stelios and Elias Papaioannou. 2013. "Precolonial Ethnic Institutions and Contemporary African Development." *Econometrica* 81(1):113–152.

Michalopoulos, Stelios and Elias Papaioannou. 2020. "Historical Legacies and African Development." *Journal of Economic Literature* 58(1):53–128.

Michels, Robert. 1915. *Political Parties: A Sociological Study of the Oligarchical Tendencies of Modern Democracy*. London: Jarold and Sons.

Migdal, Joel S. 1988. *Strong Societies and Weak States: State-Society Relations and State Capabilities in the Third World*. Princeton, NJ: Princeton University Press.

Miguel, Edward and Mary Kay Gugerty. 2005. "Ethnic Diversity, Social Sanctions, and Public Goods in Kenya." *Journal of Public Economics* 89: 2325–2368.

Miller, Rory. 1982. "The Coastal Elite and Peruvian Politics, 1895–1919." *Journal of Latin American Studies* 14(1):97–120.

Mitchell, Timothy. 1999. "Society, Economy, and the State Effect." In *State/Culture: State-Formation after the Cultural Turn*, ed. George Steinmetz. Ithaca, NY: Cornell University Press, pp. 76–97.

Muller-Crepon, Carl, Philipp Hunziker, and Lars-Erik Cederman. 2020. "Roads to Rule, Roads to Rebel: Relational State Capacity and Conflict in Africa." *Journal of Conflict Resolution*.

Murdock, George P. 1967. *Ethnographic Atlas*. Pittsburgh, PA: University of Pittsburgh Press.

Murray, Francis J. 1972. "Land Reform in the Philippines: An Overview." *Philippine Sociological Review* 20(1):151–168.

Myers, Robert J. 1940. "Errors and Bias in the Reporting of Ages in Census Data." *Transactions of the Actuarial Society of America* 41(104):394–415.

Nathan, Noah L. 2019. *Electoral Politics and Africa's Urban Transition: Class and Ethnicity in Ghana*. New York: Cambridge University Press.

National Peace Council. 2017. "Draft Report for Conflcit Mapping – Northern Ghana." Memorandum of the National Peace Council of Ghana.

Nichter, Simeon. 2018. *Votes for Survival: Relational Clientelism in Latin America*. New York: Cambridge University Press.

Novaes, Lucas M. 2018. "Disloyal Brokers and Weak Parties." *American Journal of Political Science* 62(1):84–98.

Ntsebeza, Lungisile. 2005. *Democracy Compromised: Chiefs and the Politics of Land in South Africa*. Boston: Brill Publishers.

Nugent, Paul. 2010a. "Nkrumah and Rawlings: Political Lives in Parallel?" *Transactions of the Historical Society of Ghana* 12:35–56.

Nugent, Paul. 2010b. "States and Social Contracts in Africa." *New Left Review* 64:35–68.

Nunn, Nathan. 2008. "The Long-Term Effects of Africa's Slave Trades." *Quarterly Journal of Economics* 123(1):139–176.

Nunn, Nathan. 2010. "Religious Conversion in Colonial Africa." *American Economic Review: Papers & Proceedings* 100:147–152.

Nunn, Nathan and Leonard Wantchekon. 2011. "The Slave Trade and the Origins of Mistrust in Africa." *American Economic Review* 101(7): 3221–3252.

O'Brien, Dan. 1983. "Chiefs of Rain. Chiefs of Ruling: A Reinterpretation of Pre-Colonial Tonga (Zambia) Social and Political Structure." *Africa: Journal of the International African Institute* 53(4):23–42.

O'Donnell, Guillermo. 1993. "On the State, Democratization and Some Conceptual Problems: A Latin American View with Glances at Some Postcommunist Countries." *World Development* 21(8):1355–1369.

Olson, Mancur. 1993. "Dictatorship, Democracy, and Development." *American Political Science Review* 87(3):567–576.

Osafo-Kwaako, Philip and James A. Robinson. 2013. "Political Centralization in Pre-Colonial Africa." *Journal of Comparative Economics* 41(1):6–21.

Ostby, Gudrun, Ragnhild Nordas, and Jan Ketil Rod. 2009. "Regional Inequalities and Civil Conflict in Sub-Saharan Africa." *International Studies Quarterly* 53(2):301–324.

Ostrom, Elinor. 1990. *Governing the Commons: The Evolution of Institutions for Collective Action*. New York: Cambridge University Press.

Paglayan, Agustina S. 2020. "The Non-Democratic Roots of Mass Education: Evidence from 200 Years." *American Political Science Review*.

Paine, Jack. 2019. "Ethnic Violence in Africa: Destructive Legacies of Pre-Colonial States." *International Organization* 73:645–683.

Palik, Julia, Siri Aas Rustad, and Fredrik Methi. 2020. "Conflict Trends: A Global Overview, 1946-2019." PRIO Working Paper.

Paller, Jeffrey W. 2019. *Democracy in Ghana: Everyday Politics in Urban Africa.* New York: Cambridge University Press.

Pellow, Deborah. 2012. Chieftaincy, Collective Interests and the Dagomba New Elite. In *Development, Modernism and Modernity in Africa*, ed. Augustine Agwuele. New York: Routledge, pp. 43–61.

Pierskalla, Jan, Alexander de Juan and Max Montgomery. 2019. "The Territorial Expansion of the Colonial State: Evidence from German East Africa 1890–1909." *British Journal of Political Science* 49(2):711–737.

Pinkston, Amanda. 2016. Insider Democracy: Poverty and the Closed Political Class in Democratic Africa PhD Thesis, Harvard University.

Posner, Daniel N. 2004. "The Political Salience of Cultural Differences: Why Chewas and Tumbukas Are Allies in Zambia and Adversaries in Malawi." *American Political Science Review* 98(4):529–545.

Posner, Daniel N. 2005. *Institutions and Ethnic Politics in Africa.* New York: Cambridge University Press.

Pul, Hippolyt A. S. 2003. Exclusion, Association, and Violence: Trends and Triggers of Ethnic Conflicts in Northern Ghana. Master's Thesis Duquesne University.

Querubin, Pablo. 2016. "Family and Politics: Dynastic Persistence in the Philippines." *Quarterly Journal of Political Science* 11:151–181.

Ramirez, Susan E. 1986. *Provincial Patriarchs: Land Tenure and the Economics of Power in Colonial Peru.* Albuquerque: University of New Mexico Press.

Ranger, Terence O. 1983. "The Invention of Tradition in Colonial Africa." In *The Invention of Tradition*, ed. Terence O. Ranger and Eric J. Hobsbawm. New York: Cambridge University Press.

Rathbone, Richard. 2000. *Nkrumah and the Chiefs: Politics of Chieftaincy in Ghana, 1951–1960.* Ohio University Press.

Rattray, R. S. 1932. *The Tribes of the Ashanti Hinterland.* Oxford, UK: Clarendon Press.

Ricart-Huguet, Joan. 2021a. "Colonial Education, Political Elites, and Regional Political Inequality in Africa." *Comparative Political Studies* 54(14): 2546–2580.

Ricart-Huguet, Joan. 2021b. "The Origins of Colonial Investments in Former British and French Africa." *British Journal of Political Science.* Online FirstView.

Riedl, Rachel Beatty. 2014. *Authoritarian Origins of Democratic Party Systems in Africa.* New York: Cambridge University Press.

Robinson, Amanda Lea. 2019. "Inventing Traditional Authority: Lhomwe Chiefs in Malawi." Working Paper.

Robinson, Amanda Lea and Jessica Gottlieb. 2021. "How to Close the Gender Gap in Political Participation: Lessons from Matrilineal Societies in Africa." *British Journal of Political Science* 51(1):68–92.

Roessler, Philip, Yannick I. Pengl, Kyle Titlow, Robert Marty, and Nicolas van de Walle. 2020. "The Cash Crop Revolution, Colonialism and Legacies of Spatial Inequality: Evidence from Africa." Working Paper.

Rudolfsen, Ida. 2017. "State Capacity, Inequality, and Inter-Group Violence in Sub-Saharan Africa: 1891–2011." *Civil Wars* 19(2):118–145.

Rueda, Miguel R. 2016. "Small Aggregates, Big Manipulation: Vote Buying Enforcement and Collective Monitoring." *American Journal of Political Science* 61(1):163–177.

Salehyan, Idean, Cullen S. Henrdrix, Jesse Hamner, Christina Case, Christopher Linebarger, Emily Stull, and Jennifer Williams. 2012. "Social Conflict in Africa: A New Database." *International Interactions* 38(4):503–511.

Savannah News. 2018. "I Have no Hand in Najong killing – Solomon Boar." *Savannah News*, 7 January.

Schatzberg, Michael G. 1980. *Politics and Class in Zaire: Bureaucracy, Business, and Beer in Lisala.* New York: Africana Publishing.

Scheuer, Florian and Joel Slemrod. 2019. "Taxation and the Superrich." NBER Working Paper #26207.

Scott, James C. 1998. *Seeing Like a State: How Certain Schemes to Improve the Human Condition Have Failed.* New Haven, CT: Yale University Press.

Scott, James C. 2009. *The Art of Not Being Governed: An Anarchist History of Upland Southeast Asia.* New Haven, CT: Yale University Press.

Shami, Mahvish. 2017. "Connectivity, Clientelism and Public Provision." Forthcoming, *British Journal of Political Science.*

Shefter, Martin. 1977. "Party and Patronage: Germany, England, and Italy." *Politics and Society* 7:403–451.

Sidel, John T. 1999. *Capital, Coercion, and Crime: Bossism in the Philippines.* Stanford, CA: Stanford University Press.

Sidel, John T. 2008. "Social Origins of Dictatorship and Democracy Revisited." *Comparative Politics* 40(2):127–147.

Skocpol, Theda. 1985. "Introduction." In *Bringing the State Back In*, ed. Peter B. Evans, Dietrich Rueschemeyer and Theda Skocpol. New York: Cambridge University Press.

Slater, Dan. 2008. "Can Leviathan Be Democratic? Competitive Elections, Robust Mass Politics, and State Infrastructural Power." *Studies in Comparative International Development* 43:252–272.

Slater, Dan. 2010. *Ordering Power: Contentious Politics and Authoritarian Leviathans in Southeast Asia.* New York: Cambridge University Press.

Slater, Dan and Diana Kim. 2015. "Standoffish States: Nonliterate Leviathans in Southeast Asia." *TRaNS: Trans-Regional and National Studies of Southeast Asia* 3(1):25–44.

Smith, Daniel M. 2018. *Dynasties and Democracy: The Inherited Incumbency Advantage in Japan.* Stanford, CA: Stanford University Press.

Soifer, Hillel. 2008. "State Infrastructural Power: Approaches to Conceptualization and Measurement." *Studies in Comparative International Development* 43:231–251.

Soifer, Hillel. 2015. *State Building in Latin America.* New York: Cambridge University Press.

Spear, Thomas. 2003. "Neo-Traditionalism and the Limits of Invention in British Colonial Africa." *Journal of African History* 44(1):3–27.

Stacey, Paul. 2014*a*. "Political Structure and the Limits of Recognition and Representation in Ghana." *Development and Change* 46(1):25–47.

Stacey, Paul. 2014*b*. "'The Chiefs, Elders, and People Have for Many Years Suffered Untold Hardships': Protests by Coalitions of the Excluded in British Norhtern Togoland, UN Trusteeship Territory, 1950–1957." *Journal of African History* 55(3):423–444.

Staniland, Martin. 1975. *The Lions of Dagbon: Political Change in Northern Ghana*. New York: Cambridge University Press.

Stasavage, David. 2005. "Democracy and Education Spending in Africa." *American Journal of Political Science* 49(2):343–358.

Stoecker, Helmuth. 1986. *German Imperialism in Africa*. London: C. Hurst and Company.

Stokes, Susan C., Thad Dunning, Marcelo Nazareno, and Valeria Brusco. 2013. *Brokers, Voters, and Clientelism: The Puzzle of Distributive Politics*. New York: Cambridge University Press.

Sundberg, Ralph, Kristine Eck, and Joakim Kreutz. 2012. "Introducing the UDCP Non-State Conflict Dataset." *Journal of Peace Research* 49(2):351–362.

Suryanarayan, Pavi and Steven White. 2021. "Slavery, Reconstruction, and Bureaucratic Capacity in the American South." Forthcoming, *American Political Science Review*. 115(2):568–584.

Tait, David. 1961. *The Konkomba of Northern Ghana*. London: Oxford University Press.

Talton, Benjamin. 2010. *Politics of Social Change in Ghana: The Konkomba Struggle for Political Equality*. Palgrave Macmillan.

Tignor, Robert L. 1971. "Colonial Chiefs in Chiefless Societies." *Journal of Modern African Studies* 9(3):339–359.

Tignor, Robert L. 1976. *The Colonial Transformation of Kenya: The Kamba, Kikuyu, and Maasai from 1900 to 1939*. Princeton, NJ: Princeton University Press.

Tilly, Charles. 1990. *Coercion, Capital, and European States: AD 990 – 1992*. Cambridge, MA: Wiley-Blackwell Publishers.

Tollefsen, Andreas Foro and Halvard Buhaug. 2015. "Insurgency and Inaccessibility." *International Studies Review* 17:6–25.

Tonah, Steve. 2002. "Fulani Pastoralists, Indigenous Farmers, and the Contest for Land in Northern Ghana." *Africa Spectrum* 37(1):43–59.

Tonah, Steve. 2004. "Defying the Nayiri: Traditional Authority, People's Power, and the Politics of Chieftaincy Succession in Mamprugu – Northern Ghana." *Legon Journal of Sociology* 1(1):42–58.

Tonah, Steve. 2012. "The Politicisation of a Chieftiancy Conflict: The Case of Dagbon, Northern Ghana." *Nordic Journal of African Studies* 21(1):1–20.

Trejo, Guillermo and Sandra Ley. 2018. "Why Did Drug Cartels Go to War in Mexico? Subnational Party Alternation, the Breakdown of Criminal Protection, and the Onset of Large-Scale Violence." *Comparative Political Studies* 51(7):900–937.

Vail, Leroy. 1989. Introduction: Ethnicity in Southern African History. In *The Creation of Tribalism in Southern Africa*, ed. Leroy Vail. Berkeley: University of California Press.

van de Walle, Nicolas. 2001. *African Economies and the Politics of the Permanent Crisis, 1979–1999*. New York: Cambridge University Press.

van de Walle, Nicolas. 2009. "The Institutional Origins of Inequality in Sub-Saharan Africa." *Annual Review of Political Science* 12(1):307–27.

Van der Linde, Ada and Rachel Naylor. 1999. *Building Sustainable Peace: Conflict, Conciliation, and Civil Society in Northern Ghana*. Oxford, UK: Oxfam International.

Walker, Andrew. 2015. "From Legibility to Eligibility: Politics, Subsidy and Productivity in Rural Asia." *TRaNS: Trans-Regional and National Studies of Southeast Asia* 3(1):45–71.

Wantchekon, Leonard, Marko Klasnja, and Natalija Novta. 2015. "Education and Human Capital Externalities: Evidence from Colonial Benin." *Quarterly Journal of Economics* 130(2):703–757.

Weber, Eugen. 1976. *Peasants into Frenchmen: The Modernization of Rural France, 1870–1914*. Stanford, CA: Stanford University Press.

Weber, Max. 1946 [1919]. "Politics as a Vocation." In *From Max Weber: Essays in Sociology*, ed. H. H. Gerth and C. Wright Mills. New York: Oxford University Press.

Wickberg, Edgar. 1964. "The Chinese Mestizo in Philippine History." *Journal of Southeast Asian History* 5(1):62–100.

Wig, Tore. 2016. "Peace from the Past: Pre-Colonial Political Institutions and Civil Wars in Africa." *Journal of Peace Research* 53(4):509–524.

Wilfahrt, Martha. 2018. "Precolonial Legacies and Institutional Congruence in Public Goods Delivery: Evidence from Decentralized West Africa." *World Politics* 70(2):239–274.

Wilfahrt, Martha. 2021. *Precolonial Legacies in Postcolonial Politics: Representation and Redistribution in Decentralized West Africa*. New York: Cambridge University Press.

Wilkinson, Steven. 2004. *Votes and Violence: Electoral Competition and Ethnic Riots in India*. New York: Cambridge University Press.

Wilks, Ivor. 1975. *Asante in the Nineteenth Century: The Structure and Evolution of a Political Order*. New York: Cambridge University Press.

Wilks, Ivor. 1989. *Wa and the Wala: Islam and Polity in Northwestern Ghana*. New York: Cambridge University Press.

Wilks, Ivor, Nehemia Levtzion and Bruce M. Haight. 1986. *Chronicles from Gonja: A Tradition of West African Muslim Historiography*. New York: Cambridge University Press.

Williams, Martin J. 2017. "The Political Economy of Unfinished Development Projects: Corruption, Clientelism, or Collective Choice?" *American Political Science Review* 111(4):705–723.

Williams, Martin J. 2019. "Beyond State Capacity: Bureaucratic Performance, Policy Implementation, and Reform." Working Paper.

World Bank. 1997. *World Development Report 1997: The State in a Changing World*. Washington: The World Bank.

Yaro, Joseph Awetori. 2010. "Customary Tenure Systems under Siege: Contemporary Access to Land in Northern Ghana." *GeoJournal* 75:199–214.

Ying, Luwei. 2020. "How State Presence Leads to Civil Conflict." *Journal of Conflict Resolution.*

Young, Alwyn. 2013. "Inequality, the Urban-Rural Gap, and Migration." *Quarterly Journal of Economics* 128(4):1727–1785.

Young, Crawford. 1994. *The African Colonial State in Comparative Perspective.* New Haven, CT: Yale University Press.

Young, Crawford. 2004. "The End of the Post-Colonial State in Africa? Reflections on Changing African Political Dynamics." *African Affairs* 103:23–49.

Zarazaga, Rodrigo. 2014. "Brokers beyond Clientelism: A New Perspective through the Argentine Case." *Latin American Politics and Society* 56(3):23–45.

Zolberg, Aristide R. 1966. *Creating Political Order: The Party-States of West Africa.* Chicago: Rand McNally.

Index

David Knoke, Franz Urban Pappi, Jeffrey Broadbent, and Yutaka Tsujinaka, eds., *Comparing Policy Networks*

Ken Kollman, *Perils of Centralization: Lessons from Church, State, and Corporation*

Allan Kornberg and Harold D. Clarke, *Citizens and Community: Political Support in a Representative Democracy*

Amie Kreppel, *The European Parliament and the Supranational Party System*

David D. Laitin, *Language Repertoires and State Construction in Africa*

Fabrice E. Lehoucq and Ivan Molina, *Stuffing the Ballot Box: Fraud, Electoral Reform, and Democratization in Costa Rica*

Benjamin Lessing *Making Peace in Drug Wars: Crackdowns and Cartels in Latin America*

Janet I. Lewis *How Insurgency Begins: Rebel Group Formation in Uganda and Beyond*

Mark Irving Lichbach and Alan S. Zuckerman, eds., *Comparative Politics: Rationality, Culture, and Structure*, 2nd edition

Evan Lieberman, *Race and Regionalism in the Politics of Taxation in Brazil and South Africa*

Richard M. Locke, *The Promise and Limits of Private Power: Promoting Labor Standards in a Global Economy*

Julia Lynch, *Age in the Welfare State: The Origins of Social Spending on Pensioners, Workers, and Children*

Pauline Jones Luong, *Institutional Change and Political Continuity in Post-Soviet Central Asia*

Pauline Jones Luong and Erika Weinthal, *Oil is Not a Curse: Ownership Structure and Institutions in Soviet Successor States*

Doug McAdam, John McCarthy, and Mayer Zald, eds., *Comparative Perspectives on Social Movements*

Gwyneth H. McClendon and Rachel Beatty Riedl, *From Pews to Politics in Africa: Religious Sermons and Political Behavior*

Lauren M. MacLean, *Informal Institutions and Citizenship in Rural Africa: Risk and Reciprocity in Ghana and Côte d'Ivoire*

Beatriz Magaloni, *Voting for Autocracy: Hegemonic Party Survival and its Demise in Mexico*

James Mahoney, *Colonialism and Postcolonial Development: Spanish America in Comparative Perspective*

James Mahoney and Dietrich Rueschemeyer, eds., *Historical Analysis and the Social Sciences*

Scott Mainwaring and Matthew Soberg Shugart, eds., *Presidentialism and Democracy in Latin America*

Melanie Manion, *Information for Autocrats: Representation in Chinese Local Congresses*

Isabela Mares, *From Open Secrets to Secret Voting: Democratic Electoral Reforms and Voter Autonomy*

Isabela Mares, *The Politics of Social Risk: Business and Welfare State Development*

Isabela Mares, *Taxation, Wage Bargaining, and Unemployment*

Cathie Jo Martin and Duane Swank, *The Political Construction of Business Interests: Coordination, Growth, and Equality*

Anthony W. Marx, *Making Race, Making Nations: A Comparison of South Africa, the United States, and Brazil*

Daniel C. Mattingly, *The Art of Political Control in China*

CPSIA information can be obtained
at www.ICGtesting.com
Printed in the USA
BVHW032335210223
658948BV00003B/45